1-2-3® Graphics Techniques

Stephen W. Sagman

CORPORATION

LEADING COMPUTER KNOWLEDGE

1-2-3® Graphics Techniques

Copyright © 1990 by Que® Corporation.

Library of Congress Catalog No.: 89-63558

ISBN: 0-88022-515-7

93 92 91 90   8 7 6 5 4 3 2 1

Interpretation of the printing code: the rightmost double-digit number is the year of the book's printing; the rightmost single-digit number, the number of the book's printing. For example, a printing code of 90-1 shows that the first printing of the book occurred in 1990.

1-2-3 Graphics Techniques is based on 1-2-3 Releases 2.01, 2.2, and 3.

DEDICATION

For my mother and father:
They gave me the desire to read and the confidence to write.

Publishing Director

David P. Ewing

Acquisitions Editor

Terrie Lynn Solomon

Indexed by

Hilary Adams

Book Design and Production

Dan Armstrong
Bill Basham
Claudia Bell
Brad Chinn
Don Clemons
Sally Copenhaver
Tom Emerick
Denny Hager
Tami Hughes
Bill Hurley
Jodi Jensen
David Kline
Larry Lynch
Lori A. Lyons
Jennifer Matthews
Cindy L. Phipps
Joe Ramon
Dennis Sheehan
Louise Shinault
Bruce Steed
Mary Beth Wakefield
Nora Westlake

Production Editor

Jeannine McDonel

Editor

Tim Huddleston

Technical Editors

David A. Knispel
David Maguiness
Joyce J. Nielsen
Shelley O'Hara
Timothy S. Stanley
Charles O. Stewart III

Editorial Assistant

Stacey Beheler

Composed in Garamond and Excellent No. 47
by Que Corporation

Stephen W. Sagman

S tephen W. Sagman is a free-lance technical writer and PC educator based in New York. He has written hundreds of articles and product reviews, often relating to graphics, which have appeared in *PC Week, PC Computing, PC Magazine,* and others. He writes documentation, user guides, marketing and training materials. He has taught thousands of students in the classroom and executives in seminars on computer topics ranging from the basics to advanced graphics and desktop publishing subjects.

Prior to his computer writing, Mr. Sagman edited *MIDI Marketer*, an electronic musical instrument marketing newsletter, and served as marketing manager for several high-technology companies. Mr. Sagman graduated from Hamilton College and has an M.B.A. from the City University of New York.

Mr. Sagman co-wrote Que's *Using Harvard Graphics*.

TABLE OF CONTENTS

ACKNOWLEDGMENTS

I am earnestly grateful to a host of people who helped create this book. Jeannine McDonel, at Que, toiled with a gratifying passion over its words. She masterfully rewove the fabric, yet preserved the original patterns. Terrie Lynn Solomon offered unceasing optimism and encouragement when I needed it most. David Ewing made this book possible and provided helpful guidance and critical contributions. Tim Stanley donated his technical expertise throughout the book. I am particularly grateful for his considerable contribution in the chapter on macros for graphing. The material in this chapter is largely his.

I am grateful to the many technical editors who reviewed portions of the manuscript and to Bruce Stark for reviewing portions of the final chapter. I want to thank these people who helped at the many companies whose products are described: Barbara Brooker, Allison Parker, Mary Ann Singleton, and Alexandra Trevelyan at Lotus Development Corporation; Steve Malkiewicz at IBM; Colleen Terry at Brightbill-Roberts; and Lynne Killey at Harvard Systems. I am also grateful to Michael Dunn and David Mayer for their research assistance, and Eric Weinberger for his patience and support.

TRADEMARK ACKNOWLEDGMENTS

Que Corporation has made every attempt to supply trademark information about company names, products, and services mentioned in this book. Trademarks indicated below were derived from various sources. Que Corporation cannot attest to the accuracy of this information.

Introduction

You are a manager being called to justify your upcoming budget, or a Parks official hoping to convince the town council to allocate funds for a new playground. Perhaps you are an economist expected to explain your predictions for the future, or an astronomer sifting through hours of radio telescope data for more evidence to support your theory. Whatever your task, you use the enormous power of 1-2-3 to organize and interpret your data and search out an indisputable conclusion.

But, as you add, average, and adjust what seems to be endless columns of figures, their significance refuses to emerge. With just a few keystrokes, you arrange your data into a 1-2-3 graph, and a pattern, hidden before, appears. A single line rises above the rest, a set of bars dwarfs its companions, or a pie slice proves disproportionately large compared to the rest. The graph you create reveals what the raw numbers could not.

1-2-3 graphs have always served as a fresh perspective on your data, a composite view that illuminates trends or aberrations. But, as the business environment surrounding 1-2-3 rapidly evolves, 1-2-3 graphs are being prodded more toward duties of presentation rather than analysis.

The reason behind the surging demand for presentational graphics is clear. Prominent graphs have traditionally accompanied stories with a numeric bent in newsmagazines. They deliver the numbers succinctly and let the text simply explain why. Now, flashy graphs have become just as indispensable to television news and highly graphic contemporary newspapers, such as *USA Today*. What was once communicated through long and boring recitations of numbers or cryptic tables of figures is capsulized in succinct graphs. Whether you call this new highly visual field graphing, business graphics, or presentation graphics, the demand for provocative graphics has never been stronger. But, some say this demand has outstripped the ability of 1-2-3 to produce graphics.

When 1-2-3 was born in 1982, the IBM PC had just emerged. Even later, when 1-2-3 was updated, not many personal computers existed with the hardware to create impressive color graphs. The advent of IBM's Personal System/2 line of computers, all with built-in color and graphics on their screens, marked a fundamental change in the computer industry and ushered in an era when most new computer models include high-resolution color graphics as standard.

New spreadsheets such as Excel, Quattro Pro, and others take advantage of that technology to create eye-catching, colorful graphs so that users can assemble clear and persuasive presentations. Graphs made with these programs have large, attractive text typefaces and brightly colored bars and lines. 1-2-3's graphs look rudimentary in comparison. Even 1-2-3's latest incarnation, 1-2-3 Release 3, which offers substantially better-looking graphs than earlier releases of 1-2-3, lacks the flashy three-dimensional graphs and huge graph type assortment of its competitors. The 1-2-3 family line, as a whole, remains more adept at analyzing data than presenting it.

Some users, frustrated by what they perceive as 1-2-3's shortcomings, have left 1-2-3 in favor of products that create flashier graphs. But they often abandon 1-2-3 at substantial cost: both the expense of purchasing new software and the value of time spent enduring a new learning curve.

1-2-3 Graphics Techniques explores a number of alternate paths to getting the graphics that today's analytical and presentational needs require without deserting 1-2-3. The text suggests ways to capitalize on 1-2-3's strengths in data management and analysis and still obtain highly polished graphs suitable for presentation. It suggests methods of using 1-2-3 to create simple analytical graphs, then continuing with complementary programs which can add professional luster to 1-2-3's basic output.

One such program is the 1-2-3 add-in Allways, bundled with 1-2-3 Release 2.2 and available separately for 1-2-3 Release 2.0 or 2.01. Allways can substantially upgrade the appearance of a standard 1-2-3 graph, giving it big, bold titles. Those who use 1-2-3 Release 3, instead, can also get many of the graph formatting improvements offered by Allways, simply by using its special commands for designing graphs.

But the capabilities of Allways, and the graphing enhancements of 1-2-3 Release 3, are only the first step toward transforming 1-2-3's simple graphs into slick presentation vehicles. A host of dedicated graphics programs can let you import and then dress up completed 1-2-3 graphs using the special tools they make available. With just a few steps, you can give a graph a makeover, changing its text typeface, livening its colors, or adding a three-dimensional effect to its bars or lines. If the graph's message might be enhanced with an illustration, you can add a predrawn figure taken from an electronic clip-art library.

For even greater effect, you might want to add motion and special effects to static graphs by including them in animated desktop presentations. Desktop presentation software, one of the newest classes of personal computer software, can fade from one graph to the next in a presentation or cause the bars or lines of individual graphs to grow or move across the screen. If your need is to incorporate eye-catching graphs in printed materials, you can use many word processors and desktop publishing systems to mix both text and graphs on attractively laid-out pages.

Whatever your need, you can obtain professional-quality graphs by assembling a system that uses the basic graphmaking abilities of 1-2-3 as its core. This book tells you how.

Who Should Read This Book

1-2-3 Graphics Techniques is written to meet the needs of a wide range of 1-2-3 users, from those just starting out with 1-2-3 graphing to 1-2-3 experts who seek to enhance their 1-2-3 graphs, present them as slides or animated sequences, or integrate their 1-2-3 graphs into printed documents. The book assumes knowledge of the most basic 1-2-3 terminology. So before you proceed, you should be familiar with such 1-2-3 concepts as entering values and labels into worksheet cells, entering simple formulas, and selecting ranges of cells.

For those who are familiar with 1-2-3 worksheets but new to graphing, the first six chapters serve as an introduction to making the basic 1-2-3 graph types that are available in all current versions of 1-2-3.

For those who are experienced 1-2-3 graphmakers, the later chapters cover such specialized topics as making slides from 1-2-3 graphs, animating graphs, choosing hardware for graph presentations, and using 1-2-3 PIC files to export completed graphs to desktop publishing software.

How This Book Is Organized

1-2-3 Graphics Techniques covers all current versions of 1-2-3: Release 2.0, 2.01, 2.2, and Release 3.0. Procedures specific to one version, such as those exclusive to 1-2-3 Release 3.0, are clearly indicated as such in the text.

The first chapter offers a quick tour through the graphics capabilities of your version of 1-2-3, whether you use 1-2-3 Release 2.0, 2.01, 2.2, or Release 3. Use it to get an overview of the way 1-2-3 converts numeric data into several different graph types. The chapter that follows offers a number of guidelines to keep in mind as you plan your graphs. By following its advice, you can be sure to create graphs that are both expressive and credible, and you can avoid some of the pitfalls many innocent graphmakers encounter. Chapters 3 through 6 offer step-by-step instructions for creating each of the graph types of 1-2-3 and for using both Allways and the advanced graphing commands of 1-2-3 Release 3 to enhance the graphs you make.

Chapters 7 and 8 offer specialized information on two topics related to making 1-2-3 graphs: using macros and add-ins to help make graphs. Chapter 9 gives you a list of troubleshooting suggestions for some common problems known to frustrate less experienced 1-2-3 graphmakers.

Chapters 10 through 14 help you convert 1-2-3 graphs into materials suitable for presentation. Chapter 10 deals with printing and plotting graphs, and Chapter 11 gives a wealth of information about importing 1-2-3 data into various types of graphing software programs. Chapter 12 is devoted to making slides to display your graphs. Chapter 13 tells you how to animate your graphics presentations with popular desktop presentation programs that create impressive visual effects, such as making graphs fade into view or making their bars appear to grow or their lines appear to travel on-screen. Chapter 14 surveys the most popular hardware that you can select to present your completed 1-2-3 graphs to an audience.

Chapter 15 describes the many possible paths for PIC file versions of your graphs. If your goal is to incorporate your graphs into printed presentations, you'll find much detailed advice for incorporating PIC files into the leading word processors and desktop publishing programs. The chapter also surveys a number of illustration programs that you can use to enhance the appearance of your PIC files and utilities you can use to translate your PIC file graphs into other graphic file types for use in other software.

Conventions Used in This Book

A number of conventions are used in *1-2-3 Graphics Techniques* to help you learn the techniques described in the text.

References to keys in the text are as they appear on the keyboard of the IBM.

Information you are asked to type is printed in **boldface**.

The first letter of each command from 1-2-3's menu system appears in **boldface**: **/G**raph **T**ype **B**ar indicates that you type /gtb to select this command if you are entering it manually.

The function keys, F1 through F10, are used for special situations in 1-2-3. In the text, the function key name is usually followed by the number in parentheses: Graph (F10).

Ctrl-Break indicates that you press the Ctrl key and hold it down while you press the Break key. Other hyphenated key combinations, such as Alt-F4, are performed in the same manner.

1

A 1-2-3 Graph
Quick Start

If you have never created graphs in 1-2-3, this chapter is for you. By following its step-by-step instructions, you can get a sense of using 1-2-3 graphing capabilities in real-world settings. You'll plan and create basic graphs, and then enhance them either with the add-in program Allways or with the special commands of 1-2-3 Release 3. By the close of this Quick Start tutorial, you will have progressed from the planning stage to the printed graph.

But before you proceed, take a moment to be sure your notion of graphs corresponds with the definition of graphs, as produced by 1-2-3. Graphs in 1-2-3 visually depict numeric information, illuminating trends and tendencies to communicate the meaning behind sets of numbers found in a worksheet. Graphs can be as simple as a single line, a sectioned circle, or a set of bars, just as long as the fundamental geometric shapes represent quantities with clarity and precision.

Keep in mind that unless the graph you create symbolizes a set of numbers in a manner that is quickly comprehended, you're no better off than you were with the numbers alone. So, as you proceed through this chapter, your goal will be to create some preliminary graphs that exhibit the best traits of 1-2-3 graphing—clarity and expressiveness.

To start, take a few moments to recreate the worksheet shown in figure 1.1 with your own copy of 1-2-3. This worksheet will serve as the basis for all the demonstrations in this chapter. After you have the sample worksheet on your screen, you can follow the exercises using any version of 1-2-3, including 1-2-3 Release 3.

When you have produced the figure 1.1 worksheet, save it on disk as a file called Cooper. You'll be using Cooper as the basis for several graphs.

G19:   `READY`

	A	B	C	D	E	F	G
1	Cooper Canning						
2	Consolidated Data						
3		Jul	Aug	Sept	Oct	Nov	Dec
4	Revenues						
5	Eric	22300	23250	24900	26700	29000	33100
6	Sabina	18600	18700	20000	23600	26400	29200
7	David	34500	35200	38800	40100	44700	49250
8							
9	Total Sales	75400	77150	84500	90400	100100	111550
10							
11	Expenses						
12	Operations	17000	17000	17000	17000	17000	17000
13	Marketing	14200	14400	15100	15700	17200	17800
14	Personnel	16100	16100	16100	17920	17920	17920
15							
16	Total Expenses	47300	47500	48200	50620	52120	52720
17							
18							
19							
20							

16-Oct-89 08:48 AM   `UNDO`

Fig. 1.1. The Cooper Canning worksheet.

Now, as you create your first graph, you find yourself in the following scene:

As usual, Cooper Canning has let its annual presentation to the board of directors slide until the very last minute. It's not that their procrastination has been any worse this year. The staff has been fully preoccupied with Cooper's wild business upswings over the last several months.

Of course, the office staff has been gathering data for the presentation as a routine duty all year, and they anticipate nothing less than stellar-looking graphs from the compiled figures, but the company's data still resides in raw form in 1-2-3 worksheets. The presentation is just an hour away.

Nevertheless, over the next little while, Cooper needs to transform its data from baffling columns of numbers into informative visuals with a warm and positive tone. That's where you come in. You have been summoned on an emergency basis for your 1-2-3 expertise, and you have mere minutes to produce the graphs Cooper must have.

You begin your work eagerly. Within a few moments you consolidate data from a dozen 1-2-3 worksheets into one summary worksheet— from this single worksheet, you can generate all the graphs you need. That worksheet is the Cooper worksheet you now see on your screen.

Normally, Cooper keeps separate worksheets calculating sales totals for each of its three salespeople, Eric, Sabina, and David. Cooper also tracks a number of expense categories in separate worksheets. The summary you have created now brings together all of these sales and expense figures into a single worksheet.

After a quick meeting with Cooper's staff, you learn that the company needs three graphs for the big presentation. These graphs must show three sets of data:

☐ The relative sales of the three salespeople each month.

☐ The general trends of sales and expenses over the previous six-month period.

☐ The contribution of each salesperson to the total sales from July through December. (End-of-the-year bonuses are based on third- and fourth-quarter sales contribution.)

You begin by planning the first graph, the sales comparison of three salespeople over six months, for which you decide on a bar graph.

Creating the Bar Graph

Your first task—determining the appropriate graph type for the message you must convey—resulted in a bar graph choice. Why? You have several reasons. Bar graphs are familiar and easily interpreted by most people. More importantly, bar graphs compare results at specific points in time. Unlike line graphs, which display general data trends across time, a bar graph is a series of snapshots, freezing a situation at successive moments. Each snapshot records a set of events that become bars in a graph. This graph will contain six snapshots—six sets of bars that compare three salesperson's results at monthly intervals.

To create the actual graphs, you follow your usual efficient series of operations. Your plan is to begin with the basic bar graph produced by 1-2-3. This is the graph 1-2-3 produces on its own if you specify no more than the graph type and the data chosen to be graphed. The result is a simple representation, without title, legend, aesthetic adornment, or other elements that enhance the expressiveness of your graph.

After you have the basic graph, you will edit the components that are already part of the graph, and you will add the lacking elements: the title, the legend, and the labels to identify the axes.

When you complete the graph, you will save your work through either of two methods. You can name the graph for recall by that name the next time you retrieve the worksheet for editing. Or you can save the graph as a separate PIC file on disk. Then you can print the PIC file or use it in other software.

Now with a plan fixed in mind, you can begin the hands-on process of creating the bar graph. On your screen now should be the worksheet that you will produce the graph from, the Cooper Canning worksheet shown at the beginning of this chapter (see fig. 1.1).

All the commands you need for creating graphs in 1-2-3 are located under the graph menu, so begin by selecting /**Graph**. You should see the menu and graph settings screen shown in figure 1.2. If you use 1-2-3 Release 3, you won't see a graph settings screen; you will see the menu illustrated in figure 1.3.

Select **G**raph **T**ype **B**ar as the style for your first graph. Nothing appears to change on the menu, but as soon as you specify the data you want graphed, 1-2-3 will create a bar graph with no further intervention from you.

A typical bar graph contains a number of components common to most graphs. This Quick Start introduces the terminology you will see throughout this book to describe the components of the graph. These terms are illustrated in figure 1.4. The graph has a set of *titles* centered at the top, *x*- and *y-axes*, *axis titles*, a *legend*, and *bars*. Other graphs may have still more elements, described later, such as grid lines and data-labels.

Your next step in preparing the bar graph is to designate the three sets of sales data you want graphed. 1-2-3 can graph six sets of data simultaneously, but to plot all six could create a graph that is complicated and hard to interpret.

If you have used graphing software before, you may be more familiar with the term *series* to describe a set of data. A series is a succession of

```
G19:                                                                    MENU
Type X A B  C  D  E  F  Reset View  Save  Options  Name  Group  Quit
Line  Bar  XY  Stack-Bar  Pie
                              ── Graph Settings ──────────────
   Type: Line                    Titles: First
                                         Second
   X:                                    X axis
   A:                                    Y axis
   B:
   C:                                         Y scale:          X scale:
   D:                                 Scaling  Automatic        Automatic
   E:                                 Lower
   F:                                 Upper
                                      Format     (G)             (G)
   Grid: None        Color: No        Indicator  Yes            Yes

      Legend:            '  Format:  Data labels:             Skip: 1
   A                        Both
   B                        Both
   C                        Both
   D                        Both
   E                        Both
   F                        Both

16-Oct-89   09:01 AM
```

Fig. 1.2. The graph menu and graph settings screen in 1-2-3 Release 2.2.

```
A:G23:                                                                  MENU
Type X A B  C  D  E  F  Reset View  Save  Options  Name  Group  Quit
Line  Bar  XY  Stack-Bar  Pie  HLCO  Mixed  Features
A         A           B        C        D        E        F        G
 1 Cooper Canning
 2 Consolidated Data
 3                     Jul      Aug      Sept     Oct      Nov      Dec
 4 Revenues
 5           Eric     22300    23250    24900    26700    29000    33100
 6         Sabina     18600    18700    20800    23600    26400    29200
 7          David     34500    35200    38000    40100    44700    49250
 8                   ------------------------------------------------
 9    Total Sales     75400    77150    84500    90400   100100   111550
10
11 Expenses
12     Operations     17000    17000    17000    17000    17000    17000
13      Marketing     14200    14400    15100    15700    17200    17800
14      Personnel     16100    16100    16100    17920    17920    17920
15                   ------------------------------------------------
16 Total Expenses     47300    47500    48200    50620    52120    52720
17
18
19
20
21
22
23
24
25
26
27
28
29
COOPER.WK1
```

Fig. 1.3. The graph menu in 1-2-3 Release 3.

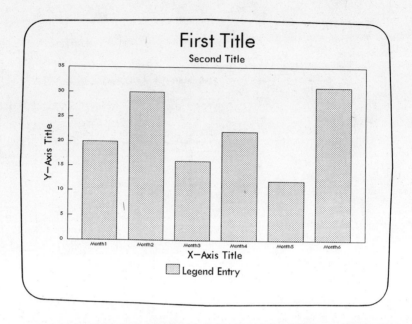

Fig. 1.4. *The major elements of a bar graph.*

results or measurements over time. 1-2-3 keeps the data for a series in a worksheet data range, so 1-2-3 calls a series a *data range*. 1-2-3 can plot six data ranges simultaneously, except when producing graph styles where this would be inappropriate—in pie graphs or the High-Low-Close-Open (HLCO) graphs available with 1-2-3 Release 3. You can see the six data-range names displayed on the 1-2-3 graph menu. Each data range is assigned a letter of the alphabet, from A through F. Another series, the *X data range*, holds the labels that appear along the horizontal axis of the graph, the x-axis.

For this first graph, the A, B, and C data ranges will be drawn from the half-year's sales results for Eric, Sabina, and David, the three Cooper salespeople. But before you assign one individual's results to one of the ranges, you may want to assign the X data range, so that you can set up the structure of the graph before entering the graph's data.

The month names for the x-axis are in worksheet range B3..G3. If you assign range B3..G3 to the X data range, the x-axis will plot six months, July through December. To do so, select **X** from the graph menu and point to the range B3..G3 or type in **B3..G3** and press Enter. (You point to a range by moving the cell pointer to the first cell in the range, pressing the period key, and then moving the pointer to the last cell in the range and pressing Enter.) While you are pointing to B3..G3, the worksheet looks like the one shown in figure 1.5.

```
G3: "Dec                                                          POINT
Enter x-axis range: B3..G3

            A          B        C        D        E        F        G
1  Cooper Canning
2  Consolidated Data
3                      Jul      Aug     Sept      Oct      Nov      Dec
4  Revenues
5              Eric    22300    23250    24900    26700    29000    33100
6            Sabina    18600    18700    20800    23600    26400    29200
7             David    34500    35200    38800    40100    44700    49250
8
9        Total Sales   75400    77150    84500    90400   100100   111550
10
11 Expenses
12         Operations  17000    17000    17000    17000    17000    17000
13          Marketing  14200    14400    15100    15700    17200    17000
14          Personnel  16100    16100    16100    17920    17920    17920
15
16      Total Expenses 47300    47500    48200    50620    52120    52720
17
18
19
20
   16-Oct-89   09:13 AM
```

Fig. 1.5. *Assigning the month names to the X data range.*

Now, assign the three sets of data you want graphed to the first three data ranges A, B, and C. Begin by selecting **A** from the graph menu. Point to range B5..G5 or enter the range address manually. Use the same method to assign data range B to the worksheet range B6..G6 and then to assign data range C to worksheet range B7..G7.

If you are using Release 2.2, you will see the graph settings sheet shown in figure 1.6. Notice that Bar is shown as the graph Type and that data ranges X, A, B, and C are set to the worksheet ranges you specified.

With Release 3, you do not see a graph settings sheet on your screen. Instead, you see the actual worksheet. To check the setting for a data range with Release 3, select the letter for the data range again on the graph menu. You will see the worksheet range for that data range highlighted. Press Enter to confirm your choice and return to the graph menu.

Now, you have supplied all the elements necessary for 1-2-3 to create a graph. Before you instruct 1-2-3 to display the graph on-screen, select **B&W** for black and white from the /Graph Options menu even if you are using a color monitor. The B&W option forces 1-2-3 to fill the graph bars with hatch patterns rather than colors. That way, what you see on-screen will approximate the illustrations in this chapter. Now, to

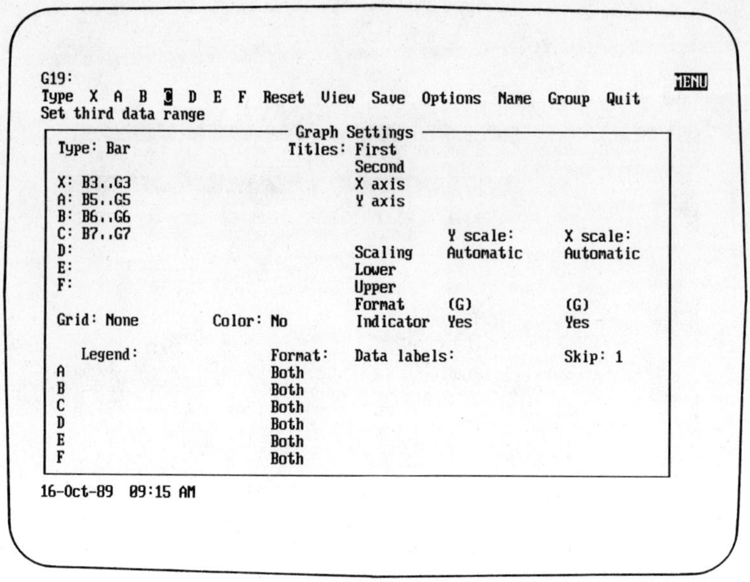

```
G19:                                                              MENU
Type X A B C D E F  Reset View Save Options Name Group Quit
Set third data range
                            ┌─── Graph Settings ───────────────────┐
   Type: Bar                │        Titles: First                 │
                            │                Second                │
   X: B3..G3                │                X axis                │
   A: B5..G5                │                Y axis                │
   B: B6..G6                │                                      │
   C: B7..G7                │                       Y scale:    X scale:
   D:                       │        Scaling  Automatic   Automatic
   E:                       │        Lower                         │
   F:                       │        Upper                         │
                            │        Format      (G)         (G)   │
   Grid: None    Color: No  │        Indicator Yes        Yes      │
                            │                                      │
      Legend:               │  Format:  Data labels:      Skip: 1  │
   A                        │  Both                                │
   B                        │  Both                                │
   C                        │  Both                                │
   D                        │  Both                                │
   E                        │  Both                                │
   F                        │  Both                                │
                            └──────────────────────────────────────┘
16-Oct-89  09:15 AM
```

Fig. 1.6. The 1-2-3 Release 2.2 graph settings sheet.

display the graph on-screen, select **Q**uit to return to the main graph menu and then select **V**iew. The current graph looks like the one shown in figure 1.7, or slightly different if you are using Release 3. Press any key to return to the graph menu.

Adding Titles and a Legend to the Bar Graph

The graph in figure 1.7 may be an accurate representation of the sales data in the Cooper worksheet, but the board of directors may find it a bit lacking. Surely, they will notice that the graph has neither title nor legend. The board may wonder if Cooper means to hide which salesperson is responsible for which set of bars. Without a legend, your viewers have no way to match up bars or lines to the subjects that give rise to the measurements. To solve both of these shortcomings, you next add titles and a legend to the graph.

Nearly all modifications and enhancements you make to graphs are controlled by selections under the /Graph Options menu. The titles and legends you want to add are just two of the options; others are format, grid, axis scale, and data-labels.

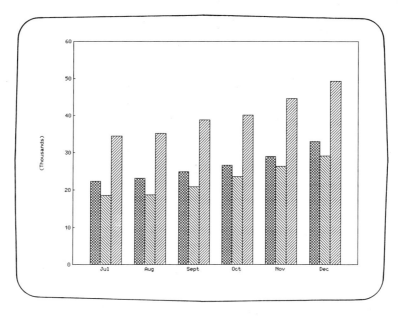

Fig. 1.7. *Your first bar graph.*

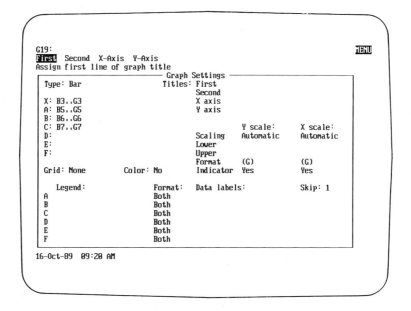

Fig. 1.8. *The /Graph Options Titles menu.*

When you select Titles under the /Graph Options menu, you see the menu shown in figure 1.8. Notice that you can enter four titles for the graph. Earlier, in figure 1.4, you saw the title positions. Select First, so you can enter a main title. Type in **David Remains a Consistent Sales Leader** and press Enter. For a second title, select Second from the titles menu and then type \A1; press Enter again. By making the title entry a cell address preceded by a backslash, you can instruct 1-2-3 to reach into the worksheet and use as a title the text found in that worksheet cell. Because you entered \A1 as the second title, 1-2-3 uses "Cooper Canning" from cell A1 as a second title immediately below the first. You can check the appearance of the revised graph by quitting from the options menu and then selecting View from the graph menu. After looking at your graph, press any key to return to the graph menu.

The legend entries should come next: select Legend on the options menu under /Graph. Later, you'll learn how to use the Range command to enter all legend entries at once. For now, enter them one by one and watch the process. Start by selecting the first data range on the legends menu, data range **A**, and typing in **Eric** when 1-2-3 prompts you for an entry. For data range **B**, enter **Sabina** as the legend entry, and for data range **C**, enter **David.**

When you next view the chart, you should see a legend at the chart's bottom center. The revised graph should now look like the one shown in figure 1.9.

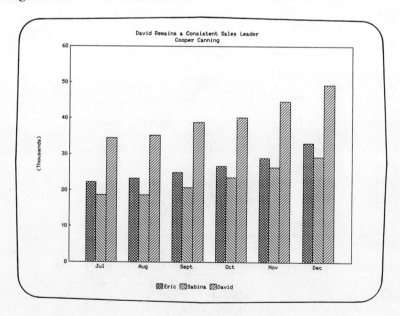

Fig. 1.9. *The graph with titles and a legend in 1-2-3 Release 2.2.*

If you are using 1-2-3 Release 3, your graph will look different. Figure 1.10 shows how your graph appears.

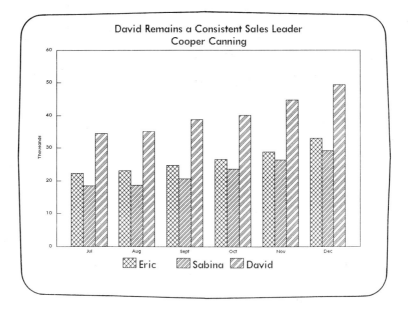

Fig. 1.10. *Graph titles and legends in 1-2-3 Release 3.*

Adding Data-Labels and a Grid to the Bar Graph

Your graph in progress now gives the board of directors the information they need to gauge the relative successes of your three salespeople, but one director you can be sure will want actual numbers. Rather than printing a copy of your data just for him, you can add the data values represented by the bars to your graph. These data values are called *data-labels.* Another option is to add a grid of horizontal lines to the background, so that your viewers can approximate the height of the bars and judge the numbers they represent. Try adding both data-labels and the grid to your graph to see which is the more effective.

To add data-labels, select **Data-labels** from the options menu under /Graph. Then you see the menu shown in figure 1.11. Notice that you can set data-labels for each of the data ranges in the graph. You can also use an option called Group to set all data-labels simultaneously. Details about using Group come in Chapter 3.

```
G19:                                                            MENU
▓ B  C  D  E  F  Group  Quit
Assign first data-range data labels
┌───────────────── Graph Settings ─────────────────────┐
│ Type: Bar              Titles: First  David Remains a Consistent ...│
│                                Second \a1                           │
│ X: B3..G3                      X axis                               │
│ A: B5..G5                      Y axis                               │
│ B: B6..G6                                                           │
│ C: B7..G7                              Y scale:      X scale:        │
│ D:                             Scaling Automatic     Automatic       │
│ E:                             Lower                                 │
│ F:                             Upper                                 │
│                                Format  (G)           (G)            │
│ Grid: None      Color: No      Indicator Yes         Yes            │
│                                                                    │
│   Legend:              Format: Data labels:          Skip: 1        │
│ A  Eric                Both                                         │
│ B  Sabina              Both                                         │
│ C  David               Both                                         │
│ D                      Both                                         │
│ E                      Both                                         │
│ F                      Both                                         │
└────────────────────────────────────────────────────┘
16-Oct-89  09:33 AM
```

***Fig. 1.11.** The /Graph Options Data-labels menu.*

To add data-labels to the bars representing data range A, select **A** from the data-labels menu, then point to the range B5..G5, containing the actual values for data range A, and press Enter. You now see another menu asking you to specify positioning for the data-labels: centered on the data point, above the data point, and so on. When you are creating bar graphs, you can add data-labels either above or below the bars. However, if you select centered, to the right or to the left, 1-2-3 automatically places data-labels above the bars. Select **A**bove so that the data-label appears just above each bar. Repeat the procedure for data ranges B and C, but point to data ranges B6..G6 and B7..G7, respectively. Choose **A**bove as the data-label position for both of these data ranges, too. Select **Q**uit to return to the options menu.

Before you view the graph, try experimenting with a grid. You can add a horizontal grid, with lines running across the width of the graph, or a vertical grid, or both. Because your viewers need to judge the height of the bars and not their position along the x-axis, select only **H**orizontal from the grid menu under the options menu. If you use 1-2-3 Release 2.2, you now see the word "Horizontal" next to the Grid entry.

The graph now looks like the one in figure 1.12. Notice that the data-labels do not fit properly above the bars. The confusion on the screen is compounded, not helped, by the horizontal grid lines. Something has got to go. You have several choices: you can remove the grid lines or the data-labels, or you can remove the bars and leave only the data points and labels. Another option is to use lines to represent the data ranges rather than sets of bars. Then, you can position some of the data-labels above the data points and others below, so that they are all easily legible. But the problem with lines is that they tend to emphasize a general progression of results over time, lessening the emphasis on individual results. For this graph, your best option may be to eliminate the data-labels and leave only the grid. The result will be less precise, but the graph will be less cluttered and have a more dramatic impact.

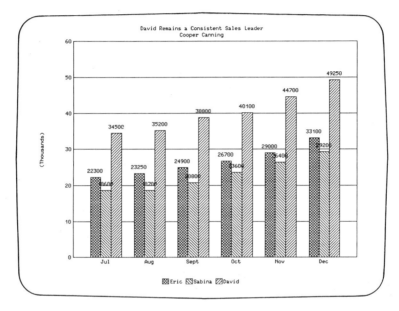

Fig. 1.12. The graph with data-labels and horizontal grid added.

To remove the data-labels, assign a blank cell as a substitute for the earlier assigned data-label series range. To accomplish this, return to the data-labels menu under /**G**raph **O**ptions and select data range **A**. Now, point to any blank cell, perhaps cell A18, and select any position for the data-label. Repeat the procedure for data ranges B and C.

The graph with only a grid now looks like the graph shown in figure 1.13. If you use 1-2-3 Release 3, your graph looks like the one in figure 1.14.

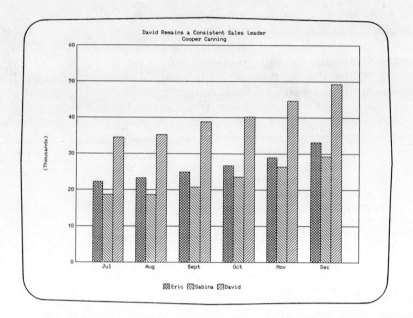

Fig. 1.13. *The bar graph with a grid and no data-labels.*

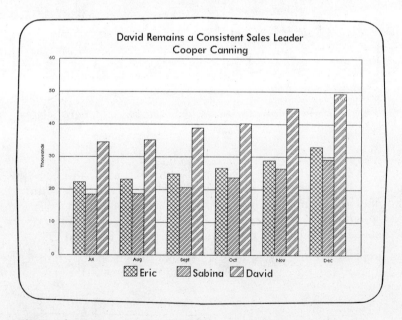

Fig. 1.14. *The bar graph with grid and no data-labels with 1-2-3 Release 3.*

Saving the Bar Graph

You could make many more alterations to the graph if you had time. Instead, stop here and save the graph. 1-2-3 offers two ways to save a graph. You can give it a name so that you can retrieve the graph later along with the worksheet it is a part of. Or you can save the graph as a separate PIC file on disk, so that you can use the file in another program. You may even decide to do both. Which method you choose depends on whether you will need to edit the graph again within 1-2-3 or whether you will need to take the graph outside of 1-2-3 to print, annotate, or add it to a document within a word processing or desktop publishing program.

For safety and security, and because it takes only a moment, you may want to use both saving methods. To name the graph, select **/G**raph **N**ame from the 1-2-3 menu. You will see the name menu shown in figure 1.15. Select **C**reate from the name menu. Type in a name for the graph and press Enter. By creating a named graph, you are saving one version of all of the graph settings. If you use 1-2-3 Release 2.2, you can think of naming a graph as saving one copy of the graph settings sheet. When you select **/G**raph **N**ame **U**se later on, 1-2-3 retrieves the graph settings and reconstructs the graph, using the current data in the worksheet. So, if the worksheet data changes, the graph is automatically updated the next time the graph appears.

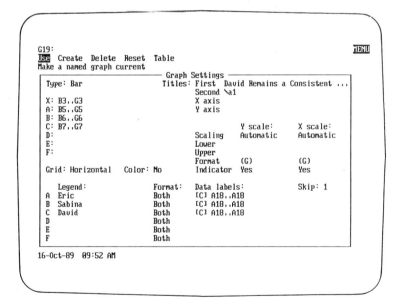

Fig. 1.15. *The /Graph Name menu.*

To give this graph a name, select **C**reate from the **/G**raph **N**ame menu, type in **SALES** and press Enter. To make sure the named graph is saved, you should use the **/F**ile **S**ave command from the 1-2-3 main menu to save the worksheet as well. Save the worksheet as COOPER. Named graphs are saved on disk only when the worksheet containing them is saved using **/F**ile **S**ave. If you quit from 1-2-3 or retrieve another worksheet before saving the current worksheet, you will lose your named graph.

Another option for saving a graph is to use the save command on the graph menu, shown highlighted in figure 1.16. After you enter a name, 1-2-3 saves the graph as a PIC file on disk. A PIC file is an essential tool for transferring a 1-2-3 graph to another program for printing, enhancement, or for incorporation into a document. PrintGraph, the separate printing program, which comes with 1-2-3 Release 2.2 and earlier versions of 1-2-3, depends on PIC files as its input (1-2-3 Release 3 lets users print a graph from within 1-2-3).

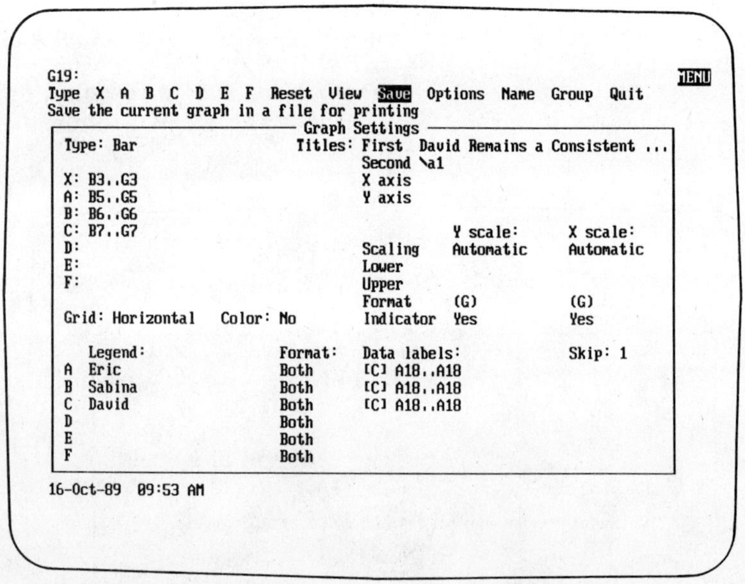

```
G19:                                                                    MENU
Type  X  A  B  C  D  E  F  Reset  View  Save  Options  Name  Group  Quit
Save the current graph in a file for printing
                           ── Graph Settings ──
  Type: Bar                  Titles: First  David Remains a Consistent ...
                                     Second \a1
  X: B3..G3                  X axis
  A: B5..G5                  Y axis
  B: B6..G6
  C: B7..G7                                 Y scale:      X scale:
  D:                         Scaling        Automatic     Automatic
  E:                         Lower
  F:                         Upper
                             Format   (G)         (G)
  Grid: Horizontal  Color: No  Indicator Yes        Yes

     Legend:        Format:  Data labels:           Skip: 1
  A  Eric           Both     [C] A18..A18
  B  Sabina         Both     [C] A18..A18
  C  David          Both     [C] A18..A18
  D                 Both
  E                 Both
  F                 Both

  16-Oct-89  09:53 AM
```

Fig. 1.16. *The /Graph Save command highlighted.*

Ironically, PIC files are inherently limited by their independence. When you save a PIC file, you break the tie between the worksheet and the graph. If you modify worksheet data, the graph within the PIC file remains unchanged. To reflect the changes in your numbers, you must create a new PIC file. As long as you keep that limitation in mind as you plan your work, you can make good use of PIC files.

To create a PIC file of your bar graph, select /Graph Save from the 1-2-3 menu, type in a file name of up to eight characters, and then press Enter. 1-2-3 automatically adds the file name extension PIC. To remind you that this graph for Cooper Canning is a bar graph, type **SALESBAR** for the PIC file name, then press Enter.

Finally, save the worksheet, so that you can retrieve it later when you create the other graphs for the Cooper presentation. Replace the existing COOPER worksheet with the revised worksheet.

If you are using 1-2-3 Release 2.2, or an earlier release, you can print your graph with PrintGraph. In this program, you can make additional formatting selections for the graph, such as the text font. But with 1-2-3 Release 2.2, you can take advantage of a special program called Allways, which attaches to 1-2-3. Allways comes as part of the package when you buy 1-2-3 Release 2.2, or when you upgrade to Release 2.2 from an earlier release. You can also buy Allways separately and add it yourself to 1-2-3 Release 2.01 or earlier.

If you use Release 2.2, or if you bought Allways separately for your copy of 1-2-3, you should follow along with the next section, which describes how you can use Allways to improve dramatically the appearance of your graphs.

If you are using 1-2-3 Release 3, you should skip the following section and pick up the Quick Start with the section, "Formatting the Graph in 1-2-3 Release 3."

Formatting the Graph in Allways

With Allways, a special add-in written for 1-2-3 by Funk Software, you can perform formatting tasks that are not possible with 1-2-3 alone. First, Allways gives you a faithful on-screen representation of your printed worksheet. You see formatting enhancements, such as bold text, on the screen as well as on the printed page. Among many enhancements made possible with Allways, you can enhance text and numbers with a variety of printer typefaces; you can underline worksheet data as you choose; or you can shade ranges of work-sheet cells.

Allways is just as helpful in formatting graphs. With Allways attached to 1-2-3, you can retrieve a graph saved as a PIC file and superimpose it over a portion of the worksheet. If that area is adjacent to one that contains data, you can send both areas to the printer side by side to get worksheet data and a graph on the same page. But using Allways to combine data and graphics on a page is only the start of what Allways can do, as you'll learn in Chapter 5, "Formatting Graphs with Allways in 1-2-3 Release 2.2."

Much of the advanced graph formatting you can perform with Allways relies on one simple fact about the way the program works. When you add a graph on top of a worksheet area, anything beneath the graph shows through from the worksheet, appearing to be integrated into the graph. With that in mind, you can omit from the graph text items such as titles and enter them into worksheet cells behind the graph. Then, using Allways, you can format the added text, selecting text typefaces and type sizes that are simply unavailable in 1-2-3. The text that you have formatted shows through to serve as graph titles. Best of all, the typefaces you select from within Allways closely approximate on-screen the printed-page form. You can design an attractive layout for your graph with the confidence that the graph will look just as good or better when printed. In fact, because your printer resolution is undoubtedly better than your screen resolution, you can expect sharper, crisper images from the printed graph.

For the Cooper presentation, you wisely decide to replace the current titles entered originally from /Graph Options Titles with new titles formatted through the services of Allways. So, retrieve the graph you created earlier, if necessary, by selecting /Graph Name Use and entering the graph name SALES. To delete the current titles, select /Graph Options Titles and then select First from the titles menu. You should see the title you typed in earlier in the edit panel. Press Esc to clear that title and then press Enter. Do the same with the second title. View the graph quickly to be sure the titles are gone.

Now that you have made a change to the graph, you must replace the current PIC file on the disk by saving the new graph as a PIC file with the same name. So, before continuing, select /Graph Save, enter the name SALESBAR, and select Replace to tell 1-2-3 to replace the current PIC file on disk with the revised PIC file.

To load Allways, you must select /Add-in Attach from the 1-2-3 main menu and then select ALLWAYS.ADN from the add-in names that appear. Unless you bought other add-ins separately, the only two that should appear are Allways and the Macro Manager. After you select Allways as the add-in to attach, 1-2-3 asks whether you want to assign it to a particular Alt-Function key combination so that you can invoke the program quickly. Select the number 7, so that you can press Alt-F7 to use Allways. Then, from the next menu, select Invoke to start an add-in and choose ALLWAYS as the add-in to invoke. In a moment, you will see your worksheet as it appears on the Allways screen. Your screen should now look like the screen shown in figure 1.17.

Try pressing the 1-2-3 menu key (/). The Allways menu pops up rather than the 1-2-3 menu. You can jump right back to 1-2-3 by pressing Esc a few times. Then, you can press Alt-F7 to return to Allways.

FONT(1) Triumvirate 10 pt						ALLWAYS	
G19:							

```
            A           B       C        D        E        F        G       H
  1   Cooper Canning
  2   Consolidated Data
  3                      Jul     Aug     Sept     Oct      Nov      Dec
  4   Revenues
  5          Eric       22300   23250   24900    26700    29000    33100
  6        Sabina       18600   18700   20800    23600    26400    29200
  7         David       34500   35200   38800    40100    44700    49250
  8                    --------  -------- -------- -------- -------- --------
  9    Total Sales      75400   77150   84500    90400   100100   111550
 10
 11   Expenses
 12     Operations      17000   17000   17000    17000    17000    17000
 13      Marketing      14200   14400   15100    15700    17200    17800
 14      Personnel      16100   16100   16100    17920    17920    17920
 15                    --------  -------- -------- -------- -------- --------
 16  Total Expenses     47300   47500   48200    50620    52120    52720
 17
 18
 19
 20
 21
 22
 23
 24
 25
 26
 27
16-Oct-89  10:12 AM
```

Fig. 1.17. The Cooper worksheet as it appears in Allways.

After you are in Allways, you can add the graph you made earlier to a clear area of the worksheet. Then you can add titles to the graph formatted with Allways. To try it, call up the Allways menu. Select **Graph** to see all the graph menu commands, as shown in figure 1.18. Next, place a copy of a graph stored as a PIC file onto the worksheet by selecting **Add** from the graph menu and then selecting the SALESBAR.PIC file, which appears on the list of PIC files.

When you choose a PIC file to add to a worksheet, Allways queries you for a graph placement range. You can type in a range address or you can use the familiar 1-2-3 pointing method to select the range. Either way, select the range B19..F34 below the worksheet. When you press Enter, the graph appears in the range that you selected, as shown in figure 1.19.

To begin reformatting your graph titles, position the cursor on the worksheet cell into which you will add the first title. Cell B18 would be about right as the starting point for the first title, so position the cursor in cell B19 and press Esc to return to 1-2-3. When 1-2-3 returns to the screen, type **David Remains a Consistent Sales Leader** and press Enter. In the cell below and to the right, C19, enter **Cooper Canning**. The worksheet should look like the one shown in figure 1.20. After the text is entered into the cells, you can press Alt-F7 to invoke Allways once again so you can format the new titles.

```
FONT(1) Triumvirate 10 pt                                    MENU
Add  Remove  Goto  Settings  Fonts-Directory  Quit
Add a graph to the worksheet
        A           B        C        D        E        F        G        H
1   Cooper Canning
2   Consolidated Data
3                     Jul      Aug     Sept     Oct      Nov      Dec
4   Revenues
5            Eric    22300    23250    24900    26700    29000    33100
6          Sabina    18600    18700    20800    23600    26400    29200
7           David    34500    35200    38800    40100    44700    49250
8                   --------  -------  -------  -------  --------  --------
9      Total Sales   75400    77150    84500    90400   100100   111550
10
11  Expenses
12      Operations   17000    17000    17000    17000    17000    17000
13       Marketing   14200    14400    15100    15700    17200    17800
14       Personnel   16100    16100    16100    17920    17920    17920
15                   --------  -------  -------  -------  --------  --------
16   Total Expenses   47300    47500    48200    50620    52120    52720
17
18
19
20
21
22
23
24
25
26
27
20-Feb-90   04:40 PM                                  NUM
```

Fig. 1.18. The Allways graph menu.

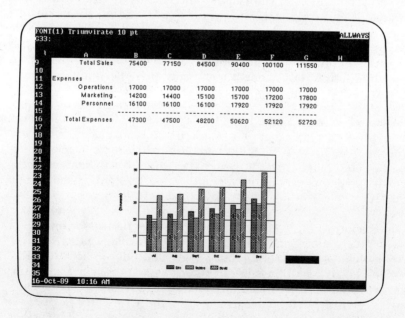

```
FONT(1) Triumvirate 10 pt                                    ALLWAYS
G33:
        A           B        C        D        E        F        G        H
9     Total Sales   75400    77150    84500    90400   100100   111550
10
11  Expenses
12      Operations   17000    17000    17000    17000    17000    17000
13       Marketing   14200    14400    15100    15700    17200    17800
14       Personnel   16100    16100    16100    17920    17920    17920
15                   --------  -------  -------  -------  --------  --------
16   Total Expenses   47300    47500    48200    50620    52120    52720
16-Oct-89   10:16 AM
```

Fig. 1.19. The SALESBAR.PIC graph added to range B19..F34.

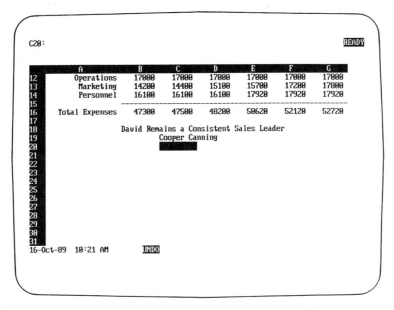

Fig. 1.20. The worksheet with labels added for graph titles.

To select a more attractive typeface for the text, position the cursor on the first of the cells holding the title text, cell B18. Next, bring up the Allways menu. Select **Format** from the menu and then select **Font**. From the list of available *fonts*, or typefaces, (see fig. 1.21) you can select a style for your text. Try highlighting Triumvirate 14 point with the cursor and pressing Enter. When Allways requests a range of cells to format, stretch the highlight so that it covers the range B18...C19 and press Enter.

The text freshly formatted in the Triumvirate font is far better looking than before. The only finishing touch needed is to move the second line of the title to the right a bit. You can move a title by padding it with spaces just as you do a worksheet label. Remember, these are true worksheet labels showing through the graph from behind. To pad the second title, return to 1-2-3 by pressing Esc; then add a few spaces at the beginning of Cooper Canning in cell C19. Six spaces should just about do it. The graph in Allways with reformatted titles appears in figure 1.22. Notice that rows 18 and 19 have increased in height to accommodate the title text.

A faster way to select a font for a text label is to position the cursor on the cell with the label, press and hold the Alt key and press one of the number keys at the top of the keyboard. Triumvirate 14 point is font

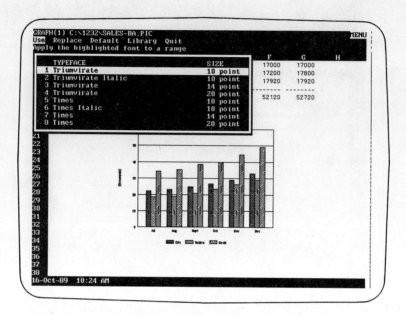

Fig. 1.21. *The list of Allways fonts.*

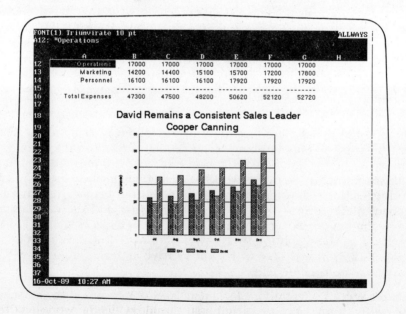

Fig. 1.22. *The titles reformatted by Allways.*

number 3, for example, so you can press Alt-3 to format the contents of a cell in this font. Try using this technique to change the font for the contents of cell B18. Position the cursor on B18 and press Alt-1, Alt-2, Alt-3, and so on through Alt-8 in order to see all eight Allways fonts. You may want to return to the font you first chose, Font 3, Triumvirate 14 point.

Allways provides still more formatting capabilities, and these you will read about in Chapter 5. For now, save your 1-2-3 worksheet and continue with the Quick Start. To save the worksheet, press Esc to leave Allways and return to 1-2-3. Save the worksheet as you normally save a file, with /File Save. All the enhancements you supplied in Allways are saved, too. When you next retrieve the worksheet and invoke Allways, you will see the same graph added to the worksheet and the same formatted titles.

You can now skip the following section, intended for users of 1-2-3 Release 3. For those readers using a 1-2-3 version prior to Release 3, the Quick Start resumes with "Creating a Line Graph."

Formatting the Graph in 1-2-3 Release 3

Many of the special graph formatting capabilities that are appended by the add-in program Allways in earlier releases of 1-2-3 are integrated into 1-2-3 Release 3. Also added into Release 3 are some graphic design possibilities normally attainable only with dedicated graphing programs.

Your graph, as created by 1-2-3 Release 3, so far resembles figure 1.23. Some of the vast improvements over Release 2 graphs you'll notice are the appropriately sized graph titles and legend text. Release 3 also uses varied hatch patterns within the bars. But one of the greatest improvements is a new tool that will help you as you make graphs, the graph window.

A 1-2-3 Release 3 graph window places a miniature version of your graph on the screen so that the graph shares the screen with your worksheet data. As you make changes to the numbers in your worksheet, the on-screen graph immediately updates to reflect those changes. The graph window makes performing visual what-ifs and data analyses easy.

Setting up a graph window is a straightforward procedure: position the cursor in the column where the graph window should start and select /Worksheet Window Graph. The graph window fills the worksheet from that column to the right edge of the screen. Of course, when you

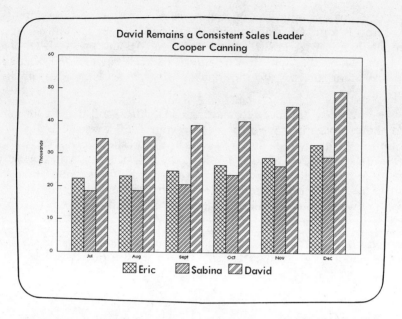

Fig. 1.23. *The Cooper Canning graph so far in 1-2-3 Release 3.*

devote over half the screen to a graph window, much less of the worksheet is available. So, to maximize the amount of the worksheet you can see, you should reduce the column widths as much as you can. Begin by setting the global column width to 8, selecting /Worksheet Global Col-Width **8**. Then, change the width of column A to **16**. Your worksheet should now look like the worksheet in figure 1.24.

To open a graph window, position the cursor anywhere within column E and select /Worksheet **W**indow **G**raph. Your graph will appear, starting at column E and continuing to the right of the screen (see fig. 1.25). You can still press Graph (F10) at any time to see a full-screen version of your graph. If you do, you'll notice a dramatic difference between how the graph appears in the window and how it appears full-screen. The window you set up with /Worksheet Window Graph is tall and narrow compared to the full-screen graph window. An elongated distortion of the graph appears in the graph window. Although the graph is still technically accurate, the impression of monthly change it gives is quite different.

You may notice other, more subtle changes to the graph. 1-2-3 reduces the size of the graph's first title to fit the graph window. 1-2-3 also truncates graph text to fit the window, cutting short titles and labels as it needs to. The graph window is a fine tool for an overall check of the

A:A1: [W16] 'Cooper Canning   READY

```
A        A            B       C       D       E       F       G       H
1   Cooper Canning
2   Consolidated Data
3                      Jul     Aug    Sept     Oct     Nov     Dec
4   Revenues
5          Eric       22300   23250   24900   26700   29000   33100
6        Sabina       18600   18700   20800   23600   26400   29200
7         David       34500   35200   38800   40100   44700   49250
8                    -----------------------------------------------
9   Total Sales       75400   77150   84500   90400  100100  111550
10
11  Expenses
12   Operations       17000   17000   17000   17000   17000   17000
13    Marketing       14200   14400   15100   15700   17200   17800
14    Personnel       16100   16100   16100   17920   17920   17920
15                   -----------------------------------------------
16  Total Expenses    47300   47500   48200   50620   52120   52720
17
18
19
20
21
22
23
24
25
26
27
28
29
```
COOPER.WK3

Fig. 1.24. *The revised 1-2-3 Release 3 worksheet.*

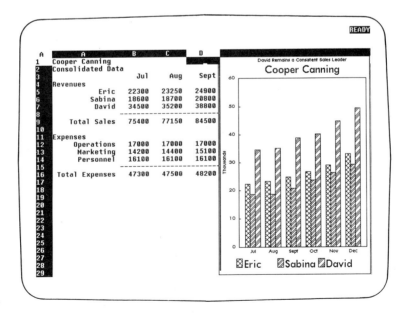

Fig. 1.25. *A 1-2-3 Release 3 graph window.*

graph features, but you should gauge the true appearance of your graph only from the full-screen view.

To see one example of the usefulness of a graph window, try modifying a single data item in the worksheet and watch how the graph changes. Add 100,000 to Eric's July sales figure so that it increases to 122,300. Note the difference in the graph, reflected in figure 1.26. 1-2-3 has automatically changed the maximum value of the vertical y-axis to accommodate your new data. Set the figure back to its original value, 22,300, so that you can continue.

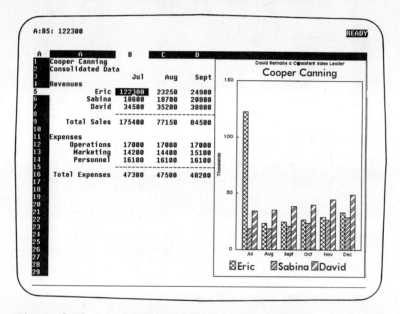

Fig. 1.26. *The window graph reflecting a data change.*

The graph window also comes in handy as you alter the graph design. Rather than switching back and forth from worksheet to graph, you can monitor instantly the effect of changes you make to the graph. To try this, experiment by changing the hatch patterns in the graph bars.

All the commands you need to modify a graph's appearance are on the /Graph Options menu. When you select Options Advanced Hatches from the graph menu, 1-2-3 supplies a menu of data ranges. Select the data range you want to modify, data range **A**, and then pick hatch pattern 1 from the menu of hatch patterns. Take a look at the graph. Select data range **A** again and try hatch pattern 2, instead. Try each of the eight available hatch patterns until you settle on one that pleases your eye. Now you can select two other hatch patterns for data ranges B and C. Your goal in picking hatch patterns is to choose side-by-side patterns that are clearly different, so that a viewer can distinguish the bars immediately. If you select hatch patterns 3, 1, and 2, your graph looks like the one you see in figure 1.27.

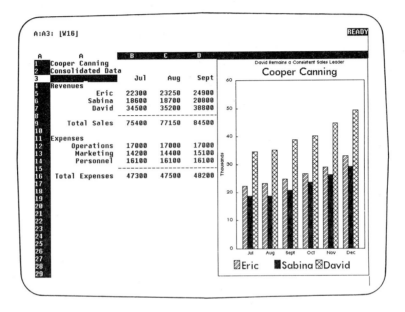

Fig. 1.27. *The bar graph with hatch patterns 3, 1, and 2.*

The hatch menu provides eight pattern choices, but you can actually select from among 14 hatches. Patterns 9 through 14 are shades of gray rather than line patterns, and, to select these, you must set up a hatches range. A hatches range also lets you specify the hatch pattern for graph bars separately. By using a contrasting hatch pattern for certain bars, you can highlight for emphasis. For instance, you might accentuate the month with the greatest sales revenue.

To set up a hatches range, you enter hatch-pattern numbers into a blank range on the worksheet spanning the same number of cells as the data range you have graphed. Your graph has three data ranges of six cells each, so your hatches ranges should match. Each cell in a hatches range corresponds to a data range cell.

For this graph, you will use the same hatch number for all bars in each data range. You can set up the hatches range so that you can enter one number in the first hatch range cell and have it copied to all other hatch range cells. To try this, enter the number 10 into cell H5. Enter +H5 in cell I5 and copy it to J5..M5. Enter the number 12 in cell H6. Enter +H6 in cell I6 and copy it to J6..M6. Similarly, enter the number 14 in cell H7. Enter +H7 in cell I7 and copy it to J7..M7.

Now that you have the hatches ranges set up, you can assign the ranges by first selecting /**Graph O**ptions **A**dvanced **H**atches, and then selecting **A**, the first data range. Select **R**ange from the next menu and point to the hatches range H5..M5. Notice the change through the graph window. Select data range **B** from the hatches menu, select **R**ange, and then point to hatches range H6..M6. Select data range **C**, select **R**ange, and then point to hatches range H7..M7. The graph in the window displays three attractive shades of gray, hatch patterns 10, 12, and 14. Remember that if you are working with a color monitor, you must choose B&W from the options menu to obtain the gray shadings. If you press Graph (F10) to preview the full-screen image, your work should look like the graph shown in figure 1.28.

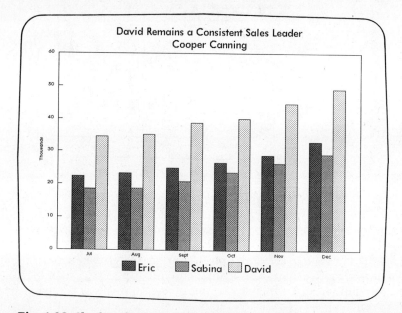

Fig. 1.28. Shades of gray set with a hatches range.

Experiment with changing the numbers in column H to modify the hatch pattern used by the data ranges. You can select any hatch number from 1 through 14. Also, you can change some of the numbers in the remainder of the hatches range and see the effect on specific bars in the windowed graph.

1-2-3 Release 3 provides a similar facility for changing the colors of a graph's bars when you create a color graph for a color printer, plotter, or slidemaker or when you need a color graph for an on-screen desktop presentation. You'll find an entire chapter later in this book on creating animated desktop presentations. 1-2-3 Release 3 provides many other advanced graph formatting features, all of which you'll find covered in detail in Chapter 6, "Advanced Graph Formatting in 1-2-3 Release 3."

For now, you should save the graph you completed with attractive gray bar shading. As always with 1-2-3, you can save the graph by two methods. You can name the graph so that you can retrieve it later when you recall the worksheet, or you can save the graph as a PIC file. When you save a Release 3 PIC file, the advanced formatting enhancements become part of the PIC file—just one of the benefits of creating graphs with Release 3.

Name the graph **SALESBAR** with the /Graph Name Create command, and then save a PIC file version of the graph with the same name using the /Graph Save command.

Creating a Line Graph

For your next feat, you must create the graph to compare Cooper's sales and revenues over the preceding six months. Easy. The focal question of this graph is "How have sales and revenue changed over the last six months?" Because this graph illustrates the general trend of data over time, you wisely decide on a line graph rather than a bar graph. The bar graph was preferable for the first assignment—when you wanted to depict results at discrete intervals. Now you are working with trends.

You don't need to start from scratch to build the line graph: you can change the current bar type to a line graph. Then you can make other changes to bring the graph in line with the current data and presentation needs. If you use Release 3, you can open a graph window on the screen and watch changes to your graph take effect immediately as you make modifications.

Start by selecting /Graph Type Line to change the graph type from bar to line. The x-axis should remain the same, so you can skip to the next step, that of redefining the data ranges. The data ranges should now constitute month-by-month total sales and total revenues rather than individual salesperson's figures. Select data range **A** on the main graph menu and select Total Revenues in worksheet range B9..G9 to supersede the range selected earlier. Select data range **B** on the main graph menu, too, and change the worksheet range to Total Expenses, B16..G16. To clear off data range C—no longer needed—select **R**eset from the graph menu and then select **C**.

Now take a look at the revised graph. The graph you see should look like the one in figure 1.29. If you are using Release 2.2, the title is missing and the legend is incorrect. If you are using 1-2-3 Release 3, both the titles and legend are incorrect. But the graph does properly display two lines, one for revenues and one for expenses. After a few choices from graph options, you will have a perfectly suitable line graph.

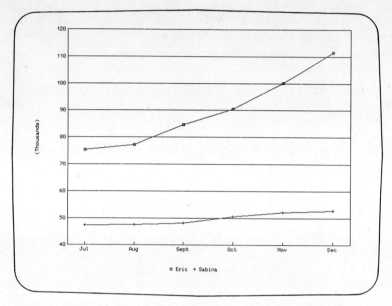

Fig. 1.29. *Revenues and expenses plotted as lines in 1-2-3 Release 2.2.*

Modifying the Line Graph

First, modify the legend by selecting /**G**raph **O**ptions **L**egend and then selecting data range **A** from the legend menu. You should see the old legend entry in the edit panel. Press Esc to clear off the old entry, type in **Revenues,** and then press Enter to set the new legend entry in place. Follow a similar procedure to change the legend for data range B to Expenses. For data range C, you can simply press Esc and then Enter to clear off the old entry without adding a new one.

Take another look at the line graph (see fig. 1.29). The presence of both horizontal grid lines and graph lines muddles the graph, making for a confusing rather than a clean and simple visual. Remember, your goal is to create a graph that communicates even at a glance. Not that the board of directors is incapable of understanding a complex graphic, but you run the risk of muting your message with a graph that takes too long to interpret. Put another way, the graph that is most easily understood is the graph with the greatest impact.

To simplify the graph, you may want to remove its grid lines altogether. You may want to offer your viewers more precise value indications than lines can provide. Why not supply the numbers themselves by adding data-labels to the graph? Data-labels display the actual data point values on the graph adjacent to the data points. They are a perfect complement to many uncluttered line graphs. The clean, clear areas in line graphs leave plenty of space for data-labels.

To add data-labels, select /Graph Options Data-labels, select data range A and then point to the worksheet range that data range A portrays, B9..G9. When 1-2-3 queries you for a position for the data-labels, select Above, so that each data-label appears above its corresponding data point. Follow the same procedure for data range B, but select the worksheet range B16..G16 and Below to place the data-labels below the data points.

The last change necessary is a new first title line that describes the new graph expressively. Select /Graph Options Titles First; press Esc only if necessary to clear off the prior title; and enter **Revenues Outpace Expenses.** Add the second title, **Cooper Canning**, if necessary. If you use 1-2-3 Release 3, you will see the title change immediately in the graph window. Notice that the new, shorter title fits easily in the graph window, so 1-2-3 uses a larger text size for it. You will see no difference in the size of the title in Release 2.2. 1-2-3 displays the graph title in small characters on the screen and prints the title in larger characters on paper. Both sizes are preset.

If you use Release 2.2, your on-screen graph should look like the one in figure 1.30. If you use Release 3, your graph looks like the figure 1.31 graph instead.

Saving the Line Graph

To save the graph, you should name it so that you can retrieve it later. Select /Graph Name Create and enter **REV-EXP** as the graph name. Save a PIC file version of the graph by using the /Graph Save command and entering **REV-EXP** as the name of the file to save. Save the worksheet once again with /File Save to be sure the named graph is saved on disk along with the worksheet.

The last-minute nature of your work now prevents any further changes. With more time, you would elaborate your work further within 1-2-3 or, outside of 1-2-3, with one of the popular dedicated graphics,

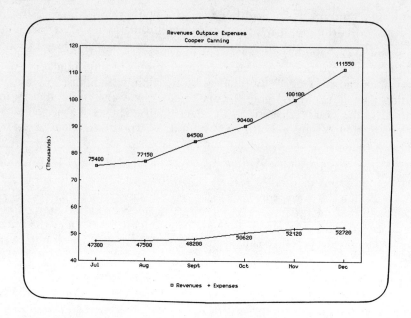

Fig. 1.30. *The line graph in 1-2-3 Release 2.2.*

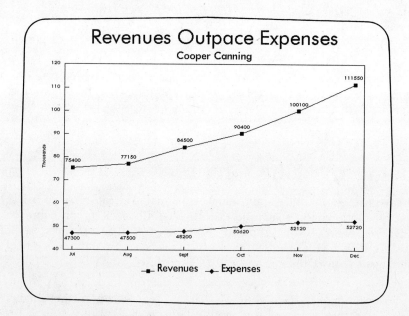

Fig. 1.31. *The line graph in 1-2-3 Release 3.*

animation, or illustration programs. You could pull the completed 1-2-3 graph into a program such as Freelance Plus or Harvard Graphics for enhancements that would make the presentation more fun to look at and more meaningful. A simple change, such as replacing the plain bars with stacks of Cooper's cans could make the graph come alive for your viewers. A can is an easy graphic to produce in most graphics programs. If your artistic abilities faded abruptly after kindergarten, you can pull an image of a can from any of dozens of clip-art libraries and add it to your graph.

If you use Release 3, you can take advantage of that program's advanced options. A new graph type offered in Release 3, the area graph, is similar to a line graph, but the areas below the lines are filled, and the data series are stacked vertically. Area graphs downplay individual results measured at time intervals in favor of the overall trend of data across the period. 1-2-3 Release 2.2 and earlier releases of 1-2-3 do not include area graphs in their repertoire.

Changing this line graph to an area graph would take only a moment, so you decide to take a quick look. Maybe the area type would give the Cooper presentation a little extra emphasis. You make the change by selecting /Graph Options Format Graph and then choosing Area from the format menu. The revised graph appears in figure 1.32.

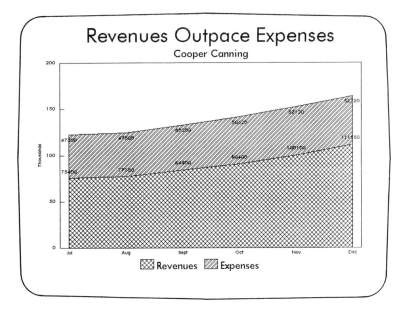

Fig. 1.32. Sales and revenues presented in an area graph.

The area graph does a fine job of showing a steady increase in revenues, but it distorts the magnitude of the increase in expenses. Because expenses are stacked on top of increasing revenues, the expense total appears to increase dramatically, also. The truth is that expenses increased only slightly at the same time revenues were skyrocketing. The area graph not only misrepresents, but it misrepresents in the wrong direction. Cooper is proud of keeping the growth of expenses moderate, so a graph that exaggerates expense growth is unwelcome, to say the least.

An area graph has another problem in this case. Because 1-2-3 area graphs stack results one on top of another, they represent not only the trend of individual results over time, but the trend of the aggregate, too. Subtracting expenses from revenues would offer a meaningful net, but adding revenues and expenses together produces no meaningful perspective.

Perhaps one of the other graphs would work well as an area graph. Think back to the initial graph you produced, the bar graph of three salesperson's revenues. Stacking those figures to produce a total would offer helpful information. From the stacked areas, you could interpret not only the sales trend of each individual, but the overall accomplishment of the sales force also. An area graph version of the data from the first graph might be worth a second look.

Before you return to the first graph, select /Graph Options Format Graph Lines to set the graph type back to line. Now, you can use the /Graph Name Use command to retrieve the previous chart and make the change.

Select /Graph Name Use and select the graph name SALESBAR. 1-2-3 will retrieve the graph settings saved as SALESBAR and reconstruct the original SALESBAR graph. To change the graph to an area graph, select /Graph Options Format Graph Area. The graph does not appear to change because the graph type is still set to Bar. Return to the main graph menu and select Line for the graph type. If you press Graph (F10) to view the full-screen graph, you will see the area graph illustrated in figure 1.33.

You can save this area graph along with the SALESBAR graph by giving it a name, too. Select /Graph Name Create and enter **SALES-AREA** as the graph name. When you next save the worksheet, both SALESBAR and SALES-AREA will be saved as part of your work.

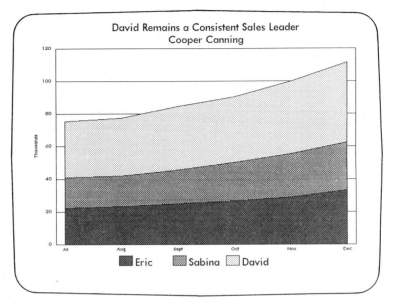

Fig. 1.33. *The SALESBAR graph converted to an area graph.*

Creating the Pie Graph

To top off Cooper's presentation in style, the staff needs one last graph. This is a breakdown of sales results for the three salespeople during July through December. Whenever you want to depict relative contributions of a series of numbers to a whole, your best choice is a pie graph. The complete circle of the pie constitutes a whole, and each pie slice represents one contributing portion.

You create a pie slice by defining two data ranges, X and A. The X data range holds the pie-slice labels, and the A data range holds the pie-slice values.

Begin the pie graph by using the /Graph **R**eset **G**raph command to clear all current graph settings. You can always recall the complete group of settings for one of the two graphs you created by using the /Graph **N**ame **U**se command. The only setting that remains unchanged after you use Reset is graph type. Select /Graph **T**ype **P**ie to change it.

Next, select the worksheet range for the X data range. The labels in the range you choose become the pie-slice labels, so select the salepeople's names, A5..A7.

Earlier, when you set up the bar and line graphs, you selected several data ranges from the worksheet. For a pie graph, you can designate only a single range of worksheet values. You assign that range to data range A. The values within that data range determine the number and sizes of pie slices. Because you can graph only a single range, you must decide between two options: 1) to create a separate pie for each month's breakdown of the salespeople's results or, 2) to add the monthly sales figures, placing the results in three cells, and then use those totals to create the pie slices.

```
H9:                                                                    READY

          A          B       C       D       E       F       G       H
 1  Cooper Canning
 2  Consolidated Data
 3                     Jul     Aug    Sept     Oct     Nov     Dec
 4  Revenues
 5            Eric    22300   23250   24900   26700   29000   33100  159250
 6          Sabina    18600   18700   20800   23600   26400   29200  137300
 7           David    34500   35200   38800   40100   44700   49250  242550
 8                    ------  ------  ------  ------  ------  ------
 9     Total Sales    75400   77150   84500   90400  100100  111550
10
11  Expenses
12       Operations   17000   17000   17000   17000   17000   17000
13        Marketing   14200   14400   15100   15700   17200   17000
14        Personnel   16100   16100   16100   17920   17920   17920
15                    ------  ------  ------  ------  ------  ------
16  Total Expenses    47300   47500   48200   50620   52120   52720
17
18              David Remains a Consistent Sales Leader
19                          Cooper Canning
20
16-Oct-89  11:50 AM          UNDO
```

Fig. 1.34. Six-month totals added to column H for the pie graph.

If you are using 1-2-3 Release 2.2, you can simply create a formula in the cells to the right of the monthly figures. In cell H5, for example, you can enter the formula @SUM(B5..G5) and then copy the formula to cells H6 and H7. Figure 1.34 shows the worksheet at this point. If, however, you are using 1-2-3 Release 3, you first must insert a column to the right of the worksheet for the sums. Now, you can specify the totals in the range H5..H7 as data range A.

After you have supplied both the X and A data ranges, you can view the graph. You now have a no-frills pie graph, with labeled pie slices and percentage figures that were calculated and added for you by 1-2-3. Titles are still to be determined. Figures 1.35 and 1.36 show this graph, first as produced by 1-2-3 Release 2.2 and, second, by 1-2-3 Release 3.

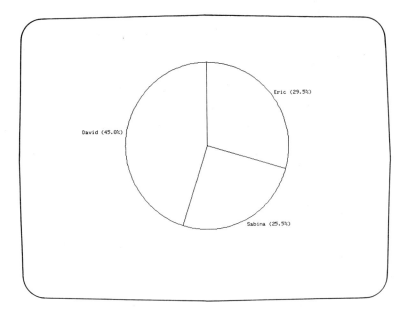

Fig. 1.35. *The basic pie graph as created by 1-2-3 Release 2.2.*

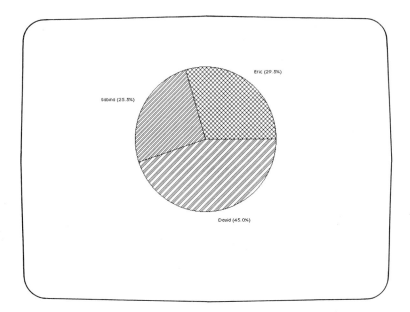

Fig. 1.36. *The basic pie graph as created by 1-2-3 Release 3.*

Observe the differences between the two graphs. 1-2-3 Release 2.2 leaves the slices unfilled, starts cutting the pie at the twelve o'clock position, and carves out new slices clockwise around the pie. 1-2-3 Release 3 fills the slices with default hatch patterns or colors, starts cutting the pie slices at three o'clock, and cuts new slices in a counterclockwise direction.

To add the titles the pie graph lacks, select /Graph Options Titles and enter something dramatic for a first title, such as **David Dominates Sales**. Enter **Cooper Canning** as the second title, so that all graphs in the presentation share a common subtitle.

Because pie graphs are the simplest of the graph types, they have the fewest options. Yet, one of the pie graph characteristics you can take artistic liberty with is pattern or color of the pie slices.

If you are using a color monitor, you should still select B&W from the main graph menu to get a display of hatch patterns. To control which hatch patterns 1-2-3 uses for the pie graph slices, enter hatch pattern numbers in a separate range on the worksheet assigned to data range B. The range you set up is the same size as the range containing the pie-slice values. The current pie-slice range is three cells, so the hatches range should contain three cells. Set up a hatches range just to the right of data range A (H5..H7). In I5..I7, enter the numbers 1, 4, and 7 and assign I5..I7 to data range B. If you are using Release 3, replace the existing numbers in cells I5..I7 with the numbers 11, 12, and 13. Figure 1.37 shows the revised worksheet.

When you press Graph (F10), you see the graph with the hatch patterns shown in figure 1.38 if you are using Release 2.2 or earlier versions. Figure 1.39 shows the graph with hatch patterns produced in Release 3. Figure 1.40 displays the hatch pattern numbers and the corresponding hatch patterns for pie graphs in Release 2.2. Figure 1.41 displays the same correspondence in 1-2-3 Release 3.

1-2-3 Release 3 offers additional hatch patterns for pie slices, just as it offers additional patterns for bar fills. The additional hatch patterns are shades of gray, which can produce a subtle look in the pie graph. Moreover, the shadings can reduce the visual vibration caused by adjacent diagonal hatch patterns of differing directions. By adding 100 to any of the hatch-pattern numbers, you can force 1-2-3 to explode the corresponding pie slice. For example, if you use 1-2-3 Release 2.2, you can explode the slice for Sabina by replacing the number 4 in the hatches range with 104. If you use Release 3, you can cut out the slice for Sabina by replacing the number 12 in the hatches range with 112. The resulting exploded pie is shown in figure 1.42.

B1·   READY

	B	C	D	E	F	G	H	I	J
2	a
3	Jul	Aug	Sept	Oct	Nov	Dec
5	22300	23250	24900	26700	29800	33100	159250		1
6	18600	18700	20000	23600	26400	29200	137300		4
7	34500	35200	38000	40100	44700	49250	242550		7
9	75400	77150	84500	90400	100100	111550
12	17000	17000	17000	17000	17000	17000
13	14200	14400	15100	15700	17200	17800
14	16100	16100	16100	17920	17920	17920
16	47300	47500	48200	50620	52120	52720

David Remains a Consistent Sales Leader
              Cooper Canning
16-Oct-89 12:07 PM   UNDO

Fig. 1.37. The worksheet with the B data range added.

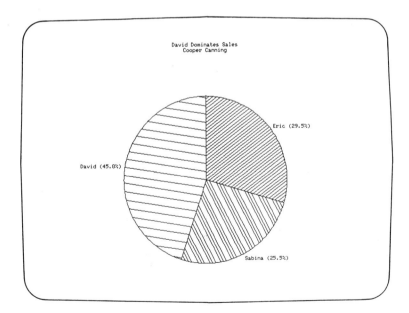

Fig. 1.38. Pie graph hatch patterns in Release 2.2.

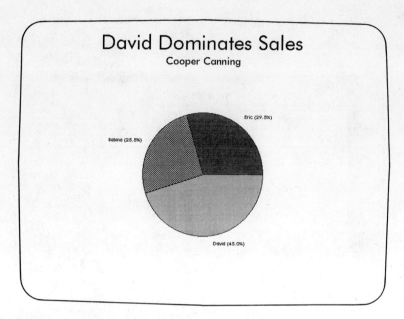

Fig. 1.39. *Pie graph hatch patterns in Release 3.*

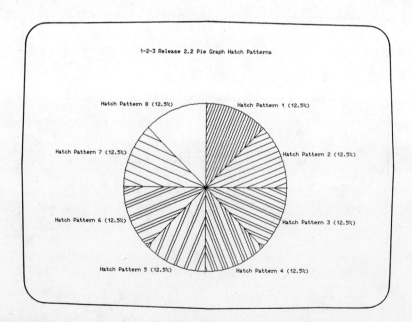

Fig. 1.40. *2.2 Pie graph hatch-pattern numbers in Release 2.2.*

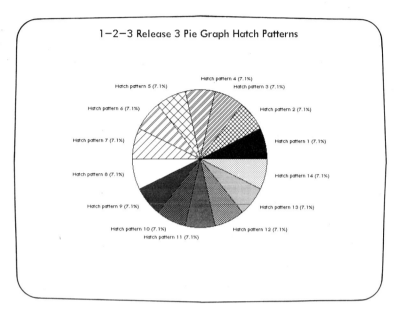

Fig. 1.41. *Pie graph hatch-pattern numbers in Release 3.*

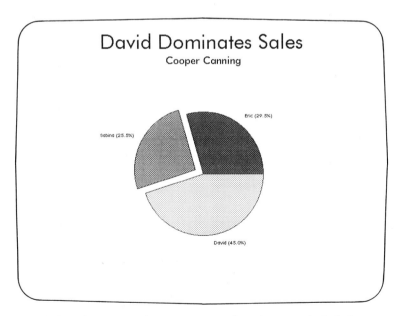

Fig. 1.42. *The 1-2-3 Release 3 pie graph with an exploded slice.*

By varying the numbers in the hatches range, you can create an attractive combination of pie-slice hatches that clearly distinguishes the sections. Adjacent slices should be of sufficient contrast so that your viewers will differentiate them without effort.

To save the pie graph for the presentation, name it SALESPIE with the /Graph Name Create command. Use /Graph Save to create a PIC file of the graph, also with the name SALESPIE.PIC. Finally, save the worksheet once again with the /File Save command to be sure you have an updated copy on the disk.

Now, you have three named graphs saved within the worksheet and three PIC files stored on disk. You can proceed to the next step. Later chapters in this book offer a host of suggestions and techniques for taking your PIC files and embellishing them in external graphics programs. For now, though, you will simply print the graphs you created within 1-2-3. Your time is short and you want to finalize the Cooper presentation.

Your final task is to print the graphs you have produced. 1-2-3 Release 2.2 and 1-2-3 Release 3 offer vastly different methods for creating printed versions of your graphs. If you use 1-2-3 Release 2.2 or an earlier version, you should follow along with the next section. If you use Release 3, you should proceed to the section titled "Printing Graphs in 1-2-3 Release 3."

Printing Graphs in 1-2-3 Release 2.2

A program included with 1-2-3 called PrintGraph has traditionally been the only vehicle for printing the 1-2-3 graphs you produce. PrintGraph is still a part of the package in 1-2-3 Release 2.2, but the add-in Allways, now included with 1-2-3 Release 2.2, not only effectively replaces PrintGraph but offers a better alternative.

PrintGraph prints PIC file versions of your graphs. That means you must save completed graphs as PIC files, leave 1-2-3, start PrintGraph, and then print the graphs, which is a long, ungainly process. Allways also prints PIC files and is accessible from within 1-2-3, so you never need to leave the program to print. Moreover, Allways provides graph formatting alternatives that are simply unavailable in either 1-2-3 or PrintGraph. To compare, try printing two graphs, one with PrintGraph and one with Allways.

Try using PrintGraph first. To start PrintGraph, you must leave 1-2-3. If you normally start 1-2-3 by typing LOTUS at the DOS prompt, you see the Lotus Access Menu before starting 1-2-3. Both 1-2-3 and PrintGraph are options on this menu. To print your graphs, select PrintGraph from the access menu rather than 1-2-3.

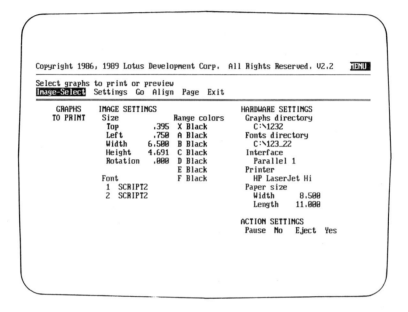

Fig. 1.43. *The PrintGraph screen.*

Figure 1.43 shows the PrintGraph main screen. Notice that this screen has space for a list of graphs you have chosen to print and three groups of settings: Image, Hardware, and Action. After you select Image-Select on the PrintGraph menu, you can modify any of the PrintGraph settings. To make your subsequent work easier, you can establish defaults for all settings options, changing selected settings only when necessary.

Before you can print with PrintGraph, you may need to modify some of the default hardware settings. In particular, you may need to modify the graphs and fonts directories and specify a printer. The graphs directory is the hard-disk subdirectory in which you store the PIC file versions of your graphs. If you have not set up a separate directory for your graphs, 1-2-3 stores your PIC files in the same directory that the 1-2-3 program resides in.

To set the default graphs directory, select Settings Hardware Graphs-Directory from the PrintGraph menu, and then enter the name of the directory where the PIC files are stored, such as C:\123. The fonts directory is where the PrintGraph text fonts reside, and it is almost certain to be the same directory in which you installed your copy of 1-2-3. Select **F**onts-directory from the hardware settings menu and then enter the appropriate directory name.

Before leaving the hardware settings menu, select **P**rinter. You should see the list of the graphics printers you chose when you first installed 1-2-3. Some printers have more than one entry on the list, one for each of the graphics printing resolutions available with the printer. The higher the graphics resolution, the clearer the image will be. Chapter 10, "Printing and Plotting 1-2-3 Graphs," deals with the issue of printing resolution in detail. Figure 1.44 shows the printer or plotter selection screen for a setup with both a Hewlett-Packard LaserJet Series II laser printer and an Epson FX-85 dot-matrix printer. Position the cursor on the entry that lists both the device you want for printing and the printing resolution you need; then press the space bar. To complete printer selection, press Enter.

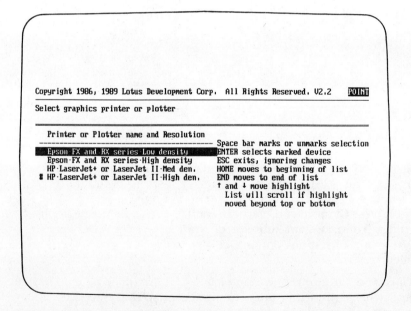

Fig. 1.44. *A PrintGraph printer/plotter selection screen.*

Select **Q**uit to return to the settings menu. Select **S**ave to save the changes you made to the PrintGraph hardware defaults and return to the main PrintGraph menu.

Because printing your graphs can be the slowest part of your work in creating graphs, PrintGraph lets you line up a group of graphs for printing. Thus, you can continue while the program and your printer work together unattended. To pick the graphs to print, choose **Image-Select** from the PrintGraph menu. PrintGraph displays a list of the PIC files in the graphs directory (see fig 1.45). Place the cursor on the first of the three PIC files, SALESBAR, and press the space bar. A number sign appears to the left of the PIC file's name. Move the space bar down to the second PIC file, REV-EXP, and press the space bar again. Now, you have selected two of the three PIC files to print, so you can press Enter and return to the PrintGraph menu.

```
Copyright 1986, 1989 Lotus Development Corp. All Rights Reserved. V2.2    POINT

Select graphs to print


GRAPH FILE  DATE      TIME     SIZE
-------------------------------------------
44          09-26-89   9:20     759        Space bar marks or unmarks selection
BLOCK1      10-02-89  13:43     755        ENTER selects marked graphs
BLOCK2      10-02-89  13:43     755        ESC exits, ignoring changes
BOLD        10-02-89  13:43     753        HOME moves to beginning of list
CTUTOR      09-10-89  22:58    1140        END moves to end of list
CTUTORA     09-10-89  23:07     829        ↑ and ↓ move highlight
CTUTORB     09-10-89  23:07    3706          List will scroll if highlight
CTUTORM     09-08-89  23:24    1140          moved beyond top or bottom
FORUM       10-02-89  13:43     754        GRAPH (F10) previews marked graph
GRAPHPIC    09-23-89   9:51    2861
ITALIC1     10-02-89  13:42     756
ITALIC2     10-02-89  13:42     756
LOTUS       10-02-89  13:42     754
PICBW       09-23-89  11:47    8123
PICCOLOR    09-23-89  11:46    2861
PICFILE     09-22-89  22:47    6887
PICGRAPH    09-23-89   9:51    2861
ROMAN1      10-02-89  13:42     755
```

Fig. 1.45. *The Image-Select PIC file list.*

To print the graphs, select **Align** and then **Go** from the PrintGraph menu. The SALESBAR PIC file, as printed by a Hewlett-Packard LaserJet Series II laser printer appears in figure 1.46. When PrintGraph finishes your graphs, select **Exit** and then **Yes** to leave PrintGraph to use Allways within 1-2-3 to print the third graph.

Start 1-2-3 again and use the **Add-in** command on the 1-2-3 main menu to first attach and then invoke Allways. Bring up the Allways menu by pressing the slash key (/). To print a PIC file from within Allways, you must first add the PIC file graph to a worksheet and then print the range containing the graph. To add the third PIC file to the worksheet,

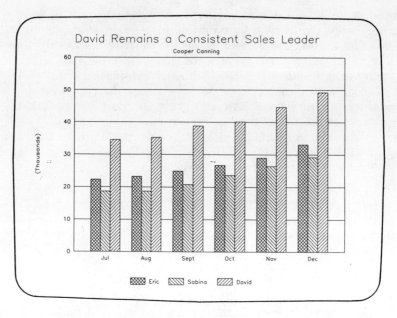

Fig. 1.46. SALESBAR.PIC as printed by PrintGraph with a laser printer.

select /Graph **A**dd and then choose SALESPIE. Specify a large enough range on the worksheet in which to add SALESPIE, such as A1..H21. The graph appears on the worksheet (see fig. 1.47).

To print the graph, you must select the range to print by selecting /**P**rint **R**ange **S**et and then pointing to the range A1..H21. When you press Enter, you see a dashed line surrounding the range you just selected. To print, select **G**o from the print menu. In figure 1.48 you see the resulting graph printed by a Hewlett-Packard LaserJet Series II without any of the enhancements possible in Allways.

Printing Graphs in 1-2-3 Release 3

Printing graphs in 1-2-3 Release 3 is far easier than with any earlier release, and the formatting flexibility is equal to using 1-2-3 in concert with Allways. To print a graph in Release 3, you merely have to select /**P**rint **P**rinter **I**mage **C**urrent **A**lign **G**o. 1-2-3 takes care of the graph printing in the background, freeing you to edit the graph, modify the worksheet data, or make any other changes you'd like within 1-2-3.

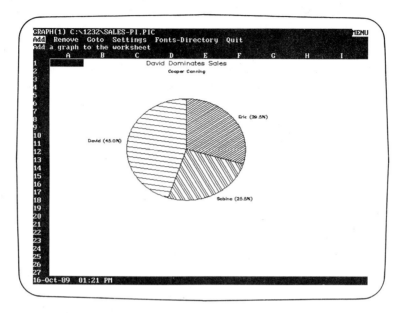

Fig. 1.47. *The SALESPIE.PIC graph as it appears in Allways.*

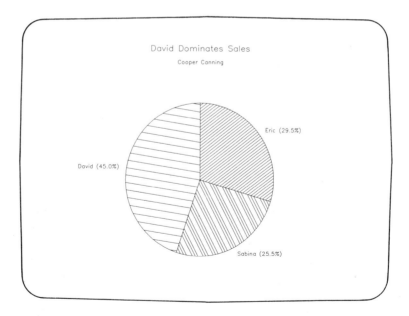

Fig. 1.48. *The SALESPIE.PIC file printed by Allways without enhancements.*

To try printing graphs, retrieve the first bar graph you made by selecting /Graph Name Use SALESBAR. You should see the full-screen graph appear. From the 1-2-3 menu, select /Print Printer Image. 1-2-3 gives you the choice of the current graph or a named graph stored on disk. First, print the current graph by selecting Current, and then Align followed by Go. In a moment, 1-2-3 will begin sending the image to the printer. When it does, you should be able to resume your work while 1-2-3 carries out its printing tasks behind the scenes. Background printing can make a significant difference in your productivity when you have a series of graphs to create.

Next, print the remaining two graphs by first selecting /Print Printer Image Named-Graph, selecting REV-EXP, and then selecting Image Named-Graph SALESPIE Align Go. 1-2-3 will absorb each of your print requests, printing the graphs as fast as it can while letting you get back to work.

Figure 1.49 shows the bar graph as printed by 1-2-3 Release 3 on a laser printer.

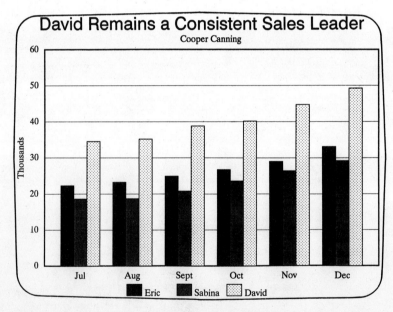

Fig. 1.49. *The bar graph printed on a laser printer by 1-2-3 Release 3.*

Summary

You should be proud of the three printed graphs you now have before you. Not only are they well chosen and well designed, but they were produced in record time. Let's hope Cooper's staff takes you for the champagne dinner you deserve.

In this Quick Start, you learned to create basic bar and line graphs. Then you learned to enhance your graphs with a few simple additions and changes. You learned how to print your graphs from 1-2-3 or from the add-in Allways. The following chapters cover in detail the procedures and techniques you should know for making graphs of all types.

Succeeding chapters cover printing and plotting graphs, making graphs in other graphing software based on 1-2-3 data, making slides, animating graphs, and selecting hardware for graphics presentations. The final chapter explains the special ways you can use 1-2-3 PIC files to transport your 1-2-3 charts into other software for embellishment and for incorporation into printed documents.

2

Graphing Expressively: Concepts and Caveats

Just as with any worthwhile and productive endeavor, creating meaningful graphs starts with thought rather than action. Too many presentation designers work the other way around. They scoop up all the data they have; they stuff the numbers into graphing programs to produce graphs visually striking and largely meaningless; finally, they sift through the graphic images to extract a message.

You can avoid all such useless activity by focusing your attention on a few straightforward principles. In this chapter, you'll find suggestions for planning the graphs your presentation entails so that you can fashion visuals both credible and persuasive—that, after all, is your goal in communication.

Creating a communicative graph can be like designing and tailoring a fine custom garment. A well-conceived garment made expressly for an individual clearly conveys a statement of personal style the wearer wishes to project. Similarly, a well-conceived graph expresses an equally ardent message about a set of numeric results that someone wishes to impart.

A garment declares unambiguously, "I am a successful business achiever"; "I am a young, upwardly mobile professional"; or "I couldn't care less about what anyone else thinks." A good graph makes an equally unambiguous statement. "The advertising campaign we began in June has led to a 25% increase in sales." To fashion such a forceful and succinct graph, you must carefully complete each of the following graphing steps:

1. Gathering, selecting, and checking the data

2. Interpreting the data

3. Uncovering the story behind the numbers

4. Determining the message to convey

5. Assessing your audience

6. Assessing the presentation method

7. Selecting an appropriate graph type

8. Constructing the graph for accuracy

9. Making the graph persuasive

After a few graphing fundamentals, this chapter will lead you through each of these steps.

A Graphing Fundamentals Refresher

Graphs visually represent numeric information, expressing the story that underlies your numbers more tellingly than the mere numbers themselves.

In high school, you learned about a graph's components: its axes, its coordinates, and its bars or lines. But not all graphs require the complete arrangement. And other graphs need little more than their pivotal line or bars to convey a tale. A jagged line moving ever higher across a page depicts overall growth in a manner that is familiar to everyone. Sets of bars compare numbers in newspapers and magazines every day.

To help such fundamental graph forms convey more information than just basic trends or turnabouts, most graphs embody a set of additional components that offer greater meaning and precision. These elements are depicted in figure 2.1.

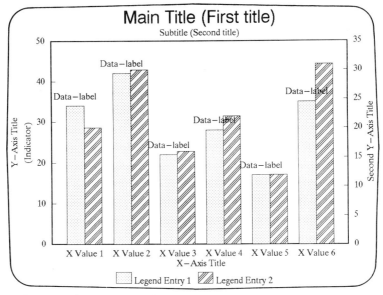

Fig. 2.1. *The elements of a graph.*

Bar and line graphs almost invariably include a set of axes, serving as scales against which the bars or lines of the graph are measured. The horizontal axis, called the x-axis, usually marks off the passage of time, but it can have any other unit of measurement assigned to it. The vertical axis, called the y-axis, usually marks off the units in which the subject of the graph is measured. If the graph depicts temperature readings, for example, the y-axis usually represents a range of possible measurements in degrees.

Each axis can be labeled with a title, which describes the scale it represents. The y-axis can also have an indicator to reveal that its increments actually represent "thousands," "millions," "thousandths," or "millionths."

Second in importance to the axes, a graph's legend tells the viewer how the information in the graph is visually represented. If the graph uses colors to differentiate the subjects of the graph, the legend indicates who or what is represented by each color. If patterns of hatch markings (hatch patterns) fill the bars or pie slices, the legend identifies which pattern corresponds to which subject.

Each number represented by a point along the line of a line graph is called a data point. And, each data point is represented by a small geometric shape called a marker. 1-2-3 uses such common markers as tiny squares, triangles, and diamonds. To indicate the precise value of

Sales, by Group

Model Name	East Coast Group	West Coast Group	Midwest Group
Elite	1,520	872	680
Cavalier	1,735	772	720
Renegade	1,020	976	530

Fig. 2.2. A table that needs no interpretation.

□ Attendance is 25% better than usual when the PTA meeting falls on the third Tuesday of every month.

□ The red ones sell better.

These are the simple declarative sentences that you strive for when you analyze the data for the underlying results. If you cannot encapsulate your analysis in a coherent statement, you simply do not have the main ingredient for a presentation graph. And when this happens, you should take another look at the data. Or construct quick and dirty graphs that help you uncover the story behind your results.

Of course, one set of worksheet numbers can yield more than a single sentence. The worksheet seen in figure 2.4 produces enough material for the following three statements.

□ Our fourth quarter was our best.

□ The Nautilus has been a consistent sales leader.

□ The profitability of the Marine Division has increased dramatically.

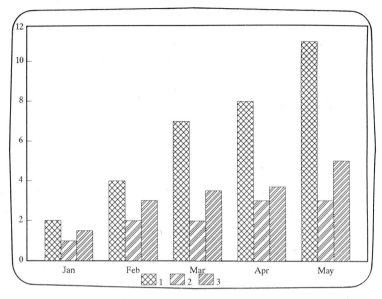

Fig. 2.3. Four quick graphs used for data analysis.

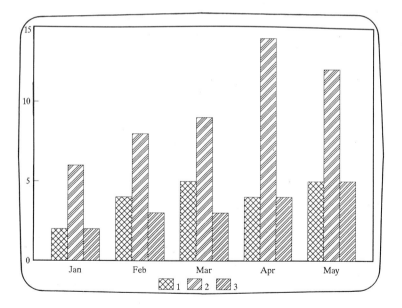

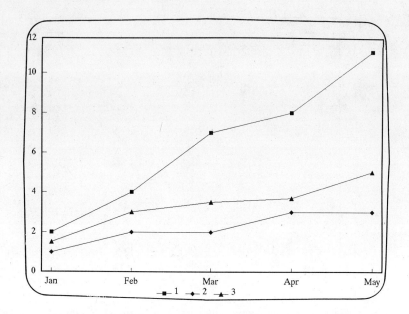

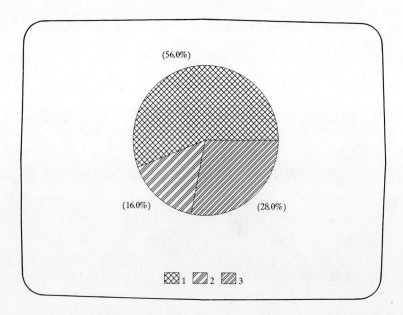

Profits, Marine Division

	Quarter 1	Quarter 2	Quarter 3	Quarter 4	Year 2
Intrepid	35,230	34,180	36,166	38,210	143,786
Dauntless	41,750	38,120	39,740	41,120	160,730
Nautilus	61,000	57,180	63,450	71,691	253,321
Pinafore	26,130	24,910	27,300	31,210	109,550
Santa Maria	17,200	9,950	22,180	26,450	75,780
Total	181,310	164,340	188,836	208,681	

Fig. 2.4. Sample worksheet data.

Determining the Message To Convey

The declarative statement or set of statements that you formulate to interpret the data serves two purposes. First, it sets a sharp focus for the graph. Fixing your sights on a single important message early helps you attain a graph with substance as well as style. To hone the message still further, you can construct a second sentence that starts "I would like to convince my audience that . . . "

The central statement you come up with can also serve as the basis for the title of the graph. A graph title should summarize the essential message, helping the viewer come to the intended conclusion about the data.

Assessing Your Audience

Now, you have analyzed the data and developed your interpretations. You have examined and characterized your data, but not your audience.

Who will see the graph you produce? Are these viewers already in search of a solution to an existing problem, or do you need first to attract them to your data? Can you sketch out the central concept behind your data, or do you need to cover the full history and background? Is the audience hostile to the idea? Will you need humor to win them over? The answers to these questions make a dramatic difference in your approach to the graph.

Assessing the Presentation Method

Finally, you should consider how the graph will be presented to your audience. If the graph will be incorporated into a document with a desktop publishing system, for example, you can allow more complexity. Your readers will have the time to scrutinize the graph and study its meaning at their leisure.

If you decide to use the graph in a slide presentation or an on-screen desktop animation, you should keep the graph simple. Your audience will have little time to decipher the graph's message, so interpretation must be spontaneous. Rather than omit important information, you may want to break a single graph into a succession of graphs, each of which singles out an issue.

Whatever presentation method you decide on, you now have completed the preliminary stages of graphmaking, and you are ready to begin the physical process of producing the graph. That task begins with choosing the graph type most appropriate for the message you wish to impart.

Selecting an Appropriate Graph Type

1-2-3 offers a handful of commonly used graph types and virtually unlimited variations on a few basic themes. The program provides line, bar, pie, and XY graphs. 1-2-3 Release 3 now adds to this original set the area graph, the high-low-close-open graph, horizontal graphs, and still others. Which graph type you pick depends on two fundamental factors: the information your data represents and the interpretation you want to present.

Some data will fit naturally into one graph type. Relative proportions of several ingredients, for example, are best represented by a pie or stack-bar graph. A set of meteorological readings, on the other hand, is best demonstrated by a line graph, in which trends from the immediate past lead to projections for the immediate future.

If you want to interpret rather than merely present the data, you may choose an entirely different graph type. A set of sales results for three divisions for a single month might best be represented by the bar graph shown in figure 2.5. Here, your goal is to compare the divisions month by month and to mete out accolades and chastisements based on what you see.

A pie graph, on the other hand, that shows the relative percentage of each division's contribution for the entire period helps you plan end-of-the-year bonuses. Figure 2.6 shows such a graph. Selecting the correct graph type starts with understanding how each works to accomplish its task.

Line Graphs

Line graphs are best for revealing trends over time. These graphs deemphasize individual values in favor of a general flow. Use a line graph when you want to show the temperature variations during a month, for example, or the fluctuations of the dollar against the yen over the course of a year. Note that these graph descriptions depend on words synonymous with change: variation and fluctuation. If you find such a word in the declarative sentence you first generate, a line graph is strongly indicated for your data.

Line graphs may stress overall trends, yet they also can be precise enough to let viewers gauge specific quantities at fixed points, especially with the help of a background grid. In a line graph, line segments connect individual data points that fall at regular intervals. You can examine the placement of the data points to obtain particular readings.

Figure 2.7 shows how a line graph demonstrates the change in one- and two-bedroom condominium values in New York City over the past twelve months. The most noticeable aspect of this chart—after you recover from the initial shock of the prices—is the flatness of the price change for one-bedroom apartments. These condominiums are abundant in New York, so their price has increased little in relation to the price of two-bedroom condominiums. Just from inspecting this chart you can reasonably guess the average condominium prices three months from now. You can often simply extrapolate the lines of a line graph into the future.

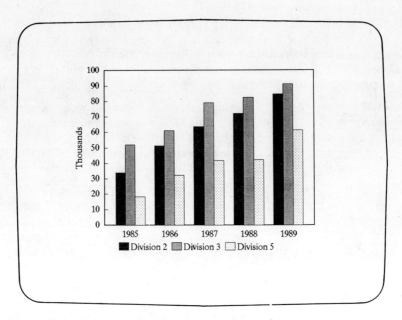

Fig. 2.5. *A bar graph showing sales by three divisions.*

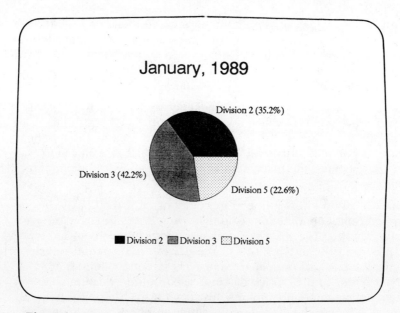

Fig. 2.6. *A pie graph showing aggregate sales at year's end.*

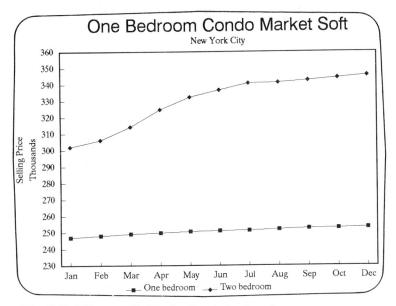

***Fig. 2.7.** A line graph illustrating price trends.*

You can construct line graphs easily, and you can depend on them to be readily understood. Line graphs, along with bar graphs, are the most commonly seen types today. To keep your line graph easy to interpret, restrict the number of lines to four. Use fewer lines if they intersect. If you have data missing, you can interrupt the line, or you can fill the space with a dashed line added in another graphics package. Do not be tempted to omit the interval. The time increments measured by the horizontal axis must be equal, and missing intervals may invite suspicion. Even if you have nothing to hide, your audience may assume otherwise.

Bar Graphs

Whereas line graphs offer just enough visual clues to let viewers compare individual results at set times, the very crux of the bar graph is its comparison of discrete points. Bar graphs clearly and unequivocally compare a set of values. The bigger the value, the taller the bar. If the bar graph tracks a set of values over time, each cluster of bars represents a set of results at an interval. Figure 2.8 shows a bar graph used to track day-by-day viewership of three popular television programs over the course of a week.

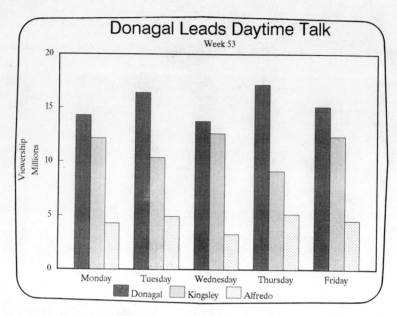

Fig. 2.8. *A bar graph as it is best used.*

Granted, the capabilities of line and bar graphs substantially overlap. Yet, each lends a unique expressiveness to the data. Line graphs give the impression of a flow of data—sales start here and end here, for example. Bar graphs give the impression of discrete measurements —sales totals are this, this, and this—because the values are expressed by the separate bars, not connected by a line that traces a sequential course for the data.

Bar graphs made by 1-2-3 Release 2.2 and earlier releases orient the bars vertically. These graphs are sometimes called column graphs. 1-2-3 Release 3 lets you flip the chart so that the bars are horizontal. Bars extended horizontally are well-suited for graphs that show progression in time or distance. Figure 2.9 shows such a graph.

The simple recommendations that apply to bar graphs are, first, to limit the number of bars each graph holds, and second, to arrange the bars in order from smallest to largest or vice versa. Figure 2.10 shows a chart so crowded with bars that it has become unintelligible.

Think of twelve bars or sets of bars as the maximum for graphs based on 12 months of data, and six bars or sets of bars as the maximum for all other data. If you must plot more data sets, ordering the bars by height can make the same graph more comprehensible. Figure 2.11 shows a well-ordered graph that simplifies comparing the results.

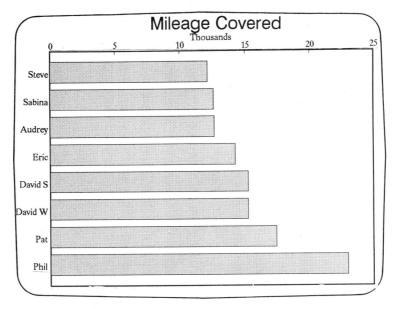

Fig. 2.9. *A graph subject appropriate for horizontal bars.*

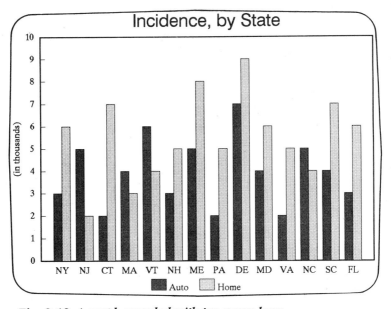

Fig. 2.10. *A graph crowded with too many bars.*

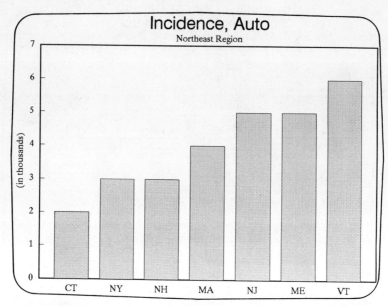

Fig. 2.11. *A well-ordered bar graph.*

Pies and Stack-Bar Graphs

Pie graphs and stack-bar graphs represent breakdowns, but each with its own emphasis. The stack-bar graph accentuates the total, and the pie graph spotlights the relative sizes of the slices. Moreover, stack-bar graphs plot several totals—usually, one for each successive interval of time. Pie graphs, on the other hand, plot only a single total. Figure 2.12 shows use of the pie graph.

The encircled zone of a pie graph represents 100%. Each pie slice represents a percentage of that whole. 1-2-3 conveniently calculates the percentage values and places them adjacent to the slices and slice labels.

Figure 2.13 shows a stack-bar graph. Each bar in the graph is broken into segments, one for each of its components. By gauging the relative sizes of the segments, you can judge the relative contributions of each to the whole. Additionally, you can gauge how the total varies over time.

Stack-bar graphs, like other 1-2-3 bar styles, can plot no more than six series at once. That sensible limit prevents you from incautiously dividing bars into segments so small as to be virtually indistinguishable.

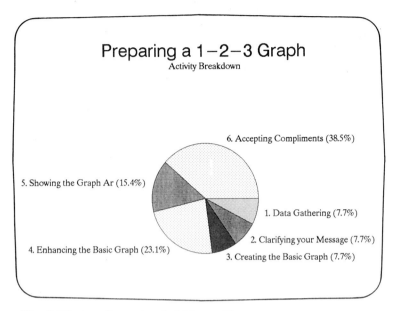

Fig. 2.12. *A well-constructed pie graph.*

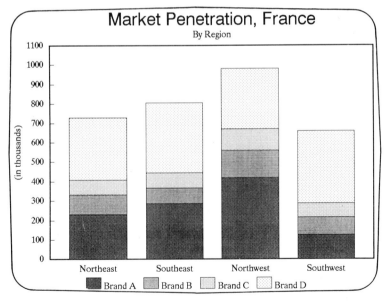

Fig. 2.13. *A stack-bar graph showing component values contributing to the overall total.*

1-2-3 pie graphs offer no such inherent limitation. You fashion a pie graph by assigning the values of a worksheet range to the pie. Each value becomes a slice. If you fail to use restraint, you can find yourself with a complex pie graph cut up into a dozen or more tiny slices. To prevent diet-sized slivers of pie, try to limit the slices in each graph to six. Certainly, impose a limit of eight slices at the most. If your data contains many small values, try to lump together several related values into one larger slice, a technique demonstrated in figure 2.14. In separate pies or with accompanying tables, you can offer further breakdowns of certain slices. Each pie will be of limited complexity so that your audience can easily interpret it.

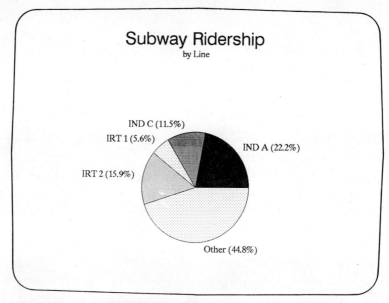

Fig. 2.14. *Many small values accumulated in a larger slice.*

To single out a slice for emphasis, separate it slightly from the rest of the pie by cutting, or exploding, it. You can cut out a slice and then further dissect it in a separate pie. Figure 2.15 shows a pie graph with an exploded slice.

XY Graphs

XY graphs plot values against two numerical axes, unlike any other graph type. By plotting results in an XY graph, you can determine or

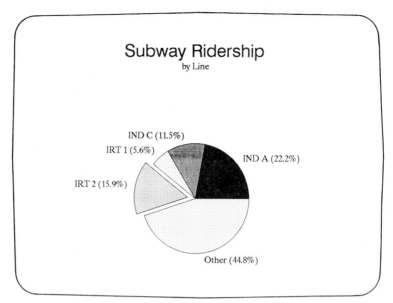

Fig. 2.15. *A pie graph with an exploded slice.*

demonstrate the correlation between two factors or forces, often called variables, measured in numerical units.

Examples of data appropriately plotted in an XY graph are price versus units sold, or cholesterol level versus age. Figure 2.16 shows an XY graph measuring the attendance at one outdoor arena at varying temperature levels.

A special form of the XY graph is the *scattergram,* or *scatterplot.* You can convert an XY graph into a scatterplot by displaying data points without connecting lines. Where the data points cluster indicates a correlation between the two variables. Figure 2.17 shows the type of scattergram you can create with a 1-2-3 XY graph.

High-Low-Close-Open Graphs

Market watchers, financial analysts, and others who track such financial instruments as stocks and bonds will be pleased to see the new High-Low-Close-Open (HLCO) graphs in 1-2-3 Release 3. No prior release of 1-2-3 offers this type. These graphs plot the high, low, closing, and opening prices of an item during an interval. The item at each interval is represented by a vertical bar, whose upper and lower extents represent the high and low price of the item. Extending to the left of

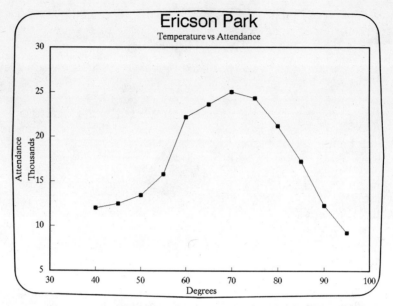

Fig. 2.16. *An XY graph measuring attendance at varying temperatures.*

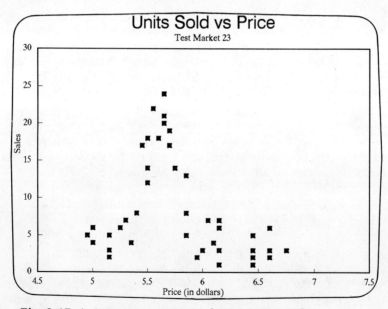

Fig. 2.17. *A scattergram version of a 1-2-3 XY graph.*

the bar is a small horizontal line representing the opening price of the item. Extending to the right is another small horizontal line representing the closing price.

To supplement the lines that represent the four prices at set intervals, the HLCO graph provides a set of bars along the bottom of the graph to track another numerical value. Stock market observers often use these bars to represent trading volume. Figure 2.18 shows a HLCO graph tracking both the price of a single stock and its trading volume over the course of one week.

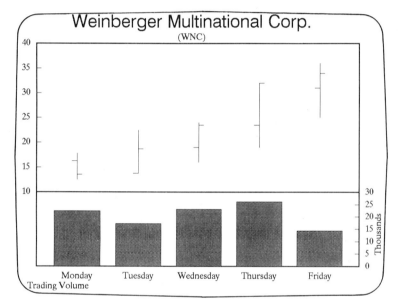

Fig. 2.18. *The HLCO graph tracking stock price and volume.*

Astute observers may recognize uses for HLCO graphs other than traditional stock tracking. Meteorologists can use HLCO graphs to record the high, low, starting, and ending barometric pressure for a set of intervals, for example. Power utility personnel might use HLCO graphs to chart hour-by-hour power demand and delivery.

Area Graphs

Area graphs, a graph type found only in Release 3 in 1-2-3, are a cross between stack-bar graphs and line graphs. Like the stack-bar graph, data values for a period are stacked, but, like the line graph, the periods are also connected by lines. The result depicts the aggregate flow of several contributing values. Figure 2.19 shows an area chart that tracks the sell-through of three products over six months.

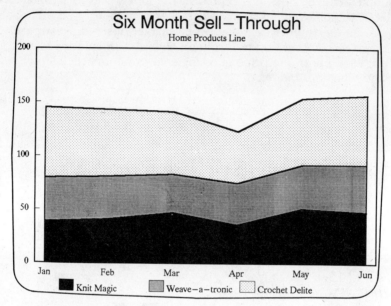

Fig. 2.19. Use of the area graph.

Notice how clearly the area graph shows the month-to-month trend of both the total and the constituent items in the total.

Constructing the Graph for Accuracy

Far too many graphs portray fiction even as they purport to show facts. Graphing is as much a science as an art, and failure to follow its laws can lead to inaccuracy, misrepresentation, and distortion.

Most of us have studied graphmaking at one time or another. In fact, you may remember plotting out a graph in school with a ruler, pencil, and graph paper. You learned how simple geometric shapes, lines, and bars can depict numbers, but you probably never learned how they can misrepresent those numbers.

The advent of computerized graphing has aggravated rather than alleviated the hazard. Graphing programs allow quick editing of every aspect of a graph, making it all too easy to inadvertently distort the message and steal the credibility from your case.

Here, then, are the guidelines and recommendations you should keep in mind as you plan and produce your graphs.

Show the Big Picture, Too

Failing to see the forest for the trees applies all too readily to graphmaking. When you target particular information without regard to how it fits into the bigger picture, you may miss long-term trends in your analysis or portrayal.

Statisticians know that the accuracy of a sample improves as its proportion to the entire population increases. The same holds true for graphing. Often, the more data you gather, the more accurate your view of the information becomes. Of course, you must exercise some restraint when you select data for graphing, balancing accuracy with simplicity. If you can amass data for 20 years rather than a mere 5, all the better, but consider showing yearly aggregates rather than monthly figures.

Figure 2.20 shows a six-month line graph alongside a second graph showing the two-year trend. Which would you prefer to see before buying the company's stock?

Select a True Scaling

Another way to take a closer look at your data is to modify the scaling of a graph. By decreasing the scope of one or both of the graph axes, you can magnify small changes in your data to see them more clearly.

Figure 2.21 shows a standard line chart. Notice that the vertical axis, the y-axis, begins at 35 and extends to 75. Now look at a different version of the graph in figure 2.22. The y-axis now begins at 0 and extends to 100. The increase in the span of the axis diminishes the appearance of change in the data.

Modifying the scale of a graph is a legitimate tool for studying the graph's data. By amplifying the magnitude of change in a line or bar graph, you can more easily discern short-term adjustments or long-term trends. But if you modify the axis scale of a presentation graph, your duty is to inform the audience of the adjustment. You can include in the graph a footnote detailing the change or you can place a second graph alongside with an unmodified scale for a fair comparison by your viewers.

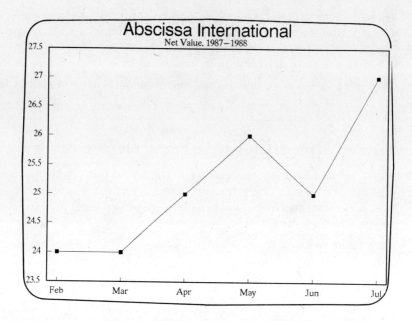

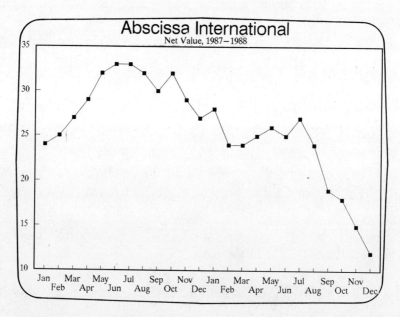

Fig. 2.20. *Six months versus two years of data.*

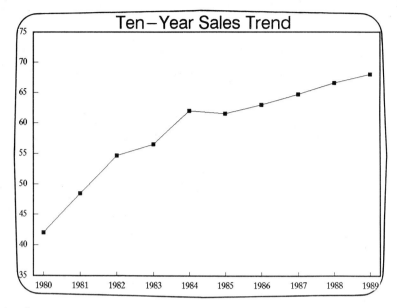

Fig. 2.21. *A vertical axis span of 35 to 75.*

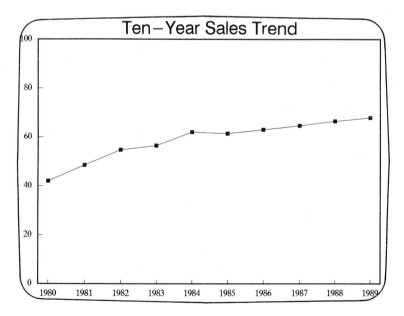

Fig. 2.22. *The vertical axis again with modified scaling.*

Maintain Equal Axis Intervals

To narrow the focus to selected data, you may be tempted to decrease intervals of time measured by points along the graph's horizontal axis, the x-axis. You plan to show yearly results for the first five years, for example, and then monthly figures for the sixth, because the results are so astounding during the sixth year. Don't do it. Even if you clearly label the x-axis, the graph's appearance is seriously distorted.

Make sure each interval along a graph axis is identical to all others. Figure 2.23 graphs irregular intervals along an x-axis. The measured growth appears to decelerate suddenly. The corrected graph, shown in figure 2.24, displays the same data with precisely equal calibrations along the entire x-axis.

Intervals should be evenly marked, even when data is missing. Suppose that you have an embarrassing gap in your documentation. Data for a certain time period simply is unobtainable. Still you must include this interval along the x-axis. Failure to do so can introduce serious unintended distortion. You may even appear to be covertly glossing over the evidence.

If you are missing data for an interval, leave the space open or connect the data points on either side with a dashed line rather than the solid line. Any sort of indication that data is missing is better than dropping the interval altogether.

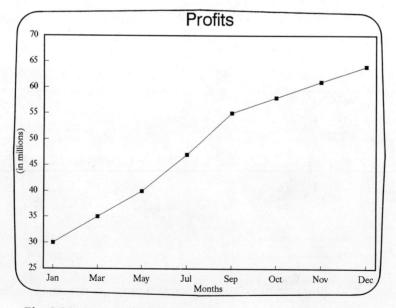

Fig. 2.23. Irregular x-axis intervals.

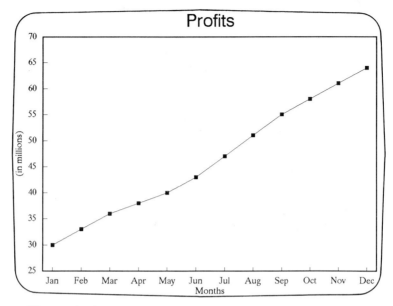

***Fig. 2.24.** The graph with equal x-axis intervals.*

With 1-2-3, you cannot connect selected points with a dashed line, but you can easily plot only the data points, then add the solid and dashed lines in virtually any graphics program. An entire chapter in this book describes pulling 1-2-3 graphs into dedicated graphing programs for enhancement.

In figure 2.25, you see that results are not present for the month of June. Rather than call attention to the absence, the graphmaker chose to drop the month altogether. Figure 2.26 shows the same graph supplied with the missing June data. The graphmaker would have done better to create the graph shown in figure 2.27.

Use Equal Scales in Side-by-Side Graphs

From time to time, you may want two graphs side by side for comparison. When you do, be certain the axes of the graphs show identical scaling, so that the basis of comparison is fair.

One such side-by-side comparison is attempted in figure 2.28. The graphmaker chose two adjacent graphs, rather than a single one crowded with data. By letting 1-2-3 perform its automatic y-axis scaling, the graphmaker mistakenly created unequal graphs. Bars measuring the same result would be of different heights on the two charts.

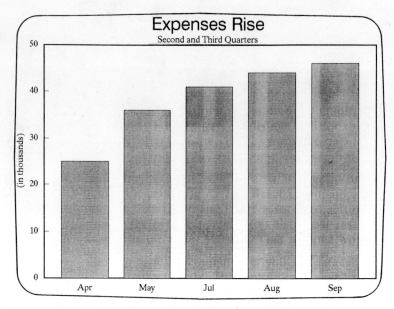

***Fig. 2.25.** A deceptive graph with missing data for June.*

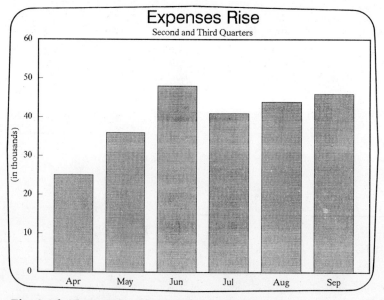

***Fig. 2.26.** The graph with the June data added.*

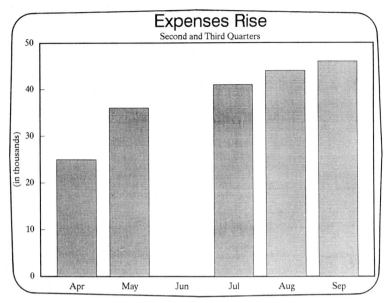

***Fig. 2.27.** Proper portrayal of a missing section of data.*

To maintain equal scaling across graphs, manually set both scales to the same upper and lower limits. You will find detailed instructions for changing graph scaling in Chapter 3, "Making Bar and Line Graphs."

Beware of Misleading Calculations

Do not blindly trust the results coming from a computer without checking the mathematical calculations behind the data. More than one company has folded as a result of an incorrectly entered formula in a spreadsheet cell. Added to mistyped formulas are calculations entered that are flawed in their construction.

Before you average a series of data, for example, be quite sure that data is measured in similar units. An average of ten dimensions, some measured in yards and others in square yards, yields information with no validity. A graphic representation of the same measurement would be just as flawed.

Correct for Variable Factors

A common error in calculation occurs when the data analyst fails to adjust the data for the effect of such factors as inflation or variations in

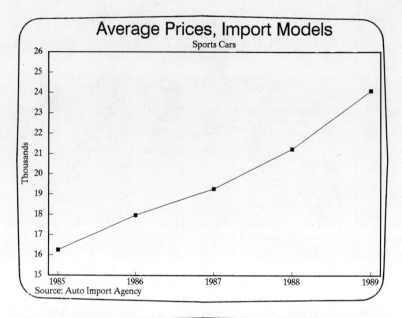

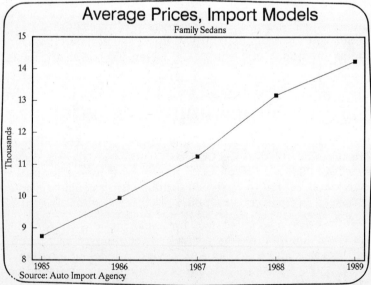

***Fig. 2.28.** An invalid comparison of graphs with discrepant scalings.*

foreign exchange. There is nothing incorrect about the graph's design or any of its elements. The underlying numbers are simply wrong because they don't mention or adjust for the overall rise in consumer prices, for example, or the changing discount rate affecting numbers in the data.

Figure 2.29 presents two graphs, one of rising home prices over twenty years and the second representing the same figures adjusted to reflect the overall rise in prices caused by inflation. The second graph represents more accurately the relative outlay homebuyers have faced then and now.

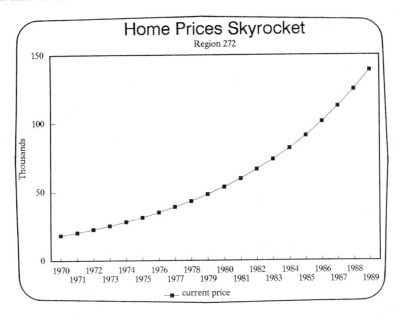

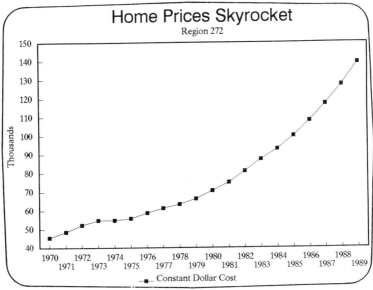

Fig. 2.29. The graph below shows numbers in constant current dollars.

Do Not Misrepresent Values with Symbols

Many illustrating and dedicated graphing programs let you import 1-2-3 graphs saved as PIC files. Once the graphs are within the graphics program, you can replace dull bars with objects of more visual interest. You have certainly seen graphs in which stacks of coins of different heights represent varying prices.

If you decide to redesign the graph with pictures, be sure to represent the values by grouping or stacking the objects that represent units, as with the coins in the example. The larger the value, the higher the stack of coins. The temptation is to draw the objects larger—one coin representing perhaps one trillion on the scale, and one coin twice as big representing two trillion. Remember, a coin stretched twice as tall also becomes twice as wide. That means it has increased in size by a factor of four rather than two. Did you intend two trillion when in fact you showed four?

Figure 2.30 shows such a misleading graph. The 1988 figure is twice that of 1984, even though the stack of coins representing 1988 is four times as large. Add coins to represent growth, as in figure 2.31.

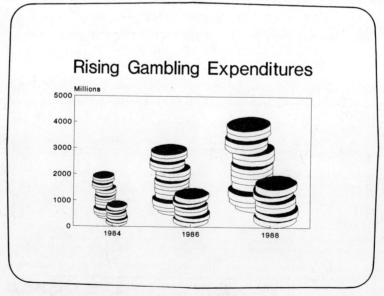

Fig. 2.30. *An unintended quadrupling of values.*

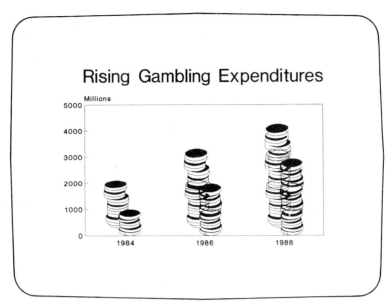

Fig. 2.31. *The corrected pictorial scale.*

Preserve the Original Aspect Ratio

As you squeeze a graph to fit a space in your newsletter or proposal, be aware that changing the *aspect ratio,* or height-to-width ratio, of a graph also changes the message it conveys.

Figure 2.32 shows a line graph in its original aspect ratio as drawn by 1-2-3. Next, figure 2.33 shows this graph squeezed to fit a short, wide space in a desktop-published business plan. Notice how the second graph portrays a slower growth than does the first.

Pie graphs are particularly hard hit by a change in shape. Squeezing a pie graph into an oval shape distorts the relative sizes of its slices and ruins the accuracy of the graph.

In figure 2.34, a pie graph with slices representing equal percentages is compressed to fit a tall space. Confirm for yourself the degree of distortion: the slices on the sides appear wider than those at the top and bottom of the pie.

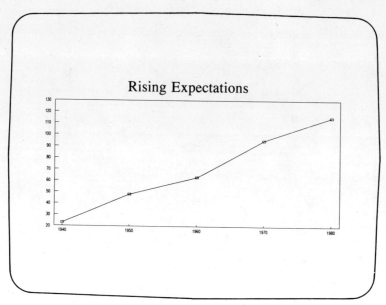

Fig. 2.32. *A line graph of correct scale.*

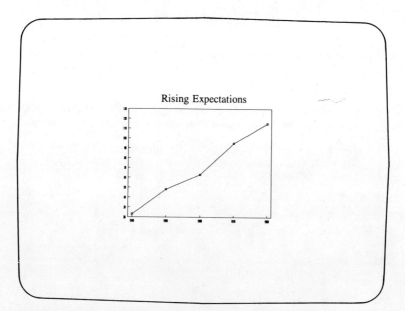

Fig. 2.33. *The line graph with distorted aspect ratio.*

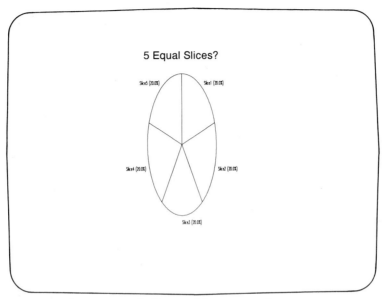

Fig. 2.34. A pie graph distorted into an oval.

Use Consistent Labeling

Inconsistent use of text can lend certain bars or pie slices greater prominence than others. Label text set in a larger size or bolder typeface emphasizes the set of bars or the pie slice it identifies. Even if the bars or slices have no greater significance than any others, the viewer's eyes are drawn to them.

Therefore, you must keep text in the graph as uniform as possible. Beyond giving the graph a clean, elegant appearance, the standardized text allocates emphasis equally among the elements of the graph. Figure 2.35 shows a graph in which equal pie slices are given unequal emphasis by differing label text sizes.

Be Vigilant Against Optical Illusions

Easily avoidable optical illusions can introduce distortion into an otherwise valid graph. Bars filled with vertical or diagonal lines appear taller than bars filled with horizontal lines, for example. Bars filled with solid black appear larger and certainly more massive than those lightly filled or with open and airy hatch patterns.

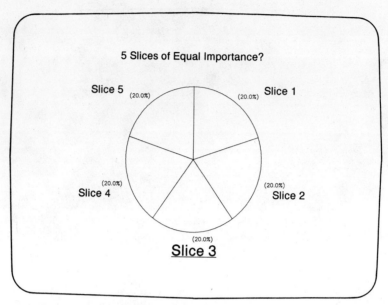

Fig. 2.35. A pie graph with unequal slice labels.

Moiré patterns produce the vibrating effect one perceives from strongly patterned areas that visually conflict, such as groups of bars with diagonal lines at different angles. With the variety of hatch patterns available to fill 1-2-3's graph bars and pie slices, you may be tempted to give each new bar a contrasting pattern. Yet, rather than making your graph more interesting, such vibrating patterns can detract from a message. Limit your use of patterns to a few simple hatches combined with solid and unfilled bars. If you use 1-2-3 Release 3, you can use shades of gray to fill bars and pie slices.

Fig. 2.36 shows a particularly poorly designed graph. It uses an overabundance of hatch patterns in an unwise combination.

Making the Graph Persuasive

The most technically accurate graph may be worthless to your cause if it is not clear and compelling. Your final step in preparing a graph is to fine-tune it to convey a critical message at a single glance. Any complexity that distracts from the communicative power of your graph saps the strength of your presentation.

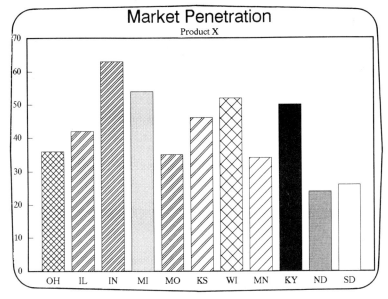

Fig. 2.36. Too many hatch patterns.

Unfortunately, the possibilities for perceptual interference are virtually limitless. A certain few types of poor graphs show up over and over, though. Here are suggestions for how to avoid them.

Use a Grid Judiciously

If you think your audience can interpret a graph without a grid, leave it out. Grids strike some graphmakers as the finishing touch. But in many cases, those graphs are already quite complete. The grid serves only to clutter the picture, distracting from the visual impact.

Be especially discriminating with grids in line graphs. The lines of the grid and the lines of the graphed data can interfere, especially if the lines intersect. Figure 2.37 shows a cluttered line graph with both horizontal and vertical grid lines.

Use Uniform Fonts

Now that 1-2-3—especially with Allways, makes it so easy to modify the typefaces of graph text, graphs are turning up all over with a dizzying assortment of text fonts. A clean and simple graph can be more

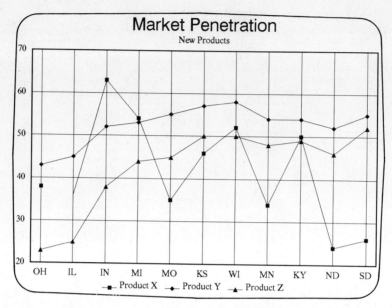

Fig. 2.37. A line graph cluttered by an unnecessary grid.

powerful than an ornate graph. For maximum impact, use no more than two text fonts in any one graph—one for the titles and one for all other graph elements. If you need more variation, use different point sizes of the same font.

Maintaining a consistency of fonts should go beyond the individual graphs you create, especially if you are assembling a number of graphs into a presentation. Then be sure to maintain a common theme and to employ the same design concepts in the graphs. Otherwise, unexpected shifts will be distracting. Furthermore, inconsistent fonts and design choices can suggest a presentation hastily borrowed from preexisting materials. Figure 2.38 shows a graph with a daunting confusion of text fonts.

Select and Limit Colors

Just as you should limit the number of fonts in a graph, you should restrict use of color. Remember, your goal is to create an elegant, simple visual in which the message takes precedence over the medium. Do not create a graph in multicolored splendor if you can communicate the same message with fewer colors. Consider using hues of a single color: shades of gray can be just as effective in communicating a message as can a rainbow of colors.

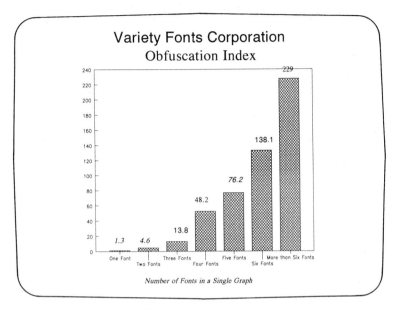

Fig. 2.38. *A graph with too many text fonts.*

You can impart added meaning just by the colors you select for your graphs, adding emotional overtones. The reds are often associated with trouble, loss, or stoppage, whereas green tones connote money, success, and opportunity. Light colors can be more eye-catching than the darker shades, so use lightly colored bars or pie slices to draw attention to special results.

Avoid coloring adjacent bars or pie slices with red and green. A surprisingly large percentage of men (4%) are red-green color blind. They simply cannot distinguish between the two colors.

Select a Brief Headline

Follow the lead of advertising copywriters. Write titles for your graphs that are short and punchy. See if you can express the graph's essential message with a few short, well-chosen words.

The title "Stock Soars" can ignite the spirit of the viewer. "Stock Posts 35% Gain During the Fourth Quarter" may sedate him. Remember, you can use the graph's subtitle, called its "Second" title, to break a long main title into two short and snappy ideas. "Debt-to-Equity Ratio," with "David Lawrence Associates" centered underneath is better as a pair of titles than the single "Debt-to-Equity Ratio of David Lawrence Associates."

Impart a Single Message

Even though two titles can capture a graph's message, be certain your graph has no more than one focal message. Don't dilute a graph by demonstrating several points with a single visual. Create a series of graphs, instead, each illustrating a separate aspect of the issue.

The creator of the graph shown in figure 2.39 attempted to prove in a single graph both that the driving age should be increased to 21 and that the drinking age should be increased to 25. The result is a chaotic clutter of graphical elements.

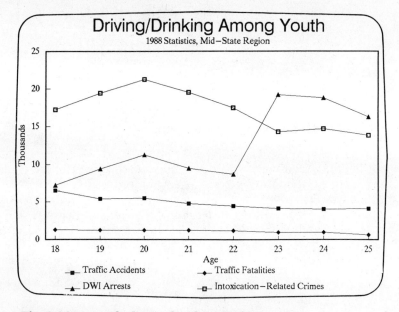

Fig. 2.39. *A graph cluttered with multiple messages.*

Limit Data Representations

In keeping with all recommendations toward simplicity, you should also limit the amount of data you portray in a graph. Too many bars, too many lines, or too many pie slices can be hard to comprehend. The more effort your viewer must expend, the more likely the graph will be misread or simply disregarded.

If you find yourself with mounds of important data, try to consolidate sets of data into totals or averages. Or consider representing the data in a series of charts, instead. In figure 2.40, you see a graph overstuffed with data.

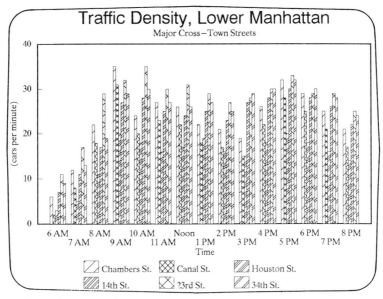

Fig. 2.40. *A graph with excessive data.*

Use Sufficient Contrast between Graph Markers

Emphasize the distinction between adjacent bars, areas within an area chart, or pie slices by selecting colors or hatch patterns that clearly contrast. Figure 2.41 shows the difficulty of distinguishing bars of a bar graph filled with similar hatch patterns.

Label All Chart Elements Carefully

Assume that your viewer has never seen a graph before and is unfamiliar with the topic presented. Label everything carefully. Choose descriptive terms for the legend, the axis labels, and the data-labels, even if they seem blatantly obvious to you. Viewers will appreciate that the graphs are pleasantly simple to interpret.

If you can place labels in the graph that identify the bars or lines, you can avoid using a legend. Legends do clarify graphs, but they also require viewers to look from the graph to the legend and back again repeatedly. That slight extra effort can detract from quick comprehension of your message. Figure 2.42 shows a graph with labels that take the place of a legend.

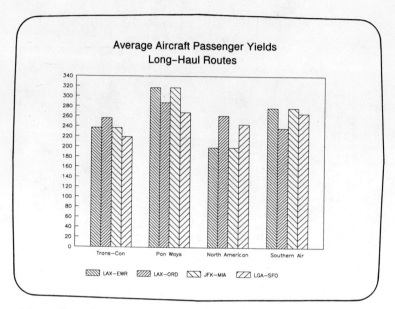

Fig. 2.41. *A bar graph with a confusion of hatch patterns.*

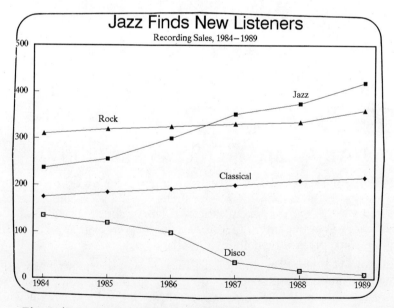

Fig. 2.42. *A graph substituting labels for a legend.*

Summary

Bearing these guidelines in mind, you can make graphs that are clear and compelling. In this chapter, you considered the fundamental principles that should guide your graphmaking and presentations. You saw how to keep graphs simple and clear, to limit data representations for an effective impression. You saw a multitude of pitfalls to avoid: how graphmakers can inadvertently mislead, or bewilder an audience when the purpose was to inform. Remember the principles illustrated in this chapter as you work through the following four chapters, first, as you create all available 1-2-3 graph types and, then, as you embellish your graphs with Allways or with 1-2-3 Release 3's special graph formatting commands.

3

Making Bar and Line Graphs

In this chapter, you learn how to create the most basic graphs, the bar and line graphs. Next, you add such important features as legends, titles, and data-labels to your graphs. Then you begin to customize and fine-tune your graphs until they clearly and accurately express the message your numbers bear.

The following chapters will show you how to create and format other types of graphs. But by learning about line and bar graphs first, you can become acquainted with the principles and techniques that underlie all 1-2-3 graphs.

Creating a Basic Graph

With 1-2-3, graph creation is an orderly process. You can develop a basic graph of your 1-2-3 data by following these steps:

1. Selecting a graph type

   Although you can change your mind at any time later, you begin creating a graph by choosing a graph type. For the graphs you create in this chapter, you will choose either **Bar** or **Line**.

2. Specifying the labels for the x-axis

   You specify the labels that will run along the *x-axis,* the horizontal axis of your graph. These labels most likely are already contained in your worksheet—the headings at the tops of columns, for example, if your data is arranged in columns. With 1-2-3, you can point to the column tops to specify the headings as labels for the x-axis.

3. Identifying the data to be graphed

   Next, you need to identify the data that 1-2-3 should graph. Data that is suitable for graphing usually is a succession of values, such as a product's sales volume shown over a number of months. This succession is called a *series* of data. 1-2-3 lets you graph as many as six series. You specify each series to be graphed by identifying it on the worksheet.

4. Viewing the basic graph

   After you choose the x-axis labels and the series to be graphed, 1-2-3 has all the information it needs to create a basic graph. Now you can view the graph and determine what needs to be added and what needs to be changed.

5. Adding informative elements to the graph, such as a title and legend

   To be sure that your graph does not leave the audience guessing, you should now add titles at the top of the graph that describe the graph's purpose. You also can add a legend that illustrates how each series within the graph is represented. Titles and legends are just a start. Many additions are possible at this stage to make the graph more communicative.

6. Customizing features of the graph for clarity and accuracy

   1-2-3 tries to set up your graph's elements appropriately. The program automatically determines the starting and ending values of the vertical y-axis, for example. But you may want to make adjustments to the graph. You can modify the graph for expressive effect, highlighting certain data to make your graph easier to interpret. At this point, you can adjust most of the graph's options until you are satisfied with the way the graph depicts your data.

This chapter and several that follow will explore each of these steps one by one. As you proceed, you'll create a variety of sample graphs to gain hands-on experience at each step. The remainder of this chapter shows you how to create and view a basic 1-2-3 bar or line graph.

Now imagine, for the purposes of this chapter, that you have been asked to help Randolph Rouges ("A Small Vineyard with Great Growth Potential Nestled in the Hills of Northern California") to create a set of graphs that convince potential investors of the profitability of Randolph's wine-making and sales. Old man Randolph himself has gathered the following summary data and has presented it to you in the 1-2-3 worksheet shown in figure 3.1.

A1:   READY

	A	B	C	D	E	F	G	H
1				Randolph Rouges				
2								
3			January	February	March	April	May	June
4	Burgundy							
5	Units sold		2630	2700	2750	3210	3370	3200
6	Price per bottle		$7.95	$7.95	$8.49	$8.49	$8.79	$8.79
7	Gross revenue		$20,909	$22,101	$23,348	$27,253	$29,622	$28,031
8								
9	Growing costs		$6,444	$6,811	$6,738	$7,223	$8,257	$8,036
10	Packaging		$3,156	$3,336	$3,300	$3,210	$3,370	$3,280
11	Marketing		$132	$139	$138	$161	$169	$164
12	Total costs		$9,731	$10,286	$10,175	$10,593	$11,795	$11,480
13								
14								
15								
16								
17								
18								
19								
20								

10-Dec-89 05:46 PM   UNDO

Fig. 3.1. The Randolph Rouges worksheet.

This worksheet collects information about the preceding six months' revenue and expenses for the vineyard's exquisite '89 Burgundy. Create this worksheet in your version of 1-2-3, so that you can create the graphs yourself.

Selecting a Graph Type

For your first graph, you decide to compare Randolph's gross revenues with total costs. What type of graph should you use? A bar graph would clearly show each month's figures so that the viewer could compare them month-by-month. A line graph, another possibility, would provide a bit more insight. Not only could viewers compare both figures for each month, but they could also see the changes in sales and expenses across the six-month time frame. Both month-by-month profits and the general trend of profitability are favorable for Randolph, so you decide to create both charts.

After you have created the worksheet shown in figure 3.1, begin creating the first chart—a bar chart. Select /Graph to bring up the graph menu, which shows these options:

Type **X A B C D E F R**eset **V**iew **S**ave **O**ptions **N**ame **G**roup **Q**uit

Press **T** to see the menu of graph types. Note that **L**ine and **B**ar are the first two graph types. **XY**, **S**tack-Bar, and **P**ie are other types covered in later chapters. The /Graph Type menu looks like this:

Line **B**ar **XY** **S**tack-Bar **P**ie

The 1-2-3 Release 3 /Graph Type menu contains a few added options:

Line **B**ar **XY** **S**tack-Bar **P**ie **HLCO** **M**ixed **F**eatures

To create a bar chart, press **B**. The sequence of keystrokes you just followed is shown in text as /Graph Type Bar. From now on, when the text tells you to make such a selection as /Graph Type Bar, you should press the slash key to bring up the 1-2-3 command menu, press **G** for the graph menu, **T** for the type menu, and then **B** for bar graph.

If you use 1-2-3 Release 2.2, the *graph settings page* appears on-screen whenever you press /G. This settings sheet, which summarizes all the settings for the current graph (see fig. 3.2), temporarily replaces your worksheet on-screen. Notice that most settings are blank; you need to specify many of these as you construct your graph. Note also that the sheet indicates you were successful in setting the graph type to Bar.

Specifying Labels for the X-Axis

While the graph menu is still on the screen, choose **X** to set the *X data range*, the worksheet range that holds the labels for the x-axis. For this graph, the x-axis should be labeled with the month names, which reside in C3..H3 in the worksheet. Point to cells C3..H3 just as you would specify any range (highlight the range's first cell, press the period key to anchor the range, and then stretch the cell pointer with the arrow keys to highlight the rest of the range); now press Enter. Notice that C3..H3 now appears next to X in the graph settings sheet on-screen. If you are using 1-2-3 Release 3, you can press **X** again to confirm the range setting.

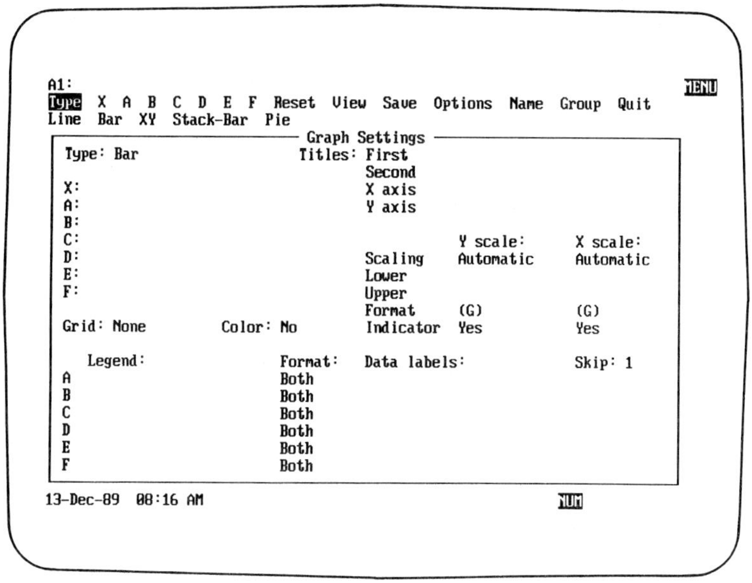

```
A1:                                                              MENU
Type X A B  C  D  E  F  Reset View Save Options Name Group Quit
Line Bar XY Stack-Bar Pie
                        ── Graph Settings ──
  Type: Bar                    Titles: First
                                       Second
    X:                                 X axis
    A:                                 Y axis
    B:
    C:                                      Y scale:       X scale:
    D:                                 Scaling Automatic   Automatic
    E:                                 Lower
    F:                                 Upper
                                       Format     (G)          (G)
  Grid: None        Color: No          Indicator Yes          Yes

      Legend:             Format:      Data labels:       Skip: 1
    A                     Both
    B                     Both
    C                     Both
    D                     Both
    E                     Both
    F                     Both

  13-Dec-89  08:16 AM                                  NUM
```

Fig. 3.2. *The 1-2-3 Release 2.2 Graph Settings sheet.*

Identifying Data To Be Graphed

So far, you have determined the type of graph 1-2-3 should create and the type of x-axis the graph should have. Now you must tell 1-2-3 which worksheet data to graph.

In the graph menu, the options **A** through **F** represent the six data ranges you can include in any one graph; each data range corresponds to one series of data. Although the six-series limit may seem like a constraint, it's a sensible one. Too many bars or lines clutter a graph, muddling its interpretation.

You can select a range by typing its address, such as **C7..H7** and pressing Enter. Or you can position the cell pointer on the first cell in the range (C7), press the period key once, use the arrow keys to stretch the cell pointer until it covers cells D7, E7, F7, G7, and H7, and press Enter.

For this graph, assign Gross revenue to series **A** and Total costs to series **B**, so that you can compare the two. The figures for Gross revenue are in C7..H7, so choose **A** from the graph menu and select the Gross revenue numbers in the range C7..H7. Do the same for series **B**, this time choosing the Total costs figures in the range C12..H12.

Viewing the Basic Graph

At this point, you have specified the minimum information 1-2-3 needs to create a basic graph. It is now time to see how the graph looks. Choose View from the graph menu to display the unadorned default graph that 1-2-3 builds from your data. Your graph should look like the one in figure 3.3.

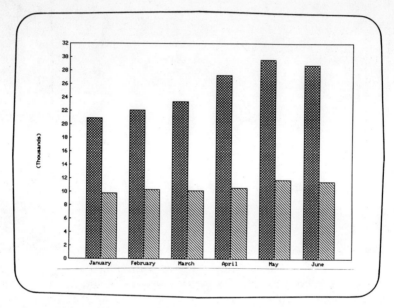

Fig. 3.3. The basic bar graph.

Notice that 1-2-3 obeyed your commands and arranged the specified X data range's contents—the month names—along the x-axis. Notice also that 1-2-3 examined the minimum and maximum values in your data and framed those numbers within a y-axis that encompasses all of your data. 1-2-3 always assigns a minimum value for the y-axis that is less than the lowest value in your data and a maximum y-axis value higher than your largest value. 1-2-3 also indicates the value unit along the y-axis, which in this case is expressed in thousands. Now, to return to the worksheet, press any alphanumeric key.

Another way to view a graph is to leave the menu system and return to the worksheet screen by pressing Esc several times. Then press Graph (F10) to instruct 1-2-3 to display a graph that uses all the currently specified settings. Press any key to return to the worksheet when you are finished viewing the graph.

Now that you have a basic graph, you can begin adding the extras to your work in progress. In practice, you will find that some of these extras are indispensable. A title and a legend, for instance, can be critical to understanding the graph's purpose. Other optional features serve to make the graph more comprehensible—the data values, grid lines, and other such enhancements. These modifications are covered later in this chapter.

Viewing through a Graph Window (Release 3)

Users of 1-2-3 Release 2.01 and Release 2.2 must be content to switch back and forth on-screen between their worksheet and their graph. Release 3 users, however, who have a high-quality graphics display, can split the screen and view the worksheet and graph simultaneously. As the user makes changes to the worksheet, modifications are displayed immediately in the corresponding graph. To use a graph window, you must have a Hercules Graphics Card, an Enhanced Graphics Adapter (EGA), or Video Graphics Array (VGA) system. Graph windows do not work with monochrome display adapters or Color Graphics Adapter (CGA) cards.

To view a worksheet and a graph together, move the cell pointer to a column about halfway across the screen and select /Worksheet Window Graph. 1-2-3 will create a window displaying the graph that extends from the cell pointer's position to the right edge of the screen.

The /Worksheet Window Graph command is extremely helpful in fine-tuning a graph. You can watch the effect on the graph as you make changes to the worksheet. Figure 3.4 shows such a window: on the left is the worksheet, on the right is the graph in progress.

To close a graph window, select /Worksheet Window Clear.

Adding to the Basic Graph

Laying the foundation of a 1-2-3 graph is simple, but the resulting graph will need some elaboration—enlightening elements added to this foundation to help the viewer read the graph. Some of these elements are virtually mandatory. Titles at the top announce the graph's contents. At the bottom of the graph, a legend provides the only key a viewer has to distinguish among the bars or lines in the graph. Other additions delve deeper into the graph's significance. Data-labels, a grid, and

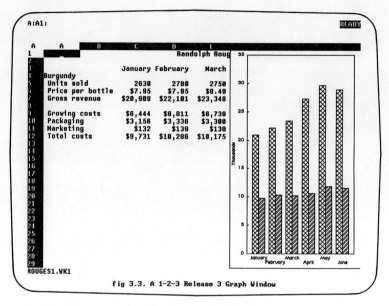

Fig. 3.4. *A 1-2-3 Release 3 graph window.*

footnotes help the viewer interpret the measurements and draw the desired conclusion from its contents.

Adding Titles

You can add four titles to any 1-2-3 graph, a main title and a subtitle, formally called the *first title* and *second title*, and you can place titles along both the x-axis and y-axis.

The first and second titles are centered at the top of the graph. To enter these titles, select /Graph Options Titles. 1-2-3 Release 2.2 responds by displaying the following titles menu:

First Second X-Axis Y-Axis

Choose First or Second, and type in the appropriate title. You can also pull a title directly from a worksheet label by typing a backslash followed by the cell address or range name of the label. Suppose, for example, that you want the worksheet title, Randolph Rouges, in cell D1, for the second title of the graph. Just enter **\D1** as the second title.

Titles for the x-axis and y-axis may be less important than the graph's title, but often they provide the only information a viewer has to evaluate the units represented by each axis. The y-axis title runs vertically, one letter under another, just to the left of the y-axis. The x-axis title runs horizontally, just below the x-axis.

For the graph you are preparing for Randolph Rouges, enter these four titles:

First: **1989 Burgundy Revenues and Expenses**
Second: **Randolph Rouges**
X-Axis: **Months**
Y-Axis: **Dollars**

You'll find that each time you enter a title, 1-2-3 returns to the options menu. You must select the titles menu again before you can enter another title. When you finish adding the titles, your graph should look like the one in figure 3.5.

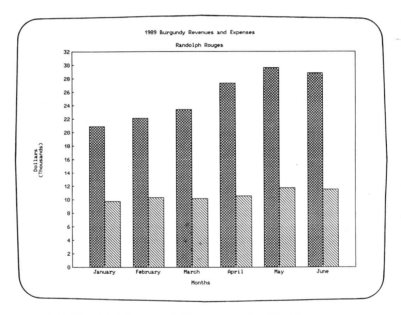

Fig. 3.5. *The 1-2-3 Release 2.2 basic graph with titles.*

1-2-3 Release 3 users will note some differences in the appearance of the graph at this point. Figure 3.6 shows how the same graph looks in 1-2-3 Release 3.

To avoid confusion, the graphs you see in this text are taken from Release 2.2. Release 3 versions of the graphs are shown only if significant differences between the two releases must be highlighted.

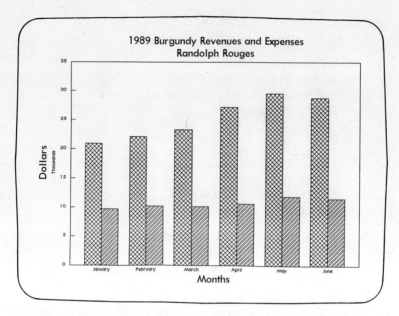

Fig. 3.6. The 1-2-3 Release 3 basic graph with titles.

Although Release 2.2 severely restricts the number and placement of the titles, you can use Allways to add further titles to a completed graph, to vary their positioning, and to obtain special fonts. You will find complete information in Chapter 5 about using Allways to add titles.

The Release 3 titles menu offers three additional choices for a total of seven possible titles:

First Second X-Axis Y-Axis 2Y-Axis Note Other-Note

☐ The **2Y-Axis** option allows a title for the second y-axis. Instruction for using this option comes in a later section of this chapter titled "Adding a Second Y-Axis."

☐ The **Note** lets you place a footnote at the lower left corner below the graph.

☐ The **Other-Note** option lets you place a second footnote below the first.

Figure 3.7 shows the positions of all seven possible titles in 1-2-3 Release 3.

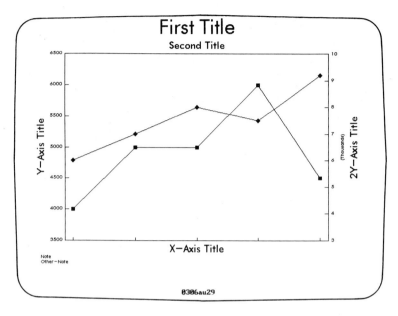

Fig. 3.7. *All possible titles in a 1-2-3 Release 3 graph.*

If you use Release 3, you might use the Note option to enter a footnote such as "Company Confidential."

If you want to change a title on a graph, use /Graph Options Titles, choose the title you want to edit, and then edit the title text in the control panel. If you borrowed a title from the worksheet by entering its cell address or range name, you must change the title in the worksheet to change the title in the graph. To remove a title, display the title in the control panel as though you want to edit it, but press Esc and then press Enter.

Adding a Legend

In graphs having more than one series, a legend lets your audience know which bars or lines depict which series. To assign legend text to data series, select /Graph Options Legend. The legend menu offers the following options:

   A B C D E F Range

To use this menu, select a data range (A-F) that needs a legend entry, and then type descriptive text for the legend. If you use Release 2.2, the text appears near the bottom of the graph settings page. If suitable text for the legend appears in a worksheet cell, you can use that text by typing a backslash followed by the cell address or range name. If, for example, cell A4 contains appropriate text for the legend entry, you can simply type \A4 as the entry for the legend.

You can select **R**ange if all the legend entries reside in a single range on the worksheet. If you are graphing three series that lie in successive rows in the worksheet, for example, and each series has a label in column A at the beginning of the row, you can specify the range containing the labels as the legend entries. 1-2-3 automatically enters backslashes, followed by the cell address of each of the legend entries.

For the Randolph Rouges graph, enter **Gross revenues** as the legend text for data range **A**. Next, enter **Total costs** as the legend text for data range **B**.

To edit or delete a legend entry, follow the same sequence you used to enter the text. The legend text, cell address, or range name appears in the control panel, ready to be edited. Edit the text and press Enter, or delete the text by pressing Esc and then pressing Enter.

Certain graphs do not require legends. Bar and line graphs need no legend if they display only one series. Pie graphs, which by their design can display only a single series, are not helped by a legend.

Adding Data-Labels

Although your sole purpose for making a graph may be to escape a dry presentation of numbers, you still may want the actual numbers to be expressed in your graph. Numbers in a graph, called *data-labels*, are attached to bars or to the data points on the lines to show the precise values. Data-labels let viewers interpret the graph with a precision they cannot attain by merely eyeballing its bars or trend lines. Nevertheless, you should use data-labels sparingly. They can clutter a graph and make it harder to interpret at a glance.

To add data-labels, select /Graph **O**ptions **D**ata-labels. The data-labels menu offers these options:

   A B C D E F Group Quit

Select one of the six data ranges, **A** through **F**, and then highlight the range of numbers on the worksheet that should appear with the bars or line associated with the range. Repeat the procedure for other data ranges that should be labeled.

1-2-3 next displays a submenu that enables you to specify the position of the data-label relative to the actual data point on the graph. The submenu contains the following options:

Center Left Above **Right** **Below**

These options are self-explanatory, but note that you are setting the position for all data-labels in a series at once. This means that you cannot place some data-labels above the data points and others below. This restriction makes sense. A viewer might easily be confused about which numbers belong to which series if you were to position data-labels in an inconsistent pattern.

To add data-labels to the current graph, take the following steps:

1. Select /**Graph** **Options** **Data-labels**.

2. Select **A** and point to the worksheet range that contains the actual values for data range A. In the sample worksheet, this range is C7..H7.

3. Select **Above** when the submenu appears.

To view the graph with data-labels, you must select **Quit** twice: once to return to the options menu and once again to return to the graph menu. You then can select **View** to see the graph.

Data-labels placed in a graph take on the same formatting as the values in the worksheet. If a data range is formatted as currency to two decimal places, for example, the data-labels appear formatted as currency to two decimal places, as well.

If you are creating a line graph, a special trick you can play with data-labels is to place centered data-labels along the line and then drop out the lines altogether. This technique results in free-floating numbers at the data point positions. To try this, follow these steps:

1. Change the graph type to **Line** from **Bar**.

2. Select /**Graph** **Options** **Data-labels** and specify the range **C7..H7** as the data-labels for data range **A**, if you have not already done so.

3. When the submenu appears, select **Center** to place the data-labels directly on their data points.

4. Specify the worksheet range **C12..H12** for the labels for data range **B**.

5. Select **Above** from the submenu to place the data-labels directly over their data points.

6. Select **Quit** to return to the options menu.

7. Select **Format** from the options menu.

8. For data range A, choose **Neither** (neither lines nor symbols) to omit both lines and symbols for the first data range.

9. Select **Q**uit twice, once to return to the options menu and again to return to the graph menu. Finally, select **V**iew to look at the graph, which should appear as shown in figure 3.8.

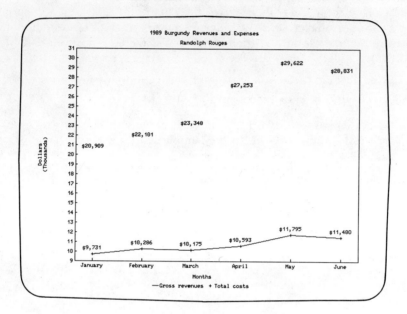

Fig. 3.8. The graph with free-floating data-labels.

Another special data-label technique is to restrict placement of data-labels to certain data points that you want to highlight. To add only selected data-labels to a data range, copy the entire range of values for the series to another area of the worksheet. Then use **/R**ange **E**rase to delete the values you want to omit. Now, you can use this edited range as the data-label range for the series. Figure 3.9 shows a graph with data-labels for only the high and low points of the Gross revenue series.

Here are the precise steps to follow for adding selected data-labels to your current graph:

1. Return to the worksheet by pressing Esc a few times.

2. Make a copy of the contents of range C7..H7. You can do this by entering **+C7** in cell C18 and copying C18 to D18..H18.

3. Erase the contents of all cells in the copied range, except for the cell with the lowest value for the six months (January, in cell C18) and the cell with the highest value (May, in cell G18).

Your worksheet should look like the one shown in figure 3.10.

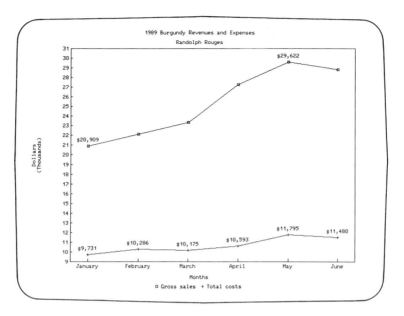

Fig. 3.9. *Graph with selected data-labels.*

A1:   READY

	A	B	C	D	E	F	G	H
1				Randolph Rouges				
2								
3			January	February	March	April	May	June
4	Burgundy							
5	Units sold		2630	2700	2750	3210	3370	3280
6	Price per bottle		$7.95	$7.95	$8.49	$8.49	$8.79	$8.79
7	Gross revenue		$20,909	$22,101	$23,348	$27,253	$29,622	$28,831
8								
9	Growing costs		$6,444	$6,811	$6,738	$7,223	$8,257	$8,036
10	Packaging		$3,156	$3,336	$3,300	$3,210	$3,370	$3,280
11	Marketing		$132	$139	$138	$161	$169	$164
12	Total costs		$9,731	$10,286	$10,175	$10,593	$11,795	$11,480
13								
14								
15								
16								
17								
18			$20,909				$29,622	
19								
20								

10-Dec-89   05:44 PM   UNDO

Fig. 3.10. *Worksheet used for selected data-labels.*

Next select /Graph Options Data-labels and specify the range C18..H18 as data-labels for data range A. When the submenu appears, select Above. Select /Graph Options Format and set the display of data range A back to its default setting (Both). Select Quit twice to return to the graph menu, and select View to view the graph. Your graph should match the one seen in figure 3.9.

If you need to remove data-labels from a series on your graph, substitute the address of any single blank worksheet cell for the current data-label range. Then select any of the choices from the data-label position submenu.

You also can select /Graph Reset and specify a data range in order to remove the data-labels. But using the /Graph Reset command also simultaneously resets the data range and other associated settings. So, if you use /Graph Reset to remove data-labels, you also must reselect the data range series as well as the other settings. That is extra work.

The Group option on the data-labels menu lets you set data-labels for a number of data ranges simultaneously. This option is covered in the section titled "Using Group Commands and Automatic Graphing."

Adding a Grid

1-2-3 graphs normally have a clear background, but you have the option to add a background grid to a graph. A grid can help the viewer to estimate values by visually lining up data points with the x-axis and y-axis.

To add a grid, select /Graph Options Grid. The following menu appears:

Horizontal Vertical Both Clear

☐ The Horizontal option enables you to add horizontal lines across the graph. The lines correspond with the tick marks on the y-axis.

☐ The Vertical option adds vertical lines to the graph. These lines correspond with the tick marks on the x-axis.

☐ The Both option adds both horizontal and vertical lines.

☐ The Clear option removes all grid lines from the graph.

Figure 3.11 shows the sample graph with both horizontal and vertical grid lines.

1-2-3 Release 3 users will see an additional option on their grid menu. If you use 1-2-3 Release 3, your grid menu looks like this:

Horizontal Vertical Both Clear Y-Axis

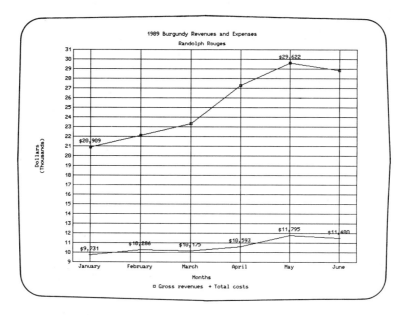

Fig. 3.11. The graph with Grid set to Both.

The **Y**-Axis option is used for a graph showing two y-axes. This option lets you specify whether the horizontal grid lines are to correspond to the first y-axis or the second. The next section shows you how to set up a second y-axis.

To try adding horizontal grid lines to your graph, select /Graph Options Grid, and then select Horizontal. Next, press **Quit** once to return to the graph menu, and select View to see the graph. You will probably agree that this simple graph is best presented without grid lines. Select /Graph Options Grid Clear to clear the grid lines.

Adding a Second Y-Axis (Release 3)

The basic graphs that 1-2-3 produces have a single y-axis at the left. But, with 1-2-3 Release 3, you can add a second y-axis on the right. This second axis is useful in comparing two or more data series of greatly differing value ranges. It also helps when you want to graph two sets of values that are measured in different units. Two examples follow for which dual y-axis graphs would be appropriate:

☐ You want a graphic comparison of the sales of two products. Over the course of six months, one product sold between 10,000 and 20,000 units. Over the same period of time, the other product sold between 250,000 and 300,000 units.

□ You want to compare the sales volume of a product against its selling price. The sales volume is measured in units sold and the selling price is measured in dollars.

To set up a second y-axis in 1-2-3 Release 3, select /Graph Type Features. The following menu appears:

Vertical Horizontal Stacked 100% 2Y-Ranges Y-Ranges Quit

Select 2Y-Ranges to set up a second y-axis, and 1-2-3 responds with this menu:

Graph A B C D E F Quit

□ The Graph option assigns all data ranges in the graph to the second y-axis.

□ A through F enable you to move specific data ranges from the first y-axis to the second y-axis.

□ The Y-Ranges option on the features menu operates in reverse. It lets you move all or selected data ranges back to the first y-axis.

If you use 1-2-3 Release 3, you can try setting up two y-axes in a graph. Revise the graph you created in this chapter so that it compares "Units sold" and "Total costs" in a line graph. If modern economics hold, you should see decreasing costs as quantities increase. Of course, the Units sold category is measured in units, with Total Costs in dollars, so you need to set up two y-axes, one for each scale of measurement.

For this example, select Line as the type of graph you want 1-2-3 to create. Then, reassign data range A so that it represents units sold rather than gross sales. To reassign data range A, follow these steps:

1. Select **A** from the graph menu to set data range A.

2. Press Esc; then you can point to the Units sold range (C5..H5) and press Enter.

3. Select /Graph Options Legend, so that you can modify the legend to reflect the new assignment for data range A.

4. Select /Graph Options Data-labels, so that you can change or remove the data-labels for data range A.

Now your graph should look like the one shown in figure 3.12. When you examine the graph, however, you will see two problems. First, the y-axis is labeled "Dollars," but the measurement for units sold should be "Units." Further, the resulting graph makes it appear at first glance that total costs are substantially higher than units. Units and costs are plotted against the same y-axis for an apples-to-oranges comparison. What you need is a graph that compares the two sets of data, with each

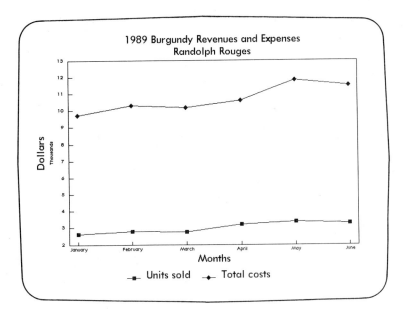

***Fig. 3.12.** Graph with units sold compared to total costs.*

plotted against its own axis. Total costs should be plotted against the first axis, with dollar units; units sold should be plotted against the second axis, which shows the amounts in "units."

To set up an appropriate second y-axis, take the following steps:

1. Select /Graph **Type** Features 2Y-Ranges.

2. Select **A** (the data range for Units sold) to assign data range A to the second y-axis.

3. Select **Quit** twice, so you can view the resulting graph, shown in figure 3.13.

Watch for a second y-axis appearing at the right side of the graph. Notice also that the minimum and maximum values of the second y-axis fit the units sold data plotted against it. The result is a graph that shows the variance of the two series of data over time, so that you can compare one against the other. The revised graph shown in figure 3.13 makes it clear that total costs have increased at a slower rate than units sold. Once again, you can see the economy of scale in action.

If you use two y-axes, you must always label your graph so that the viewer can discern which data has been plotted against which y-axis. For the present graph, you may want to revise the title of the first y-axis to read "Total costs (in dollars)" and revise the second title to

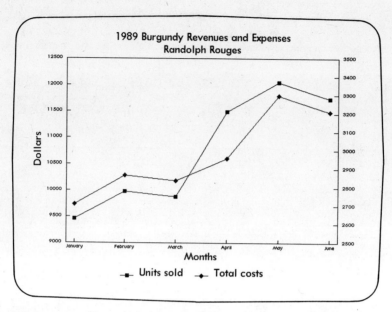

Fig. 3.13. *A graph with dual y-axes.*

read "Units sold (in units)." For the final icing-on-the-cake touch, you can format the numbers along the left y-axis to currency, in keeping with its representation of units in dollars. For detailed instructions on changing the axis number formatting, refer to "Changing the Y-Axis and X-Axis," later in this chapter.

Adding Footnotes (Release 3)

With 1-2-3 Release 3, you can add two footnotes to a graph by selecting /Graph Options Titles. This sequence presents a menu that offers the Note and Other-Note options. The single line of text that you enter for a note appears in the lower left corner of the graph. Text that you enter for Other-Note appears just below Note text.

Customizing the Basic Graph

Now that you have added an assortment of informative enhancements to the graph, you may want to alter some of the graph's design characteristics. You may think of these adjustments as mere fine-tuning, but they can amplify the graph's impact or alter its meaning considerably.

Changing Hatch Patterns and Line Symbols

In 1-2-3 graphs, bars or lines are differentiated by their colors, symbols, or hatch patterns. If you choose color on the graph menu, each series of bars or lines will appear in a different color. If you choose black and white, the bars will be differentiated by their hatch fills, the diagonal lines, stripes, or other patterns that fill the bars. When a line graph is set for black and white, each line has an identifying symbol that represents its data points.

1-2-3 Release 2.2 uses a set of hatch patterns and colors that is different from that of Release 2.01. Table 3.1 summarizes the symbols used with lines and the hatching and colors used with bar graphs and displays the differences between the two versions of 1-2-3.

Table 3.1
Release 2.01 and 2.2 Graph Symbols and Shading

Data Range	Line Graph Symbol	Bar Graph B&W Shading Release 2.01	Release 2.2	On-screen Color CGA (2.2)	EGA/VGA
A	□			Red	Yellow
B	+			Blue	Violet
C	◇			White	Blue
D	△			Red	Red
E	×			Blue	Cyan
F	▽			White	Green

1-2-3 Release 3 uses a different combination of symbols, hatch patterns, and colors altogether, as shown in table 3.2.

These tables can help you select a combination of hatch patterns for bar graphs or to choose specific symbols for line graphs. Use the tables as you assign series in the worksheet to data ranges. Rather than use data ranges A and B for two series, for example, you may want to assign the two series to data ranges A and D on the graph menu. Data ranges A and B use clearly different hatch patterns, but the pattern for data range A is so markedly unlike the one for data range D that the two series will be more easily distinguishable when printed on a black-and-white printer.

Table 3.2
Release 3 Graph Symbols and Shading

Data Range	Line Graph Symbols	Bar Graph B&W Shading	On-Screen Color
A	■	▨	Red
B	◆	▨	Green
C	▼	▨	Blue
D	▫	▱	Yellow
E	◇	▨	Magenta
F	▲	▱	Light Blue

Before proceeding further in this chapter, revise your graph, if necessary, so that it compares units sold (data range A) and total costs (data range B). Set the graph type to **B**ar and be sure to revise the legends and data-labels so that they match the series to be graphed. Figure 3.14 shows the graph settings sheet that appears if you use Release 2.2. If you use another version of 1-2-3, you can use this illustration to check all your graph settings.

Also, assume for a moment that you are using a black-and-white printer and you want to see the graph on-screen as it will appear when printed. Even if you are using a color monitor, select **B&W** from the graph options menu for the purpose of this exercise. Notice that Color is set to No on the settings sheet. Afterward, select **Q**uit to return to the graph menu.

In your graph, the series Units sold (C5..H5) is now assigned to data range A and the series Total costs (C12..H12) is assigned to data range B. Try reassigning the second series, Total costs, to data range D and look at the resulting change in the graph.

To reassign the series, follow these steps:

1. First, double-check to see if you have the graph type set to **B**ar, so that you can follow along with this exercise.

2. Select **D** from the graph menu, point to the Total costs range (C12..H12) on the worksheet, and press Enter. Now, if you use Release 2.2, you should see C12..H12 after both **B:** and **D:** on the graph settings page.

3. Clear C12..H12 from data range B by selecting **R**eset and then **B** from the graph menu. Now, the Total costs series is assigned to data range D.

4. Select **Quit** to return to the graph menu.

5. Select **View** to take a look at the revised graph. Note that both series are now filled with a diagonal grid, one grid filled more densely than the other.

```
H18:                                                          MENU
Type  X  A  B  C  D  E  F  Reset  View  Save  Options  Name  Group  Quit
Line  Bar  XY  Stack-Bar  Pie
                              ┌──── Graph Settings ────────────────────────┐
  Type: Bar                   Titles: First  1989 Burgundy Revenues and ...
                                      Second Randolph Rouges
  X: C3..H3                           X axis Months
  A: C5..H5                           Y axis Dollars
  B: C12..H12
  C:                                             Y scale:      X scale:
  D:                          Scaling   Automatic      Automatic
  E:                          Lower
  F:                          Upper
                              Format      (G)          (G)
  Grid: None      Color: No   Indicator  Yes          Yes

     Legend:        Format:   Data labels:            Skip: 1
  A  Units sold     Both
  B  Total costs    Both
  C                 Both
  D                 Both
  E                 Both
  F                 Both

  10-Dec-89  06:01 PM
```

Fig. 3.14. The graph settings sheet for the current graph.

Figures 3.15a and 3.15b illustrate the graph before and after these changes. Notice how the hatch pattern for total costs varies when the data series is reassigned from B to D.

Now that you have reassigned a data series, you need to readjust the legend to show that total costs is now data range D. If you do not change the legend, an entry for total costs will be missing from the legend.

Edit the legend by following these steps:

1. Select **/G**raph Options Legend, so that you can edit the legend.

2. Select **B** to edit the legend for data range B, press Esc to erase the legend's contents, and then press Enter.

3. Select **Legend** from the options menu again and enter **Total costs** as the legend for data range D.

Now, view the graph once again and check the legend to make sure that it is accurate.

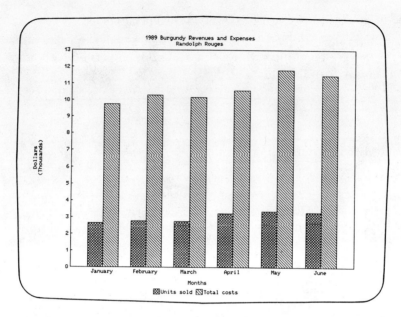

Fig. 3.15a. *Reassigning the data ranges. In this graph you see the A and B ranges.*

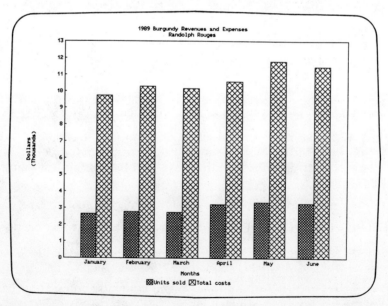

Fig. 3.15b. *In this graph you see the ranges assigned to A and D.*

Removing Connecting Lines and Symbols

Earlier in this chapter, you removed the connecting lines from line graphs, leaving only free-floating data-labels to mark the progression of values. The /Graph Options Format menu gives you the option of turning on or off the lines and symbols appearing at data points. This option is available both for line graphs and XY graphs. When you select /Graph Options Format, 1-2-3 displays the following menu:

Graph **A B C D E F** Quit

You can select the **Graph** option from this menu to turn on or off all graph lines and symbols in the graph at once. Or, you can pick each data range, **A** through **F**, from the menu and set it independently.

When you pick a data range, this menu appears:

Lines Symbols Both Neither

☐ The **Lines** option displays connecting lines between the data points for a series. Symbols do not appear at the data points on the line.

☐ If you select the **Symbols** option, on the other hand, only symbols are displayed at the data points of a series. The connecting lines between the data points do not appear.

☐ The **Both** option displays both the connecting lines and the symbols. **Both** is the default setting for data ranges.

☐ **Neither** displays neither the connecting lines nor the symbols. You can use this last option to display free-floating data-labels by assigning data-labels to the series and then selecting Center to center the labels on the data points.

The graph shown in figure 3.16 displays one series set to Line, one series set to Symbols, and one series set to Neither with free-floating data-labels.

Changing the Y-Axis and X-Axis

You may not have noticed it, but 1-2-3 automatically sets upper and lower limits on the values represented by the y-axis. In fact, if you look at the chart you are now building, you will notice that the lower limit of the y-axis is 0 and the upper limit is 13,000 (see fig. 3.17). Further, 1-2-3 automatically rescales the y-axis. If you change the graph type to a line graph, the y-axis is rescaled so that its minimum value is 2,000.

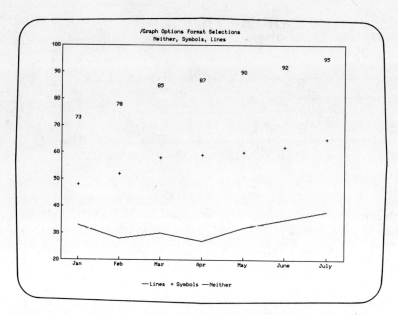

Fig. 3.16. *Three series, formatted to Line, Symbols, and Neither.*

Figure 3.17 shows how the line chart looks when you plot two data ranges against a single y-axis.

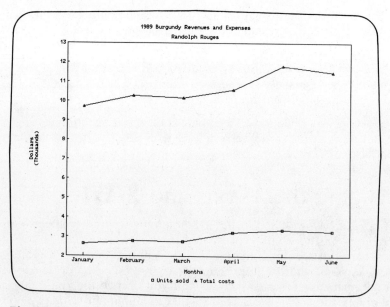

Fig. 3.17. *Line chart showing y-axis with a 2,000 minimum and a 13,000 maximum.*

How did 1-2-3 choose 2,000 and 13,000 as y-scale limits? The program examined the data you provided for graphing and determined that the graphed data contains no value less than 2,000 and no value higher than 13,000.

The scale command on the /**Graph Options** menu holds all the controls you need to adjust the x- and y-axes, including setting their extents. For most graphs, you can vary only the y-axis. XY chart types are the exception to this rule, allowing modification to the x-axis, as well.

When you select /**Graph Options Scale**, this menu appears:

> **Y**-Scale **X**-Scale Skip

You can use **Y**-Scale to vary the scale and other aspects of the y-axis. The **X**-Scale option, for XY charts, lets you vary the scale and other aspects of the x-axis. You can use Skip to set an increment between the points along the x-axis. Skip is covered later in this chapter.

To modify the y-axis, choose **Y**-Scale from the scale menu. A new menu appears:

> Automatic Manual Lower Upper Format Indicator Quit

If you use Release 3, you will see additional menu choices; the Release 3 scaling menu looks like this:

> Automatic Manual Lower Upper Format Indicator Type Exponent Width Quit

Automatic is the default choice that sets lower and upper axis limits based on the range of data that you present to 1-2-3 for graphing.

If you select **Manual**, 1-2-3 sets the lower and upper axis limits to zero, so that you must manually enter both limits. Be sure to enter an upper limit that is higher than the lower limit. Also, be aware that you can use negative numbers for the limits of line, XY, and bar graphs, whenever this is appropriate. You cannot use negative limits in stack-bar or pie graphs. If you inadvertently choose limits that are too small for the range of data you need to graph, 1-2-3 will omit data points that are beyond these limits without warning you.

Changing the scaling of a graph's y-axis can dramatically affect the impact of the graph. To see how striking adjustments to the axis scales can be, try removing Total costs from the graph and displaying only Units sold. Then take the following steps:

1. Select **Reset** from the graph menu.

2. Select the data range that contains Total costs (this probably is data range D).

3. Select **Quit** to return to the graph menu.

Take a look at the graph, shown in figure 3.18, by selecting View. Notice how healthy your sales growth looks when the y-axis is automatically scaled to a range of 2.6 to 3.5 in thousands.

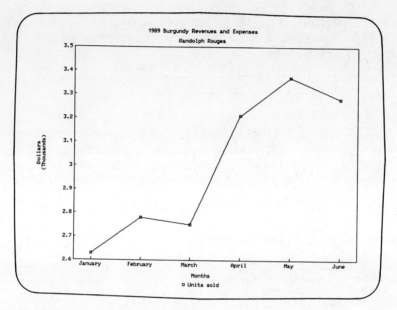

Fig. 3.18. Graph displaying only the units sold series.

Now, using the procedure that follows, manually set the graph's lower and upper limits to 0 and 5,000, and take another look. The resulting graph is shown in figure 3.19.

1. Select /Graph Options Scale Y-Scale.

2. Select Manual and then select Lower.

3. Type 0 for the lower y-axis limit and press Enter.

4. Select Upper, type 5000 for the upper y-axis limit, and press Enter.

5. Select Quit twice to return to the graph menu. Finally, select View.

Compare this graph with the previous one. In the new graph, sales growth looks remarkably modest.

You can modify the scaling of the y-axis to emphasize or deemphasize data fluctuations. The scaling you choose depends on the message you want to communicate about your data.

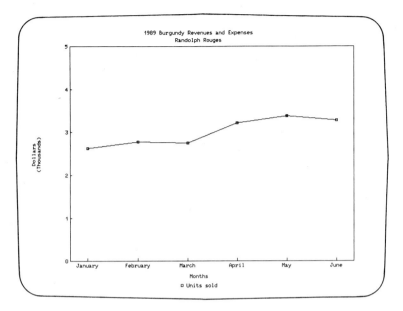

Fig. 3.19. A line graph with a manually scaled y-axis.

The Format option on the Y-Scale and X-Scale menus lets you
determine a format for the values along the axes. The default format is
General, but you can choose formats to match the value of ranges in
the worksheet.

The Indicator option lets you suppress the automatic scale indicator
that informs the viewer about how the y-axis is measured. When the
term "thousands" appears along the y-axis, for example, the viewer
knows that values on the y-axis are measured in thousands. You might
want to suppress the indicator if you always enter dollar amounts in
millions—that is, if 3,000 is customarily understood in your
organization to mean 3,000,000, or if you plan to indicate the scale
measurement in a subtitle or footnote, noting for example that "All
figures are in millions."

The remaining Release 3 options for scaling from this menu appear in
Chapter 6, "Advanced Graph Formatting with 1-2-3 Release 3."

Although you can modify the limits of the axes, you cannot tamper
with the value increments on the y-axis. If 1-2-3 displays all numbers
that are multiples of 1,000 between 10,000 and 50,000 (10,000,
11,000, 12,000, and so on), you cannot choose to display only
increments of 10,000 (such as 10,000, 20,000, 30,000, 40,000, and
50,000). 1-2-3 chooses an increment that is appropriate for the graph.

Skipping X-Axis Labels

Although you cannot vary the increment for the y-axis, you can to some degree modify the increment for the x-axis by using Skip on the /Graph Options Scale menu. This option controls display of the x-axis labels, letting you determine which to display and which to skip over. Skip allows you to set every second, third, fourth, or more label (technically, up to 8,192) along the x-axis for display. Every data point still appears in the graph, but the x-axis skips certain labels.

Skipping x-axis labels can be helpful when you have so many axis values that the labels become crowded. Both Release 2.2 and Release 3 will stagger x-axis labels if necessary, as you see in figure 3.20.

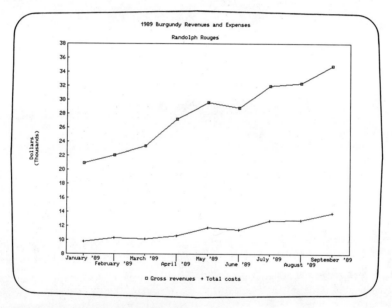

Fig. 3.20. The x-axis with staggered labels.

To display every other x-axis label so that the axis becomes more legible, enter a skip value of 2. Figure 3.21 shows the Randolph Rouges graph displayed with an x-axis skip of 2.

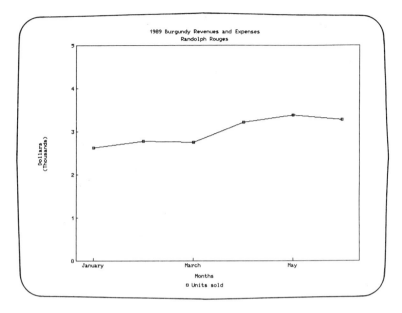

Fig. 3.21. A line graph with the x-axis skip set to 2.

Displaying Data-Labels below the X-Axis

Another labeling technique lets you use the x-axis to display data-labels for data points occurring within the graph. You may also want to use the x-axis data for the data-labels. Figure 3.22 illustrates the result. Notice that the x-axis labels and the data-labels have been switched. The values that were within the series now appear along the x-axis; and the labels that were along the x-axis now appear above the data points.

To use actual data values along the x-axis, select the **X** option from the main graph menu. Assign the data-labels to the X data range. The data-labels now appear along the x-axis in the same format they had on the worksheet.

To try placing the data-labels along the x-axis of your graph, select **/Graph X**. Next, point to the Units sold data range (C5..H5) and press Enter. View the graph to see the result. To use the month names as the data-labels for the series, as shown in figure 3.22, use **/Graph Options Data-labels** and assign the data range containing the month names (C3..H3) to data range A.

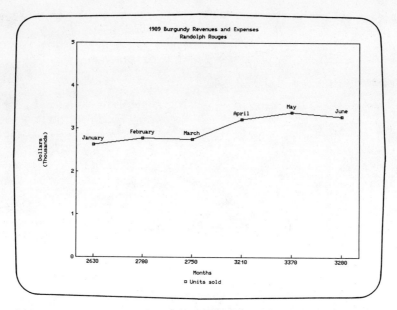

Fig. 3.22. Data-labels displayed along the x-axis.

If the data-labels along the x-axis are so long that they overlap, both
Release 2.2 and Release 3 stagger them. Release 2.01 users will need to
adjust formatting of the data range on the worksheet to get correctly
formatted x-axis data-labels.

Saving Your Graph

You have completed the basic formatting steps that are common to all
releases of 1-2-3. Release 2.2 allows you to format the graph further by
using Allways. Release 3 provides additional menu selections for
advanced formatting options. Chapters 5 and 6 cover these topics in
detail.

Before you go on to those chapters, however, you should learn how to
save a graph through two methods. You should know how to save a
graph along with a worksheet so that you can print it, view it again, or
continue to make modifications to it. You also should learn how to save
the graph as a separate file on disk.

Saving the Graph with the Worksheet

You can save your completed 1-2-3 graph in either of two ways. First, you can save it along with the worksheet by giving it a name. This enables you to recall the image at any time, to view it, and to make modifications. What's more, if you make any changes to the graphed numbers in your worksheet, the graph is automatically updated to reflect those changes. The second method is to save the graph as a separate file on disk. Then you can print the graph with the PrintGraph program or pull the graph file into other software packages. Some graphics packages, such as Freelance Plus from Lotus, let you import for modification and enhancement any 1-2-3 graph you have saved as a file. Some desktop publishing programs and word processors let you incorporate into documents the 1-2-3 graphs you have saved as files.

To save a graph with the worksheet, use /**Graph Name Create**. You can assign a name to each graph that you create. If you use Release 2.2, you can think of using /**Graph Name Create** as saving one version of the graph settings sheet. In other words, each named graph is a complete set of graph settings. You can save as many versions of the graph settings sheet as you want. Later, when you select one of the names with /**Graph Name Use**, 1-2-3 recalls all the settings on the graph settings sheet for a particular graph.

When you select /**Graph Name**, 1-2-3 responds with the following menu:

> **Use Create Delete Reset**

If you use either Release 2.2 or Release 3, the following menu appears:

> **Use Create Delete Reset Table**

After you use **Create** to save a named graph settings sheet, you can recall the sheet and the resulting graph with /**Graph Name Use**. To delete a graph name, use /**Graph Name Delete**. /**Graph Name Reset** is dangerous; this command clears all graphs from the worksheet. Be extremely cautious when you use **Reset**. With one press of the R key, you can wipe out all your graphing work.

The **Table** command, available with both Release 2.2 and Release 3, lets you set up a table showing the name, type, and first title of the graph.

Try saving your current graph by selecting /**Graph Name Create**. Supply a name for the graph and press Enter. Your graph is now saved with the worksheet. To confirm this, return to the name menu and select **Use**. The graph's name should appear in the control panel. If you are slightly more adventurous, you can return to the main graph menu, select **Reset**, and then select **Graph**. This clears all settings for the current graph. Now, return to the name menu and select **Use**. You can now press F3 to display all the graph names in columns on the screen. Pick the graph name you created earlier; your graph should reappear. If you press Esc, the program returns to the graph settings sheet; all the graph's settings should be there, just as you left them.

The most important caveat for saving graphs with **/Graph Name Create** is the same as for saving range names with **/Range Name Create**. Graph names become a permanent part of the worksheet only when you use **/File Save** to save the worksheet. Until then, if you erase the worksheet or retrieve a different worksheet, you lose the graphs you have created.

If you use Release 2.2 or Release 3, you can use the **Table** option from the graph name menu to have 1-2-3 set up a three-column table displaying the name, type, and first title of the graphs associated with the current worksheet.

When you select **/Graph Name Table**, 1-2-3 prompts you for a range in which it can create the table. Point to an unused and unprotected cell in a clear area of the worksheet and press Enter. Leave plenty of room below the cell for the list of graph names. After you have saved a few graphs, your graph name table will look something like the one in figure 3.23.

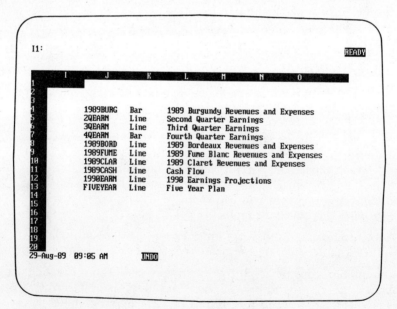

Fig. 3.23. *A graph name table.*

After you have a number of graphs named, you can quickly repeat the /Graph Name Use command several times to create a slide show of existing graphs. A simple macro can execute a series of /Graph Name Use commands for you and make it easy to display a slide show. You will find that macro and others for graphing in Chapter 7, "Using Macros for Graphing."

Saving a Graph Separately as a PIC File

To save a graph as a separate file on disk, use /Graph Save. The /Graph Save command creates a PIC (Lotus PICture) file on disk. This file is suitable for importing into other software or for printing with the PrintGraph program. 1-2-3 Release 3 users do not need to create PIC files to print their graphs. They can print directly from within 1-2-3.

1-2-3 Release 3 users also have the option of creating a different type of graphics output file, a *Computer Graphics Metafile (CGM)*. CGM is a widely used method of interchanging graphics files among software. If a program does not import Lotus PIC files, it may very well import CGM files, instead.

Remember, when you save a graph as a separate file, you permanently sever the link between the worksheet and the graph. Should you make a change in the worksheet, 1-2-3 does not automatically update the graph.

To save a graph as a separate file, select /Graph Save. 1-2-3 prompts for a file name and displays the names of existing PIC files already on the disk. If you want to overwrite an existing file, select its name by moving the highlight with the arrow keys and pressing Enter when the correct name is highlighted. If you are overwriting an existing file, 1-2-3 displays the Cancel/Replace menu. Choose **R**eplace to overwrite the file, or **C**ancel to return to the worksheet. To create a new file, enter a new file name of up to eight characters.

You can save a graph file to a special subdirectory by selecting /Graph Save and then pressing Esc twice to erase the existing directory name. When the old directory name is gone, you can supply another. You can also use the /File Directory command to change directories before saving a graph file.

Release 3 users can save graphs in either PIC or CGM file formats. If you use Release 3, select /Worksheet Global Default Graph, and then select either **M**etafile (CGM) or **P**IC. You can check the current default graph setting with /Worksheet Global Default Status.

Chapter 15 covers PIC files in greater detail.

Using Group Commands and Automatic Graphing

Both Release 2.2 and Release 3 provide special commands that can greatly speed up graphing operations. Release 2.2 provides a series of group commands that enable you to specify a group of data ranges, data-labels, or legend entries simultaneously. Release 3 provides a special automatic graph capability that can define an entire graph with a single keystroke when your data is suitably arranged.

Using /Graph Group

If the data ranges that you want to graph are arranged in your worksheet in adjacent rows or columns, you can use the /Graph Group command. This command specifies the x-axis labels and data ranges A through F simultaneously.

To try the /Graph Group command, use /File Save to save the worksheet you have been creating, and then create the new worksheet shown in figure 3.24. This worksheet compares a set of figures for four varieties of Randolph's wine.

A1: [W22]   READY

	A	B	C	D	E
1			Randolph Rouges		
2			Costs of Production		
3					
4					
5		Burgundy	Bordeaux	Chardonnay	Fume Blanc
6	Planting	1230	1160	1380	1640
7	Fertilizing	2570	2630	2730	2400
8	Grape picking	1370	1350	1450	1250
9	Grape stomping	760	670	690	620
10	Storage	40	30	30	50
11	Bottling	1850	1380	1820	2700
12	Labeling	180	120	290	480
13	Sampling	20	30	30	40
14					
15					
16					
17					
18					
19					
20					

29-Aug-89 09:15 AM   UNDO

Fig. 3.24. *Worksheet comparing four Randolph Rouges.*

Notice that, in this worksheet, all data for each step in wine production happens to fall in consecutive rows. Each row has a heading at its left, which describes the row's contents. Further, there are no blanks between rows, and data is conveniently arranged in the order in which you want to graph it.

To use the /Graph Group command on this data, follow these steps:

1. Select /Graph Group.

2. Enter the range address, range name, or point to the rectangular range containing the row headings and data. In this case, that range is A6..E13.

3. Select either Columnwise (the first column contains the x-axis labels) or Rowwise (the first row contains the x-axis labels). In this case, select Columnwise, because x-axis labels are in the first column.

Now, examine the settings for each of the data ranges, X and A through D. Notice that the following assignments have been made automatically:

X: A6..A13
A: B6..B13
B: C6..C13
C: D6..D13
D: E6..E13

Figure 3.25 shows the graph that appears if you select Bar as the graph type and then select View. Notice how the x-axis labels are staggered because of their length.

Using /Graph Options Data-Labels Group

If you are graphing just a few series, you can supply the ranges for data-labels using a group command, too. To do so, follow these steps:

1. Select /Graph Options Data-Labels Group.

2. Enter the range address, or the range name, or point to the rectangular range containing the data-labels you want to include within the graph. To add data-labels to the graph you are making, point to the range B6..E13.

3. Choose Columnwise or Rowwise. You should make the same choice here that you made when specifying data ranges using the group command.

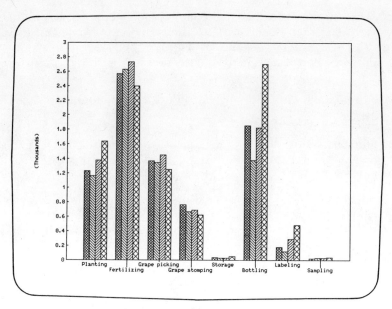

Fig. 3.25. *A basic graph created with the /Graph Group commands.*

4. Select **C**enter, **L**eft, **A**bove, **R**ight, or **B**elow for the positioning of the data-labels. For this example, choose **A**bove.

5. Select **Q**uit twice to return to the graph menu and view the graph.

The resulting graph appears in figure 3.26. Obviously, this technique is appropriate when you have only a few series.

To remove all these data-labels, select **/G**raph **O**ptions **D**ata-labels **G**roup again. This time, however, select a single blank cell, choose either **C**olumnwise or **R**owwise, and pick any position for the data-label.

Using /Graph Options Legend Range

You can use a similar approach when setting up a graph legend. Rather than specifying each legend entry individually, use **/G**raph **O**ptions **L**egend **R**ange and enter the range address or range name, or point to the range of cells containing the legend entries. In this case, that range is B5..E5.

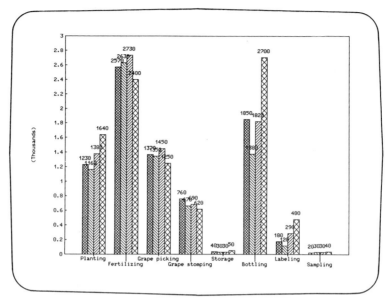

Fig. 3.26. Data-labels added with the /Graph Options Data-labels Group command.

Automatic Graphs (Release 3)

Automatic graphs are a special feature of 1-2-3 Release 3. This feature lets you create certain graphs with a single keystroke. In many cases, you need only position the cell pointer anywhere within the range of data to be graphed and then press Graph (F10) or select /Graph View. You can use this technique as long as you are graphing worksheet data that conforms to the following rules:

1. The /Graph X and data ranges A through F settings are cleared. Use the /Graph Reset Range command to clear these settings, if necessary.

2. The data to be graphed must be arranged in columns or rows with the X data range first, followed by data range A, followed by data range B, and so on.

3. Data for the automatic graph must be separated from other worksheet data by at least two blank columns and rows.

If these restrictions are met, you can position the cell pointer anywhere within the data and press Graph (F10). The resulting graph is formatted according to whether /Worksheet Global Default Graph is set to

Columnwise, dividing data into columns, or **R**owwise, which places the data in rows. By default, 1-2-3 creates a line graph, but you can easily select another graph type.

In figure 3.24, the worksheet data is ideal for an automatic graph. If you use Release 3, try creating this automatic graph. To do so, reset all the graph settings with /**G**raph **R**eset **G**raph, place the cell pointer anywhere within the data, and press F10. You should see the graph shown in figure 3.27. All the data ranges are automatically set. Now you are ready to change the graph type and add titles, data-labels, a legend and other enhancements covered earlier in this chapter.

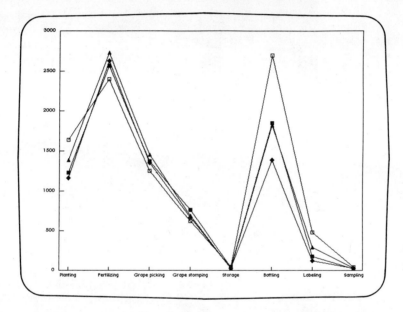

Fig. 3.27. An automatic graph.

You should be aware of the following rules regarding automatic graphs:

☐ If you plan to use automatic graphing to produce an XY graph (XY graphs are covered in a later chapter), you should know that the first column or row containing numbers becomes the X data range.

☐ For all graph types other than XY graphs, the first column or row that contains numbers is used as the A data range.

☐ Any labels found in ranges used for automatic graphing are treated as zeros.

☐ In order for an automatic graph to assign x-axis labels, the first column or row must contain only labels. If this is not the case, the automatic graph does not assign a range for the x-axis.

Summary

In this chapter, you learned to follow an orderly series of steps to create bar and line graphs: selecting a graph type, choosing x-axis labels and data to be graphed, clarifying the graph with such elements as data-labels and a legend, then customizing the graph features for greater communication. The principles that underlie creating the bar and line graphs you learned about in this chapter also underlie the construction of other graph types you will read about in the next chapters.

In the next chapter, you will turn your attention to the four remaining graph types on the 1-2-3 menu. In Chapters 5 and 6, you will learn about using Allways in 1-2-3 Release 2.2 and the advanced graph formatting commands in 1-2-3 Release 3 to enhance your graphs further.

4

Making Stack-Bar, XY, Pie, Area, and HLCO Graphs

I n Chapter 2, you learned about the principles to keep in mind as you plan graphics presentations. Among the key ideas of that chapter were the importance of isolating the data that best presents your case and choosing a graph type appropriate to the significance of your data.

Next, in Chapter 3, you began experimenting with the two most popular 1-2-3 graphs, the bar and the line graph. You learned that line graphs are preferable when you want to show a data series changing over time and that bar graphs compare results at discrete intervals. A line graph would be your best choice to depict how the sales of a product has increased over the last six months, for example. A bar graph would best illustrate the relative sales of eight products during week 8 of a 13-week campaign.

Not all numerical comparisons are best presented by line and bar graphs. 1-2-3 offers a repertoire of graph types, each with its own range of uses. The present chapter moves the focus to the lesser recognized graphs that 1-2-3 makes available to you: the *stack-bar* variation on the bar graph, the *XY graph* that gives you a dual scale to display your data against, the *pie graph* that reveals proportions in dramatic simplicity, the *area graph* that combines mass with trend, and the *high-low, close-open* type that no stock analyst could do without. This chapter picks up with a style of intriguing potential, the stack-bar.

Comparing Totals with a Stack-Bar Graph

Stack-bar graphs, sometimes called *stacked* bar graphs, are available with both 1-2-3 Release 2.2 and Release 3. This graph type is handy when you want to show how totals and their breakdowns vary over time. Stack-bar graphs pile one bar representing a portion of the total on top of the next. This graphic scheme makes it easy to compare ingredients as well as the stacked wholes. Figure 4.1 illustrates the stack-bar graph. Consider how the graph design facilitates the dual comparison: you quickly see how much each product contributed to the entire product line each month, and you see the month-by-month sales for the product line as a whole.

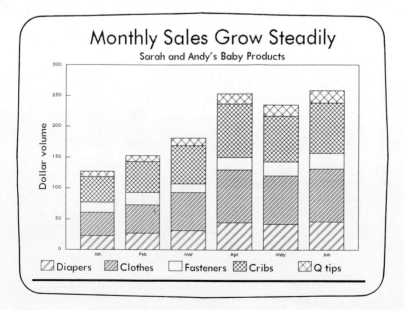

Fig. 4.1. *A stack-bar graph.*

To set up a stack-bar graph, you will follow the same procedures described in Chapter 3 for creating a standard bar graph. To review the process, follow these steps:

Select a range of labels or data on the worksheet that can serve as labels for the x-axis. Assign this data range to X on the /Graph menu. Select one worksheet range for each of the series of data you want graphed. Assign these ranges to data range A, data range B, and so on. Rather than select Bar for the Graph Type, though, select Stack-Bar.

The stack-bar graph's data ranges appear in a specific order. Data range A is closest to the x-axis; data range F is farthest from the x-axis. If a data range contains negative values, the bars extend below the x-axis rather than above, but the same rule holds true—data range A is still closest to the x-axis, at the top of the stack extending downwards, and data range F is farthest from the x-axis.

In stack-bar graphs, data-labels always appear above the corresponding bars if the graphed numbers are positive. The labels are placed below the bars if the numbers are negative. This is true no matter what data-label position setting you choose.

So that you can try creating a stack-bar graph, set up the small worksheet shown in figure 4.2. This worksheet tracks the marketing expenses of A. Cohen's Consulting Division by quarter.

```
A1: 'Marketing Expenses, A Cohen Consulting Division                    READY

          A        B        C        D        E        F        G        H
1    Marketing Expenses, A Cohen Consulting Division
2    (All numbers in millions)
3                                Q1       Q2       Q3       Q4
4                             -------------------------------------
5    Print advertising           975     1200     3900     4600
6    Broadcast advertising      3250     3900     2000     1700
7    Sales                      6375     6300     5700     6800
8    Promotion                  1660     1660     1750     2400
9    Direct Mail                   0        0     1700     1200
10                            -------------------------------------
11                    Total   12260    13140    15130    16700
12
13
14
15
16
17
18
19
20
04-Sep-89  11:13 PM         UNDO
```

Fig. 4.2. *Worksheet data for the stack-bar graph.*

To create the basic graph, specify the quarter names as the X data range (the x-axis labels) and the figures for each expense category as data ranges A through E. Use the following commands:

/Graph Type Stack-Bar
X: D3..G3
A: D5..G5
B: D6..G6
C: D7..G7
D: D8..G8
E: D9..G9

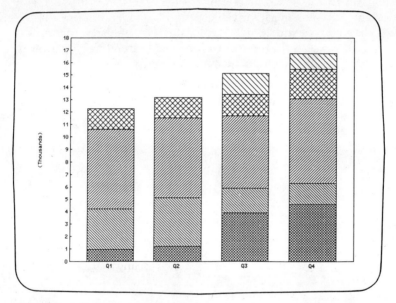

Fig. 4.3. *A basic stack-bar graph.*

Figure 4.3 shows the basic graph that results if you use 1-2-3 Release 2.2. Some improvements, such as titles and a legend, are obviously needed. Use the following commands to add both:

/Graph Options Titles
First: \A1
Second: \A2

Y-Axis: Expenditures
Legend
Range: A5..A9

Figure 4.4 shows the completed stack-bar graph produced by 1-2-3 Release 2.2.

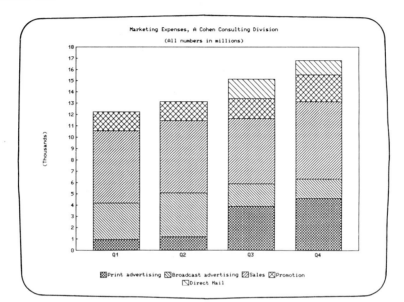

Fig. 4.4. The completed stack-bar graph.

Notice how clearly visible is the steady increase in A. Cohen's total marketing expenses from one quarter to the next. And notice that it is just as apparent how each expense category contributes to that increase. Take note of the reallocation of funds during the third and fourth quarters from broadcast to print advertising. You can see the effect in total marketing expenditures of the direct mail campaign carried out during the third and fourth quarters.

The graph in figure 4.4, however, has two flaws: one of design and one of scale. First, the hatch patterns for the broadcast advertising and sales segments of the bars are so similar that the two segments may not be easily distinguished. To correct this minor fault, you can move one series to another data range to obtain a different hatch pattern. In Chapter 3, tables 3.1 and 3.2 display all the hatch patterns used by the data ranges in all three versions of 1-2-3. Fig. 4.5 shows a revised graph with the broadcast advertising series reassigned to data range F.

You see in the figure that the segments have been reordered. Data range A is always nearest the x-axis and data range F is always farthest from the x-axis.

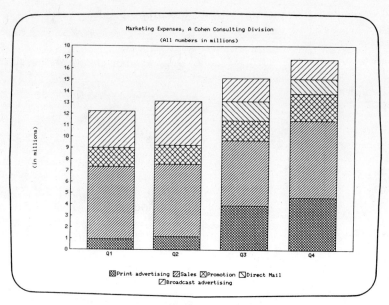

Fig. 4.5. The stack-bar graph with designated hatch patterns.

You may run into a similar problem if you want to display or print a stack-bar graph in color. If so, reassign one or more series to other data ranges to heighten the color contrasts. Make sure that adjacent bar segments use clearly distinguishable colors.

The second problem with the graph in figure 4.4 was that the y-axis indicates thousands, whereas the numbers represent millions. You must remove the y-axis indicator with /Graph Options Scale Y-Scale Indicator No. You can then tag the y-axis "in millions."

If you use Release 3, you can create a stack-bar graph by using the /Graph Type Features Stacked command to manually stack the bars.

Correlating Numbers with an XY Graph

In the types of graphs discussed so far, the x-axis usually represents the passage of time, whether measured in days, weeks, months, quarters, or years. The stack-bar graph that was created earlier in this chapter, for example, used the x-axis to represent the four quarters of a year. Similarly, the bar and line graphs created in the previous chapter used the x-axis to represent months.

The XY graph gives you a double scale—the x-axis and y-axis both represent numeric values. Each data point, therefore, is the intersection of x-axis and y-axis values. By examining clusters of data points, you can detect the presence of a relationship between the two items, factors, or forces represented by the axes. If you are already aware of a dependence of one set of numbers on another, you can use an XY graph to present your findings.

What makes XY graphs unique is that both the x- and y-axes represent numeric ranges of values. The graph shown in figure 4.6 takes advantage of the XY graph capability. The graph displays sales results against advertising expenditures, both of which are numeric values. A quick glance at this graph reveals that when Audrey spends no money on advertising, she sells only a couple of shoe polish tins to her friends. But when her advertising expenditures reach a critical threshold of $160 per week, sales of her award-winning product jump.

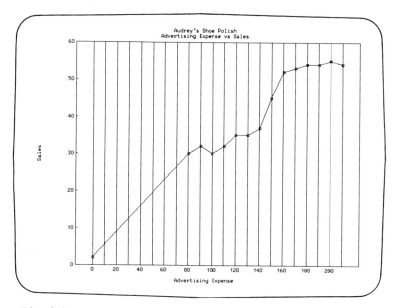

Fig. 4.6. *An XY graph comparing advertising expenditures and sales.*

To create an XY graph, select **XY** on the graph type menu. For the X data range, specify the range of values that you are testing or that you have some control over. These X values measure what is traditionally called the *independent variable* because it is not dependent on any other numbers in the case. The independent variable in this case, and therefore the series assigned to the X data range, is Audrey's advertising expenditure, the variable over which she has control.

Once the independent variable is assigned, assign *dependent variables* to the other data ranges, A through F. These dependent variables in some way depend on the numbers in the X data range. In this case, Audrey hopes to see a positive correlation of sales to advertising expenditures. Therefore, assign sales, the first dependent variable, as the A data range. You can plot additional dependent variables in data ranges B through F.

After you assign data series to data ranges, you can use titles and legends just as you did when you created bar and line graphs to label the graph and to distinguish the series for the viewer.

To create an XY graph, first recreate the worksheet for Audrey's Shoe Polish that is shown in figure 4.7. Audrey is very methodical. Month by month, she has been gradually increasing her weekly advertising expenditure by ten dollars and noting the effect in sales.

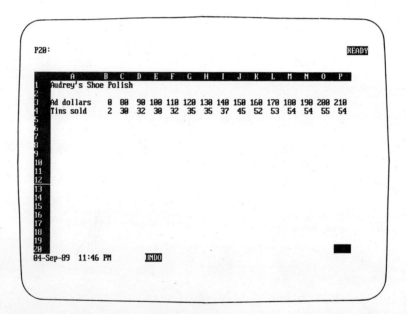

Fig. 4.7. Audrey's shoe polish data.

Use the following commands to create and look at the basic XY graph for Audrey's Shoe Polish (see fig. 4.8):

/Graph Type **XY**
X: **B3..P3**
A: **B4..P4**
View

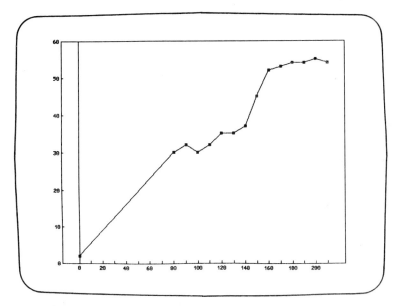

Fig. 4.8. The basic XY graph.

Because the X and Y ranges are numeric indicators, 1-2-3 automatically scales both. As this graph plots only one data series against the x-axis, no legend is really needed to distinguish among the series. The only enhancements you might consider are titles, data-labels and grid lines. Because both of its axes are labeled only by numbers, the XY graph needs titles describing the axes.

Look again at the completed XY graph in figure 4.6. See how clearly the graph illuminates the relationship between advertising expenses and shoe polish sales. This graph explicitly demonstrates that a $160 weekly advertising expense would be a good investment for Audrey. Any more than that, however, would cause little further increase in sales.

With the XY graph type, you can plot a trend line. Suppose that you want to determine the trend of the changes in an independent variable. Suppose further that it would help you determine the speed at which sales increase in relation to increased advertising expenditures. You can track such trends by using 1-2-3's built-in *linear regression* capabilities. A *linear regression* calculates a single straight line that best fits all of a set of data points.

The best-looking representation of a linear regression is with the connecting lines between the independent variable's data points removed and the linear regression values plotted as a line through the scattered independent variable data points.

To create this effect, first use /Graph Options Format **A** Symbols to leave only symbols at the data points. Then calculate a linear regression line using /Data Regression and add it to the graph as an additional data range. For this second data range, choose /Graph Options Format **B** Lines. The resulting graph shows a trend line plotted through the middle of the suspended data points.

Figure 4.9 shows Audrey's data plotted with a best-fit trend line. If you want to perform a regression, you must use /Range Transpose to transpose the two data series to obtain two vertical ranges (regression calculations require their input data to be in columns). Then you can calculate the data points for the regression line by multiplying the X coefficient by each value of the independent variable (the X data range) and adding the constant to the result. Specify the resulting range as data range B and use /Graph Options Format to set this range's format to Lines.

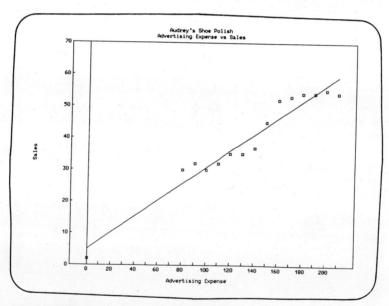

Fig. 4.9. The XY graph with a trend line.

Presenting Proportions with Pie Graphs

When your numbers are the portions of a single total, a pie graph can visually represent their relative contributions to the whole. Pie graphs display only one series of data; each number in the series adds its one slice to the pie. Figure 4.10 shows a pie graph that displays the caseload breakdown of a personnel consulting firm.

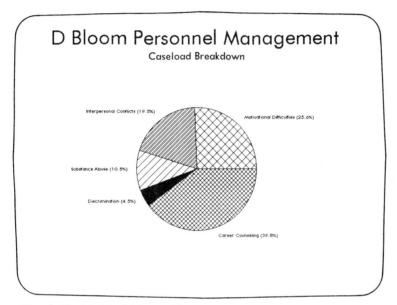

Fig. 4.10. *A typical pie graph use.*

1-2-3 creates a pie graph by adding together the values assigned to data range A and then calculating each value's percentage contribution to the total. For each value, 1-2-3 creates one pie slice, which is sized according to the value's percentage in the breakdown.

Figure 4.11 shows a pie graph used by DLS Neurological Services to analyze the breakdown of its patients by age. To create this graph, DLS used the numbers shown in figure 4.12.

The range A4..A8 is specified as the X data range to provide a label for each of the pie slices. The actual age data, which appears in the range B4..B8, is assigned to the A data range.

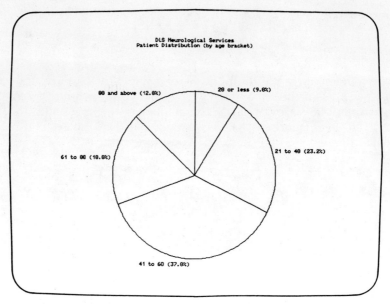

Fig. 4.11. *A pie graph showing breakdown of DLS patients by age.*

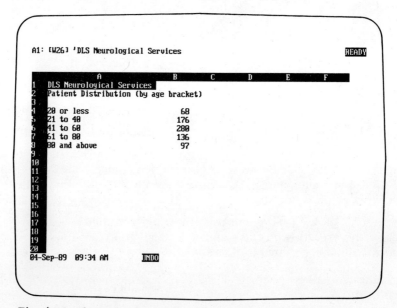

Fig. 4.12. *The DLS patient distribution data.*

You can create the same pie graph by using the following commands:

/Graph **T**ype **P**ie
X: A4..A8
A: B4..B8

1-2-3 automatically places its percentage calculation for each of the slices in parentheses next to the label for that slice. If you use Release 3, the basic pie graph looks somewhat different. Figure 4.13 shows the Release 3 version of this pie graph.

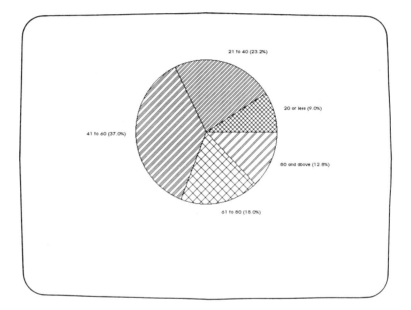

Fig. 4.13. *The basic pie graph as created by Release 3.*

When generating pie graphs, 1-2-3 Release 2.01 and Release 2.2 plot values in the A data range starting at 12 o'clock and continuing clockwise around the pie. Further, the pie's slices are not filled with hatch patterns.

Release 3, on the other hand, plots the A data range's values starting at 3 o'clock and continuing counterclockwise around the pie. By default, Release 3 pie slices are filled with hatch patterns.

You cannot vary the starting angle of the pie slices or the direction in which values are plotted around the pie. You can add or modify hatch patterns, however, by entering values in the B data range that correspond to the appropriate hatch patterns. Figures 4.14 and 4.15 show the B data range entries and corresponding hatch patterns for all versions of 1-2-3.

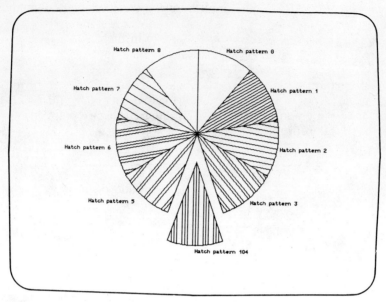

Fig. 4.14. *1-2-3 Release 2.2 hatch patterns.*

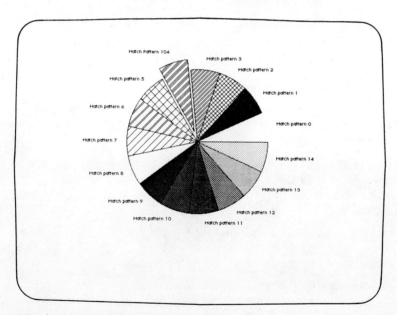

Fig. 4.15. *1-2-3 Release 3 hatch patterns.*

You can cut slices of the pie to emphasize certain values by adding 100 to the B data range value for the slice. If you want hatch pattern 4 for the slice, for example, enter 104 (100 + 4) in the corresponding B data range entry to cut the slice. To hide a slice, make its value negative.

If you use Release 3, you can omit the display of percentage numbers in parentheses next to slice labels. To do so, set up a separate range with one cell for each pie slice. Enter a zero in a cell to suppress the percentage figure for the corresponding slice. Then assign the range to data range C. In neither Release 2.01 nor Release 2.2 can you omit the percentage figures.

Another technique to clarify a pie graph is to add data values to pie slice labels. 1-2-3 places the result of its percentage calculation for each slice next to the slice label. You can further enhance the label by adding each slice's actual data number (in this case, the number of patients in each age group) to the label.

To perform this trick, you need to use 1-2-3's string function called *concatenate,* which joins two labels into one long string of characters. Remember, however, that data for the pie exists as values rather than labels. Thus, before you can join them to the pie slice labels, you need to copy the data values with **/R**ange **V**alue to another range on the worksheet. There, you can reformat the copied values as labels by placing apostrophes in front of them.

In the worksheet, range B4..B8 contains the actual data values. Range C4..C8 contains the numbers that specify hatch patterns for the pie slices. Range D4..D8 contains the copied data values, which have been reformatted as labels. In cell E4, enter the formula **+A4&**": "**&D4**. Copy this formula to the range E5..E8. Figure 4.16 shows how the worksheet should look after the formula is copied. Notice in the figure that the formula for cell E4 is visible in the control panel.

Finally, reassign the range E4..E8 as the X data range. The finished graph should look like the one shown in figure 4.17.

Showing Volume with an Area Graph

Area graphs are a special feature of 1-2-3 Release 3. Think of an area graph as a stack-bar graph with lines rather than bars. Like the stack-bar graph, the area graph compares the components of a whole. Unlike a stack-bar graph, however, the area graph emphasizes changes over time rather than measurements at specific intervals.

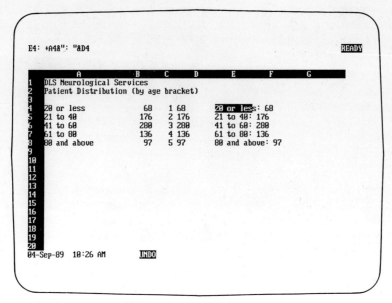

Fig. 4.16. *Worksheet for the completed graph.*

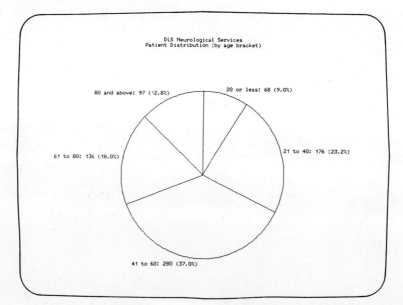

Fig. 4.17. *The completed DLS pie graph with enhanced slice labels.*

To create the simple area graph shown in figure 4.18, use the data shown in figure 4.19 for Sarah and Andy's Baby Products.

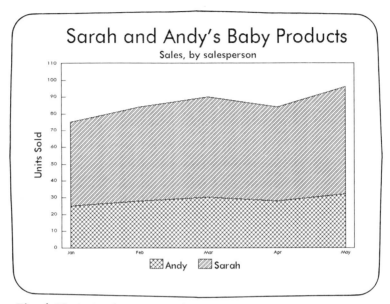

Fig. 4.18. *A simple area graph.*

A:F20: READY

	A	B	C	D	E	G
1	Sarah and Andy's Baby Products					
2	Sales, by salesperson					
3						
4		Jan	Feb	Mar	Apr	May
5	Andy's sales	25	28	30	28	32
6	Sarah's sales	50	56	60	56	64
7						
8						
9						
10						
11						
12						
13						
14						
15						
16						
17						
18						
19						

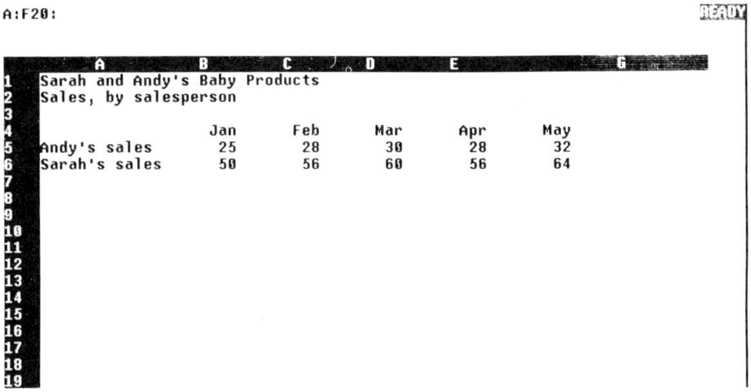

Fig. 4.19. *Data for the area graph in figure 4.18.*

Use the following commands to set up the basic graph and add titles and a legend:

/Graph Type Line
X: B4..F4
A: B5..F5
B: B6..F6

Options Titles
First: **\A1**
Second: **\A2**
Y-Axis: **Units Sold**

Options Legend
A: **Andy**
B: **Sarah**

Quit

View

Before you go any further, notice on the worksheet that Sarah has made exactly twice as many sales as Andy. This relationship, however, is not truly reflected in the graph, as shown in figure 4.20. In this example, 1-2-3 automatically scales the y-axis to a minimum of 20 and a maximum of 70, making Andy's sales seem far less than half of Sarah's sales. If you set the minimum y-axis to zero, instead, the true proportion of sales becomes evident.

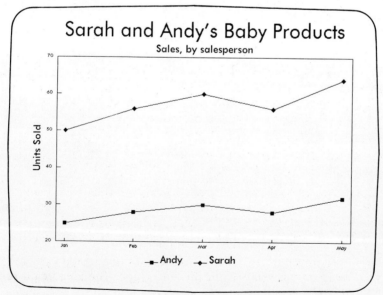

Fig. 4.20. *A line graph for Sarah and Andy's Baby Products.*

To scale the y-axis manually, use the following commands:

/**Graph Options Scale Y-Scale Manual**
Lower: **0**
Upper: **70**

This scaling brings the graph much closer to reality, as shown in figure 4.21.

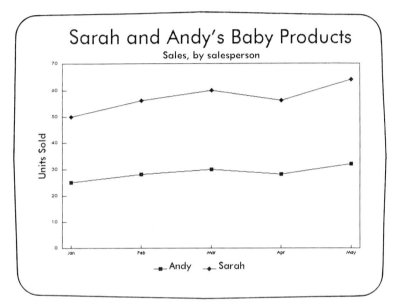

Fig. 4.21. The revised line graph.

By making one small change, you can easily convert the current graph to an area graph. An area graph not only displays the month-by-month relationship between Andy's and Sarah's sales, but it also shows how the total company sales varied over the period.

To convert the line graph in figure 4.21 to an area graph, use /**Graph Options Format Graph Area.** This sets the format for all data ranges in the graph to **Area.**

Now view the graph, which is illustrated in figure 4.22. The space under the line for Andy's sales has been filled with a hatch pattern and Andy's data looks fine. But Sarah's data seems to have filled the rest of the graph. What's wrong with the way you've plotted Sarah's data?

The answer lies in the manual y-axis scaling you performed earlier, when you modified the y-axis to fit the line graph. The area graph now stacks the two sales results one on top of the other; therefore, the

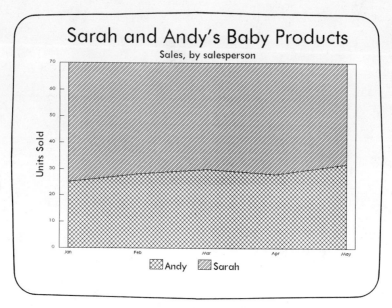

Fig. 4.22. Line graph with Options Format set to Area.

graph needs a maximum y-axis value higher than 70. Your manual
y-axis scaling was appropriate then but not now. Why not let 1-2-3
calculate an appropriate y-axis maximum by setting the y-axis scaling
back to automatic? You can do this by selecting /Graph Options Scale
Y-Scale Automatic.

Now, view the complete area graph and note that it displays Andy's
sales in proportion to Sarah's sales. The graph also displays the
company's healthy sales growth based on the combined sales of the two
owners. Area graphs emphasize not only the individual contributions to
a total, but the progress of the total over time. Figure 4.23 shows the
completed graph.

Tracking Stocks with a High-Low-Close-Open Graph

Another new graph type added to 1-2-3 Release 3 is the High-Low-
Close-Open Graph (HLCO graph), which is designed for stock market
participants and observers. HLCO graphs enable you to track the high,
low, closing, and opening prices of stocks and other financial
instruments during an interval of time.

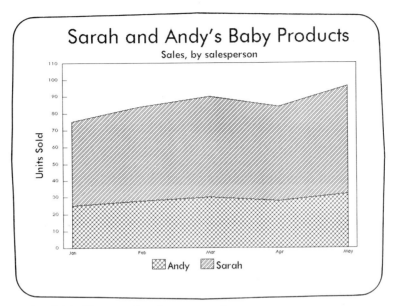

Fig. 4.23. *The completed area graph.*

But this graph style also works well with other measurements. The parameters that comprise the HLCO are first, measurements that fluctuate over time and, second, values that have discrete highs and lows during the graphed period. Consider the HLCO graph type for meteorological readings of temperature and air pressure, or scientific readings of elasticity, density, power, and so forth.

On the HLCO graph, you can also track an additional series as bars below or a line through the HLCO portion of the graph. Usually the line or bars are used to represent the overall trading volume during the period. Figure 4.24 illustrates a typical HLCO graph, which shows the fluctuations of EHW Corporation's stock over the course of one week and the trading volume of the market each day.

To create the HLCO graph, you should assign the data ranges X through F as follows:

Data Range	Worksheet Values
X	Time: days, weeks, quarters, etc.
A	High value
B	Low value
C	Closing value
D	Opening Value
E	Values for the bars
F	Values for the line

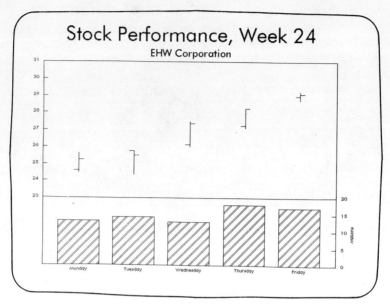

Fig. 4.24. EHW Corporation's HLCO graph.

Figure 4.25 shows the worksheet that contains stock market data for the HLCO graph in figure 4.24. In your stock-tracking worksheet, you should maintain stock price information as values rather than labels. In this case, however, the data was downloaded over the phone as labels from an information service. To graph this data, you first must use the @VALUE function to convert the data from labels to values.

To employ the @VALUE function, enter **@VALUE(B5)** in cell B11. Then, copy B11 to the range B11..F15. Now you have duplicated the cells as values in the range B11..F15. To identify the series, you can copy the row headings in A5..A9 to A11..A15. Figure 4.26 shows how the worksheet should look.

Fig. 4.26. The revised HLCO worksheet.

Now that your worksheet is ready, you can use the following commands to set up the HLCO graph:

    /Graph Type HLCO
    X: A:B4..A:F4
    A: A:B12..A:F12
    B: A:B13..A:F13
    C: A:B14..A:F14
    D: A:B11..A:F11
    E: A:B15..A:F15

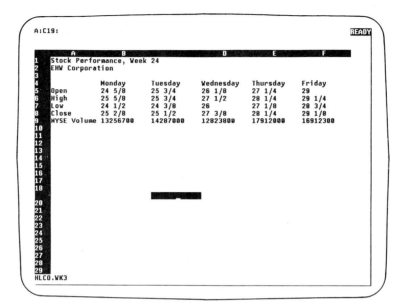

Fig. 4.25. *Data downloaded for the HLCO graph.*

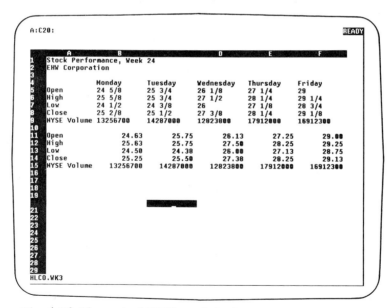

Fig. 4.26. *The revised HLCO worksheet.*

Your graph should look like the one shown earlier in figure 4.24. Notice that each vertical line has a tick mark extending to the left (the opening price) and a tick mark extending to the right (the closing price). You can enhance the graph with titles and axis labels just as you would any other graph.

Although HLCO graphs are designed for tracking financial instruments, you can use this type of graph to display scientific measurements or measurements from instruments if there are recorded highs and lows in the measured data during a time period. Meteorologists might use an HLCO graph, for example, to display daily high and low temperatures for the region.

Mixing Bars and Lines with a Mixed Graph

1-2-3 Release 3 provides one more type of graph: the mixed graph. A mixed graph is actually a combination of a bar graph and a line graph. In a mixed graph, series assigned to data ranges A, B, and C are plotted as bars and series assigned to data ranges D, E, and F are plotted as lines.

Mixed graphs are appropriate when you need to graph data with different measurement scales, such as units sold and retail cost. In such a case, you can assign one series to data range A, B, or C and assign the second series to data range D, E, or F. Then you can plot the second series against the second y-axis.

Mixed graphs are discussed in detail in Chapter 6, "Advanced Graph Formatting in 1-2-3 Release 3."

Summary

In this chapter and the preceding chapter, you learned that creating a basic graph is simply a matter of selecting a graph type and assigning data ranges. After that, you can examine the graph and decide which enhancements to add and which aspects of the graph to modify to emphasize the story your graph will tell.

If you use 1-2-3 Release 2.2 or 1-2-3 Release 3, you should read one of the next two chapters so you can learn to turn the graphs (which are now perfectly respectable just as they are) into visuals that are nothing less than compelling.

5

Formatting Graphs with Allways in 1-2-3 Release 2.2

The graphs you produce using the 1-2-3 graph menu are adequate for simple presentations, perhaps to a coworker or even to supervision. These simple graphs also provide an important tool for data analysis: relationships, hidden behind columns of inscrutable numbers can emerge from a line or bar graph. Yet, the unadorned graphs that come out of 1-2-3 are not ready for presentation, where style is as important as substance.

To dress up your 1-2-3 graphs, you have several alternatives. First, you can bypass 1-2-3's built-in graphics module altogether and pull your raw data from 1-2-3 into a separate presentation graphics package. Chapter 11 discusses several dedicated graphics programs, such as Freelance Plus and Harvard Graphics, which take 1-2-3 data and create superb graphs of all types.

Another choice is to step up to 1-2-3 Release 3, if you are currently using Release 2.01. The graphing capabilities of Release 3 are far improved, and its finished graphs approach those produced by many dedicated graphics packages. You will find information about 1-2-3 Release 3's advanced graph formatting commands in the following chapter.

Yet without upgrading to Release 3 or turning to a dedicated graphics package, users of earlier 1-2-3 versions have a special alternative. If you purchased your copy of 1-2-3 Release 2.01 recently or have upgraded to Release 2.2, you will find a companion product included in the package that bridges the gap between the rudimentary graphing of the 2.01 and 2.2 versions and the presentation graphics of Release 3. Funk Software's Allways, The Spreadsheet Publisher, has been available as an add-in to 1-2-3 since early 1989. You can buy it separately, attach it to 1-2-3, and suddenly benefit from impressive worksheet formatting capabilities. Allways is now integrated into 1-2-3 Release 2.2, though, and the enhancements it adds make a dramatic difference in your graphs. Figures 5.1 and 5.2 show the before-and-after effects of using Allways to spruce up a graph.

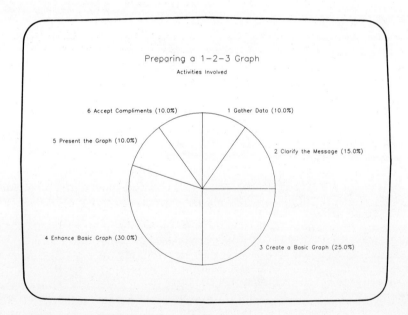

Fig. 5.1. A graph formatted without Allways.

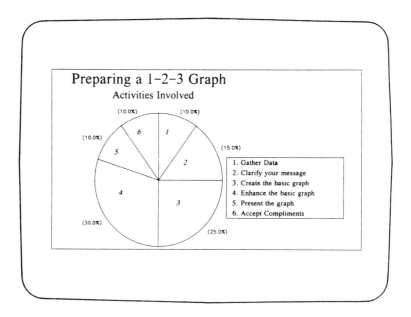

Fig. 5.2. *The graph formatted with Allways.*

This chapter explores techniques for using Allways to enhance the appearance of your graphs and even to create new graph types not available within 1-2-3 Release 2.2.

What Is Allways?

Allways adds a host of worksheet formatting possibilities to 1-2-3 Release 2.01 and Release 2.2. With Allways, you can underline the contents of cells, shade ranges, print cells or cell ranges in colors, and choose from text typefaces that are far superior to those of the 1-2-3 PrintGraph module.

But more importantly for graphics use, Allways lets you pull a completed 1-2-3 graph, saved on disk as a PIC file, into a worksheet. Then, on a single page you can combine a graph and the data it represents. Because these graphs are transparent, you can annotate the worksheet cells that show through the graph from behind. These notes, comments, or callouts appear within the graph when it is printed. With this in mind, you may prefer to omit titles when you create the graph, adding them later as text formatted by Allways. You have far greater control over the positioning, size, and typeface of titles formatted by Allways.

Allways takes full advantage of the capabilities of today's high-resolution laser printers and 24-pin dot-matrix printers. 1-2-3 on its own serves some needs well enough, but its printed output pales in comparison to what Allways can produce.

One critical limitation of Allways you should understand is its dependence on completed graphs saved as PIC files. Even if you store a graph with a worksheet by using the /Graph Name Create command, Allways cannot access the graph until you save it on disk as a PIC file with the 1-2-3 /Graph Save command. Allways pulls a PIC file graph on top of an on-screen worksheet. Of course, once you save a graph as a PIC file, the link between the numbers in your worksheet and the bars or lines in your graph is broken. Change a number or two in the worksheet and the PIC file graph stays the same.

You can see, then, that graphs in Allways and graphs in 1-2-3 play very different roles. Within 1-2-3, you can use graphs to enhance what-if analyses. Not only can you check the effects that ripple throughout a worksheet after a few changes to your data, but you can view an instant graph reflecting those changes. The result may be more immediately apparent in the graph than from the raw numbers. An Allways graph, on the other hand, is meant for presentation only. By the time you get to the Allways stage, you have interpreted the data within 1-2-3 and ascertained the message it conveys. You use Allways to communicate that message effectively.

Starting Allways

After you have installed Allways, using its AWSETUP program, you are ready to attach Allways to 1-2-3. Release 2.01 requires that you use the Lotus Add-In Manager to access Allways. When you do so, you will obtain the Add-in menu by pressing Alt-F10.

If you use 1-2-3 Release 2.2, you can select /Add-in from the main 1-2-3 menu. Then, one of your choices will be to Attach an add-in. Select Attach and then choose ALLWAYS.ADN. You can specify an Alt-function key combination that invokes Allways at the next prompt or select No-Key if you want to invoke Allways by manually selecting /Add-in Invoke from the 1-2-3 menu.

When you invoke Allways, either by the Alt-function key combination or by selecting /Add-in Invoke from the 1-2-3 menu, you will see the Allways opening screen (see fig. 5.3).

When Allways is active, the Allways horizontal bar menu replaces the standard 1-2-3 menu when you press the slash key (/). You see this menu in figure 5.4.

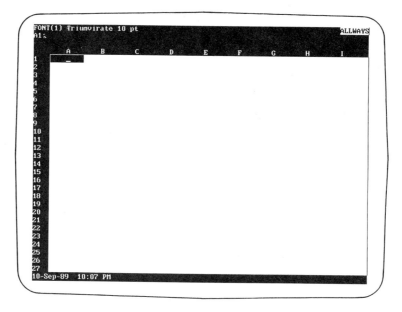

Fig. 5.3. *The Allways opening screen with 1-2-3 Release 2.2.*

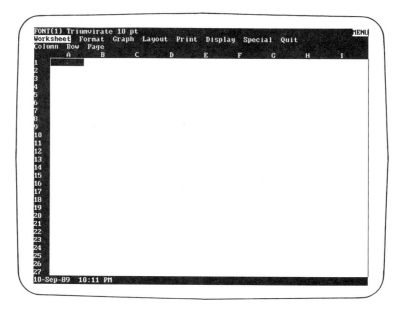

Fig. 5.4. *The Allways main menu.*

Merging Worksheet Data and Graphs

A powerful feature of Allways is its capability of merging a worksheet with one or more of the worksheet's graphs and then displaying the result on-screen or on paper. 1-2-3 alone lets you print worksheet data, of course, and the 1-2-3 PrintGraph module lets you print graphs, but Allways lets you print both on the same page. Only 1-2-3 Release 3 can perform a similar feat. In the following paragraphs, you will learn how to use merging to your advantage.

Adding a Graph to a Worksheet Range

To merge a section of a worksheet and a graph in Allways, you must add the graph to a blank area of the worksheet by using the Allways /Graph Add command. Allways then presents a list of the PIC files on disk in the same directory as the current worksheet. Choose a PIC file and then specify the worksheet range into which the graph should fit. The size and shape of the range determine the size and shape of the graph.

After you select a worksheet range for the graph, either of two displays will appear: a graph or a box filled with a crosshatch pattern. If a pattern shows up, press F10 or select /Display Graphs Yes from the Allways menu to see the graph. The graph now appears on-screen.

Why don't graphs appear automatically? Because they take far longer to draw than the usual numbers and text. Displaying a graph on-screen while you work slows down the screen activity considerably. Allways assumes that you don't need to see the graph until you are ready to print it, so it doesn't waste time redrawing the graph after every change to the screen. To toggle the graph display back off, you can press F10 again.

Try merging a worksheet and a graph by following this example. Computer Tutor Industries wants to create a page for its annual report that compares its two profit centers, Training and Consulting. Bruce, the president of Computer Tutor, has assembled the data in the worksheet shown in figure 5.5. He has saved the worksheet on the disk as CTUTOR.WK1. Also, Bruce has created a simple line graph that makes the comparison you see in figure 5.6. After creating the graph, he saved it as a PIC file called CTUTOR.PIC.

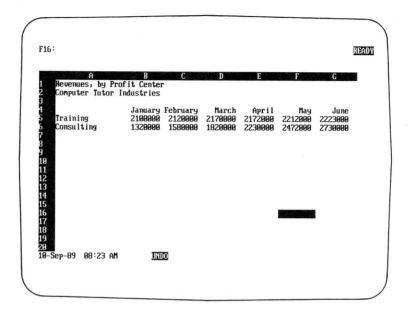

Fig. 5.5. *The Computer Tutor worksheet.*

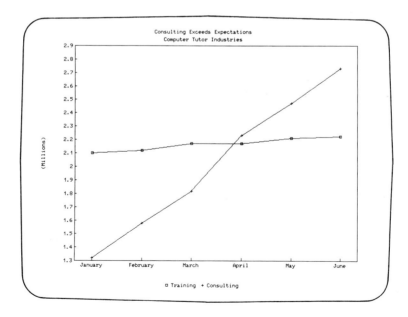

Fig. 5.6. *The Computer Tutor CTUTOR.PIC line graph.*

Create the worksheet shown in figure 5.5. Then you can create the CTUTOR graph and save it on disk. Use the following commands:

/Graph Type Line
X: B4..G4
A: B5..G5
B: B6..G6

Options Title
First: Consulting Exceeds Expectations
Second: **\A2**

Options Legend
A: Training
B: Consulting

Quit

Name Create CTUTOR

Save CTUTOR.PIC

Quit
/File Save CTUTOR.WK1

Now, two separate files exist on the disk: CTUTOR.WK1, the worksheet, and CTUTOR.PIC, the graph. Remember, Allways will pull the PIC file from disk and overlay it on the worksheet file. Suppose that Bruce were to revise the numbers in the CTUTOR worksheet. He would need to recreate the graph and save it once again as CTUTOR.PIC to be sure that the revised graph is on disk and that the worksheet and graph match. Let's hope that he named the graph with **/Graph Name Create** before he saved the worksheet, as you did. If so, he can quickly recall the graph later and resave it rather than redoing it from scratch.

To pull the graph into the blank area below the worksheet data, invoke Allways and then select **/Graph Add** and pick CTUTOR.PIC from the list of PIC files that appears. Now, select the range A8..E21 below the worksheet data range and press Enter. The graph will show up in the range. If a crosshatch pattern appears, press F10 to see the graph. The screen now looks like the one shown in figure 5.7.

If your video card is incapable of displaying graphics, you will see G's on the screen at the location of the graph. If you see this display and your video card can produce graphics, you may have Allways set to text-only mode. Press F6 to switch to Graphics mode or select **/Display Mode Graphics** from the Allways menus.

To remove a graph from a worksheet in Allways, you can use the **/Graph Remove** command. If you have many graphs on a worksheet—

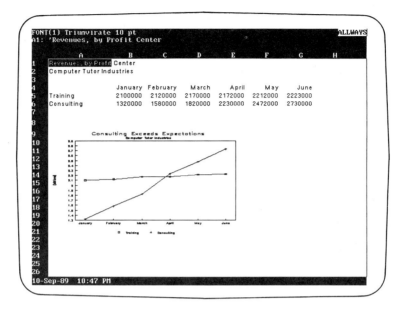

Fig. 5.7. The CTUTOR.PIC graph added to the CTUTOR worksheet.

Allways allows up to 20 per worksheet—you can use the /Graph GoTo command to quickly find the graph you want. The /Graph GoTo command works just like GoTo (F5) within 1-2-3.

Changing the Location and Size of a Merged Graph

After you have positioned a graph on top of a worksheet with Allways, you can move or resize it before you add enhancements. To move a graph, you have two options. You can remove the graph and add a new one somewhere else on the worksheet. Or, much better, you can specify a new range for the worksheet with the /Graph Settings Range command. Before you select this series of menus, though, be sure to position the cursor within the graph range. Should you fail to do so, and should you have several graphs on a worksheet, Allways will display a list of worksheet graphs offering you a choice.

With the Range command, you can do more than simply move a graph. By specifying a new range for the graph, you can change its size and shape as well as its location on the worksheet. If the new range is shaped differently from the old range, Allways will readjust the size of the graph to fit. To reset the range that shows up on the graph settings sheet, press Esc and then type in a new range, or point to that range on the worksheet.

Of course, if you are placing a pie graph, you want to select a range that is somewhat square. Otherwise, your round pie graph will become oblong and the relative shapes of the slices may be misleadingly stretched. The same holds true when you add any graph style. A tall, thin bar graph will create a different impression from a short, squat graph. Figure 5.8 illustrates this distortion.

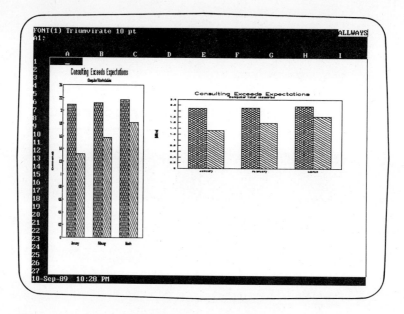

Fig. 5.8. *A graph set in differently shaped ranges.*

Try modifying the range occupied by the CTUTOR graph, so that the graph fills the space below the worksheet. To change the size of the graph, use these commands:

/Graph Settings **R**ange
Esc
A8..G21

Now, the screen should appear like the one shown in figure 5.9.

If you need to make minor adjustments to the size of a graph, you can use the /**W**orksheet **R**ow and /**W**orksheet **C**olumn commands. These

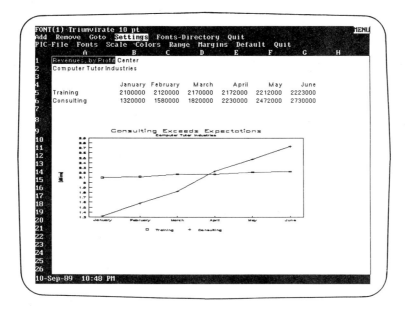

Fig. 5.9. *The graph widened with* **/Graph Setting Range.**

commands will increase or decrease the widths of whatever column or row within the graph range you specify.

Range is only one of the options on the Allways /Graph Settings menu. The complete menu is a full array of graphic design settings:

PIC-File Fonts Scale Colors Range Margins Default Quit

/Graph Settings Margins lets you make minor adjustments to the size of the graph within the range. By increasing the margins, you can add a little blank space around the edges of the graph and reduce its size within the range. The default is 0 inches for top, bottom, left, and right margins, but you can enter a value in inches between 0 and 9.99 for any of the margins.

Embellishing Graphs

After you add a graph to a worksheet in Allways, you can enhance the graph in a variety of ways. Many of the basic choices you can make in Allways are similar to the choices you make when you print the graph with the 1-2-3 PrintGraph module. For example, you can select two fonts, one for the main title, and a second for the subtitle and other text within the graph. You can also specify colors for the six graphed data ranges and the X data range.

These choices are important if you plan to use Allways to print a worksheet and graph combination. Allways will use a combination of default settings for certain aspects of the graph unless you specify otherwise. All these settings are maintained on a settings sheet with each graph. When you position the cursor within the graph range and select /Graph Settings from the Allways menu, you will see the settings sheet for the graph (see fig. 5.10).

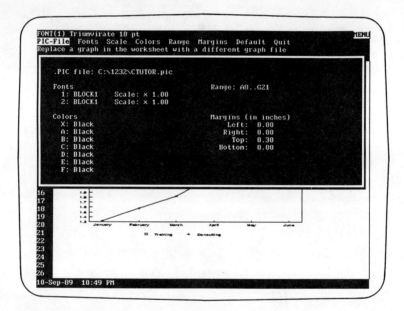

Fig. 5.10. *The default settings sheet for the CTUTOR graph.*

If you leave the default fonts in effect, Allways will use the same font for all text, the PrintGraph BLOCK1 font. And, even if you specify Display Colors for ranges while still in 1-2-3, you must set printing colors for ranges in Allways. The default printing color for all ranges is black.

The complete /Graph Settings menu follows:

PIC-File Fonts Scale Colors Range Margins Default Quit.

The /Graph Settings PIC-File option lets you replace an existing graph with a new PIC file. To use this option, position the cursor within the first graph you want to replace, and then select /**Graph Settings PIC**-File and choose a new PIC file from the list.

The /**Graph Settings Fonts** option lets you specify the two fonts Allways uses when it displays or prints the graph. Allways looks for these fonts in the hard disk directory you specify as the fonts directory. You choose the fonts directory with the /**Graph Fonts**-Directory command. Font files with the extension .FNT are supplied by PrintGraph, so when you select a fonts directory, you should choose the directory PrintGraph is in.

When you select /**Graph Settings Fonts**, you must decide whether to set the font for 1, the first title line of the graph, or 2, the remainder of the graph text. Then, from the list of fonts that appears, you can pick one of the choices you see in figure 5.11.

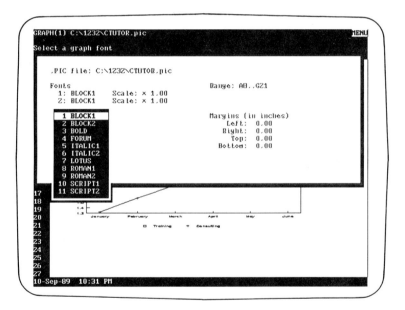

Fig. 5.11. *The fonts available for graph text.*

The option /**Graph Settings Scale** lets you change the printed text in your graph, by multiplying its size by a scale factor between 0.5 and 3.0. The setting of 0.5 reduces the size of text by one-half. Choose 3 to triple the text size. A scale factor of 1 is the default. Using this menu option, you can dramatically improve the appearance of a graph just by increasing the size of its title text. Figure 5.12 shows the result of choosing several different scale sizes for the text in the main title (Font 1).

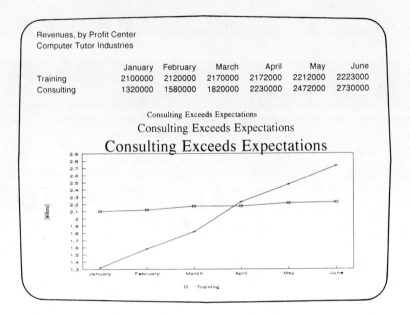

Fig. 5.12. Font 1 text set with a range of scale settings.

Selecting /Graph Settings Default lets you return the settings for any of the graph's attributes back to their defaults. This command also updates the defaults, replacing them with the current settings. You can decide to print all future graphs with the LOTUS font as Font 1, for example. To do this, change Font 1 to LOTUS on one graph, and then choose /Graph Settings Default Update.

Modifying the settings on the graph settings sheet is the quickest way to enhance a graph, but not the most flexible. The remainder of this chapter describes alternatives to various options on the graph settings menu and several techniques you can use to make further improvements.

Enhancing Graph Text

When you import a PIC file, Allways can do little for the titles and text already present in the graph. What it can do is to change titles from one PrintGraph font to another or to scale them uniformly in a larger or smaller point size. But, through a technique that takes advantage of the transparency of Allways graphs, you can use Allways to create titles of all sizes, fonts, and positions.

Remember that a graph in Allways is superimposed on a range of cells in a worksheet. Thus, as you type text into worksheet cells located under the blank graph areas, the text shows through, appearing to be integrated into the graph itself. Because this text actually is composed of worksheet labels, Allways can perform all sorts of stylish formatting tricks on it: showing it in special text font styles and sizes, making it bold, underlining it, or enclosing it in a box or shadow box. Of course, if you add graph text on the worksheet, don't duplicate it by adding it also to the graph.

Try replacing the CTUTOR graph titles with text titles on the worksheet. Then you can select a font from the wide Allways font selection. In order to place new titles on the graph, you must remove the old titles first; clear these away by pressing Esc to return to 1-2-3 and deleting the existing titles under /Graph Options Titles. Then, save the graph as a new PIC file. Following are the specific commands to use:

> Esc to return to 1-2-3
> /Graph Options Titles
> First: Esc, then Enter
> Second: Esc, then Enter
> Quit
> Save CTUTOR.PIC Replace

Now, invoke Allways using /Add-In Invoke Allways or the Alt-function key combination you specified earlier. Notice that the graph reappears on the worksheet, less the titles you deleted. If you still have the unrevised graph on-screen, you must take either of two courses of action. You can save the worksheet and then retrieve it, so that Allways can retrieve the revised PIC file. Or you can use the /Graph Settings PIC-File option to replace the current graph with the revised PIC file on disk. The second option is probably easier, so try using this command to replace the graph with the new version:

> /Graph Settings PIC-File CTUTOR.PIC

To place the main title at the top center of the graph, position the cursor in cell B8. Now, return to 1-2-3 by pressing Esc. Notice that the cursor remains at the same cell address. This constancy as you cross from 1-2-3 to Allways and back helps you position titles and other text properly. Into the current cell (B8) type **Consulting Exceeds Expectations** and press Enter. In the cell below, type **Computer Tutor Industries**. Now, return to Allways by pressing the Alt-function key combination or by using /Add-In Invoke Allways. Note that the second text line appears to overlay part of the graph (see fig. 5.13).

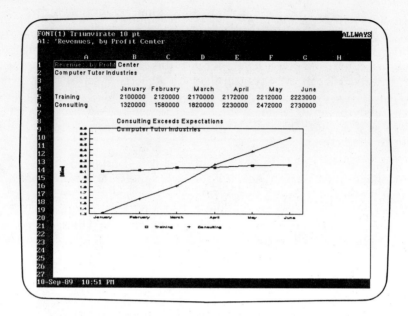

Fig. 5.13. *Titles added as text to the worksheet.*

You can solve this problem in two ways. Either you can increase the top margin of the graph, or you can specify a new range for the graph that is slightly shorter. The first option is probably easier, and it provides finer control over the graph's exact placement. So, select /Graph Settings Margin **T**op from within Allways and enter .3. Then, press **Q**uit twice to view the graph again.

Now you can use the Alt-1 through Alt-7 font selection shortcut keys, or you can select /**F**ormat **F**ont and choose one of the eight fonts to reformat the main title and the subtitle. To set both titles to an attractive 14 point Times, select /**F**ormat **F**ont from the Allways menu and pick Times 14 point from the menu that appears. Then highlight B8..B9 as the range to format. You may need to drop back to 1-2-3 to center the titles above the graph, moving them to the right by adding spaces in front of the titles in their cells. Your screen should now look like the figure 5.14 display.

Annotating a Graph with New Text

To add text annotations to the graph, you can use the same technique you used for titles in the previous section. By adding text to blank worksheet cells behind the graph, you can create the illusion that the text is part of the graph.

Try adding a short statement next to each line on the graph that highlights the results of the line. This technique is seen in figure 5.15.

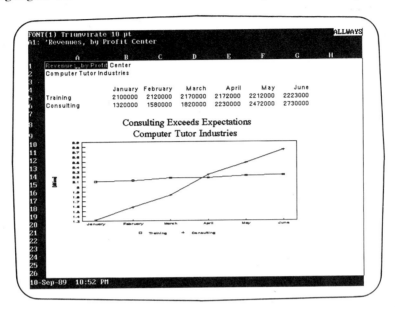

Fig. 5.14. *Titles added to the worksheet and formatted with Allways.*

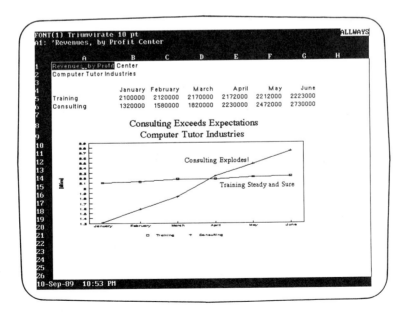

Fig. 5.15. *Annotations added to the graph.*

Start by positioning the cursor where the first text line ("Consulting Explodes") should appear within the graph. Position the cursor in cell D12. Now, press Esc to return to 1-2-3 so that you can type the text into the cell. Then, reinvoke Allways and check the position and font of the text. You may need to make changes to both.

Return to 1-2-3. Enter the second text line ("Training Steady and Sure") into cell E15 on the worksheet, and then invoke Allways. Now, to finish off, you can modify the text font for the two annotations quickly and easily. Position the cursor on each annotated cell and press Alt-5 (the quick keystroke combination to select Font 5). Or you can position the cursor on cell D12 and select /Format Font, choose Font 5 (Times 10 point), and then specify a range that includes both cells D12 and E15, the two cells with text lines.

Overlaying Two Graphs

The graph you insert into a worksheet can be so illuminating and impressive, why stop with one? You can add several graphs to illustrate numbers from various worksheet areas, or you can overlay two graphs, one on top of the other, to combine two graph types in one mixed graph. 1-2-3 Release 3 makes creating mixed graphs a simple process, and most dedicated graphing packages include mixed graphs as a standard feature. But without Allways, earlier releases can produce only a single graph type at a time. By overlaying a bar graph and a line graph in Allways you can create a mixed graph that shows both bars and lines.

To mix graphs of different types, first you need to create and save them on disk separately as two PIC files. Then, you can add both graphs to the same worksheet range with Allways. As long as you ensure that the axes of the graphs are equally scaled, the two should overlay well, giving the effect of a single graph with both bars and lines.

Some small but easily solved problems may show up in the x-axis and legend of the combined graph. 1-2-3 centers x-axis labels under the bars of a bar graph, but left-aligns x-axis labels in a line graph. This is the reason your labels will align imperfectly at first in a double vision; you have two labels slightly offset for each x-axis point. And, if you include a legend with each graph, the two legends may overwrite each other, trying to occupy the same space below the x-axis.

The solution to the x-axis problem is to display the x-axis for the first graph in white. The second x-axis remains black, so it appears alone. There is no simple solution to the overwriting legend problem, but you can omit the legends and substitute text annotations, as described in the previous section, to distinguish among the series.

To try this procedure, modify the Computer Tutor graph you have displayed in Allways so that it graphs one series as a line and one series with bars. Of course, to start, you need to return to 1-2-3. Then create the graphs separately and save them as PIC files. To begin, follow these steps:

1. Press Esc until you have returned to 1-2-3; then recall the graph you created with /Graph Name Use CTUTOR. Before you proceed, notice that the y-axis scaling is from 1.3 to 2.9 million. That will be important later.

2. Modify the graph so that it displays data range A with a line only. To do this, clear off data range B with /Graph Reset B.

3. Select Quit to return to the main graph menu.

4. From the graph menu, select Options Legend B to remove the legend for data range B; then press Esc, followed by Enter.

Now, view the graph and notice its automatic y-axis scaling from 2.1 to 2.23 million, as shown in figure 5.16.

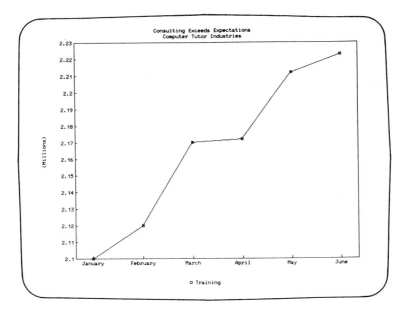

***Fig. 5.16.** The line graph showing data range A only.*

Because you checked the scaling of the earlier graph and know that you need a y-axis range of between 0 and 3 million to accommodate the second series, you should now manually scale the y-axis. As it stands, the narrow y-axis range chosen by 1-2-3's automatic scaling makes the modest growth in training look phenomenal. Yet the purpose of this graph is to display a message to the contrary: Consulting has done much better than Training. To scale the axis, follow these steps:

1. Select /**Graph Options Scale Y**-Scale **Manual** to manually scale the y-axis.

2. Set a lower limit of **0** and an upper limit of **3000000**; then press **Quit** twice to return to the main graph menu. Before you save the resulting graph, check it for accuracy, and then name it by using /**Graph Name Create** CTUTORA. To create the PIC file you need for Allways, use /**Graph Save** and supply the name CTUTORA. 1-2-3 will supply the PIC extension.

Now, to create the second graph, recall the original graph with /**Graph Name Use** CTUTOR. Then, follow these steps to set up the bar graph:

1. Select /**Graph Type Bar** to change the graph type to bar.

2. Clear data range A with /**Graph Reset A**.

3. Clear the corresponding legend by selecting /**Graph Options Legend A** and then pressing Esc, followed by Enter. Take a quick peek at the bar graph and notice how 1-2-3 has automatically scaled the y-axis.

4. Modify the scale of the y-axis by using /**Graph Options Scale Y**-Scale **Manual**.

5. Set the lower y-axis limit to **0** and the upper limit to **3000000**.

The resulting graph is not so dramatic, but still shows impressive growth and will work better in your combined graph. Save the graph as CTUTORB by naming it with /**Graph Name Create**. Then, save the graph as a PIC file on disk called CTUTORB with /**Graph Save**.

Now, you are ready to pull the two graphs into a worksheet range. But before you invoke Allways, examine the worksheet and verify that the old titles and text annotations are still in place. You can leave the title and simply erase the text annotations, which may no longer be suitably placed (see fig. 5.17). Use /**Range Erase** to remove just the annotations, "Consulting Explodes!" and "Training Steady and Sure."

To begin overlaying the two graphs, invoke Allways. Replace the current graph, which shows both series as lines, with the first of the two graphs. Then, add the second graph on top of the first. To perform these tasks, follow these steps:

1. Select /**Graph Settings PIC**-File in Allways and choose CTUTORA.PIC.

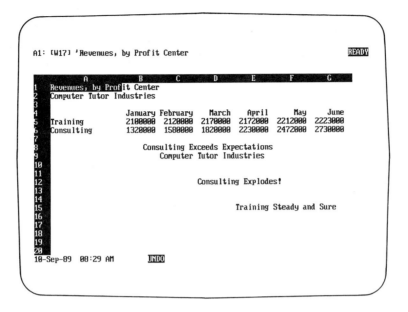

A1: [W17] 'Revenues, by Profit Center   READY

```
           A          B        C        D        E        F        G
1  Revenues, by Profit Center
2  Computer Tutor Industries
3
4             January February   March    April     May     June
5  Training   2100000 2120000  2170000  2172000  2212000  2223000
6  Consulting 1320000 1580000  1820000  2230000  2472000  2730000
7
8                Consulting Exceeds Expectations
9                 Computer Tutor Industries
10
11
12                    Consulting Explodes!
13
14
15                   Training Steady and Sure
16
17
18
19
20
   10-Sep-89  08:29 AM        UNDO
```

Fig. 5.17. The worksheet showing titles and annotations.

2. Press Esc if necessary to view the worksheet and to verify that the only graph shown is the line graph.

3. Position the cursor at the top left corner of the graph range (cell A8) and select /Graph **A**dd.

4. Choose CTUTORB.PIC and then specify the same graph range for this graph as for the first (A8..G21).

So that the two graphs will have the same margins, set the top margin for the second graph to **.3** inches:

1. Select /Graph **S**ettings and specify CTUTORB.PIC as the graph you want to modify.

2. Select **M**argins **T**op and enter **.3**.

Now, the screen display should look like the one in figure 5.18.

If you use the Allways command /**D**isplay **Z**oom **H**uge to examine the graph components in detail, you will see the two problems with the x-axis and the legend described earlier. Both elements are slightly out of position. To resolve the problem, try displaying the X data range for one of the graphs in white so that only one set of x-axis labels is visible. Follow these steps:

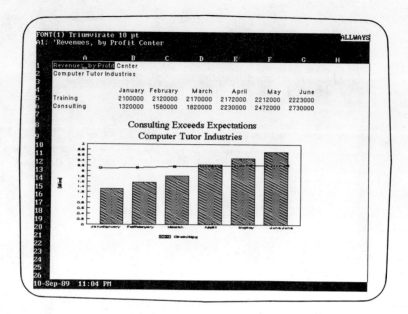

***Fig. 5.18.** Two graphs placed in the same range.*

1. Select /**G**raph Settings and then pick CTUTORA.PIC to modify.

2. Choose **C**olors from the Graph Settings menu and then **X** to set the color for the X data range.

3. Select **W**hite by moving the highlight and pressing Enter or by typing the number **8** for white and pressing Enter.

4. Select **Q**uit twice and view the graph.

But now there is another problem. Note that the white x-axis labels of CTUTORA are overwriting the black x-axis labels of CTUTORB. Looks like you should have set the labels of CTUTORB to white, instead, because it is drawn first. So, using the same series of commands, set the X data range for CTUTORA back to its default of black. Now, use the /Graph Settings Colors menu to set the X data range of CTUTORB to white. View the graph and observe that now the white x-axis labels are drawn first and the black labels are drawn on top. The labels look great.

The only remaining correction is to remove the legends from both graphs and to identify the series with annotations. To remove the legends, return to 1-2-3 and save two new PIC files with the legends removed, then return to Allways.

Your completed mixed graph should look like the one you see in figure 5.19.

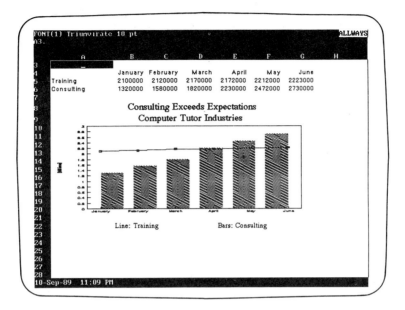

Fig. 5.19. *The mixed graph.*

Creating a Graph Data Table

One last idea when combining graphs and worksheets is to let the graph tell the story and use the worksheet numbers as a data table beneath the graph. (This is not the same as using the /Data Table command.) Figure 5.20 displays the mixed graph above a data table composed of the worksheet data.

A data table can help the viewer determine the precise values the graph reflects, and combining the graph with a data table has the same benefit as including a worksheet portion and graph in separate sections of a report.

To align the columns of data and bars in the graph, you will need to play around with the column widths and the graph range until you get the right combination.

Adding a Graph Border

You can use Allways to enclose a graph in a rectangular frame called a *border.* To draw a border around a graph, position the cursor above and to the left of the graph, select /Format Lines Outline and then highlight the graph range.

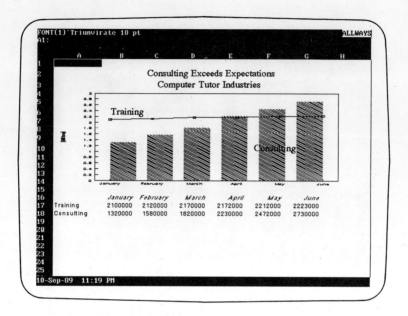

Fig. 5.20. The mixed graph with a data table.

Follow these steps to draw a border around the CTUTOR graph:

1. Position the cursor at cell A8.

2. Select /Format Lines Outline from the Allways menu.

3. Point to the graph range or enter **A8..G22**.

Shading a Graph

Just as you can place a border around a graph with the Allways /Format Lines command, you can shade a graph using the /Format Shade command. To shade a range of cells containing the graph, position the cursor at the top left corner of the range to be shaded. Now select /Format Shade, choose a shade level, and then highlight the range.

Shading only the interior of the graph is tricky, but possible. You need to align the edges of the graph to coincide with the edges of cells. Then you can specify a range of cells for shading that corresponds to the interior region of the graph.

Creating Text Charts with Allways

Some estimates have it that almost three quarters of all graphs produced are composed of text only. Text chart pages, transparencies, or slides display lines of text while a speaker summarizes key points of a presentation. To make text charts to accompany the pictorial graphs, you can simply enter text into the cells of a blank worksheet and format it with Allways.

Figure 5.21 shows a text chart that Bruce at Computer Tutor will use for his next presentation to stockholders. The chart summarizes the information he will show in the next slide, a graphic comparison of training and consulting revenues.

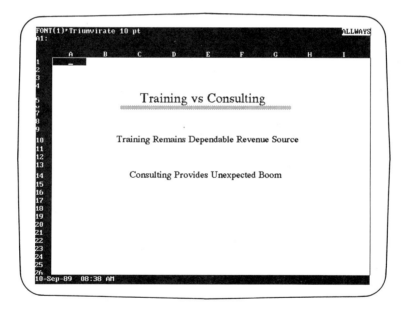

Fig. 5.21. *A text chart formatted with Allways.*

Printing Graphs with Allways

You will find more detailed information about printing with Allways in Chapter 10, but following is the information you need to print the graphs you have created here. By using Allways to print graphs, you can avoid leaving 1-2-3 to use the PrintGraph program. Allways provides all the capabilities that PrintGraph does. In fact, once you have Allways installed, you may consider deleting the PrintGraph files from your 1-2-3 directory to free up some disk space.

Printing a graph with Allways merely entails including the graph range when you specify an Allways print range with /**Print R**ange **S**et. Figure 5.22 shows the worksheet and mixed graph that you created earlier, now as printed with Allways on a Hewlett-Packard LaserJet Series II.

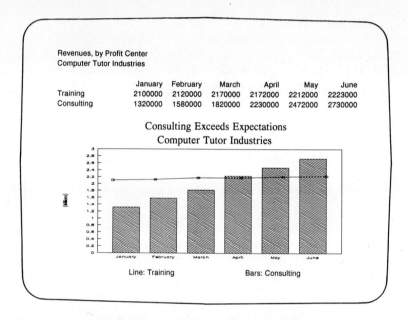

Fig. 5.22. The worksheet and mixed graph printed with Allways.

In order to print the mixed graph you just finished, you need to change the colors of the x-axis of both graphs. When you overlay two graphs, they write to the screen in a different order than they print to the printer. Before, the x-axis of CTUTORA.PIC was white and the x-axis of CTUTORB.PIC was black. Now, you must reverse the colors, making the x-axis of CTUTORB.PIC white and the x-axis of CTUTORA.PIC black. The graph will not appear correctly on the screen, but it will print properly.

The Allways Print Configuration menu has several options that can directly affect the appearance of graphs. Orientation lets you print a graph in *Landscape,* or sideways, rather than *Portrait,* which is the normal upright—and default direction.

Resolution lets you set the quality of printing your printer should perform. The higher the resolution, the sharper the image. If you use a laser printer, you may run out of memory trying to print a large graph at high resolution. In that case, you must reduce the size of the graph, choose a lower resolution, or, of course, add more memory to your printer.

Summary

For simple data analysis, 1-2-3 graphs on their own are usually sufficient. But for presentations, Allways can turn bland and boring bar graphs into interesting and impressive illustrations.

In this chapter you learned how to start Allways, use its capabilities to merge graphs and worksheet data on the same page, and use its commands to enhance the titles and text within graphs. You also learned how to use Allways to create mixed graphs and text charts.

The next chapter covers the special advanced graph formatting commands in 1-2-3 Release 3 that incorporate into 1-2-3 many of the capabilities you have with Allways. You may want to skip the next chapter if you don't use 1-2-3 Release 3 and proceed directly to Chapter 7, which covers macros especially designed for graphing.

6

Advanced Graph Formatting in 1-2-3 Release 3

The features Lotus added to 1-2-3 Release 3 substantially augment the program's ability to create graphs. The basic graphs produced with 1-2-3 Release 3 are a dramatic advance over those from previous versions of 1-2-3. In fact, 1-2-3 Release 3 gives you most of the superior formatting options that are provided by the add-in Allways, covered in the preceding chapter.

This chapter covers in detail each of the graph formatting features that are exclusive to 1-2-3 Release 3. You see how to combine bars and lines in a mixed graph. Then you learn to use colors and hatch patterns for special effects. You learn the special text settings available in Release 3 and how to control the axes and their scales. You will complete the chapter with two interesting graph variations, the stacked and the 100% graph versions.

195

Mixing Bars and Lines in a Graph

With 1-2-3 versions prior to Release 3, you could create graphs with bars or with lines, but not both. 1-2-3 Release 3's /Graph Type menu adds a new graph type called *mixed,* which combines bars and lines in the same graph. When you choose this graph type, any series you assign to data ranges A, B, and C are represented as bars; any series you designate as data ranges D, E, and F are represented as lines.

When should you use a mixed graph? When you particularly want to emphasize the difference between two series. Perhaps the data series are measured in different units. Or they represent two separate years of data. The mixed graph can illustrate these discrepant categories, so that each is measured against its own meaningful scale: let's say that you have apple sales, measured in thousands of dollars, and orange sales, measured in hundreds of dollars. The common element is fruit sales in dollars, and this can be shown in a single mixed graph.

Setting up a mixed graph is simply a matter of choosing **Mixed** from the /Graph **Type** menu. Then designate the series you want represented as bars to data ranges A, B, or C, and those you want represented as lines to data ranges D, E, or F. Try creating a mixed graph by working through the example that follows.

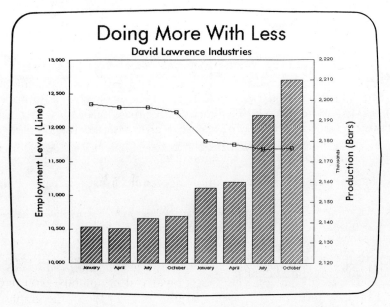

Fig. 6.1. *The David Lawrence Industries mixed graph.*

The new management team of David Lawrence Industries (DLI) chose a mixed graph to astound their audience at the annual stockholders' meeting. After all, the results of the company's reorganization have been nothing less than impressive, and the graph displaying this should be equally impressive. The graph should show that in only two years, the size of the workforce has substantially reduced, while production has substantially increased. Things couldn't be better at David Lawrence. The graph that proves this is shown in figure 6.1.

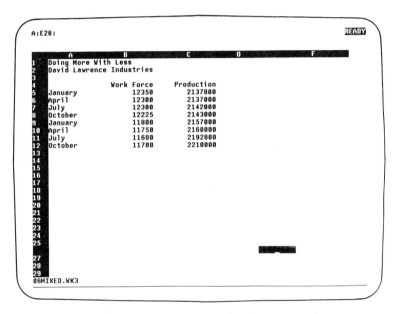

Fig. 6.2. Worksheet data for the DLI graph.

To construct the DLI graph, you will first create a simple bar graph using the worksheet shown in figure 6.2. Because this data is arranged in consecutive columns, you can use the automatic graphing feature of Release 3. This option sets up the basic graph. Try it by positioning the cursor anywhere within one of the data columns and pressing F10 (Graph).

But this automatically produced graph needs adjustments. Although 1-2-3 successfully assigns the X, A, and B data ranges to the row labels, the workforce level series, and the production series, respectively, the resulting graph is anything but successful. Because the two series use different scales of measurement—workforce size is measured in tens of thousands and production capacity is measured in millions—you need to set up two separate y-axes, one to plot each series on the graph.

Try assigning the production series to a second y-axis by using this command sequence:

/Graph Type Features 2Y-Ranges B

The revised graph should look like the one in figure 6.3.

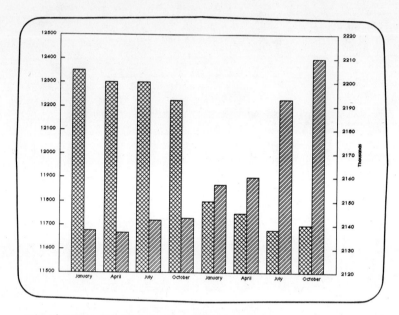

***Fig. 6.3.** The David Lawrence Industries graph with two y-axes.*

Now, here is where the special features of a mixed graph come in handy. To emphasize that the graph compares two very different units, you can represent one series with bars and one series with a line. To select a mixed graph, use **/Graph Type Mixed**.

When you choose a mixed graph, the series assigned to data ranges A, B, and C are represented as bars, even if you started with a line graph. To represent one of the series as a line, then, reassign it to data range D, E, or F. Move the workforce series to data range D by using **/Graph D A:B5..A:B2** and then using **/Graph Reset A** to clear data range A. Now, take another look at the graph. The resulting graph is shown in figure 6.4.

Although this graph is technically accurate and does clearly distinguish between the two series, it makes its point to excess. The rise in production, represented by bars, looks astonishing, whereas the relatively minor reduction in the company's workforce, represented by a line, looks like a case of wholesale slaughter. To diminish the

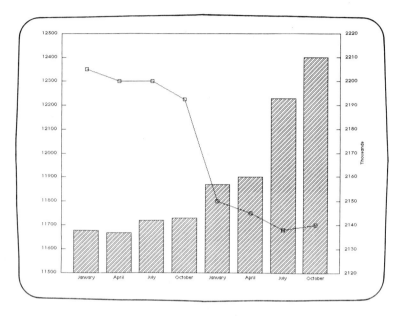

***Fig. 6.4.** The David Lawrence graph converted to a mixed graph.*

magnitude of change portrayed, you can change the scaling of the two y-axes. By extending the upper and lower scale limits, you can stretch out and thus deemphasize indications of change in your data.

To rescale the y-axes, use these commands:

/Graph **Options** Scale **Y**-Scale Manual
Lower: **10000**
Upper: **13000**

2Y-Scale Manual
Lower: **2000000**
Upper: **2250000**

Figure 6.5 shows the final graph with appropriate titles and a legend.

Setting Graph Colors

With 1-2-3 Release 3, you can choose colors for the data ranges portrayed in a graph. To set the color for a range, use /Graph **Options** **Advanced** Colors. This menu of data ranges will appear:

A B C D E F Quit

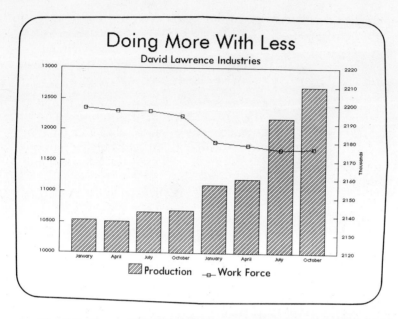

Fig. 6.5. *The completed David Lawrence Industries graph.*

Select the data range you want to modify from the menu and then select one of the eight color numbers presented in the following menu:

1 2 3 4 5 6 7 8 Hide Range

The color that corresponds to each number depends on the graphics display system (graphics card and monitor) and the color printer you use.

Picking a number from the color menu lets you assign a certain color to a series. But, using the **R**ange command, you can do more. You can specify a color for each data point in the series. The Range option lets you set up a *colors range* on the worksheet. By entering color numbers from 1 through 14 in the cells of this range, you can set colors for corresponding data points in the data range. Of course, the number of cells in the color range must equal the number of cells in the data range.

Experiment to see how the color numbers correspond to colors available with your color graphics display system or color printer. Use a colors range to assign numbers to each value in a dummy worksheet range; then view the resulting graph. Or print the trial graph with **/Print Printer Sample**.

To assign additional colors to data points, you can use a colors range to specify a full 14 different colors for any range—as opposed to 8 if you pick from the menu of colors. You can even use a colors range to assign specific colors to data points within a series depending on their value. This special technique is covered later in this chapter.

To try a colors range to modify the bar colors in the David Lawrence graph, set up a third range in the graph to the right of the other two ranges. This will be the colors range. Try setting the first four bars to color 4 by entering the number 4 in the first four cells of the range. Then set the remainder of the bars to color 5. Your worksheet should now look like the worksheet in figure 6.6.

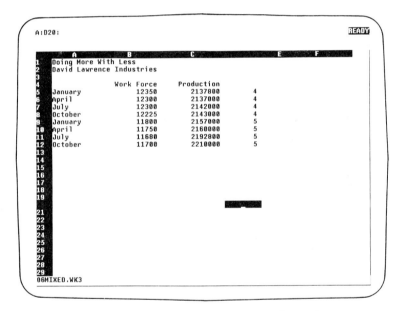

Fig. 6.6. *The David Lawrence worksheet with a colors range.*

Now, assign the colors range to data range B (the Production figures) by selecting /Graph **O**ptions **A**dvanced **C**olors **B** **R**ange. For the range, specify **A:D5..A:D12.** The default colors for data ranges A through F are numbers 2 through 7. If you use a negative value in a colors range, the corresponding data point is hidden.

You may wonder how 1-2-3 determines a color for the legend if you are using several colors to display a data range. 1-2-3 uses the first number in the range for the legend color for that series.

You can use a colors range for a pie graph when the graph display is set to color rather than B&W and when you have no B data range. If you add 100 to a color number that refers to a pie slice, the slice will be cut, or exploded, from the pie.

Using Conditional Colors To Highlight Special Results

Rather than manually assigning colors to data values, you can use the 1-2-3 @IF function to assign colors to data points based on their value. With this procedure you could, for example, assign all data points above 2,175,000 to color 2 and all data points 2,175,000 or below to color 5.

To try this, enter the formula **@IF(C5>2175000,2,5)** into cell D5 and then copy it to A:D6..A:D12. If you haven't already done so, assign this range as the colors range by selecting **/Graph Options Advanced Colors B Range** and then specifying **A:D5..A:D12.**

Hiding Data Series

The Hide option on the /Graph Options Advanced Colors [Range] menu lets you hide a range from view in the current graph. With Hide, you can drop out a certain series from the display. You can use Hide advantageously when you need to create a series of graphs that compare combinations of up to six series, the maximum number of data ranges available in 1-2-3. Using Hide, you can display a single pair of data ranges for a comparison and then save the graph. Then you can use Hide to display a different pair of series and save that graph, too, and so on.

To use Hide, select **/Graph Options Advanced Colors**, select a data range, and then **Hide** from the colors menu.

To hide only the Production data series in the example above, select **/Graph Options Advanced Colors B Hide.** Then press F10 to view the resulting graph.

Setting Graph Hatch Patterns

Hatches, another choice on the /Graph Options Advanced menu, lets you specify the hatch patterns for bar, stack-bar, mixed, and HLCO graphs. This option also is used for the filled areas of an area graph and for the slices in a pie graph.

The hatch submenus offer the same options as the /Graph Options Advanced Colors [Range] menu. You first select a series and then a hatch-pattern number for the series. You can set up a hatch range, just as you can set up a colors range. When you use a hatch range, you can specify 14 choices in all: 8 hatch patterns and 6 shades of gray.

Just as with a colors range, if you enter a negative number in a hatch range, the corresponding range value is hidden on the graph. And, also as with a colors range, the first hatch pattern in the range is the hatch pattern used for the legend for that series. You can use an @IF function to set a hatch pattern based on the value of the data point, just as you did earlier to determine a color for the data point.

If you are using a hatch range to set hatch patterns for the slices of a pie, verify that the graph display is set to Color and that hatch patterns are not specified in the B data range when the graph display is set to B&W.

Figure 6.7 shows all the hatch patterns in 1-2-3 Release 3.

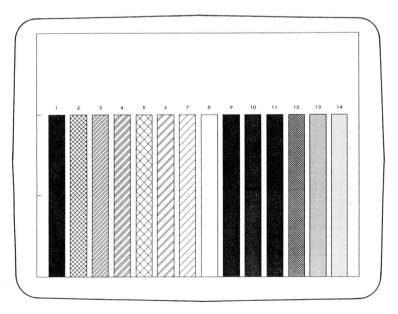

Fig. 6.7. 1-2-3 Release 3 hatch patterns.

Setting Text Color, Font, and Size

Before Release 3, 1-2-3 users had to be content with two text fonts for all graph text, unless they used special add-ins, such as Allways. 1-2-3 Release 3 lets you specify a separate text color, font, and size for each of three text groups within each graph:

First: The first line of the graph title.

Second: The second line of the graph title, the titles for both the x- and y-axes, and the text in the legend.

Third: The axis labels, data-labels, footnotes, and axis scale indicators.

Figure 6.8 demonstrates each of these text groups.

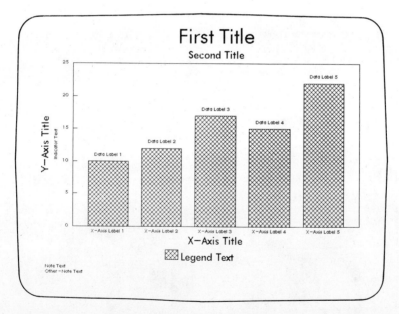

Fig. 6.8. *Three text groups. First: first title; Second: x- and y-axis titles, legend text; Third: x-axis label, data-labels, notes, indicator.*

To modify the text format, select /Graph Options Advanced Text. The following menu will appear:

First Second Third Quit

Select the text group you want to modify. Then, from the next menu, choose whether you want to modify the text's color, font, or size.

Setting Text Color

After you select /Graph Options Advanced Text (title) and choose whether you want to modify the first, second, or third text group, you can select Color from this menu:

Color Font Size Quit

The color menu gives the same eight choices you have when setting the color of data ranges. The specific color assigned to each number depends on your graphics hardware. If you choose Hide from the color menu, 1-2-3 will hide all the text in the selected text group.

Setting Text Font

If you choose Font from the /Graph Options Advanced Text (Title) menu, you will see the following choices:

Default 1 2 3 4 5 6 7 8

Each number, 1 through 8, assigns a different *font,* or character style, to the selected text.

Normally, you will see your font selection when you print the graph, but not when you view the graph on your screen. This is an important point to keep in mind. You do not see the result of your font choices on the screen, because the graph as displayed can use only a standard display font.

The number and selection of fonts available to you will vary with the printer, plotter, or other output device you are using. 1-2-3 may not provide a full eight fonts for your printer. You will find more information about printer and plotter fonts in Chapter 10, "Printing and Plotting 1-2-3 Graphs."

Figure 6.9 shows the four standard fonts available with a commonly used printer, the Hewlett-Packard LaserJet Series II laser printer.

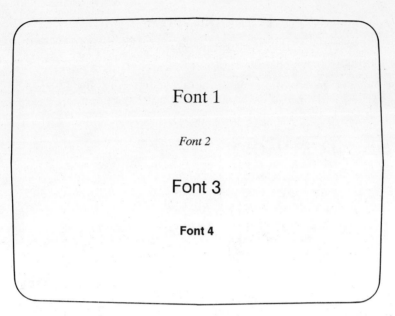

Fig. 6.9. Printer fonts available with a LaserJet Series II printer.

The default font for the first text group is Font 3. The default font for the second and third text groups is Font 1. Try modifying the David Lawrence Mixed Graph so that the first line of its title will print in Font 2. To modify the font of the first title, use these commands:

   /Graph Options Advanced Text First Font 2

Setting Text Size

Just as you can make independent color and font settings for the three text groups in 1-2-3 graphs, you can set the text size for each group. If you leave the defaults, 1-2-3 assigns a size of 8 to the first text group, a size of 4 to the second text group, and a size of 2 to the third text group. These numbers fall along an arbitrary scale used by 1-2-3 for text size. Unfortunately, they do not represent a familiar unit, such as printers' points.

The Size menu under **/Graph Options Advanced Text** offers nine sizes. The larger the number, the larger the text size. You will see, however, only three text sizes on the screen: small, medium, and large. Actual sizes 1 through 3 appear in small on the screen, sizes 4 through 6 appear in medium, and sizes 7 through 9 appear in large.

How many sizes you can use when you print or plot the graph depends on the printer or plotter you are using—just as your output device selection may also limit color and font selection.

Figure 6.10 displays the text sizes available with a Hewlett-Packard LaserJet Series II.

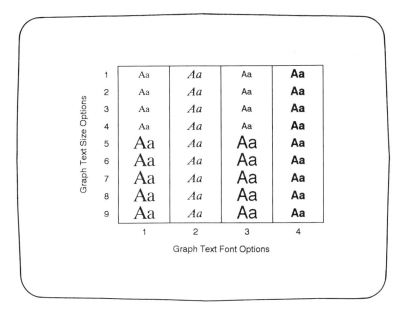

***Fig. 6.10.** Text sizes available for fonts with a LaserJet Series II.*

Try reducing the size of the first title line of the David Lawrence mixed graph by two. Then print the graph to see the result.

Changing the Axis Number Format

1-2-3 Release 3 lets you change the formatting of one or more of the axis labels, just as you can change the formatting of values in a range by using /Range Format. In fact, the same menu of formatting selections appears:

Fixed Sci Currency, General +/− Percent Date Text Hidden

Normally, numeric axis labels appear in General format, which is the default format for values in a worksheet. But you can change axis number formatting by selecting /Graph Options Scale, choosing an axis, and then selecting Format. After you pick a format style from the menu above, you must specify how many decimal places the axis number should display.

The two y-axes of the DLI graph might look better if you choose comma (,) and zero decimal places to format their numbers. Try using these commands to format the y-axes:

/Graph Options Scale
Y-Scale Format , 0
2Y-Scale Format , 0

Notice the result (see fig. 6.11). The numbers of both y-axes are formatted now with commas separating the thousands position.

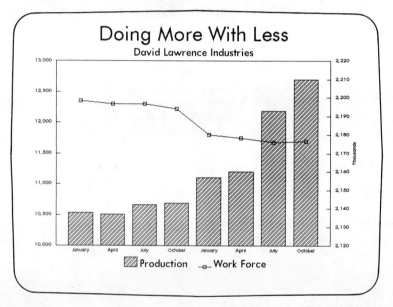

Fig. 6.11. *The DLI graph with comma-formatted axes numbers.*

Scaling the Axes Logarithmically

By selecting /Graph Options Scale, choosing an axis, and then selecting Type, you can choose from either Standard (linear) or Logarithmic scaling. Linear scaling places equal increments between each value marker along the axis—100, 200, 300, and so on. Logarithmic scaling uses values that increase by a factor of 10 along the axis, as with the progression 10, 100, 1000,...

Logarithmic scaling lets you graph numbers that span a wide range, yet retain visible changes in numbers at the low end of the scale. Logarithmic scaling also lets you graph two or more sets of numbers covered by different ranges.

The graph in figure 6.13 uses a standard y-axis to display the data in figure 6.12, average income levels and average home costs over a period of ten years. Notice how difficult it is to see changes in income levels because of the span of the y-axis scaling. You could make the graph more clear by plotting one of the data series against a second y-axis scaled appropriately. Then again, you could scale the single y-axis logarithmically.

By using a logarithmic scale, as shown in figure 6.14, you can see both the variation in number of loans and the variation in down-payment amounts plotted against a single axis.

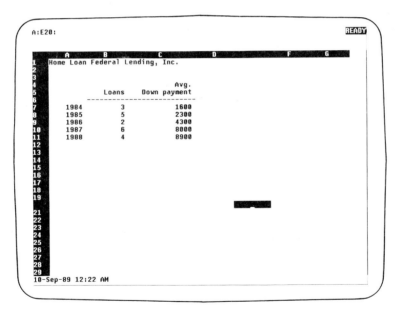

Fig. 6.12. *Worksheet data for figures 6.13 and 6.14.*

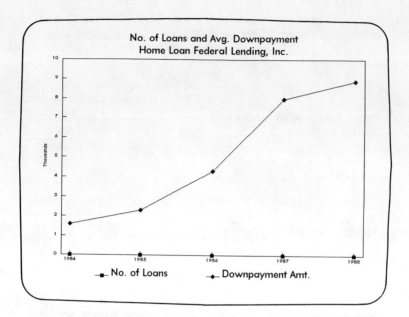

Fig. 6.13. Graph with standard y-axis scaling.

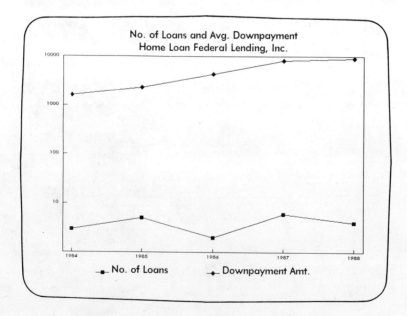

Fig. 6.14. Graph with logarithmic y-axis scaling.

Setting a Scale Number Exponent

Changing the scale number exponent determines by what power of 10 the values on an axis are measured. If 1-2-3 displays your y-axis numbers in "Thousands," for example, you know you must multiply the numbers on the y-axis by 1,000. Because 1,000 is 10 to the third power, the scale-number exponent in this case is 3. You can choose any number from -95 to 95.

To change the scale number exponent, select /**G**raph **O**ptions **S**cale, select the axis to modify, and then select **E**xponent. You can choose **A**utomatic to let 1-2-3 determine an appropriate exponent; choose **M**anual to enter an exponent of your preference.

To display the actual numbers on the second y-axis of the DLI graph rather than the numbers in "Thousands," use this series of commands:

/**G**raph **O**ptions **S**cale **2**Y-Scale **E**xponent **M**anual **0**

The resulting graph is shown in figure 6.15. Notice that the actual numbers represented by the second y-axis are displayed next to the axis, and the thousands indicator is automatically removed.

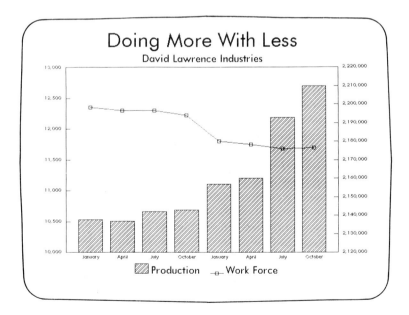

***Fig. 6.15.** The second y-axis with an exponent of 0.*

Setting the Scale Number Width

To change the maximum width of the numbers displayed along an axis, select /Graph Options Scale, select an axis, and then choose **Width**. The unit of measurement for width is the width of the letter 0 in the current text font. An entry of 3, for example, is the width of three zeroes side by side. You can enter any number from 1 to 50, or you can let 1-2-3 calculate a maximum width when you select **Automatic**.

Try setting the width of the numbers along the second y-axis to 7 and check the result. Use these commands:

/Graph **O**ptions **S**cale **2**Y-Scale **W**idth **M**anual **7**

Your displayed graph should match the one seen in figure 6.16. Notice that asterisks appear, because the y-axis numbers do not fit into a space that is 7 zeroes wide.

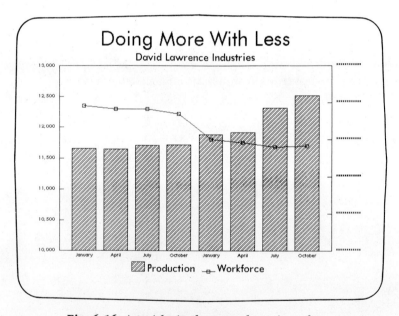

Fig. 6.16. *Asterisks in the second y-axis scale.*

Now, correct the problem by changing the width of the scale numbers to 8. Notice that even though there are nine characters in the numbers, they still fit into a space 8 zeroes wide.

Displaying the Graph Horizontally

Certain graphs lend themselves to a horizontal orientation rather than a vertical layout. Fortunately, 1-2-3 Release 3 can switch the orientation of your graph. By selecting /**G**raph **T**ype **F**eatures **H**orizontal, you can instruct 1-2-3 to make the x-axis of your graph the vertical axis and the y-axis the horizontal axis. Bar graphs are particularly appropriate for a horizontal direction, although you can use this option effectively with a number of graph types.

Figure 6.18 shows a perfectly acceptable graph comparing 1989 passenger air miles for four little-known but upcoming airlines. The data for the graph is given in figure 6.17. Data-labels identify the bars, and hatch numbers 10 through 13 placed in a hatch range cause the four attractive shades of gray hatching.

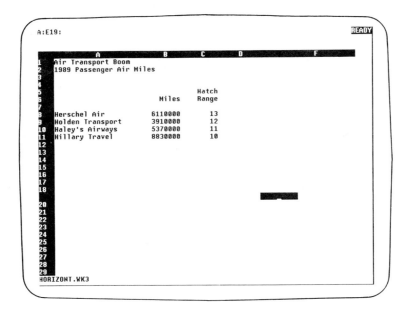

Fig. 6.17. *The worksheet for the air transport graph.*

But figure 6.19 displays the same graph set to Horizontal. Now, the graph makes more immediate visual sense. The horizontal axis represents distance traveled, so the bar extending farthest to the right represents the greatest distance. If you were to pull this graph into a dedicated graphing package such as Freelance Plus or Harvard Graphics, you could incorporate art into the graph by adding a jet to the right end of each bar, giving a far more dynamic impression.

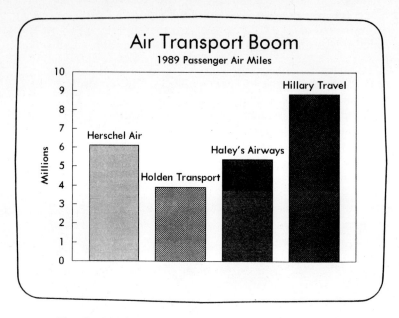

Fig. 6.18. *A bar graph with the normal orientation.*

Creating Stacked and 100% Graph Versions

Two further options on the /Graph Type Features menu, Stacked and 100%, let you stack the series of a graph one on top of the next, or display the series as percentages of the total. The graph in figure 6.20 displays three passenger air mileage figures for the same four airlines graphed over four years using bars. Figure 6.21 shows the same three series with the Stacked option turned on.

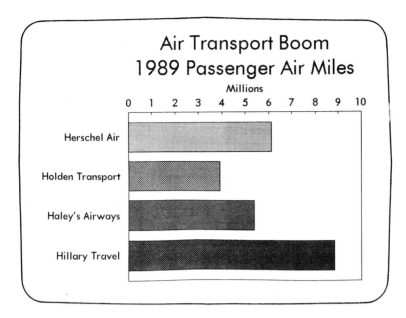

Fig. 6.19. *The air transport graph oriented horizontally.*

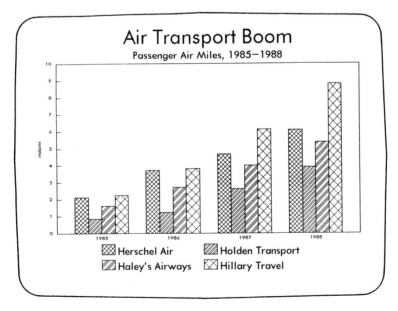

Fig. 6.20. *A simple bar graph showing three sets of mileage figures.*

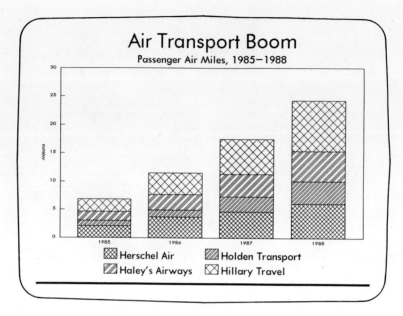

Fig. 6.21. *The same bar graph with the stacked feature.*

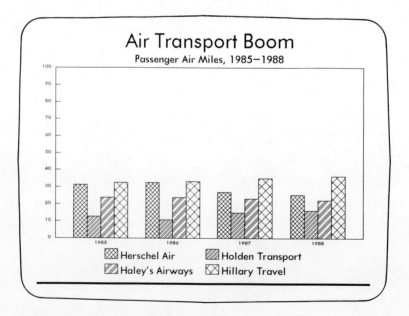

Fig. 6.22. *The same bar graph with the 100% feature.*

To display how the four airlines have each contributed to the total flown by all four, select /Graph **Type** Features **100% Yes**. Figure 6.22 displays the resulting 100% graph.

You can combine the 100% and stack features to illustrate the relative contributions of each airline by showing the relative sizes of the bar segments. Figure 6.23 shows a combined 100% and stacked graph.

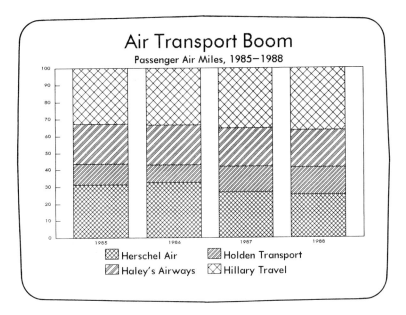

Fig. 6.23. *The graph with both 100% and Stacked set to Yes.*

Summary

By using the special formatting commands that are unique to 1-2-3 Release 3, you can create presentation quality graphs. In this chapter, you explored the advanced capabilities of Release 3. You learned how to create and use mixed graphs, and then you learned about the special options for colors, hatch patterns and text fonts. You learned how Release 3 helps you control the axes. Finally, you saw how some of these advanced options were used in stacked and 100% graph types. The following two chapters cover special macros for graphing and add-ins designed for making graphs.

7

Using Macros for Graphing

Macros in 1-2-3 can automate the mundane tasks you perform over and over again in graphmaking, especially when you create the same graph types routinely. A macro is a chain-reaction sequence of commands that you can initiate with just a few keystrokes. Once started, the macro races through the series of steps that you would otherwise need to enter manually.

Of course, you do need to carry out all the steps the first time to enter the routine. Then 1-2-3 can copy your keystrokes into a range specified for the macro. Or, you can type the macro in step by step, using special keyword macro commands and menu command letters for the actions you usually perform while working in 1-2-3. With either method, the end product is a macro that accomplishes an entire set of tasks without assistance from you.

Understanding Macro Fundamentals

Before you study the graphing macros offered in this chapter, you may first want to become more familiar with the basic principles of 1-2-3 macros. If you are already somewhat familiar with macros, you may find the following basic description of macros a helpful refresher.

Macros are composed of strings of abbreviations for 1-2-3 commands entered into a column of worksheet cells. As 1-2-3 reads down the column, the program sequentially runs all the macro steps it finds. Most macro abbreviations are simply keystroke equivalents. The macro **/wcs12~**, for example, is the same as pressing the keys /, **w**, **c**, and **s** for /Worksheet Column Set-Width, typing the number **12**, and pressing the Enter key (signified by the ~). **{RIGHT 2}** is the same as pressing the right arrow key twice. Macros also contain commands that have no menu command equivalents. The WAIT command, for example, waits for a specified time before letting the macro carry out the next task.

The macros found in this chapter are limited to graphics use. For a comprehensive treatment of macro abbreviations and commands, refer to Que's *Using 1-2-3 Release 2.2*, Special Edition, *Using 1-2-3 Release 3*, or *1-2-3 Macro Library*.

You can use either of two methods for creating 1-2-3 macros. The first is to jot down all the keystrokes that you would normally type to accomplish a task. Then, type the keystrokes as a macro into cells in the worksheet.

To illustrate the first method, let's say that you want to create a macro to insert columns into the worksheet. To insert a column, you normally move the cell pointer to the column to be inserted. Next, you type the command /Worksheet Insert Column Insert and press Enter to insert a column at the location of the cell pointer. So, the keystrokes that you write down are /, **w**, **i**, **c**, and ~ (remember, the tilde (~) is used to signify Enter in a macro). This, then, is the complete macro that you enter:

/wic~

A second and often easier way of creating a macro is to instruct 1-2-3 to "learn" your keystrokes as you type them. By carrying out the procedure once with 1-2-3 recording it as you go, you can have your keystrokes entered into a macro range automatically. Then, you need only to name the range to complete the macro. Later, when you play back that macro, 1-2-3 will play back your keystrokes just as you typed them earlier. This second method is preferable when a macro automates a simple series of keystrokes.

How you use the Learn mode depends on whether you are using 1-2-3 Release 2.2 or 3. With Release 2.2, you issue the command /Worksheet Learn to obtain this menu:

Range Cancel Erase

First select **R**ange and assign a range on the worksheet to place the recorded keystrokes into—AB1..AB10, for example. 1-2-3 now returns to Ready mode. After you assign a range to store the keystrokes, turn on Learn using the key combination Alt-F5. You will see the Learn indicator appear at the bottom of the screen. Next, type the command /Worksheet **I**nsert **C**olumn and press Enter. Shut off the Learn mode by pressing Alt-F5 again. Move to cell AB1, to confirm your keystroke entry of /wic~.

If you turn on the Learn mode again, additional keystrokes can be added to those already in the range. If you fill the Learn range, you will see the error message **Learn range is full.**

Use /Worksheet **L**earn **E**rase to erase the keystrokes in the learn range so that you can record new keystrokes. The /Worksheet **L**earn **C**ancel command will reset the learn range.

1-2-3 Release 3 always records keystrokes. To access the keystrokes, press the key combination Alt-F2, Record. When you do, a menu appears offering these options:

Playback Copy Erase Step

Following is a description of each option:

Playback is a "temporary" macro. You can select keystrokes that you would like to use again.

Copy lets you select keystrokes to copy to the worksheet for use as a macro.

Erase clears the keyboard record buffer.

Step turns on the Step mode to debug a macro.

To copy keystrokes to the worksheet, first type the keystrokes that you want to copy, such as /Worksheet **I**nsert **C**olumn. Next, press Alt-F2, Record. Your screen will look like figure 7.1.

Press the Tab key, and, using the left arrow key, highlight the keystrokes and press Enter. Respond to the prompt to place the cell pointer in the cell to copy the keystrokes; then press Enter. The keystrokes will be copied to the appropriate worksheet cell.

After you create a macro by typing a list of menu command letters and macro commands into a column of worksheet cells, you must name the macro. To give a macro a name, you use the /**R**ange **N**ame **C**reate command to name the range that encompasses all the cells that are part

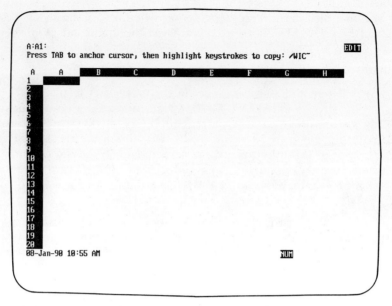

A:A1:
Press TAB to anchor cursor, then highlight keystrokes to copy: /WIC~

EDIT

08-Jan-90 10:55 AM

NUM

Fig. 7.1. *Recorded keystrokes in 1-2-3 Release 3.*

of the macro. 1-2-3 Release 2.01 requires that you give the macro range a name of any single letter or number preceded by a backslash (\ ). A typical designation would be \p for a macro that prints a graph. Then, to start the printing macro found in a range named \p, you must press the Alt-P key combination. 1-2-3 Release 2.2 and Release 3 enable you name a macro with up to 15 characters, so that a full name such as *makeagraph* is possible. By pressing Run (Alt-F3) you can view a list of all the macros you have previously named.

This chapter provides instructions sufficient to enter each of the suggested macros, to name the macros properly, and to start them. You'll see that macros, by standard convention, begin in cell AA of a worksheet. This procedure keeps the macro far from your worksheet data to avoid inadvertent data deletions.

Column AA contains all range names to be used in the macros. You will then issue the /**R**ange **N**ame **L**abel **R**ight command to assign these names to their adjacent cells to the right. Column AB contains the actual macro statements. A third column contains information about each macro line. Providing the names of ranges in column AA and entering information about each macro line are not necessary for running the macros. This information, however, serves to document the macro.

The macros covered in this chapter use a combination of techniques. The first macro, for example, automates the keystrokes required to create a simple graph. To produce this macro, you can use 1-2-3's learn feature.

In the sections that follow, you will find 14 utility macros that you can combine into a useful graphics macro library. These utility macros help you to make changes or additions easily to the current graph. Following is a list of the macro names with a description of the function of each macro.

Macro Name	*Macro Function*
\f	Assigns a graph's first title.
\s	Assigns a graph's second title.
\x	Assigns a graph's x-axis title.
\y	Assigns a graph's y-axis title.
\l	Assigns a group of data-labels to a graph.
\h	Uses a horizontal grid in a graph.
\v	Uses a vertical grid in a graph.
\b	Uses both a horizontal and vertical grid in a graph.
\o	Displays a graph in color.
\w	Displays a graph in black and white.
\c	Creates a graph name.
\d	Deletes a graph name.
\u	Uses a graph with a name.
\t	Creates a graph name table.

Also given in this chapter are five application macros that enable you to create, view and print graphs. These macros are described in the following list.

Macro Name	*Macro Function*
\c	Creates a graph from a worksheet with contiguous ranges.
\n	Creates a graph using a worksheet with noncontiguous ranges.
\m	Creates a menu of graphs so that you can select one for viewing.
\g	Creates a slide show.
\p	Prints a graph from 1-2-3 Release 3.

As you type each macro into a worksheet and try it, you will no doubt find ways to modify it to fit your worksheets.

A Macro for Creating a Simple Graph

The easiest macro to create, but one that can make your graphing work far easier, is a simple macro to make a basic graph. To use this macro, certain conditions must be met. The macro assumes that your worksheets are laid out in the same manner. For example, your graph's first title must be in cell A1, and the second title in cell A2. Also, your data must be laid out in a rowwise format. For example, each person or item comprising the set of data should be in a separate row. Each row of data can then be specified as a data range.

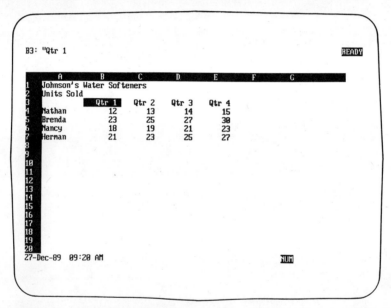

Fig. 7.2. A sample worksheet.

Refer to the sample worksheet shown in figure 7.2. The worksheet is laid out in a rowwise format, with each data range in its own row. Row 3 defines the X range of quarterly time intervals; rows 4 through 7 define ranges A through D, showing units sold by each person.

In cells A1 and A2 are the titles that will be used in the graph. For use with this macro, it is important that you maintain fixed locations on the worksheet for the first and second titles. Then, if you decide to change a title, you only have to move the cell pointer to the appropriate cell and type a new title.

The following is a list of steps the macro performs when you run the macro to create a graph.

1. Enter the graph menu.

2. Choose the type of graph.

3. Select **Group** to set all data ranges at once.

4. Highlight the group range; select rowwise for group.

5. Choose the graph's legends.

6. Highlight the range of the legends.

7. Set the first title.

8. Set the second title.

9. View the graph.

As you set up this macro, notice how each step is accomplished.

Setting Up the Macro
To Create a Graph

Look at the macro shown in figure 7.3. This macro will work with 1-2-3 Release 2.2 or Release 3.

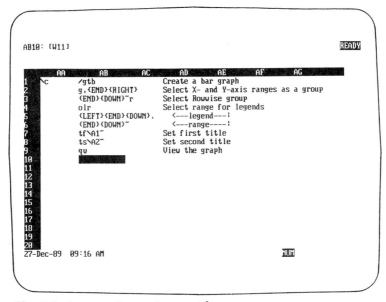

Fig. 7.3. *A macro to create a graph.*

Prior to running the macro, you must place the cell pointer on cell B3 in your worksheet. Notice that cell B3 is the upper left cell to be used in your graph data. Placing the cell pointer on this cell will enable the macro to issue the /Graph Group command and assign all data ranges simultaneously. If you place the cell pointer in any other cell, the data ranges will be set incorrectly. When you use this macro, then, always place the cell pointer on the cell that is the upper left corner of the data to graph.

Another thing to remember before running this macro is that no other graph should exist as the current graph. There is no problem, however, if you have other graphs named in the worksheet. Before running this macro, type /Graph Reset Graph Quit to reset the current graph settings and return to the Ready mode.

Creating a Range Name for the Macro

There is only one range name used with this macro—that is \c, the name of the macro. To create the range name, place your cell pointer on cell AA1, which should contain the label \c. Type the command sequence /Range Name Label Right and press Enter. This will assign the label \c as a range name to the cell AB1. Pressing Alt-C will start the macro.

The /Range Name Label Right command is an easy way to quickly create range names. A range name created by this command can be no more than one cell large. If the range name must contain the contents of more than one cell, use the command /Range Name Create, type the range name, then type the range of cells to assign the range name to.

Running the Macro To Create a Graph

When you type Alt-C, the macro begins by calling the /Graph menu and selects bar as the type of graph, using the commands from cell AB1. In cells AB2 and AB3, Group is selected to assign all data ranges, the x-axis and the y-axis. The period anchors the cell pointer for highlighting a range, and the End-Right, End-Down cursor sequences select B3..E7 as the group range. The group of ranges is selected Row-wise so that row 3 will be the X range, row 4 the A range, and so on.

The commands in cells AB4..AB6 select A4..A7 as the legend range. The range AB7..AB8 selects the first and second titles and AB9 causes the graph to appear on the screen. Figure 7.4 shows the resulting graph.

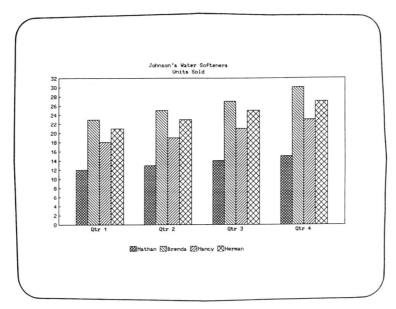

Fig. 7.4. *The graph created by the macro.*

This macro will work no matter how many columns or rows of data you have in your worksheet. You must, however, keep each column and row contiguous; that is, there can be no breaks between rows and columns.

Revising the Macro for Noncontiguous Ranges or for Release 2.01

Sometimes you cannot use the Group menu command to assign all axis ranges at once. You may create a worksheet that does not have contiguous ranges—each row to be graphed may not be contiguous as in figure 7.5. Or, if you use Release 2.01, you do not have the Group menu command. Note the revised macro in figure 7.6.

This macro will allow you to create the same graph that was shown in figure 7.4. The macro is a little more complex, however, and not quite so automatic in its assignment of ranges.

Stepping through the Revised Macro

The procedure for revising this graph macro differs from the set of steps to create the original. Notice the differences:

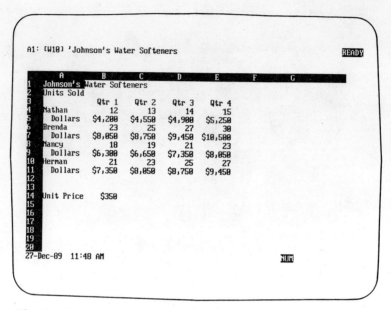

Fig. 7.5. *A worksheet with noncontiguous rows to graph.*

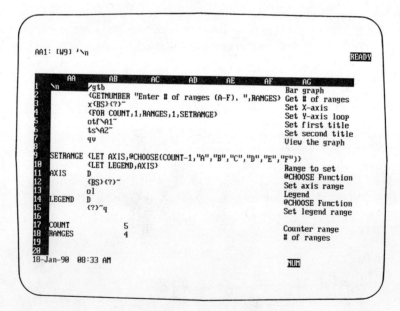

Fig. 7.6. *A revised macro for creating graphs.*

1. Enter the /Graph menu.

2. Select the type of graph.

3. Determine the number of y-axes to assign.

4. Set the x-axis range.

5. Start a loop to set all ranges determined by step 3.

6. Set the first title.

7. Set the second title.

8. View the graph.

Step 5 started a loop to assign all y-axis ranges. The following lists the steps for this loop:

1. Determine which y-axis is being set, A-F.

2. Assign the range letter to two range names.

3. Allow user to set the y-axis range manually.

4. Set the legend for the y-axis.

5. Allow user to set the legend range manually.

These steps will create a graph that contains noncontiguous ranges.

Running the Revised Macro

The macro first selects a bar graph. Next, you are asked how many ranges will make up your graph by the GETNUMBER macro command in cell AB2. The number you type is stored in cell AB18, a range named RANGES. Next you are instructed to enter the range for your x-axis. Enter the range either by typing it or by using the point method. Press Enter to continue.

Cell AB4 starts a FOR looping process to assign each of the y-axis ranges. The subroutine that repeats is called SETRANGE, and its number of repetitions depends on the number of ranges that you entered. When SETRANGE is completed, the first and second titles are set, and the graph is displayed on the screen.

If you entered the number 4 at the prompt **Enter # of ranges (A-F)**. SETRANGE will be repeated four times. The FOR looping statement counts the number of times it runs SETRANGE in a range name called COUNT. So the first line of SETRANGE uses COUNT to determine which range needs to be set. The function

@CHOOSE(COUNT-1,"A","B","C","D","E","F")

is placed at the range names AXIS and LEGEND. This function selects A through F depending on the value of COUNT-1. A is returned if COUNT-1 equals 0; B is returned if COUNT-1 is 1, and so on.

For each repetition of SETRANGE, the macro prompts you to enter a data range for each y-axis range. The macro stops, allowing you to type the data range or to point to the range using the cursor keys. You then press Enter to accept the range. The next prompt lets you enter a legend corresponding to the data range you just entered. Press Enter after you enter the legend.

Creating a Macro Library for Setting Up Graphs

When you create graphs, you will always perform certain tasks. For instance, you normally will create titles for the graph. Or you will assign the graph data-labels or name the graph for later recall. You will find that developing a macro library so that utility macros are at your disposal will aid your graph building. If you have the Macro Library Manager Add-in, you can place these utility macros in memory without entering them first in your worksheet.

Follow these steps to create a graph macro library:

1. Load the Macro Library Manager into memory. Using 1-2-3 Release 2.2, type /Add-In Attach and select MACROMGR.ADN and press Enter. Select a function key to call the Macro Manager, choosing a number from 7 through 10 to designate a left key. Choose **Q**uit to return to the Ready mode.

2. Type all 14 macros shown into the worksheet starting at cell AA1. Leave one blank row between each macro. The cells you should use are AA1..AD34.

3. Issue the command /**R**ange Name Label **R**ight; highlight cells AA1.AA34 and press Enter.

4. Press Alt and the function key you assigned to start the macro manager. For example, if you selected 7 when loading the macro manager, you can press Alt-F7. You will see the following menu:

    Load Save Edit Remove Name-List Quit

5. Select **S**ave.

6. When prompted **Enter name of macro library to save**, type the name GRAPHMAC and press Enter.

7. When prompted **Enter macro library range**: highlight the range AA1..AD32 and press Enter. Select **N**o to avoid password protecting the file.

The macros will disappear from the screen, but because the macro manager is still loaded in memory, the macros remain in memory. Try to run one of the macros and you will see that they are still available.

Each time you start 1-2-3, you must load the macro library in memory. Do this by loading the macro manager in memory; then from the macro library manager menu, select Load. When prompted **Enter name of macro library to load:** select the macro library and press Enter.

Macros for Assigning Titles to a Graph

Even if a graph does display meaningful information, the graph can be meaningless to others without explanatory titles. You normally assign a first title to your graph and quite often a second title, as well as x- and y-axis titles.

The macros shown in figure 7.7 enable you to assign titles to your graph more easily. The macros are named \f, \s, \x and \y, to signify *f*irst, *s*econd, *x*-axis and *y*-axis, respectively. Prior to starting a macro, the worksheet must be in Ready mode. If you are in the middle of a menu when you start a macro, you will hear a good deal of beeping.

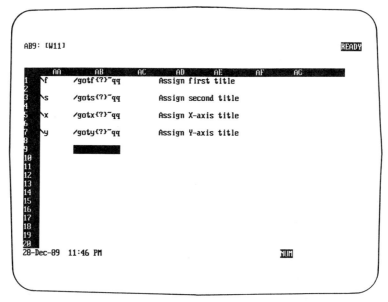

Fig. 7.7. *Four macros for setting graph titles.*

The macros are straightforward in the way that they work. For example, if you press Alt-F, the command /Graph Options Title First is executed. The {?} halts the macro for your response. You may type the actual text of a title, or you may refer to a cell in the worksheet by typing a backslash and a cell address (\A1). When you are certain that you have entered the title or cell reference correctly, press Enter. The tilde (~) enters the title; then the two q's at the end of the macro return the worksheet to Ready mode. To view the graph press the Graph key, F10.

Each of these four macros works in the same manner, varying only as you enter the first, second, y- or x-axis title.

Macros for Setting Data-Labels, Grids, and Color

Often, to make a graph more descriptive or easier for others to read, you add data-labels and grids or change to color from black and white. The macros given in figure 7.8 enable you to accomplish these tasks.

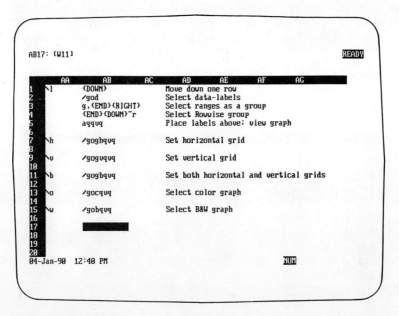

Fig. 7.8. *Macros for assigning data-labels, grids and changing between color and black and white.*

The Data-Labels Macro

To use the macro that assigns data-labels, first you position your cursor, just as you did with the macro that creates a graph. As an example, look back at figure 7.2. Place your cell pointer on cell B3, the upper left corner of your graph's data range. Press Alt-L to start the macro.

The first line moves the cell pointer down to the row of your A-data range. The menu command /Graph Options Data-labels Group is issued. The period anchors the cell pointer in the upper left cell of the Group range, which in this case is cell B4. The {END}{RIGHT}{END}{DOWN} combination selects B4..E7 as the group range. The tilde accepts this range, then **R**owwise is selected, telling 1-2-3 that the data-label ranges are in rows rather than columns. The labels are placed above the data points, and the graph is displayed on the screen.

You can press Enter or Esc to remove the graph from the screen. When you press one of these keys, you return to the Ready mode.

The Grid Macros

The next three macros in figure 7.8 are used to add grids to a graph, horizontal or vertical, or both. The macros are named to correspond to function, designated by \h, \v and \b.

All three of these macros work in a similar manner. When you start these macros, they issue the command /Graph Options Grid. At this point, however, the macros vary: each macro now selects the appropriate type of grid. Finally, the graph is viewed on the screen. Pressing Enter or Esc returns the worksheet to Ready mode, as the graph disappears from the screen.

Once again, these macros assume that you are starting them from Ready mode. If you start these macros while you are in a menu, you will accomplish only a series of beeps.

Selecting between Color and Black and White

If you have a color monitor, you may often find yourself changing back and forth between color and black and white. When you view the graph on-screen, using color is naturally more pleasing. But, if your printer prints only in black and white, you must change your graph back to black and white to save the graph for printing. The \o and \w macros shown in figure 7.8 enable you to switch easily between color and black and white (here, the macros are named \o and \w instead of \c and \b to avoid a naming conflict with the macro that sets both grids).

These two utility macros are procedurally quite forthright. The \o macro issues the command **/Graph Options Color**, then displays the macro on the screen. When you press Enter or Esc, the graph will vacate the screen, returning you to Ready mode. The \w macro, on the other hand, issues the command **/Graph Options B&W**, then causes the graph to appear on the screen. Again, when you press Enter or Esc, you return to the Ready mode.

Macros for Using Graph Names

To create a second graph without losing the settings of the first, you must give the first graph a name. The graph settings, then, are saved with the worksheet and are tied to the graph name. So you may find yourself creating, using, and deleting graphs from your worksheet. Also, after you create several graphs in a worksheet, you may want to keep a listing of those graphs. For this, you can create a table of graphs in your worksheet.

Look at the macros \c, \d, \u and \t in figure 7.9. These four macros enable you to create a graph name, delete a graph name, use a graph name and create a table of graphs.

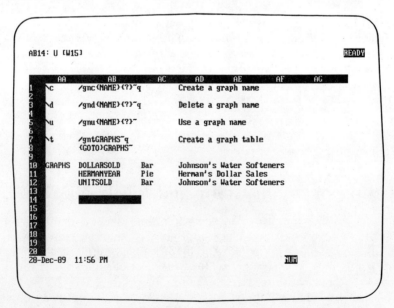

Fig. 7.9. *Macros for managing graph names.*

Creating a Graph Name with a Macro

To use the \c macro in figure 7.9, first create a graph. Then, press Alt-C. The command sequence /**G**raph **N**ame **C**reate now starts. The macro prompts you to enter a name for your graph. Any preexisting names are displayed at the top of the screen. Only five graph names can be displayed at a time, however, so the {NAME} keyword is included in the macro. The NAME key uses the full screen to display graph names.

Rather than typing a new name for a graph, you may wish to overwrite an existing graph with the new settings of the current, active graph. You can either type the name of an existing graph or use the cursor keys to highlight one of the graph names on the screen. Press Enter to accept the graph and return to the Ready mode.

Macros To Delete and Use a Graph Name

The delete macro, \d, works similarly to the create macro. With this macro, however, the graph name that you type or select is deleted from the worksheet. To recall the graph, you must completely recreate it, entering all of the settings. Use this utility macro with care.

The macro to use a graph is similar to the one for creating a graph name. The name that you select is displayed on the screen, and the settings for the graph become active so that you can make changes as you wish. When you press Enter or Esc to remove the graph from the screen, you are left in the /Graph menu on the assumption that you are using a graph to make additional changes. Remember, if you do change a graph, you must use the /**G**raph **N**ame **C**reate command (the \c macro) and save the new settings under the same or a new name.

A Macro for Creating a Graph Table

You can create more than one graph in a worksheet and may find it difficult to remember all the graphs in your worksheets. Knowing this, Lotus provides the /**G**raph **N**ame **T**able command, which places a list of your graph names in cells on your worksheets.

When you create a graph name table, place it in an out-of-the-way area of the worksheet. If you select an area where there is data, you risk overwriting the data with the table. The \t macro shown in Figure 7.9 places a graph name table in a safe area of the worksheet.

When you press Alt-T, the menu command **/Graph Name Table** is performed. The location for the table is the range name GRAPHS. You should make the range name GRAPHS in an out-of-the-way place on the worksheet. Finally, the cell pointer is moved to graphs so that you may view the graph names.

A Macro for Creating a Menu of Graphs

This macro is an elaboration on the previous one. The macro shown in figure 7.10 will not only create a graph table, but will allow you to select the graph to view from the table.

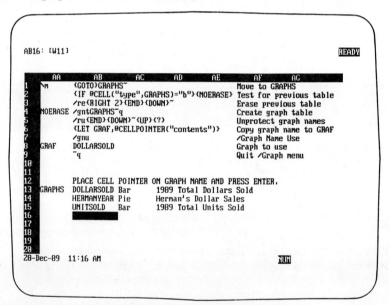

Fig. 7.10. *A macro for creating a graph menu.*

The menu macro will follow seven steps:

1. Go to the location where the graph name table will be created.

2. Test to see if the location chosen is blank; if the location is not blank, erase the information.

3. Create the graph name table.

4. Unprotect the column containing the names.

5. Allow user to move the cell pointer to the graph name to view.

6. Copy the graph name to be used by the macro.

7. Issue the /Graph Name Use command to view the graph.

Note that step 2 uses an IF test. If the location being tested is not blank, the location will be erased. However, if the location is already blank, one line of the macro will be skipped. Review the macro to see how the IF test works.

Setting Up the Macro

This macro takes advantage of the Release 2.2 and Release 3 command /Graph Name Table. This command makes a table containing graph names, the type of graph, and the first title of the graph. Note the table created in cells AB9..AD11 in figure 7.10. You may need to make your worksheet column wider, depending on your graph names. The width of column AB was changed to 11 to accommodate the names.

Four range names are used with this macro:

\m	AB1
NOERASE	AB4
GRAF	AB8
GRAPHS	AB13

How the Graph Menu Macro Works

To start the macro, press the key combination Alt-M. The cell pointer moves to the range name GRAPHS. The IF statement in cell AB2 tests GRAPHS to see if graph table information is already present. Any information in the GRAPHS range is erased by the macro statement in cell AB3. If no data is found in GRAPHS, the macro skips its erasure step and continues with the range name NOERASE, cell AB4.

The graph table is created at GRAPHS. Next, the /**R**ange Unprotect command is issued to unprotect the cells containing the graph names. If you are using a color monitor, the graph names change to green, while the other text on the screen remains white. If you are using a monochrome monitor, the graph names appear brighter than the other text on-screen. This is done simply to make the names of the graphs stand out.

The cell pointer moves up to the cell containing the instruction

PLACE CELL POINTER ON GRAPH NAME AND PRESS ENTER.

At this point, the macro halts. Next move the cell pointer to the graph name that you wish to view and press Enter. The name is copied to GRAF. The command /Graph Name Use is issued and the graph you choose appears. Press Enter or Esc to remove the graph from the screen and return to the worksheet.

One change you may want to make is to move GRAPHS to an out-of-the-way location of the worksheet, for instance cell AA21. Then, when the cell pointer moves to GRAPHS, the user of the macro sees only the graph table.

An Alternate Macro for Viewing Graphs

The macro shown in figure 7.10 works as well in Release 3 as it does in Release 2.2. But you cannot use this macro with Release 2.01, because that version does not contain the /Graph Name Table command. An alternate macro, useable with Release 2.01, was shown previously in figure 7.9, the \u macro.

Notice that this macro is simple, using only the /Graph Name Use command. The macro does not create a table on the screen, as did the previous macro, so you do not see the type of graph or the first title.

A Macro for Running a Slide Show

Making graphics presentations during meetings can help you make your point much better than by simply using numbers. In Chapter 12 you see how to use programs to create a slide show presentation. The next macro lets you use 1-2-3 to help create a slide show.

Before you get started on the slide show presentation, you must create the graphs and save each one using /Graph Name Create. Do not save with the /Graph Save command. For each graph you create and save, you must assign a sequential name. For example, if you plan to create 10 graphs, name the graphs GRAPH1, GRAPH2, and so on. You will see how the macro uses these sequential names in a moment.

Slide Show Macro Principles

The slide show macro is a bit more complex than some of the other macros, as it builds two of its lines "on the fly." Here is the step-by-step procedure:

1. Create a two-column table of graph numbers including the time that each graph should stay on the screen.

2. Range name the table.

3. Enter a formula that counts the number of graphs listed in the table.

4. Use a FOR loop for display of graphs on-screen.

Now that the steps for the main macro are complete, you must follow these steps for the loop that places each graph on the screen for a designated time.

1. Create each sequential graph name to display.

2. Determine, from the table, how long the graph from step 1 is to display.

3. Display the graph on the screen.

4. Keep the designated graph on the screen for the appropriate amount of time.

5. Continue with the next graph.

As you look through the macro, notice how steps 1 and 2 of the loop are done.

Range Names Used with the Slide Show Macro

After you create and save your graphs, you can start the macro by typing Alt-G. The slide show macro is shown in figure 7.11.

Before starting the macro, you must take a few preliminary steps. First, create the range names using the /**R**ange **N**ame **L**abel **R**ight command; highlight cells AA1..AA9; and press Enter. Next, create the two-column table shown at AB11, AC11. The first column contains a number for each graph, so for a 10-graph slide show, enter the numbers 1 through 10. In the adjacent column, enter the time in seconds that each graph should appear on the screen. You see in figure 7.10 that graphs 1, 2, 3, 6, and 7-10 each remain on-screen for five seconds. Graph 4 stays on the screen for eight seconds, and graph 5 for ten. Give this table the range name TIMETABLE. In figure 7.11, the range for TIMETABLE is AB11..AC20.

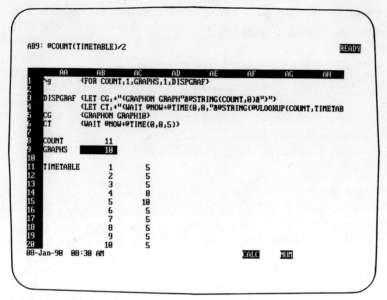

Fig. 7.11. *A slide show macro.*

The range name table is as follows:

\g	AB1
DISPGRAF	AB3
CG	AB5
CT	AB6
COUNT	AB8
GRAPHS	AB9
TIMETABLE	AB11..AC20

A formula for GRAPHS is entered:

@COUNT(TIMETABLE)/2

This formula counts the number of cells in the range TIMETABLE and divides by two. This number is used by the macro to display all the graphs on the screen.

One macro line in cell AB4 does not appear completely in the figure:

{LET CT,+"{WAIT   @NOW+@TIME(0,0,"&@STRING(
@VLOOKUP(COUNT,TIMETABLE,1),0)&")}"}

Running the Slide Show Macro

The slide show macro starts with a FOR loop that calls the subroutine DISPGRAF once for each graph to display. If, for example, the number 10 is in the cell GRAPHS, DISPGRAF will be run 10 times.

The DISPGRAF subroutine actually places each graph on the screen. The first line of DISPGRAF places in the cell range named CG this formula:

+"{GRAPHON GRAPH"&@STRING(COUNT,0)&"}"

This formula is a string used to develop the graph name. Each time the FOR loop runs DISPGRAF, FOR places a number in the range name COUNT to track how many times the subroutine has run. This formula takes advantage of COUNT, changing the number to a string and combining the string with the name GRAPH. So, if COUNT contains the number 1, the result of the string formula is {GRAPHON GRAPH1}.

The second line of DISPGRAF is similar to the first. This line places a formula at the cell range named CT. The formula is

+"{WAIT @NOW+@TIME(0,0,"&@STRING(
@VLOOKUP(COUNT,TIMETABLE,1),0)& ")}"

This string formula determines how long the graph stays on the screen. The @VLOOKUP function returns the number of seconds that a graph should remain on-screen. COUNT determines which graph the macro displays. If COUNT contains the number 5, then the @VLOOKUP function returns the number 10. The result of the string formula is {WAIT @NOW+@TIME(0,0,10)}.

This statement causes the macro to wait ten seconds from the current time (@NOW) before continuing. When the appropriate amount of time has passed, the graph is removed from the screen and the FOR loop determines whether to display another graph. This macro will not work with Release 2.01, but can be used with Release 2.2 and Release 3.

A Macro for Printing a Graph with Release 3

Because with Release 3 you can print graphs from inside the worksheet, you may find helpful a macro to aid you in printing graphs. The macro shown in figure 7.12 is a variation of the macro to create a graph menu. In fact, it is identical to the graph menu macro with the exception of three lines.

Before printing a graph, you must select the graph to print, much in the same way you select a range from the worksheet to print. This macro develops a menu of graphs in the worksheet to choose from. As the macro runs, you select the graph to print. The graph name is copied to GRAF.

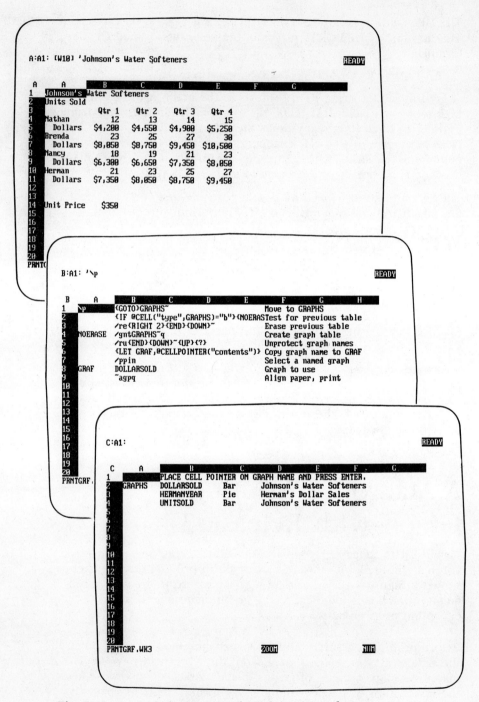

```
A:A1: [W10] 'Johnson's Water Softeners                              READY

    A      A        B        C        D        E       F       G
 1  Johnson's Water Softeners
 2  Units Sold
 3           Qtr 1    Qtr 2    Qtr 3    Qtr 4
 4  Nathan      12       13       14       15
 5    Dollars $4,200   $4,550   $4,900   $5,250
 6  Brenda      23       25       27       30
 7    Dollars $8,050   $8,750   $9,450  $10,500
 8  Nancy       18       19       21       23
 9    Dollars $6,300   $6,650   $7,350   $8,050
10  Herman      21       23       25       27
11    Dollars $7,350   $8,050   $8,750   $9,450
12
13
14  Unit Price  $350
15
16
17
18
19
20
PRNTG
```

```
B:A1: '\p                                                          READY

   B      A         B         C         D        E      F       G      H
 1  \p        {GOTO}GRAPHS~                              Move to GRAPHS
 2            {IF @CELL("type",GRAPHS)="b"}{NOERAS Test for previous table
 3            /re{RIGHT 2}{END}{DOWN}~               Erase previous table
 4  NOERASE   /gntGRAPHS~q                            Create graph table
 5            /ru{END}{DOWN}~{UP}{?}                  Unprotect graph names
 6            {LET GRAF,@CELLPOINTER("contents")}     Copy graph name to GRAF
 7            /ppin                                   Select a named graph
 8  GRAF      DOLLARSOLD                              Graph to use
 9            ~agpq                                   Align paper, print
10
11
12
13
14
15
16
17
18
19
20
PRNTGRF.
```

```
C:A1:                                                              READY

   C      A         B         C         D        E      F      G
 1          PLACE CELL POINTER ON GRAPH NAME AND PRESS ENTER.
 2  GRAPHS  DOLLARSOLD     Bar       Johnson's Water Softeners
 3          HERMANYEAR     Pie       Herman's Dollar Sales
 4          UNITSOLD       Bar       Johnson's Water Softeners
 5
 6
 7
 8
 9
10
11
12
13
14
15
16
17
18
19
20
PRNTGRF.WK3                              ZOOM              NUM
```

Fig. 7.12. *A macro that prints 1-2-3 Release 3 graphs.*

The two cells that are different from the menu macro are in cell B7 (AB7 in the graph menu macro) and B9 (AB9 in the graph menu macro). The line in B7 selects the graph image to print. B9 aligns the paper to the top of the form, prints the graph, and page advances the paper.

Summary

As a rule, macros make tedious tasks easy. Using the command language and building command lines with formulas, you can create useful programs. In this chapter, you saw how to create a number of utility macros that you can use in your own graphmaking. These utility graphs perform tasks you frequently repeat in creating graphs. You learned several application macros of special use in graph presentations, such as the 1-2-3 slide show macro.

8

Using Add-Ins
for 1-2-3 Graphs

G raphing in 1-2-3 is not without its shortcomings, as many people are
quick to point out. But some of the more conspicuous gaps have
been plugged by add-ins designed expressly for making 1-2-3 graphs.

This chapter introduces you to three of the most popular add-ins for 1-2-3
graphmaking. If you have not yet acquired these products, this will serve
as a preview of the capabilities you can expect. If you now have these
products in hand, the following text can serve as a jumpstart to using one
of them. In either case, this chapter is not intended to be an exhaustive
review of these programs' features. Instead, it highlights their more
important benefits and gives you a hands-on chance to try a few graphs.

Impress

Impress, from PC Publishing, Inc., fulfills the same need as does Funk
Software's Allways, which is now bundled with 1-2-3 Release 2.2 in the

U.S., and which has gotten the lion's share of the publicity. But despite that disadvantage, Impress carries on and offers features that Allways simply cannot match. In fact, in Europe Lotus Development Corporation bundles Impress rather than Allways with copies of 1-2-3 Release 2.2.

Impress, billed as "the ultimate worksheet publisher for 1-2-3" adds into 1-2-3 Release 2.01 and 2.2 just as Allways does. Allways forces you to toggle back and forth between the standard 1-2-3 view of your worksheet and a special display on which you can make formatting adjustments. When you are working with your data in standard 1-2-3, you cannot use the Allways formatting options, but then when you invoke Allways to format your worksheet you lose access to standard 1-2-3 commands. When you invoke Allways, for example, you cannot edit the contents of cells nor can you copy or move data from one range to another.

Unlike Allways, when you invoke Impress, your worksheet appears in a graphical representation on-screen, and you can continue to use all of the standard 1-2-3 commands. Alternately, when you toggle back to the customary 1-2-3 screen, you can still use all of the Impress formatting commands. This dual access to 1-2-3 and Impress commands means that you can make content and appearance changes simultaneously.

Impress also is superior to Allways in its handling of 1-2-3 graphs. To display and format a graph in Allways, you must save a completed graph in 1-2-3 as a PIC file before invoking Allways. Then, once Allways is invoked, you can pull the PIC file back in and overlay it on a portion of a 1-2-3 worksheet. PIC files, by their nature, are static snapshots of your data, representing how the data last stood when you created the PIC file. They do not vary with subsequent changes in the data. Impress, on the other hand, lets you embed a live graph within a 1-2-3 worksheet, one that continues to update as you modify the data it depicts. Without doubt, that ability to retain a live link between your data and its graph is the primary advantage of Impress in graphmaking.

Yet Impress offers other advantages. The program's full-screen preview lets you view an entire page of your worksheet/graph combination, as does Microsoft Excel. The program also can automatically fit the print range you choose on paper by scaling larger or smaller.

For use, Impress requires one of the following four graphics card types: CGA, Hercules, EGA, or VGA. If you are without one of these graphics cards, you can still use Impress to format a worksheet, but you will not see a graphic view of your worksheet.

To start Impress, you select /**Add-in Attach** from the 1-2-3 menu and select IMPRESS.ADN from the list of available add-ins that appears. Then assign an Alt-number key combination—Alt-F7 for example. Then, you can use Impress at any time as you work in 1-2-3 just by pressing Alt-F7.

The following example shows how to use Impress to add a graph to a worksheet, format the graph titles, and then print both the worksheet data and the graph.

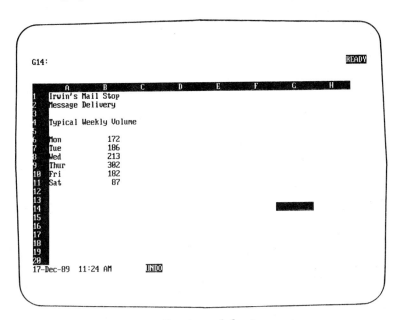

Fig. 8.1. *The Irwin's mail stop worksheet.*

Charles Irwin needs to track his daily message-delivery volume to help assign additional couriers. For that, he's set up a simple 1-2-3 worksheet to track total day-by-day deliveries. Set up the the Irwin worksheet as you see it in figure 8.1. Charles has already created a simple 1-2-3 graph that lets him view the data graphically, but he wants to combine both the data and graph in a single, attractively formatted printout for his records. To see the graph Charles created, follow these steps:

1. Select **/Graph Type B**ar to create a bar graph.

2. Select **X** from the /Graph menu and select the range **A6..A11** to include the days of the week.

3. Select **A** from the /Graph menu and select the range **B6..B11** to include the day-by-day figures.

4. Select **/Graph O**ptions **T**itles **F**irst and enter **\a4** as the main graph title.

5. Select **/Graph Options Titles Second** and enter **\a1** as the graph subtitle.

6. Select **View** from the /Graph menu to see the graph; then press Esc several times to return to the worksheet.

Now it is time to add in Impress so that you can mix the worksheet and the graph on a single screen. If you are using 1-2-3 Release 2.01, be sure the Add-in Manager is added to your driver set by typing **ADD-MGR 123.SET** at the DOS prompt. If you use a driver set other than 123.SET, substitute its name for 123.SET. Also, make sure 123.DYN exists in the directory in which 1-2-3 is installed. If not, you may need to copy it from the PrintGraph disk. To start Impress, follow these steps:

1. Press Esc then select **Quit** to return to your worksheet.

2. Select **/Add-in Attach** and choose IMPRESS.ADN from the list of add-ins that appears.

3. Select **7** from the next menu so that you can invoke Impress in the future with the Alt-F7 key combination.

Now, Impress is attached. Notice that the screen looks different (see fig. 8.2.). The worksheet background has changed color, and the worksheet text now appears in a different typeface on the screen. If you press the 1-2-3 menu key (/), the standard 1-2-3 menu appears and you can carry out the full array of 1-2-3 commands.

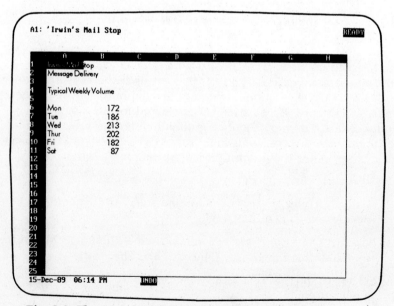

Fig. 8.2. *The 1-2-3 worksheet as it appears in Impress.*

If, instead, you invoke Impress, the Impress menu appears on the screen, as shown in figure 8.3. To invoke Impress, press Esc to return to the Ready mode. Then, press Alt-F7.

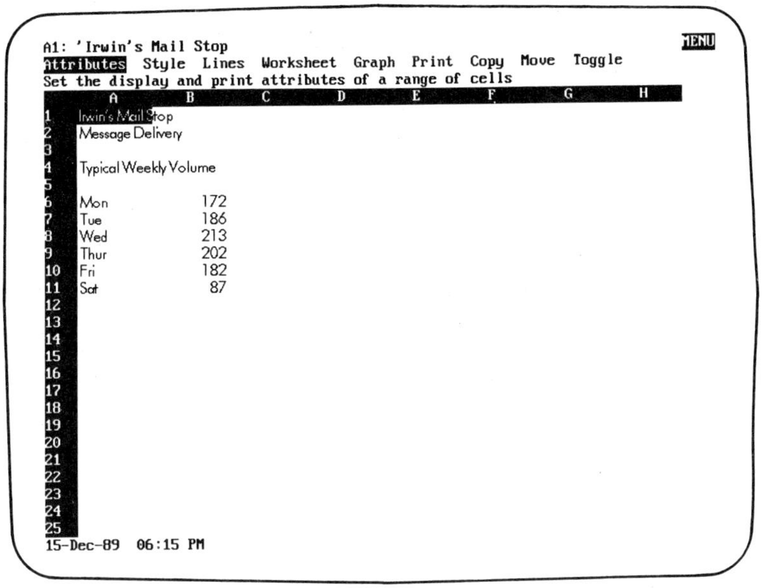

A1: 'Irwin's Mail Stop   MENU
Attributes Style Lines Worksheet Graph Print Copy Move Toggle
Set the display and print attributes of a range of cells

	A	B	C	D	E	F	G	H
1	Irwin's Mail Stop							
2	Message Delivery							
3								
4	Typical Weekly Volume							
5								
6	Mon	172						
7	Tue	186						
8	Wed	213						
9	Thur	202						
10	Fri	182						
11	Sat	87						

15-Dec-89 06:15 PM

Fig. 8.3. The Impress menu.

Most of the options on the Impress menu pertain to improving the appearance of worksheets for printing. The Graph option lets you add a graph to the worksheet, so go ahead and select Graph. When you do, you'll see a new menu with a set of eight choices for working with graphs. The first choice, Add, allows you to add an existing graph—the current graph, a named graph, or a PIC file graph—to a blank area of the worksheet. To add the graph you prepared for Irwin earlier, select Add and then Current. Then, when prompted, point to the range in which Impress should fit the graph. Select **C1..G12** as the range for the graph and press Enter. You will see the graph appear, as shown in figure 8.4.

Because the current graph is linked to the data also visible on the screen, you should be able to modify a data value and see an immediate change in the graph. Try it by adding 100 to the value for Thursday. Replace the current figure, 202, with 302, and note the new appearance of the graph, as seen in figure 8.5. The ability of Impress to display both worksheet data and a graphic depiction of that data offers the same benefits as the graph window feature of 1-2-3 Release 3. You can perform visual what-ifs, modifying data and immediately inspecting the differences in the resulting graph.

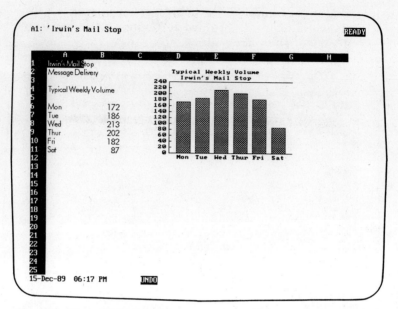

Fig. 8.4. *The current graph superimposed on the worksheet.*

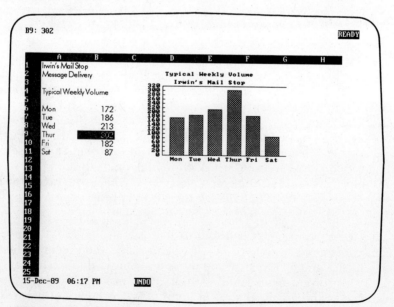

Fig. 8.5. *The revised graph.*

As with Allways, Impress offers no direct manipulation of the graph elements superimposed on worksheets. You cannot directly modify the positioning and font choices for the text in your graphs, for example. Instead, you must rely on the capability of Impress to format text on the underlying worksheet. To create the illusion of modifying text in the graph, you can actually add text to the worksheet underneath and format it with the commands of Impress. To replace the default text font used for the current Charles Irwin graph titles, you can delete the current graph titles and add new titles in worksheet cells at the same location. Then, you can use Impress to select an attractive bold font for the titles.

To try setting up titles you can format with Impress, you must first delete the existing graph titles. To do so, press the slash key (\) to bring up the 1-2-3 menu. Select /Graph Options Titles First and then press Esc followed by Enter to clear the current first title. Return to the Titles menu to remove the graph's Second title also. Then, select Quit twice to return to the worksheet screen. To see the change take effect, press Recalculate (F9).

Now, in cell E1, you can enter the text **Irwin's Mail Stop**. The title appears in the default Helvetica font. To select a different font, bring up the Impress menu with Alt-F7, select **Attributes**, and then select **Font**. Try selecting G-TMS12, a 12-point Times Roman font. When Impress prompts you for a range to format, press Enter to accept the current range, E1..E1. The new Times Roman font is surely an improvement, but an even better step would be to select a bold version of the same font. Again, bring up the Impress menu with Alt-F7, select Attributes, and then select Bold. Press Enter to format E1..E1.

To finish the graph, enter the text **Typical Weekly Volume** below the graph into cell E12. Format it with the 12-point Times Roman font by selecting Alt-F7 Attributes Font G-TMS12 and then pressing Enter to accept the range E12..E12. The finished worksheet/graph combination is shown in figure 8.6.

To print both the worksheet and graph side by side on a page, select Print from the Impress menu. Check Hardware Printer under the Print menu quickly to be sure Impress uses the correct driver for your printer. If you move the cell pointer from one cryptic printer driver name to the next with the arrow keys, you will see a full description of the printer driver in the edit panel at the top left corner of the screen. Move your cell pointer to the name of your printer and press Enter. You will return to the Print menu. Before you can print, you must specify the range you want to print, just as you do when you print a region of a worksheet in 1-2-3.

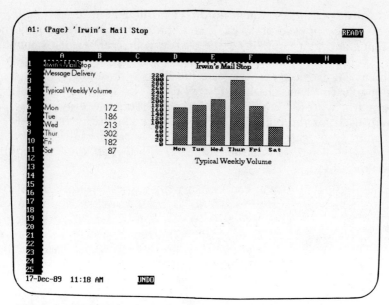

Fig. 8.6. The finished worksheet/graph combination.

Press Esc or select **Q**uit, then select **R**ange. Position the cursor at the top left corner of the range you want to print—in this case cell A1, and highlight the range A1..G12. Before you select **G**o to print the range, take a quick look at the current print settings by selecting **S**tatus from the Print menu. The Status screen appears, as shown in figure 8.7.

A second selection on the Impress Print menu, Preview, shows you a full-screen representation of how your printed output will appear. Select **P**review to see the screen shown in figure 8.8.

As you work more with Impress, you will see how it combines the best graph formatting features of 1-2-3 Release 2.2 used with Allways and 1-2-3 Release 3. Impress offers the worksheet and graph publishing features of Allways and the graph window feature of Release 3 all in one.

2D Graphics

Adding 2D-Graphics from Intex Solutions to 1-2-3 Release 2.01 or 2.2 is like giving the aging graph features of 1-2-3 a transplant. Out goes the old /Graphics menu to be replaced by a bigger, more capable, and fuller featured menu with a host of additional options. The graphs you

```
A1: {Page} 'Irwin's Mail Stop                                    MENU
Range  Status  File  Preview  Layout  Hardware  Options  Go  Quit
Toggle display of Impress printing parameters summary window

  Layout:                              Margins (in inches)
    Print range....... A1..G12
                                           Top 0.5
    Paper type....... Letter
    Dimensions....... 8.5 by 11 inches
                                       Left          Right
    Title columns....                  0.5           0.5
    Title rows.......
    Compression...... None
    Orientation...... Portrait             Bottom 0.55

    Header.......                      Options:
    Footer.......                        Begin....... 1
                                         End......... 999
  Hardware:                              Copies...... 1
    Printer..... SHP4LASR                Wait........ No
    Interface... Parallel 1              Grid........ No
    Cartridges..                         Coordinates. No




15-Dec-89  06:23 PM
```

Fig. 8.7. *The Impress Print Status screen.*

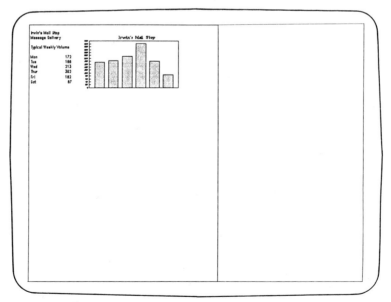

Fig. 8.8. *The Impress Print Preview screen.*

make with these options—either new graph types or graphs with new features—can be saved as PIC files and printed with the 1-2-3 PrintGraph program.

The new 2D-Graphics menu that you can use in place of the existing /Graphics menu offers five new graph types: mixed, filled-line, polar graph, circle, and hi-lo-close-open. Most of these are graph types you can find in programs dedicated to graphing, but never before have they been a part of 1-2-3. Mixed, filled-line, and hi-lo-close-open (HLCO) graphs are also in the new graphing repertoire of 1-2-3 Release 3.

The 2D-Graphics menu also offers six additional series, so you are no longer limited to the six data ranges A through F. You can enter data in a full twelve data ranges, A through L. And, in addition to the new data ranges, 2D-Graphics augments the graphing commands of 1-2-3 with a variety of graph formatting improvements and additions to the current options. 2D-Graphics lets you change the axis scaling to logarithmic, for example, and specify precise graph color combinations.

After you attach 2D-Graphics to 1-2-3, you can invoke it at any time to bring up the replacement graph menu. Figure 8.9 compares the standard 1-2-3 /Graph menu before you invoke 2D-Graphics (above) with the replacement graph menu from 2D-Graphics.

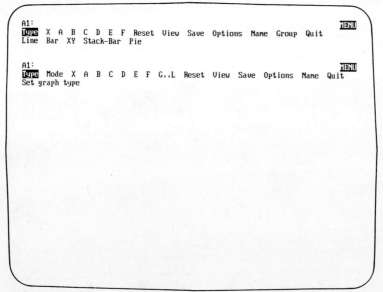

Fig. 8.9. The 1-2-3 /Graph menu (above) and the 2D-Graphics graph menu (below).

For access to the options of 2D-Graphics, you simply use the
2D-Graphics menu whenever you would normally select from the
standard 1-2-3 /Graph menu. The new menu simply augments the
standard 1-2-3 graphing commands. All of the original /Graph menu
commands are still there.

To try using 2D-Graphics to create a few new graph types, follow along
with the next example:

Charles Irwin needs a few new graphs. He needs to compare the
number of messages his service delivers each day of the week with
the number of couriers he has available. Normally, he might create a
bar graph with two sets of bars or a line graph with two lines. With
2D-Graphics, he can create a mixed graph displaying one series with
bars and the other with lines. To create the graphs for Charles, add the
new figures in column C of figure 8.10 to the previous Irwin
worksheet.

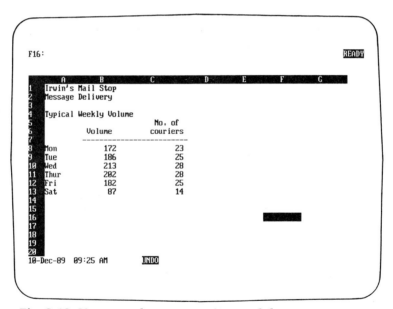

Fig. 8.10. Message volume vs. couriers worksheet.

Make sure 2D-Graphics is attached to 1-2-3. If it is not, select /Add-in
Attach from the 1-2-3 menu and then select 2D-Graphics from the
list of available add-ins. Assign the new add-in to the Alt-F8 key
combination by selecting 8 from the menu that follows. Now, you can
begin setting up the mixed graph just as you would set up any graph
within 1-2-3. First, you select a graph type, and then you assign certain
worksheet ranges to graph data ranges. By default, any worksheet range

you assign to data ranges A through F will appear in a mixed graph as bars. Any range you assign to graph data ranges G through L will appear in a mixed graph as lines. You can change this designation if you wish.

To assign a worksheet range to the x-axis, first invoke 2D-Graphics and then select **X** from the graph menu that appears. Highlight the range A8..A13 and then press Enter. To assign the volume figures to data range A, select **A** and then select the range **B8..B13**. To assign the "No. of Couriers" figures to data range G, select **G..L** on the menu, and then select **G** from the submenu that appears. Highlight C8..C13 before pressing Enter and then select **Quit** to return to the main graph menu. Set the graph type to **Bar** by selecting **Type Bar** from the menu.

Take a look at the graph with the **View** option and notice that both series are represented as bars. To set the display of the second series (the G data range) to lines, press ESC, then select **Mode Line** and then **Quit**. Now, view the graph again and notice that the graph contains both bars and a line.

When you select **Mode Line**, you were informing 2D-Graphics that you want data ranges G through L (called the *Selected* series by 2D-Graphics) to be displayed as lines.

Finish the graph by entering titles and a legend just as you would in 1-2-3 without 2D-Graphics. You can save the graph as a PIC file using the Save command on the graph menu just as you would from the standard 1-2-3 /Graph menu. Your completed graph should look like the one in figure 8.11.

Creating a Dual Y-Axis Graph

Another way Irwin might look at the same data is to plot each of the series against its own y-axis. By plotting Message Volume against the standard y-axis and creating a second y-axis against which to plot the number of couriers, you can create a graph that allows for easier comparison between the two series.

Each of the y-axes in a dual y-axis graph is scaled automatically according to the range of data plotted against it. The variation in each series is now plain to see as each is plotted against the entire height of the graph. Figure 8.12 shows the dual y-axis graph Irwin will create. No. of Couriers is plotted against the left y-axis, scaled from 0 to 30; Message volume is plotted against the right y-axis, scaled from 0 to 250. Notice how easy it is to see that the number of couriers varied in close accordance with the message volume on any single day.

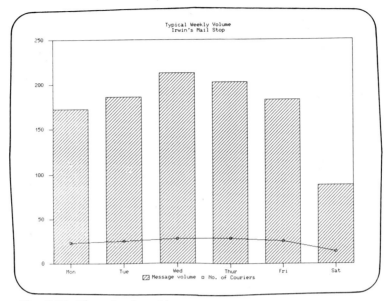

Fig. 8.11. *The mixed graph.*

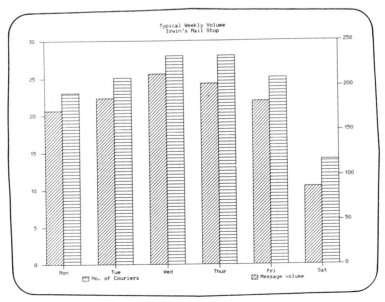

Fig. 8.12. *The dual-axis Irwin graph.*

To set up the dual y-axis graph, use the same worksheet as in the previous example. Leave all series assignments, graph type settings, and legend and title choices the same, but select **Mode Dual**-axes to set up a dual-axis graph. As soon as you do, any series in the range A through F is plotted against the left y-axis, and any series in the range G through L is plotted against the right y-axis. 2D-Graphics calls this second y-axis the *w-axis*. Notice also that 2D-Graphics automatically splits the legends so that each is positioned near the axis it relates to. The legend entry for the No. of Couriers series is near the left y-axis to indicate that the No. of Couriers data is plotted against that axis.

Creating a Filled-Line Graph

One additional type of graph Charles Irwin needs compares the relative volumes of three different types of messages delivered: PubBoard, Private, and Omnichat. He wants to show the relative breakdown of his entire pool of message traffic, the total message volume, and how both vary day to day. The filled-line graph produced by 2D-Graphics, often called an area chart, would be perfect for this task.

To create the filled-line graph, create the worksheet shown in figure 8.13.

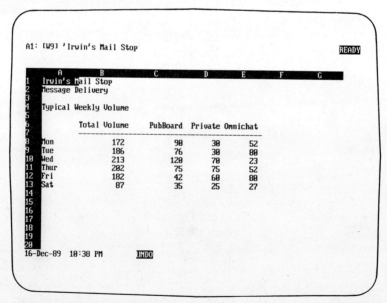

Fig. 8.13. The Irwin worksheet showing message traffic breakdown.

Begin by invoking 2D-Graphics and selecting **Type Filled-Line** to choose the area graph type. First, assign the days of the week in worksheet range A8..A13 to data range X. Then, assign the PubBoard numbers in the worksheet range C8..C13 to the A data range; assign the Private numbers in the range D8..D13 to the B data range; and assign the Omnichat numbers in the range E8..E13 to the C data range. Take a look at the graph by selecting **View**. You need only add titles and the legend to have the completed graph shown in figure 8.14.

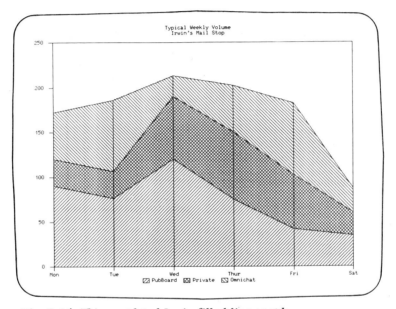

Fig. 8.14. *The completed Irwin filled-line graph.*

Examining Other 2D-Graphics Graph Types

2D-Graphics adds several other graph types to the 1-2-3 arsenal. The *circle graph,* also called a *bubble graph,* plots values against two numeric axes. The values plotted are represented by circles whose radius is determined by the value. Circle graphs can show correspondence of three different factors.

The graph shown in figure 8.15, for example, compares Irwin's pricing, profit, and volume. Irwin assigned the profit figures to the X data range and the pricing figures to the Y data range. He assigned the volume levels he observed at each price/profit point to the A data range and selected Circle as the type of graph for 2D-Graphics to create. The

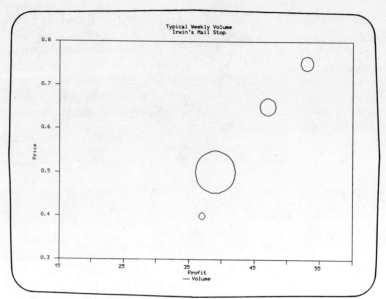

Fig. 8.15. The Irwin circle graph.

program represented the volume levels with circles of varying sizes on the graph.

The hi-lo-close-open (HLCO) graph shown in figure 8.16 depicts the performance of Irwin's stock over the preceding week. To create the HLCO graph, Irwin entered high, low, closing, and opening prices of his stocks into four ranges and chose Hi-Lo-Close-Open as the graph type. Then, he assigned the high, low, closing and opening prices in his stock-tracking worksheet to the first four data ranges, A through D. 2D-Graphics automatically creates an HLCO graph having vertical lines with tick mark extensions to the left and to the right. The upper and lower ends of the vertical bars represent the high and low prices of the stock. The tick mark to the left of the bar represents the opening price, and the tick mark to the right of the bar represents the closing price.

The *angle-radius graph,* also called the *polar graph,* is another graph type added by 2D-Graphics. Data points are arranged around a center point, with distance from the center representing value. Polar graphs are useful in highly specialized scientific applications. The graph shown in figure 8.17 represents a driver's visibility in all directions in a new-model automobile. From this graph, you can see that visibility forward and to the sides is adequate and visibility to the rear is sufficient. But two blind spots, one toward the rear on each side, may be dangerous.

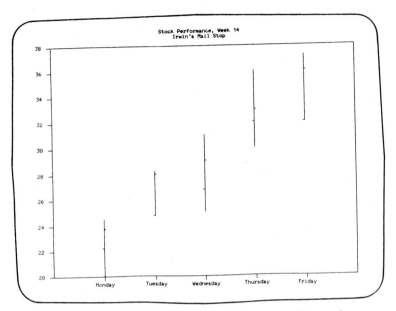

Fig. 8.16. *A Hi-Lo-Close-Open graph showing Irwin's stock performance.*

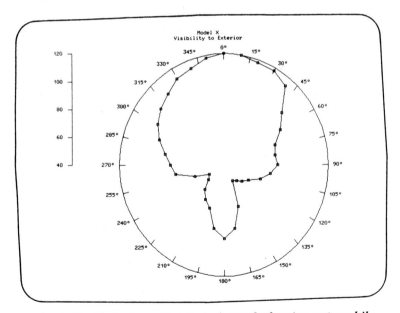

Fig. 8.17. *An angle-radius (polar) graph showing automobile driver visibility.*

3D Graphics

3D-Graphics, another add-in from Intex Solutions, also replaces the standard 1-2-3 Release 2.0, 2.01, or 2.2 /Graph menu, but this time with commands that produce three-dimensional graphs exclusively. These commands produce surface, bar, and line graphs with depth as well as width and height.

Figure 8.18 shows a sample graph produced by 3D-Graphics in combination with 1-2-3 Release 2.2. In essence, 3D-Graphics takes a standard graph and lays it on its back such that the x-axis still runs left and right, but the y-axis now recedes from the foreground. A third axis, the *z-axis*, is the new scale along which your worksheet data values are measured. In the figure 8.18 graph, the z-axis is scaled from 0 to 60, and the height of the bars represents the value for each data point.

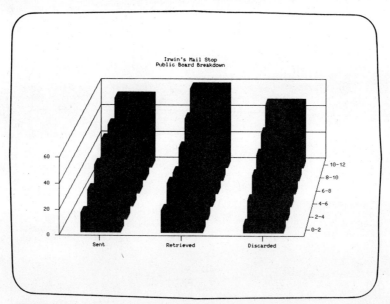

Fig. 8.18. *A sample 3D graph produced by 3D-Graphics.*

The graphs produced by 3D-Graphics are stunning in appearance, especially when displayed in color, but they provide more impact than information. Take a look at the graph in figure 8.18, for example, and guess at the number of messages retrieved in the 4-6 category. You may find it impossible to judge actual values when a graph's data is displayed in 3D, but you can get a good sense of how the values compare in relation to one another.

To see 3D-Graphics in action, try a few sample graphs using the worksheet data supplied in figure 8.19. This data represents number of callers in three age categories at two-hour intervals throughout the day and night.

```
A15: [W9] '10 PM                                              READY

          A        B        C          D          E          F
 1 Irwin's Mail Stop
 2 Usage Tracking
 3                          18-25      25-35      35 and above
 4 Midnight                  9          6          4
 5 2 AM                      3          1          1
 6 4 AM                      1          0          0
 7 6 AM                      4          2          3
 8 8 AM                      5          3          5
 9 10 AM                     3          5          2
10 Noon                      2          3          2
11 2 PM                      4          2          1
12 4 PM                      5          4          2
13 6 PM                      7          5          4
14 8 PM                      9          9          6
15 10 PM                     9          7          8
16
17
18
19
20
16-Dec-89  11:50 PM       UNDO
```

Fig. 8.19. *Irwin usage tracking worksheet.*

Begin by attaching 3D-Graphics to 1-2-3. Select /**Add-in Attach** and choose 3D-Graphics from the list of add-ins. Assign 3D-Graphics to the key combination Alt-F9 by selecting 9 from the following menu. Then, press Esc to remove the /Add-in menu to set up the figure 8.19 worksheet as you normally would in 1-2-3.

To set up the first graph, press Alt-F9 to summon 3D-Graphics. When you do, you will see the menu shown in figure 8.20. Just as with 2D-Graphics, the 3D-Graphics menu is a functional replacement for the standard /Graph menu. Start by selecting **Type** **B**ar **F**illed to set up a bar graph with solidly filled bars. Next, specify the X data range. The X data range, corresponding to the horizontal x-axis, lies horizontally on the worksheet. In this case, it is comprised of the column headings in row 3. Specify the range C3..E3 as the X data range. Next, specify the Y data range, the row labels at the left of the graph. Select A4..A15 as the Y data range.

Now, you only need to specify the A data range, the actual data values. The data values in this worksheet fill the range C4.. E15, so specify **C4..E15** as the A data range. To see the graph, select **View**. You can use

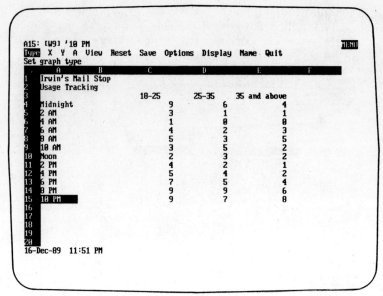

Fig. 8.20. *The 3D-Graphics menu.*

the Options Titles menu choices to enter x-, y-, and z-axis titles. The graph with titles added appears in figure 8.21. If you don't see the left and right "walls" in the graph background, select **Display Axis Yes** on the 3D-Graphics menu to turn them on and then view your graph again.

3D Graphics is somewhat rigid in the way it plots your data. Because you can specify only data range A as the single worksheet range, you must conform to the way the program arranges your data. You should be sure to specify the column headings that lie in a row at the top of your data as the x data range and the row labels that lie in a column to the left of your data as the y data range. The result, in this case, is a graph with three data series that progress from the front of the graph toward the back.

To make this graph much easier to read, it would be helpful to rotate the graph on its bottom to view it from the side. Indeed, 3D-Graphics offers Rotation as one of the choices under its Display menu. To rotate the graph, press Esc to return to the 3D-Graphics menu if you need to, and then select **Display Rotation**. Select 90 to rotate the graph 90 degrees and then view the graph once more. Now the graph looks like the one shown in fig. 8.22.

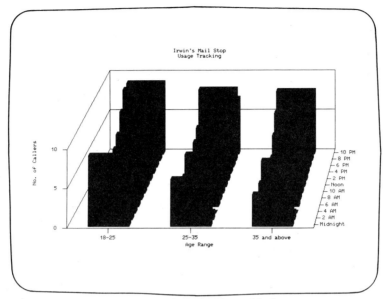

Fig. 8.21. *The 3D bar graph with titles added.*

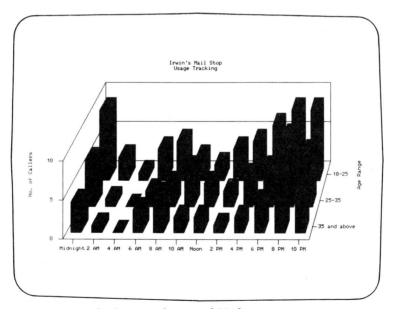

Fig. 8.22. *The bar graph rotated 90 degrees.*

The individual data points in the graph are now much easier to read, and the progression of time now proceeds right to left. The graph's meaning is easier to interpret.

Perhaps a better representation of this data would be with lines rather than bars. With lines, the viewer could see the trend across time more easily. To try a line graph, select **Type Lines Filled** on the 3D-Graphics Menu. You will see the graph shown in figure 8.23.

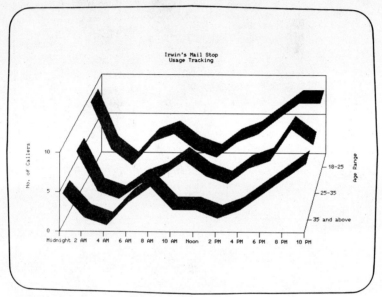

Fig. 8.23. The usage tracking data represented with lines.

Still another choice for displaying the same data might be with a joined bar graph, as shown in figure 8.24. This graph, which displays a solid mass under the lines of a line graph conveys a sense of volume, ideal for this graph. To create the joined bar graph in figure 8.24, select **Type Joined-Bar Filled.** Another selection on the 3D Graphics menu, Financial-Bar, is similar to a standard bar chart, except that negative values are shown in color or protruding from the bottom of the graph.

A fourth representation for the same data is the surface graph, shown in figure 8.25. This graph also represents volume while emphasizing the general pattern of your observations from one category to the next. To display a surface graph, select **Type Surface** from the 3D Graphics menu. Then, select either **Visible** or **Hidden** to determine whether you will see those "hidden" parts of the surface that are obscured by higher parts in front.

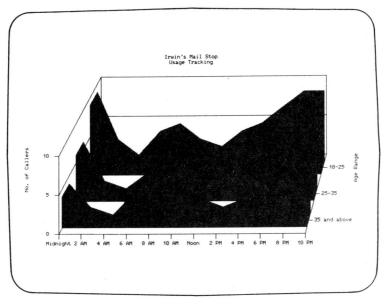

Fig. 8.24. *The Irwin data represented in a joined bar graph.*

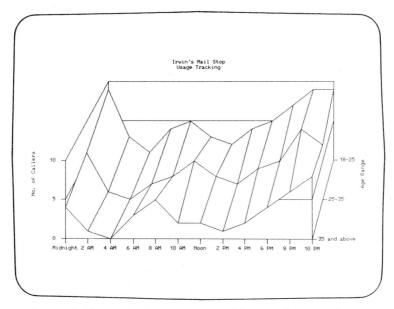

Fig. 8.25. *The Irwin data represented in a surface graph.*

After you select an appropriate graph type, you can make some fine-tuning adjustments to the appearance of the graph with other Display options besides Rotation. Viewpoint gives you a choice of three angles of view on the graph: **H**igh, **M**edium, and **L**ow. Medium is the default. Figure 8.26 shows the result of the three viewpoint settings.

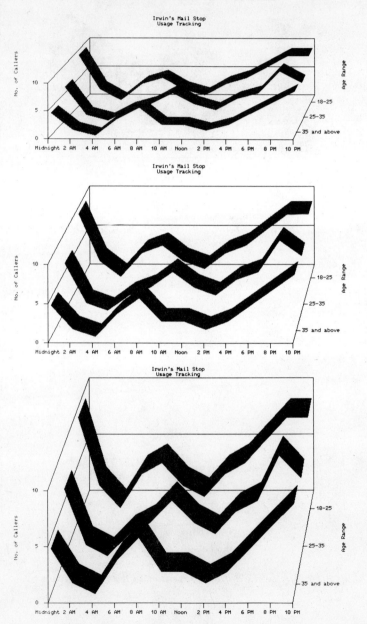

Fig. 8.26. *Top to bottom: Low, Medium, and High Viewpoint settings for a line graph.*

When you finish a graph made with 3D-Graphics, you can save it as a standard 1-2-3 PIC file using the Save command on the menu. Later, you can print the file using PrintGraph just as you would any 1-2-3 PIC file.

Summary

Using the add-ins described in this chapter, you can redress a few of the shortcomings of graphmaking in 1-2-3. Impress gives you an interactive graphics screen with which you can format both a worksheet and a graph for printing. 2D-Graphics and 3D-Graphics offer useful new graph types you can make and save as PIC files for printing.

The following chapter lists some of the more common complaints heard from 1-2-3 users when creating graphs. You will learn troubleshooting techniques for these common problems.

9

Troubleshooting Graphs

Even veteran 1-2-3 users sometimes run into snags while creating graphs. Some of the problems they come across stem from simple lapses of memory. They forgot to talk to 1-2-3 in the language it expects, so it refuses them some trivial task. The result can be hair-pulling frustration. But some problems you may encounter stem not from the program's inability to forgive, but from its simple idiosyncrasies. You may need a method of getting around 1-2-3's interpretation of your data. The troubleshooting tips in this chapter forewarn you of some of 1-2-3's more frustrating foibles in graphmaking.

Graph Problems: General

"I saved a graph, but I can't retrieve the graph with the worksheet for editing."

The /Graph Save command saves a graph on disk as a PIC file. You cannot pull a PIC file back into 1-2-3 for editing. To save a graph to

271

retrieve it later within 1-2-3, name it using the /Graph Name Create command. Later, when you want to edit the graph, you can use the /Graph Name Use command to retrieve the graph settings sheet.

Remember, you must save a worksheet using /File Save after you use the /Graph Name Create command. This is so that the named graph gets saved with the worksheet. Otherwise, if you retrieve another graph or quit from 1-2-3 without saving the worksheet, you will lose your named graphs.

"Recreating multiple graphs within one worksheet is too tedious."

1-2-3 can have only a single currently active graph, so you must create and name each one separately, if you want to recall automatically many graphs.

The solution is to save a library of graphs within a single worksheet. To do this, specify the first completed graph and then use the /Graph Name Create command to save the settings under a name you choose. Next, reset all graph settings with the /Graph Reset Graph command. Repeat the process for each graph, giving each a different name. Then you can recall any of these graphs with the Graph Name Use command. When you save the file, you also save the graph names and settings associated with the worksheet file.

Bar Graph Problems

"The y-axis of my bar graph is always zero no matter what lower limit I set."

In 1-2-3 Release 2.2 and earlier versions, bar graphs always have a lower limit of zero, even if you set another lower limit for the y-axis scale. 1-2-3 Release 3 lets you scale a bar graph y-axis from a starting point other than zero.

Bar graphs let you compare data by showing the relative height of bars. These heights indicate no more than the magnitude of difference between values—if the bars all start at zero. Starting the bars at any value other than zero can misrepresent, so earlier versions of 1-2-3 did not allow it.

"The data-labels are over the bars even if I select Center, Left, or Right."

Data-labels always appear above the bars of a bar graph if you choose any setting other than Below for the data-label position. If you select

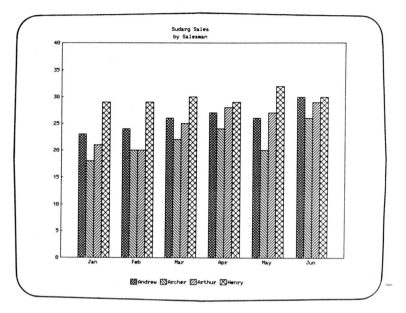

Fig. 9.1. *A bar graph with the lower limit set to 10.*

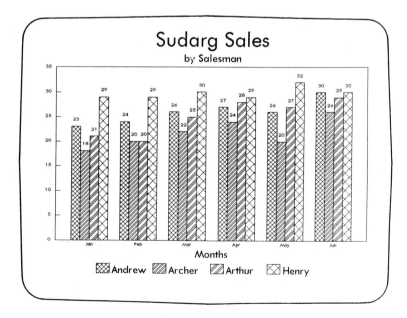

Fig. 9.2. *The data-labels here are above the bars.*

Below, the data-label for a bar appears within the bar just below the top of the bar.

If the data represented by the bars is negative, the bars point below the x-axis rather than upward, toward the top of the chart. In that case, Above and Below are exactly reversed. Any setting other than Above will cause the data-labels to appear just below the bars. Below will cause the data-labels to appear within the bars just above the bottom.

The data-labels of stack-bar charts always appear inside their corresponding bar segments.

"I don't always get a hatch pattern combination that I like."

1-2-3 sets hatch patterns by default for each graph range, A-F. Many users do not like the patterns 1-2-3 chooses for the B and C ranges. If you have fewer than six ranges to graph, just skip over those ranges whose patterns you don't want to use—you do not need to specify the ranges in order.

Another solution, available for users of Release 3, is to specify the hatch patterns manually, using the command **Graph Options Advanced Hatches**. See Chapter 6 for a comprehensive discussion of Release 3 hatch patterns in the section, "Setting Graph Hatch Patterns."

"I want the bars to appear separated, but they are placed side by side."

In a bar graph of multiple ranges, each graph range touches the one adjacent to it, even when there is enough space to spread them apart. The solution is to specify a range of blank cells, or zeroes, as a dummy range. 1-2-3 will display the dummy range as a bar with zero height, which in effect spreads apart your graph bars.

Line Graph Problems

"I can't get the lines in my line graph."

Check the data that you selected for graphing. Make sure none of the cells in the data ranges you chose are blank or formatted as labels rather than values. If 1-2-3 encounters a blank cell or a label in the middle of a data range, the program may draw only the data points for the line and not its connecting lines.

Blank cells in the range are obvious. Cells formatted as labels take a little more sleuthing to find. Check each cell individually by positioning the cursor on it; press Edit (F2), and check the edit panel. Make sure

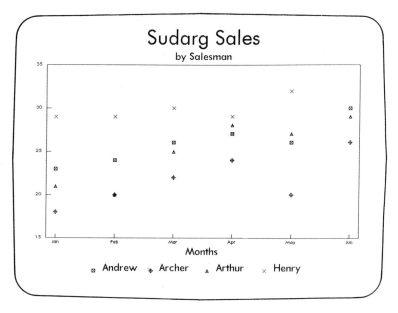

Fig. 9.3. *A line graph without lines.*

that its contents are not preceded by one of the three label prefixes: ', ", or ^.

Also verify that /Graph Options Format is set to either **B**oth or **L**ines. If /GOF is set to **S**ymbols or **N**either, you will see only the data points in the graph, or you will see neither lines nor data points.

"OK, I used /Graph Options Format to get Both or Lines, and I got neither."

Be careful not to press Esc to leave the /Graph Options Format Graph menu. If you press Esc after selecting Lines, Symbols, Both, or Neither, 1-2-3 defaults to Neither when you exit the menu. Instead, leave the menu by choosing **Q**uit.

Bar and Line Graph Problems

"The y-axis lower limit I choose becomes the upper limit, too."

You must enter a value for both the upper and lower scale values if you want to manually select the axis scaling. If you enter a value for

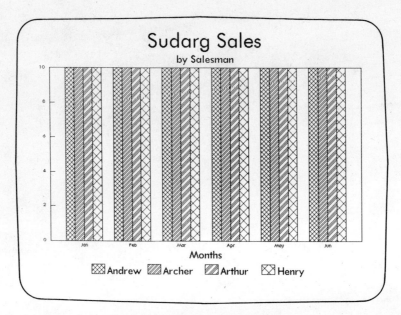

Fig. 9.4. *A bar graph with a lower limit set to 10.*

the lower limit only, 1-2-3 may use that value for the upper limit, instead. 1-2-3 assumes you meant to set the y-axis upper limit.

If you set a lower limit of 10, for example, and fail to set an upper limit, 1-2-3 scales the y-axis from 0 to 10.

"My x-axis title is not centered."

If you find that the x-axis title you entered is not properly centered, you must add blank spaces manually in front of the the title to push it to the right. The problem is most noticeable when an indicator appears with the x-axis titles—most commonly with XY graphs.

If the graph has a legend, you will want to center both the x-axis title and the legend. You cannot move the legend, so you should leave the title centered over the legend, even if the two are improperly aligned.

"The y-axis of my graph displays asterisks."

If you manually set a y-axis value width with the /Graph Options Scale **Y**-Scale **W**idth **M**anual command, that width may be too narrow to accommodate the current y-axis numbers. Try letting 1-2-3 select a width for you automatically. Use the /Graph Options Scale **Y**-Scale **W**idth **A**utomatic command. If you still want to use the manual-width setting, type in a larger number for the width, or use the right-arrow

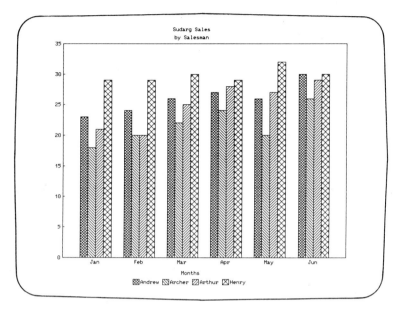

Fig. 9.5. *A graph with an improperly centered x-axis title.*

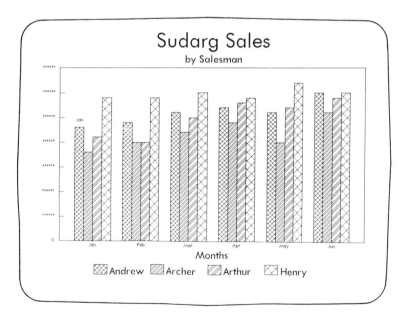

Fig. 9.6. *Asterisks replacing numbers as y-axis labels.*

key to increase the width until the numbers appear when you view the graph. Unexpected asterisks in place of y-axis labels can stem from the same cause. If the Y-Scale exponent is incorrectly set, 1-2-3 may multiply your y-axis values by a power of 10, making a scale too great to fit your manual-width setting. Try using /Graph Options Scale Y-Scale Exponent Automatic to correct the problem.

Pie Graph Problems

"There's no crosshatching in my pie slices."

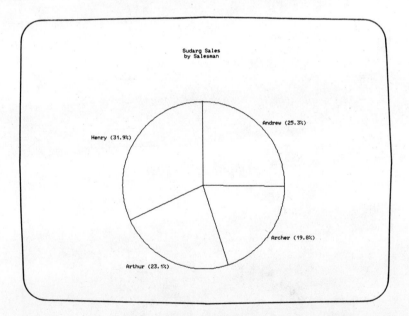

Fig. 9.7. *A graph without its hatch patterns.*

Missing pie-graph hatch patterns may occur if the range numbers you assigned to the B data range are formatted as labels rather than values. Remember, 1-2-3 uses numbers you assign to the B data range to set the hatch patterns for pie slices.

Check the B data range numbers by highlighting one of the cells and pressing Edit (F2). The contents of the cell will appear in the edit panel near the top of the screen. The number you entered should not be preceded by a label prefix (', ", or ^).

Release 3 Graph Problems

"The y-axis indicator reads Thousandths or Millionths, not Thousands or Millions. How can I get rid of the 'ths'?"

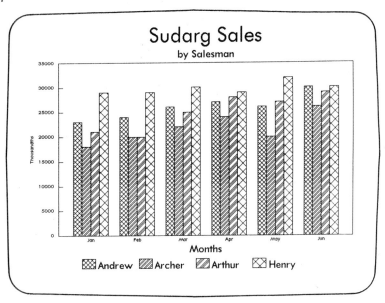

Fig. 9.8. *An indicator reading "Thousandths."*

If you enter a negative number rather than a positive number when you set the exponent for an indicator in Release 3, 1-2-3 will add the "ths." This assumes that you want the viewer to multiply the graphed numbers by a negative exponent of 10 rather than a positive 10. For example, to instruct viewers to multiply the values by 1,000 to get the actual numbers, you can enter an exponent of 3. As a result, 1-2-3 divides the numbers by 1 to the third power (1,000) and supplies an indicator of "Thousands." If you enter a negative 3 as an exponent, 1-2-3 multiplies the numbers by 1,000 and supplies an indicator of "Thousandths." In fact, the numbers along the y-axis may become so wide that they are replaced by asterisks until you increase the width of the y-axis labels.

To resolve the problem, select /Graph Options Scale Y-Scale Exponent Automatic to let 1-2-3 determine the most appropriate exponent setting.

"My graph doesn't appear in the window."

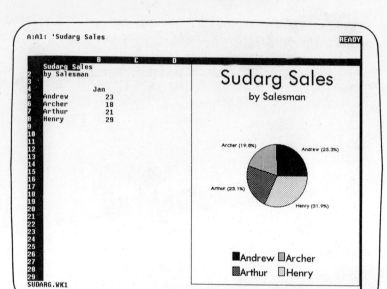

Fig. 9.9. *A graph in a graph window.*

Not all graphics cards support the display of graph windows in 1-2-3 Release 3. Among the cards that do not display graph windows are the IBM Color Graphics Adapter (CGA) and the Hercules Graphics Card in 80 x 25 mode. If you have one of these cards, you can display a graph using the entire screen with /Graph View, but the graph will not appear in a window. If you use a Hercules Graphics Card, you can select its 90 x 45 resolution mode for a graph window. Of course, the IBM Monochrome Display Adapter (MDA) simply does not display graphics.

If you are using a graphics card that supports graph windows, be sure to check /Worksheet Global Default Status to make sure the correct screen display is chosen.

If everything looks right, check these possibilities:

☐ Make sure you set both the upper and lower limits of the y-axis scale if you chose to manually scale the y-axis.

☐ Make sure you set the lower y-axis scale limit lower than the upper y-axis scale limit if you manually scale the y-axis.

☐ Make sure you defined an A data range for a pie graph.

☐ Make sure you defined a range other than the X data range for an XY graph.

☐ Make sure you designated either the A and B data ranges or the E and F data ranges for the HLCO graph.

"My graph text is cut short in the graph window display."

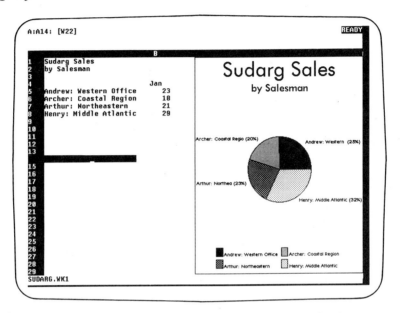

Fig. 9.10. *Pie-slice labels truncated in graph window display.*

1-2-3 may cut short some of the text in your graph when it is displayed if it cannot fit properly in the graph window. 1-2-3 will not cut short the same text when you print the graph, and it never cuts short the actual text you have entered for the graph.

To alleviate this problem, you can make the graph window larger, or you can use shorter text. Another remedy is to use the /Graph View command to display your graph using the full screen.

"Automatic Graphing mistook my worksheet columns for rows."

To instruct 1-2-3 Release 3 to correctly interpret the layout of the data within a range, you can use the /Worksheet Global Default Graph menu option and select either Columnwise or Rowwise. Columnwise instructs 1-2-3 that the data in the worksheet is arranged in columns. Rowwise instructs 1-2-3 Release 3 that the data is arranged in rows. To make your selection a default for future 1-2-3 sessions, select Update.

You can manually select either columnwise or rowwise when you automatically create a graph. Use the /**Graph G**roup [Range] **Columnwise** or /**Graph G**roup [Range] **Rowwise** menu options.

Note that after you use /**Graph G**roup, automatic graphing is no longer available for another range within the worksheet. You must first clear the old graph data ranges with /**Graph R**eset before you can use automatic graphing or /**Graph G**roup again. If you try to create an automatic graph with the F10 key, 1-2-3 Release 3 creates a graph using the ranges defined as part of the previous automatic graph, not the new range of data that the cursor is resting on.

"Automatic graphing omitted some data selected with Graph Group."

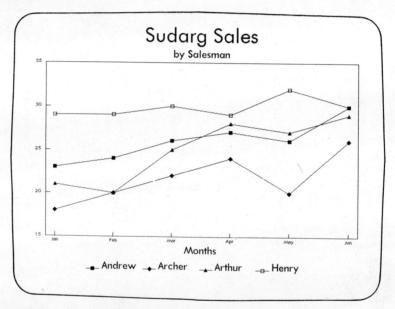

Fig. 9.11. *A /Graph Group graph showing the first row used as x-axis labels.*

Automatic Graphing (using the F10 key to generate a graph) and the /**Graph G**roup command fundamentally differ in how they treat the first column or row of data you have selected.

With Release 3, when you use the /**Graph G**roup key to create a graph automatically, 1-2-3 interprets the first column or row as the X data range. Therefore, values entered in the first column or row appear as the x-axis data-labels rather than as a graphed range.

When you use the automatic graphing option instead, 1-2-3 uses the first column or row as a data range if any of its cells contain values rather than labels. That means that data in the first column or row appears as another set of bars or a line in the graph rather than as x-axis labels. If the first column or row contains labels only, it will be assigned to the X data range automatically and used for x-axis labels.

Whether the first column or row is treated differently depends on whether you have set automatic graphing to Columnwise or Rowwise.

"I don't see my font selection in the graph display."

Even though the /**G**raph **O**ptions **A**dvanced **F**ont menu lets you pick nine font sizes, 1-2-3 Release 3 displays only three sizes. You can change the font size for the graph text and still see no corresponding change on the displayed graph. The actual fonts available to you depend on the capabilities of your printer.

"My area chart does not show the negative numbers in my data."

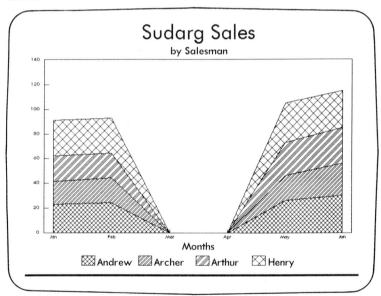

Fig. 9.12. *An area chart with negative results for the third and fourth months.*

Negative numbers that you may graph correctly with a line or bar chart do not appear in an area chart. Area charts simply do not represent numbers less than zero. You cannot have a negative area, of course, unless you live in a parallel universe. To represent negative numbers, use a line or bar chart.

"Not all the text in my graph prints or displays."

If some of the text you entered does not appear when you display or print the graph, you should check several things. First, see if the MEM indicator is displayed at the bottom of the screen. Second, check the amount of available memory using /Worksheet Status. If the memory available to 1-2-3 is low, some of the graph may not be displayed or printed.

You can check also the CONFIG.SYS file of your computer and verify that Files is set to at least 20. You should see a line reading "Files = 20" or more than 20. If you do not, add the line or edit the existing line and reboot your computer.

Summary

This chapter offered a list of the most frequent snags en route to a finished graph. Getting 1-2-3 to produce what you ask for—or think you have asked for—is usually a matter of going back through the process logically and remembering how the program interprets your data to construct a graph. In the preceding paragraphs you learned how to surmount such problems as bars that won't separate, hatch patterns that are unpleasing or nonexistent, off-center titles, and scales that don't conform to your wishes.

In the next chapter, you learn all about printing 1-2-3 graphs. You will learn about types of printers and what quality you can expect to achieve with different printers. You will learn how to set up your printer for your graphs and to preview the outcome. Then, you'll find a troubleshooting section just for printing.

10

Printing and Plotting 1-2-3 Graphs

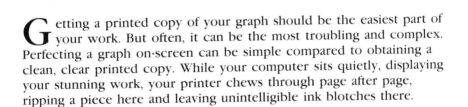

G etting a printed copy of your graph should be the easiest part of your work. But often, it can be the most troubling and complex. Perfecting a graph on-screen can be simple compared to obtaining a clean, clear printed copy. While your computer sits quietly, displaying your stunning work, your printer chews through page after page, ripping a piece here and leaving unintelligible ink blotches there.

Output does not have to be so frustrating. Getting the hard copy you want starts by choosing a printer appropriate for your needs. The first portion of this chapter addresses the variety of printing technologies available to you and the proficiencies and weaknesses of each for printing 1-2-3 graphs.

Later in the chapter, you learn the techniques to produce attractive and dependable output. Then you will find a troubleshooting section at the end of the chapter with solutions to some very specific printing problems.

Choosing an Output Device for Use with 1-2-3

Output technology is changing so rapidly that entire new categories of output devices are inevitable sooner rather than later. But even at this technological moment, a variety of dependable printers and other output devices are available with a huge array of capabilities and at a wide range of costs. The devices suitable for graphs now generally fall into one or more of four categories: dot-matrix printers, laser printers, plotters, and color printers.

Dot-Matrix Printers

Choosing the relatively inexpensive dot-matrix printer does not necessarily mean less than professional output. The latest dot-matrix models, with 24-pin print heads, offer graphics resolutions of up to 360 dots per inch, or *dpi*. This resolution far exceeds the quality of the original 9-pin dot-matrix models and that of many laser printers, as well. The 24-pin dot-matrix printers stand in the middle ground between inexpensive 9-pin printers, often under $500, and laser printers, usually at least $1,500. A few 18-pin printers represent a midpoint in quality between the 9-pin and 24-pin dot-matrix printer market.

The chief advantage of dot-matrix printers has always been their low cost. For a relatively modest outlay, you get a choice of fast draft-mode printing or a slower, near letter-quality mode, with inexpensive operation. Laser printers not only cost more initially, but they require more expensive supplies over the life of the printer.

Many dot-matrix printers offer the option of color, something only a few ultra-expensive laser printers now offer. A simple color ribbon can turn a dot-matrix printer that is prepared for it into a full-color printer. With the advent of color copiers that quickly duplicate a single-color printout, color hard copy is emerging from the realm of "just a few color pages for the board of directors" to wide distribution at a practical cost.

Most dot-matrix printers emulate the Epson FX standard 9-pin printers or the Epson LQ standard 24-pin printers. Or they are modeled after the IBM ProPrinter. Many now give you cut-sheet feeders, so you can quit the odious task of tearing apart all those perforated pages.

1-2-3 supports a host of dot-matrix printers, which, along with plotters, have been the traditional output mode for 1-2-3 graphs. A disadvantage of dot-matrix printers is their slow printing speed, even compared to laser printers, which take considerable time to construct a graph internally before printing it. And then there is the whiny noise of the dot-matrix compared to the silence of laser printers.

Laser Printers

For many users, laser printers represent the high ground in output technology. Laser printers offer quiet, dependable operation and crisp, clear graphics. In fact, a few years ago, the arrival of the laser printer heralded the quick demise of the daisy-wheel printer, formerly the best way to get professional-looking text.

The first laser printer for the personal computer, the Hewlett-Packard LaserJet, arrived at the high cost of $3,495. But later models, including Hewlett-Packard's own LaserJet Series II, have been priced substantially less, while adding more features. The original LaserJet offered 8-page-per-minute speed, but only 128K of printer memory. Because laser printers construct a bit-mapped image of a 1-2-3 graph within their own memory, the larger the memory capacity, the larger the graph can be. The capacity of 128K confines your graph to a very small image.

Even today's standard 512K laser printers can assemble only about one third of a page of high-density graphics before giving you an out-of-memory error message. To print a graph on a laser printer without added memory, you need either to reduce the size of the graph or to print it in lower resolution. As a result, there will be fewer dots in the printer's memory to transmit to the page. You also may be able to print a larger graph if you restrict your design choices: use lines rather than bars; select a hatch pattern that is less dense; and reduce the size of the titles. The general rule of thumb is that the more dark area the graph has, the more laser printer memory is required.

By adding expansion memory to a laser printer with only 512K of memory, you can increase the density and size of graphs the printer can produce. An additional half megabyte of printer memory enables you to print most graphs, and an additional full megabyte should let you print any graph, no matter how complex.

Another quality issue with lasers is print speed. Eight pages per minute is the standard, but some printers can print 10 or 12 pages per minute and more. These speeds measure the number of average text pages a laser printer can produce; printing graphics always takes much longer. Another rule of thumb is that a faster rated speed for text brings commensurately faster graphics printing.

A few expensive laser printers offer printing resolutions of 600 or 1200 dpi, two or four times higher than the standard LaserJet 300 dpi. These printers make a marked difference in the appearance of a 1-2-3 graphic, especially in the smoothness of the curved lines of a pie graph, the jagged edges of diagonal lines, and the curves in text characters. Although these printers still do not challenge the typesetters that reach 2,000 and 3,000 dpi resolutions, the current laser printers are at least in the competition and cost far less.

Laser printers were never well-supported by 1-2-3 for spreadsheet text and graphics printing until the advent of Allways, used with earlier versions of 1-2-3. You could overcome some of 1-2-3's weaknesses by using the Epson and IBM Proprinter dot-matrix printer emulations available in some laser printer models. Then came the more sophisticated printer handling of Release 3.

The most desirable laser printers incorporate PostScript, the page-description language from Adobe Systems, which appeared first in the Apple LaserWriter. PostScript provides unparalleled flexibility in printing text and graphics. PostScript printers designed for the PC are now gaining popularity, although they still account for a small percentage of the total laser printer market. Allways, for 1-2-3 Releases 2.01 and 2.2, can produce PostScript output that any PostScript laser printer can handle. Release 3 provides PostScript output suitable for the Apple LaserWriter or Apple LaserWriter Plus.

Plotters

Because plotters were the first output device to make color possible in printed graphs and because they remain one of the least expensive means of achieving color, you still find many plotters in use with 1-2-3 today.

Plotters create graphs by drawing lines on paper or film using colored pens. The best plotters automatically select colors by changing pens during operation. Less expensive plotters stop and wait for you to change the plotter's pens.

Plotters are often thought of as the output device of choice for architects and draftsmen using Computer Aided Drafting or Design (CAD) programs, because some of the larger plotters can produce extremely detailed blueprints on huge pieces of paper. E-size plotters accommodate paper that is 24 inches wide and 36 inches long. The smaller A (8 1/2″ x 11″) and B (11″ x 17″) plotters are suitable for office desktops and produce your 1-2-3 graphs in vibrant colors.

Most plotters respond to instructions provided by graphics and CAD software in the Hewlett-Packard Graphics Language (HPGL). This language contains instructions for drawing lines, circles, arcs, and other geometric shapes.

Plotters come in several physical configurations. *Flat-bed* plotters move the pen across the surface of a stationary, flat page. *Drum plotters* create a graph by moving a pen across a rotating drum to which you have attached paper. *Pinch roller, hybrid,* or *roller bed* plotters, the most popular on the desktop, move the paper under a pen, which moves side to side. No matter which way a top-quality plotter works, it is capable of extraordinarily high resolution. Many plotters have resolutions equivalent to 1000 dpi. Combine this sharp resolution with their color capabilities and you can see why plotters are so popular.

Yet plotters are beginning to lose their competitive edge to new printing technologies. Keeping the pens of plotters functional can be a nuisance. Plotters are also incapable of printing three-dimensional graphs, and they often print text slowly and poorly. Laser printers offer competitive resolution, and new desktop color printing technologies offer the color brilliance attainable with plotters. Color laser printers, now available but at a cost prohibitive to most users, may eventually replace plotters for business graphics output.

Color Printers

Pages drawn by color-pen plotters or color slides are no longer the only alternatives for color graphs. Although color printing is often two to four times more expensive than the equivalent resolution in black-and-white printing, most people consider the dramatic enhancement of color well worth the cost.

Until now, color reproduction was restricted to a few, slowly made copies. New color laser photocopiers are changing this. Color copiers can reproduce your color-printed originals more quickly and less expensively than you can produce multiple copies at the printer.

Most color printers are slower than black-and-white printers, because they require multiple passes over a page, laying down one color at a time until the complete color image is built. In addition, multiple passes require high accuracy, which necessitates slower printing.

The current crop of color printers suffer from other disadvantages. Color dot-matrix printers print slowly and produce colors that are often less than striking. Ink jet printers squirt tiny drops of colored ink onto a page, making bight colors possible, but the resolution of these printers is relatively low. Popular ink jet printers have printing resolutions from 120 to 180 dpi, which is lower than most black-and-white printers.

Thermal transfer, the latest and most expensive color printing technology, transfers heated, waxy ink to a special glossy paper. Color thermal transfer printers range in price from $10,000 to $20,000, beyond the reach of most business graphics users. Moreover, the shiny paper they require and the waxy ink they use can make graphs look amateurish, as if drawn by crayons. The advantage to thermal transfer printing in some graphics applications is its broad range of colors. Thermal transfer printers can mix dots of different colors to produce hundreds of thousands of shades. Ink jet printers overlay four colors, producing a much narrower color range, but for business graphs, this range is usually sufficient.

The two most promising color printing technologies are color laser printing and a new technology called Cycolor. Several very expensive color laser printers have appeared, which use PostScript as their control language. Look for the price of these printers to come down to a level affordable to more business users. Cycolor compresses a type of color-sensitive film onto paper. The result is high resolution and brilliant color. If Cycolor color printers emerge soon, they may become the preferred color printing method.

Fortunately, whether you are using a simple dot-matrix printer or an intricate color printer, you are detached from the complexities of operating the printer by the 1-2-3 printer driver. The driver carries out the dialog between 1-2-3 and your printer. In fact, you can expect to have immediate printing success with printers supported by 1-2-3 printer drivers. And, because the base of 1-2-3 users is so huge, manufacturers of new model printers sometimes include a 1-2-3 driver for their specialty device.

If you have access to an output device that is not supported by 1-2-3, keep in mind that you can pull a graph as a PIC file into other software that does support your printer. Then your printer can handle your 1-2-3 graphs. Both Freelance Plus and Harvard Graphics, for example, build a bridge between 1-2-3 and sophisticated output devices, including color printers, slide makers, and even the electronic screen show device VideoShow.

Nevertheless, for users of output devices supported by 1-2-3, the remaining sections of this chapter offer suggestions for printing graphs with Allways in Release 2.2 and earlier versions. Next are techniques for printing graphs in 1-2-3 Release 3. The chapter concludes with troubleshooting suggestions for specific printers and plotters.

Printing Graphs with Allways in 1-2-3 Release 2.2

The 1-2-3 add-in Allways, included with Release 2.2 and available separately for earlier versions, makes a dramatic difference in your printed worksheets and graphs.

Allways is a bonafide alternative to 1-2-3's PrintGraph program, which also prints PIC files, so you can substitute Allways for PrintGraph for your day-to-day graph printing. But Allways goes beyond replacing PrintGraph, exceeding its capabilities with a variety of advantages. First, although you can use the simple PrintGraph fonts to print titles you enter with the 1-2-3 /Graph Options Titles command, you can use the more attractive Allways text fonts. Second, you can print both a portion of the worksheet and a graph together on a page. PrintGraph prints only graphs stored as PIC files. Finally, you can print a graph from within Allways without ever leaving 1-2-3. Even though PrintGraph is just a few keystrokes away once you exit 1-2-3, you may prefer to stay within 1-2-3 for all of your work.

If you routinely choose Allways for graph printing, you may want to remove the PrintGraph files from your hard disk to conserve space. You needn't be reluctant to do so, because anything you can do in PrintGraph, you can do in Allways as well or better.

Making a Sample Graph To Print

First, create a worksheet from the data in figure 10.1. You will need this worksheet for your sample graph for printing.

Now create the Stamler graph by following these commands:

/Graph Type Line

X: B4..G4

A: B6..G6

Options Legend

A: Total Enrollment

Options Data-labels

A: B6..G6 Above

View the graph. Note that the last data-label needs just a bit more room. Rescale the y-axis by following these steps:

/Graph Options Scale **Y**-Scale Manual

Lower: **220**

Upper: **460**

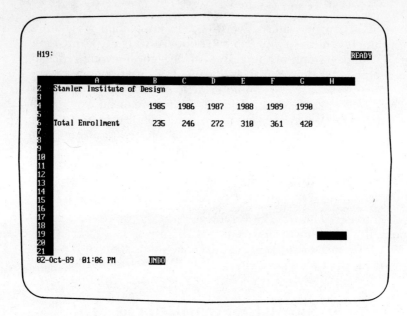

Fig. 10.1. The worksheet data for the Stamler Institute Graph.

Your graph should now resemble figure 10.2 if you use 1-2-3 Release 2.2 or earlier. If you use Release 3, your graph will look slightly different.

Do not be concerned with adding titles at this stage; you will add them in Allways, using the text formatting capabilities of Allways to choose attractive fonts and sizes. Now, save the graph with /Graph **S**ave as **STAMLER.PIC**.

Invoke Allways and move the cursor to a clear area of the worksheet. Try using the Goto (F5) command to move the cursor to cell B9. Now, use the Allways /Graph **A**dd command to add the STAMLER.PIC file to the range B9..G21. Your screen should look like the screen shown in figure 10.3.

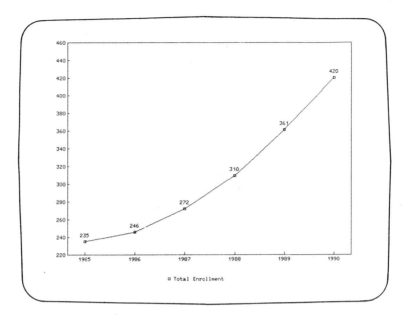

Fig. 10.2. *The Stamler graph.*

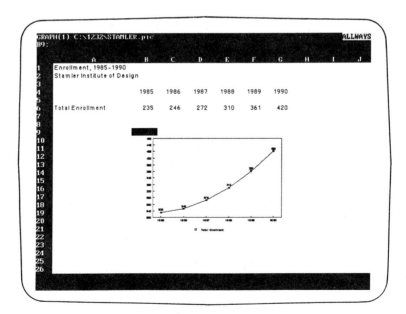

Fig. 10.3. *The Allways screen with the STAMLER.PIC graph added.*

To complete this graph, you need to add a title and subtitle. Position the cursor in cell B8, where the title should appear, and press Esc to return to 1-2-3. In cell B8, type "Enrollment Grows, 1985-1990." In the cell below, B9, type "Stamler Institute of Design." Now, invoke Allways again to format the two titles by using the Allways /Format Font command. Pick Triumvirate 14 point and specify B8..B9 as the range to format. Now, you need to enter a few spaces before each title to center the pair above the graph. Compare your screen now with the screen in figure 10.4.

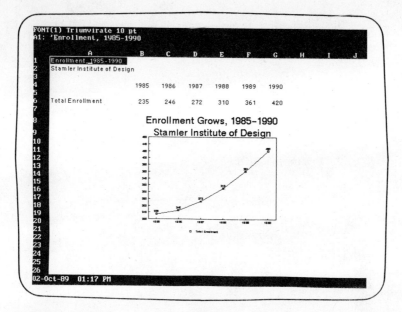

Fig. 10.4. *The Stamler graph in Allways with titles added and centered.*

Checking the Allways Print Configuration

Before you try printing an Allways graph, you should check the current Allways print configuration to verify that your printer information is correct. Because you can have several printers installed, you may need to select the appropriate printer from the list Allways presents when you select the /**Print Configuration Printer** command. The list shows you the printers you installed when you ran AWSETUP to set up Allways.

The /Print Configuration menu offers you these few additional options:

Interface lets you specify to which port the printer is attached. Parallel printers are usually attached to LPT1 (the first printer port), and serial printers are usually attached to COM1 (the first communications port).

Cartridge lets you determine which font cartridge your printer will use if your printer uses these. Both the HP LaserJets and HP DeskJet are two printers for which you can buy optional font cartridges.

Orientation lets you print a graph in the vertical direction (portrait) or in the sideways direction (landscape).

Resolution lets you specify a printing resolution for your graph. The higher the printing resolution number, the sharper the image will be. But higher resolution printing also requires more printer memory when you are using a laser printer. If you try printing a graph and receive an out-of-memory error message from a laser printer, you can try printing the graph in the next lower resolution. For example, if resolution is set to 300 x 300, try 150 x 150, instead. You may also be able to maintain the higher resolution by reducing the size of the graph. Either method will reduce the legibility of the graph. The ideal alternative is to increase the memory in your printer.

Bin lets you set how paper should be delivered to your printer. The options depend on the printer you use. If your printer uses various paper trays for pages of different sizes, you can choose a paper tray here. You can also choose to feed pages to the printer manually if that option is available with your printer. The HP LaserJet, for example, lets you choose either Paper Tray or Manual Feed.

Setting the Allways Print Range

Before you print, you must instruct Allways which region of the worksheet to print. To print a graph, simply specify the same range you specified when you added the graph, plus any cells that hold graph titles. For example, because you added the Stamler Institute graph to range B9..G21, you should set that range, plus the cells above that contain the titles, as the print range. In this case, you should specify B8..G21 as the correct print range by selecting **/Print Range Set B8..G21**. You should now see a dashed line around the print range (see fig. 10.5).

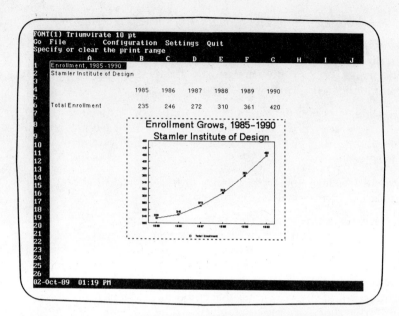

Fig. 10.5. *The Allways print range indicated by a dashed line.*

Another way to select a print range is to highlight the range before selecting **/P**rint **R**ange **S**et. Start by positioning the cursor at the top left corner of the range. Then, press the period key and extend the highlight until you have specified a rectangular range. Select **/P**rint **R**ange **S**et and you will see that range appear. Press Enter to accept the range.

Sending the Print Range to the Printer

After you set the print range, you need only select **/P**rint **G**o to have Allways send the graph to the printer. Watch the screen to see Allways send your graph to the printer row by row. Compare your printed graph with the completed Stamler Institute graph, as printed by Allways on an HP LaserJet Series II. This graph appears in figure 10.6.

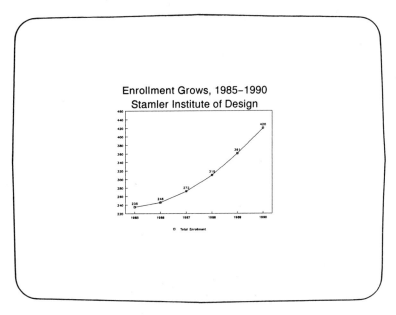

Fig. 10.6. *The Stamler graph printed by Allways on an HP LaserJet Series II.*

Printing and Plotting Graphs with PrintGraph in Release 2.2

After you have used Allways to print 1-2-3 PIC files, you may never again return to PrintGraph. The formatting options of PrintGraph are limited in comparison to those of Allways.

But PrintGraph can serve at least one useful purpose. After you have saved a batch of graphs as PIC files, you can send them all to a printer quickly. Of course, they all will have the same default PrintGraph settings—the same size and font settings, for example—but they will emerge quickly one after another supplying quick proofs of your graphs for examination.

Starting PrintGraph

If you routinely start 1-2-3 by typing **lotus** and then selecting 1-2-3 from the Access Menu, you can start PrintGraph by simply selecting PrintGraph from the same menu. If you start 1-2-3 at the DOS prompt by typing **123**, you must type **graph** to start PrintGraph when you return to the DOS prompt. If your computer has enough memory, you can start PrintGraph from within 1-2-3 by exiting to the DOS system with the /System command. Be sure you have at least 256K of memory free by checking /Worksheet Status before trying to load PrintGraph from within 1-2-3. Also be sure to save your worksheet before exiting to the DOS system, in case something goes awry when you leave 1-2-3 temporarily. If you load PrintGraph from within 1-2-3, you can return to 1-2-3 by typing **exit** after returning to the DOS prompt.

If you are using 1-2-3 with diskettes rather than a hard disk, 1-2-3 requests that you insert the PrintGraph disk when you select PrintGraph from the Access Menu. If you are using a PC or PS/2 with 3 1/2-inch diskettes, you will find the PrintGraph program on the same diskette as the main 1-2-3 program.

Setting Defaults for PrintGraph

The first time you start PrintGraph, you should make a few adjustments to the program's defaults for future PrintGraph sessions. The vital defaults are all found under the program's settings menu. Select **Settings** from the main PrintGraph menu to obtain the menu shown in figure 10.7.

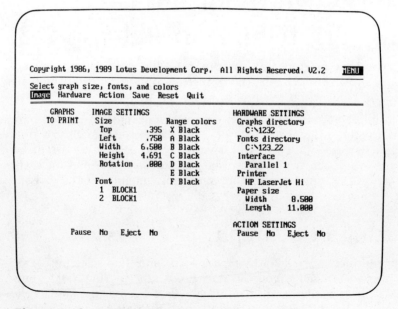

Fig. 10.7. The PrintGraph settings menu.

Take a look at the PrintGraph settings screen. Notice that the settings on the screen are divided into four groups: Graphs to Print, Image Settings, Hardware Settings, and Action Settings. The settings menu lets you set all of these except Graphs to Print.

The best policy is probably to start at the leftmost menu entry and work to the right, determining a default for each menu item as you go. Under the **Image** option, then, you will find these suboptions:

Size lets you determine a default size and the placement and rotation of the graph. Your choices for Size are Full, Half, and Manual. Full fills an entire 8 1/2-inch x 11-inch page by rotating the graph 90 degrees to the left. Half prints the graph on the top half of a vertical 8 1/2-inch x 11-inch page. Choose Manual if you set the options under Size yourself. If you choose Manual, you will need to determine entries for these settings.

Top is the margin above the graph measured in inches.

Left is the margin to the left of the graph measured in inches.

Width is the horizontal width of the graph. When Rotation is set to zero, the width is the breadth of the x-axis. When Rotation is 90 degrees, the width becomes the span of the y-axis, instead.

Height is the vertical height of the graph. The relationship between height and a specific axis is dependent on the Rotation setting, just as is Width.

Rotation is the number of degrees between 0 and 360 to rotate the graph counterclockwise.

Font lets you set one of PrintGraph's fonts for the first title of the graph and a second font for the remainder of the graph text. BLOCK1 is the initial default setting for all graph text.

Figure 10.8 shows the PrintGraph fonts available for printing with an HP LaserJet Series II printer. Select a font from the list by moving the highlight to the correct font on the list by pressing the space bar. A number 2 at the end of a font's name indicates that the font is bold. ITALIC2 is a bold version of ITALIC1, for example.

Range-Colors lets you assign printing colors to each of the ranges in a graph if you have installed a color graphics printer. If the printer currently chosen is a black-and-white printer, your only color choice will be black. You can have several graphics printers installed at once and choose one from within PrintGraph. The capabilities of the printer you choose will determine the colors available for the series on the Range-Colors menu.

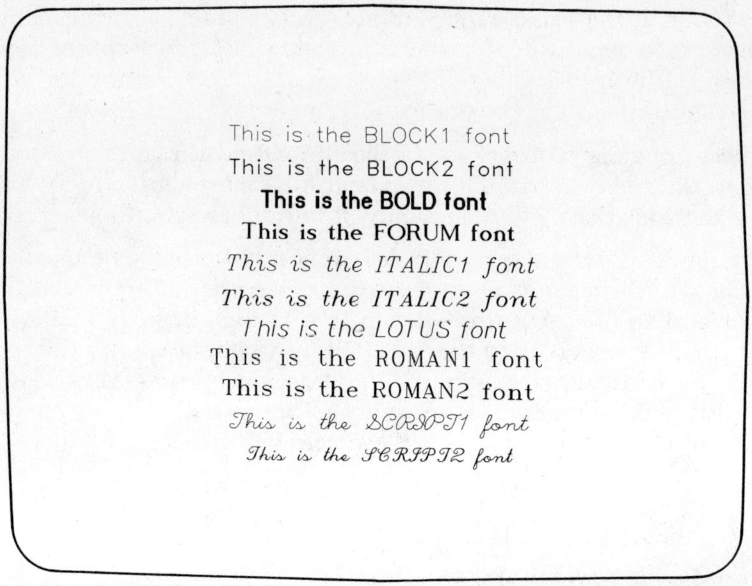

This is the BLOCK1 font
This is the BLOCK2 font
This is the BOLD font
This is the FORUM font
This is the ITALIC1 font
This is the ITALIC2 font
This is the LOTUS font
This is the ROMAN1 font
This is the ROMAN2 font
This is the SCRIPT1 font
This is the SCRIPT2 font

Fig. 10.8. *The PrintGraph font selection with an HP LaserJet Series II.*

If the graph you are printing is any style other than a pie graph, you can use the X option to set a color for the graph's frame, its background grid, and other elements except for the series, legends, and data-labels. Use the remaining options (A-F) to pick a color for each of the data ranges represented in the graph.

If the graph you are printing is a pie graph, choosing colors for its slices is more difficult. Remember that pie graphs represent data in the A data range only; thus it makes no sense to set colors for data ranges B through F. Actually, you use data ranges A through F on the Range-Colors menu to set colors for the slices of a pie. Each range corresponds to one B range code according to the following table. By linking a data range to its B range code, you can choose the color each code represents.

Range-Colors Data Range	Data Range B Code
X	Last digit is 1
A	Last digit is 2
B	Last digit is 3
C	Last digit is 4
D	Last digit is 5
E	Last digit is 6
F	Last digit is 7

If the B data range code for a slice is 106, for example, the color for Range E under Range-Colors will determine the color of the slice.

Hardware Settings let you determine where on disk to find your graphs and the PrintGraph fonts, which of the printers you have installed to use, which port the printer is connected to, and what size paper PrintGraph should prepare the graph for.

By default, the Graphs Directory and Fonts Directory are both set to drive A. Users of 1-2-3 with floppy disks do, in fact, need to get their graphs and printing fonts from a disk in drive A. If you have a hard disk, though, you can enter an appropriate directory name for each of these settings. For example, if you keep your PIC files in a special directory called \PIC within the main 123 directory, you can enter C:\123\PIC as the Graphs Directory.

PrintGraph needs one font file for each of the text font styles available when you print a graph. You can expect to find PrintGraph's font files in the same hard disk directory that holds the main PrintGraph program. If you installed 1-2-3 into a directory called C:\123, for example, both PrintGraph and the font files should be in C:\123.

Interface informs PrintGraph to which output port (on the back of your computer) your printer is physically connected. A parallel printer is usually connected to Parallel 1, and a serial printer is usually connected to Serial 1. If you have two printers connected—one black-and-white laser printer and one color plotter, for example—you can direct the PrintGraph output to one of these printers by selecting the appropriate interface.

When you examine your choices under the Printer menu option, you will see all the printers you selected as graphics printers when you installed 1-2-3. If your printer supports more than one print density, you will see these choices, too. Even if you have several graphics printers installed, you probably print on one routinely, so you can set this model as the default printer.

If you have a serial printer, you need to set a baud rate. This setting regulates how fast information travels from computer to printer. Your serial printer's manual tells you which baud rate is the fastest your printer can handle.

Paper size gives you a chance to inform PrintGraph about the paper size you are using. The default size is 8 1/2 inches x 11 inches, but if you are using legal size paper, you should set Length to 14 inches. If you are using wide paper in a wide-carriage dot-matrix printer, you should set Width to 14 inches.

Action Settings, the final group of settings on the PrintGraph settings screen and menu, lets you tell PrintGraph whether to pause between graphs, whether you are printing a series of graphs, and whether to eject the current page after printing a graph or to continue the next graph on the same page.

You should set Pause to Yes if you want to change paper between graphs or set a different printer under Hardware Settings for certain graphs. After printing each graph, PrintGraph will stop and cause the printer to beep. To tell PrintGraph to continue, press the space bar.

Saving PrintGraph Default Settings

After you have set the initial defaults for PrintGraph, you can save them as a group in a PrintGraph configuration file called PGRAPH.CNF. Then, whenever you start PrintGraph for future printing, the program will read the configuration file for all settings.

To save the current PrintGraph settings as the configuration file, select Save from the settings menu. Now, as you make future changes to the PrintGraph settings, you can select Reset to return all of the PrintGraph settings to the defaults in the revised configuration file. Only the Image-Select settings are unaffected by Reset.

Selecting Graphs To Print

Some of the settings determined under the PrintGraph settings menu are mandatory and some are optional. The Graphs Directory settings are required, for example, whereas the font settings can be set at your discretion. Yet it is certainly a good idea to check all defaults the first time you use PrintGraph. After you have established a base group of preferred settings, you can use them for printing all subsequent graphs. This system makes printing graphs simply a matter of selecting which graphs to print and then starting the printing process. PrintGraph proceeds without intervention, using the default settings you established.

Printing a batch of graphs using the default PrintGraph settings is probably the best use you can make of PrintGraph. The add-in Allways provides more options for formatting individual graphs before printing. And it offers a method to save a complete set of default graph formatting choices, as does PrintGraph. But Allways provides no method of printing a batch of graphs one after another automatically.

If you decide to print graphs one at a time with PrintGraph, you can modify the PrintGraph settings before each graph to fine-tune the graph's appearance. Otherwise, you can select a list of graphs to print by choosing **Image-Select** from the main PrintGraph menu. All graphs will share the same PrintGraph settings.

PrintGraph shows you a list of the PIC files in the current Graphs Directory (see fig. 10.9). Mark each graph you would like printed by moving the highlight to its name, using the up and down arrow keys and pressing the space bar once. A pound sign (#) appears next to the PIC file name to confirm that the graph is marked for printing. Press the space bar again to unmark a graph.

```
Copyright 1986, 1989 Lotus Development Corp. All Rights Reserved. V2.2   POINT

Select graphs to print


  GRAPH FILE  DATE     TIME    SIZE
  --------------------------------------   Space bar marks or unmarks selection
# CTUTOR      09-10-89  22:50    1140      ENTER selects marked graphs
  CTUTORA     09-10-89  23:07     829      ESC exits, ignoring changes
  CTUTORB     09-10-89  23:07    3706      HOME moves to beginning of list
  CTUTORN     09-08-89  23:24    1140      END moves to end of list
  FORUM       10-02-89  13:43     754      ↑ and ↓ move highlight
# GRAPHPIC    09-23-89   9:51    2861        List will scroll if highlight
  ITALIC1     10-02-89  13:42     756        moved beyond top or bottom
  ITALIC2     10-02-89  13:42     756      GRAPH (F10) previews marked graph
  LOTUS       10-02-89  13:42     754
  PICBW       09-23-89  11:47    8123
  PICCOLOR    09-23-89  11:46    2861
  PICFILE     09-22-89  22:47    6807
  PICGRAPH    09-23-89   9:51    2861
  ROMAN1      10-02-89  13:42     755
  ROMAN2      10-02-89  13:42     755
# SCHEER2     09-30-89  15:53    3742
  SCHEER4B    10-01-89  12:14    5874
  SCHEER4C    10-01-89  12:14    1142
```

Fig. 10.9. The Image-Select list of PIC files in the Current Graphs directory.

To preview a graph before printing, highlight the graph's name and press the Graph (F10) key. Previewing a graph allows you to verify correct graph choice, and it gives you a more accurate representation of the final printed graph than you have with the /Graph View command within 1-2-3. You may see problems that did not show up earlier. When you viewed the graph with Graph (F10) while you were creating the graph, you would not have seen that a legend was too big to print.

When you have marked the correct graphs for printing, press Enter to return to the main PrintGraph menu. Now, the graph names you selected appear under Graphs To Print (see fig. 10.10).

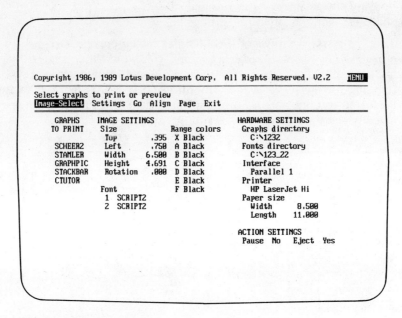

Fig. 10.10. *Selected graphs under Graphs To Print.*

To begin printing, select **A**lign from the PrintGraph menu and then **G**o. Align signals to PrintGraph that you have set the printer so that it can start printing at the top of a page. PrintGraph automatically advances the paper to a new page when it reaches the page length setting you determined when you installed the printer. If you fail to select Align before selecting Go, PrintGraph's page advance may not occur at the bottom of a page. Instead, PrintGraph may advance the paper in the middle of a page, leaving an unwanted blank area. To stop PrintGraph from printing, press Ctrl-Break. Then, press Esc to return to the PrintGraph menu.

Printing and Plotting Graphs in 1-2-3 Release 3

Printing and plotting graphs with 1-2-3 Release 3 is considerably easier than it has ever been. The capabilities of PrintGraph are now integrated into 1-2-3. You no longer need to save graphs as PIC files and leave 1-2-3 to print them. Graph printing starts right at the main 1-2-3 menu. After you complete a graph on-screen, you can select **/P**rint Printer **I**mage Current Align **G**o. Your graph now prints with the Release 3 default settings.

1-2-3 Release 3 offers a capability previously possible only with Allways attached to earlier versions. With Release 3, you can print a worksheet section side by side with a graph that illustrates the worksheet numbers. Moreover, the graph you see when you select **/G**raph **V**iew is a closer approximation of the final output than the graph you see in earlier versions of 1-2-3. Best of all, you can begin printing and then resume your work, because Release 3 offers time-saving background graph printing.

Modifying a Graph's Print Settings before Printing

Although you decide most of the formatting attributes as you design the graph with the **/G**raph **O**ptions settings, a few final print settings are reserved for the **/P**rint Printer **O**ptions **A**dvanced **I**mage menu shown in figure 10.11.

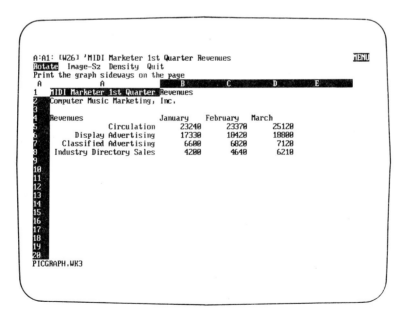

Fig. 10.11. *The /Print Printer Options Advanced Image menu.*

Image-Sz lets you enter an exact size and shape for the printed graph. By default, printed graphs extend the width of the page to the 1-inch margins on either side. 1-2-3 calculates the height of graphs by trying to maintain a strict 4:3 ratio of width to length. In other words, if the graph is 6 1/2 inches wide, 1-2-3 will make the height of the graph 5 inches.

You can use the following Image-Sz options to change the size and shape of the printed graph:

Length-Fill is measured in lines of text (6 per inch). When you enter a length, 1-2-3 prints the largest possible graph it can, while maintaining the crucial 4:3 ratio of width to length.

Margin-Fill creates a graph that extends from the left to the right margins. 1-2-3 calculates a height based on the 4:3 ratio. Margin-Fill is the default Image-Sz setting.

Reshape lets you manually enter both a height in lines and a width in standard pica characters (10 characters per inch). Even if you enter a height and width exceeding the size of the page, 1-2-3 will not print a graph beyond the boundaries of the page. Knowing this, you can intentionally enter width and height settings that are far too big to have 1-2-3 print the largest possible graph on the current page size.

1-2-3 Release 3 uses a surprising amount of built-in intelligence when it prints graphs. If you have printed part of a worksheet or another graph on a page and you try to print a graph that does not fit the remaining space, 1-2-3 prints the graph on the next page, instead.

Rotate lets you set a graph rotation on the page 90 degrees counterclockwise. Even if you set Rotate to Yes, the portion of a worksheet you are printing with the graph will print without rotation. When you rotate a graph, its width and length settings are interchanged for the purposes of the Image-Sz option.

Density lets you choose either draft or final-quality printing. *Draft* is faster, but produces an image not so dark and well-defined. *Final* prints at the best resolution that your printer is capable of. When you first print a graph, you may want to print at draft density first to check the appearance of the graph before taking the time to produce a final-density version.

Not all printers support varying density levels. If the graphics printer you have installed does not support more than one resolution, the density setting has no effect.

Printing the Graph

When you are ready to print or plot a graph, you can choose either to print the current graph in memory or to print a graph you have saved with the worksheet using the **/Graph Name Create** command. To print the current graph, select **/Print Printer Image Current Align Go**. To print a named graph, select **/Print Printer Image Named-Graph Align Go**. If you are using a laser printer, you may have to select **Page** before the graph will print.

Printing a Graph and a Worksheet Together

With Release 3, you can print both a worksheet and a named graph on the same page. To do so, you must include a semicolon after a worksheet print range, followed by an asterisk and the name of the named graph. 1-2-3 will first print the worksheet data and then print the named graph. This capability lets you combine data with a graph illustrating the data on a single printed page. Figure 10.12 shows how this combination can be used to advantage.

The graph was named Revenues with the /Graph Name Create command. Then the worksheet data was specified as a print range followed by a semicolon, an asterisk, and the name Revenues. The print range specified was A1..F8;*REVENUES. To allow some space between the bottom of the worksheet and the top of the graph, you can include a few extra blank rows in the worksheet range.

You can print a worksheet and graph side by side rather than vertically stacked on the page, but 1-2-3 Release 3 provides no automatic facility to set side-by-side printing. To accomplish this placement, you make two passes through the printer. Print either the text or graph range with a right margin of 40. Then roll the paper back up into the printer or place the page back into the paper tray. Finally, print the remaining text or graph using a left margin of 40 and right margin of 80.

Similarly, you can print four graphs to a page by printing two graphs on the left side of the page: set top, bottom and left margins to 0 and the right margin to 37. Print the first graph; select **Line** a few times to leave several blank lines between the first graph and the second; then print the second graph. Select **Page** to eject the page if you are using a laser printer. Return the page to the printer and set the left margin to 42 and the right margin to 80. Now repeat the printing procedure to place two graphs on the right side of the page.

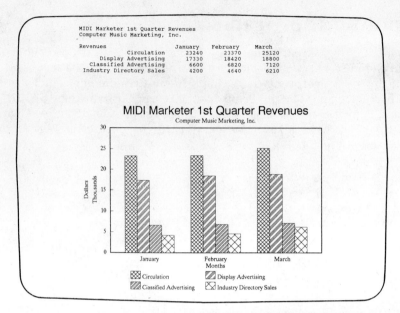

Fig. 10.12. A worksheet range and graph printed together.

Saving Print Settings

You can save any set of print settings with the **/Print Printer Options Name Create** menu selection. Later, to use the same print settings again, select **/Print Printer Options Name Use**. With this capability, you can create several complete sets of printer settings, one for each printer you use or one for each type of graph you print often.

Troubleshooting Printers and Plotters

Though most printers and plotters directly supported by 1-2-3 should give you troublefree results when you print graphs, you may encounter isolated problems with certain devices. The troubleshooting ideas in the following three sections offer specific suggestions for overcoming those occasional problems associated with graph printing.

General Printing Problems

First offered in this section on printing problems is a list of difficulties of a more general nature, or those not limited to dot-matrix, laser, or any of the more specific categories of printers that are treated separately.

Graphs do not print using the Generic printer driver.

For each printer you plan to use with 1-2-3 to print graphs, you must select a printer driver, a small file that serves as the link between 1-2-3 and your printer. A printer driver translates the printing commands sent by 1-2-3 into the specific format required by one particular model of printer. The Generic printer driver is an all-purpose driver that sends out the most commonly understood commands to any printer attached.

The Generic printer driver does not print graphs. If a graph is within the print range, 1-2-3 prints only the worksheet cells within the specified print range and leaves a blank space where the graph should have been.

When using PrintGraph in high resolution on a Novell Network, only a portion of a graph prints before the page is ejected.

To correct this problem, be sure to use the following spool command to increase the printing time-out period to 60 seconds:

Spool po ti60 nb

The printer drops some legends even though they appear on the /Graph View screen.

/Graph View displays all legends even if they are too long to print. In 1-2-3 Release 2.2 and earlier versions, the graph type and number of characters in the legend determine what legends will actually fit on the page.

In 1-2-3 Release 2.2, create a PIC file for the graph and start PrintGraph to get a more accurate view of how a graph will print. Then, mark the graph for printing with **Image-Select**. Press the Graph key (F10) to see a close approximation of the printed graph.

In 1-2-3 Release 2.2 and earlier, the following limits apply:

	Line & XY	Bar & Stack-Bar
1 legend	19 characters	19 characters
2 legends	38 characters	38 characters
3 legends	36 characters	33 characters
4 legends	30 characters	27 characters
5 legends	24 characters	21 characters
6 legends	18 characters	15 characters

1-2-3 Release 3 automatically reduces the size of the legend text as you increase the number of characters in the legend. The font size that Release 3 selects overrides the choice you made with /Graph Options Advanced Text Second Size.

If the legend text in a Release 3 graph is short, the program prints the legends on one line. If some or all of the legends are long, 1-2-3 Release 3 staggers the legends to appear alternately on a second line.

The printer left blank lines where the graph should be.

Blank lines where the graph should be printed usually indicate that the printer is incapable of printing graphs. You should inquire about whether your printer is capable of printing graphs.

Problems with Dot-Matrix Printers

The following problems are common with dot-matrix printers.

Itoh Prowriter 8510A: the PrintGraph form feed is incorrect.

After printing a graph with the C. Itoh Prowriter 8510A, Eject and Page may not work correctly. To use this model with 1-2-3, you should use the NEC 8023 printer driver, but there are some minor differences in the operation of the NEC and C. Itoh printers.

To make sure the top of form is set correctly on the C. Itoh printer, follow these steps:

1. Select **P**age in PrintGraph.

2. Take the printer off-line and adjust the paper so that the perforation is at the carriage head.

3. Set the printer back on-line.

Canon A1210: Printing moves lower on successive pages when many graphs are queued to print.

Use the Quadram Quadjet driver to solve this problem.

DEC LA50: Graphs are double-spaced in high-density mode.

To use the high-density driver with the DEC LA50 printer, the graphics aspect-ratio switch must be set in the closed position. The graphics aspect-ratio switch is switch number 5 in switch bank 1.

Epson MX Series: Double-spaces printed graphs.

Certain models of the Epson MX series of printers print double linefeeds throughout a graph when used with PrintGraph. Some call this the "venetian blind effect," because you see rows of graphics alternating with blank rows.

Epson MX printers without Graftrax Plus ROMs have this problem printing graphs. Graftrax Plus ROMs allow Epson MX printers to print high-resolution dot-addressable graphics without blank rows. All Epson FX and RX printers have Graftrax Plus ROMs installed.

To tell whether your Epson MX printer has the Graftrax Plus ROMs, turn off the printer, hold down the ON-LINE and LF buttons on the top of the printer, and then turn the printer back on. Release the buttons as soon as the printer starts printing.

If the printer starts with a line or two and then stops, you have the Graftrax Plus ROMs installed. If the printer continues the self-test without stopping, the Graftrax Plus ROMs are not installed.

Any Epson dealer can upgrade your printer ROMs.

HP2225 Thinkjet: The x-axis title and legends are dropped from a full-size graph.

Use HP Mode to print and use the PrintGraph manual size settings to change the left margin to zero and the width to 6.5. To print a half-size graph, set the left margin to .25; otherwise, the printer continuously feeds paper.

If you print graphs using Epson FX emulation, your graphs will print much smaller than you would expect.

IBM 3812 Pageprinter: Presents an unexpected "Set up plotter and press space" message.

If you see the "Set up plotter and press space" message when you select Align in PrintGraph, your IBM 3812 Pageprinter is set up to emulate a plotter rather than a dot-matrix printer. 1-2-3 recognizes the printer as a plotter and gives you messages appropriate for a plotter.

Okidata 83A: Successive queued graphs print farther down the page.

If you queue several graphs to print using the Okidata 83A, each graph prints with progressively larger top margins. The only solution is to queue no more than three graphs at a time with this printer.

Okidata 84: Large graphs print with vertical lines on the right side of the page.

The largest graph you can print on an Okidata 84 has the following PrintGraph settings:

Size:

Left Margin: 0.000
Right Margin: 0.000
Width: 13.500
Height: 19.000
Rotation: 0 or 90

Page:

Length: 20.00
Width: 14.000

If you would like to set a left margin, the sum of the graph width plus two times the left margin should not exceed 13.4. The graph width must also be less than or equal to 12.5.

Okidata 192: A graph contains unreadable characters when using the IBM Graphics driver.

Not all Okidata 192 printers are compatible with the IBM Graphics printer driver. The Okidata 192 which is not compatible with the IBM Graphics printer should instead be configured as an Okidata.

Star Micronics Gemini Printers: Extra linefeeds occur within graphs.

The Star Micronics Gemini 10X PC and 15X PC graphics printers produce the "venetian blind effect" of blank lines embedded in the graph when the Gemini 10X/15X graphics printer driver is used.

To solve this problem, use the IBM Graphics printer driver, instead.

Problems with Laser Printers

Problems often encountered with laser printers are explained in the following list.

PostScript Printers: The graph prints off the page.

Set the PrintGraph margin to greater than zero to avoid having the graph printed off the page.

PostScript Printing on a Network: Graphs do not print.

Set EJECT to YES in PrintGraph when printing using the PostScript drivers on an IBM Network.

Epson GQ-3500: The data light stays on after graph printing.

Even though the entire graph has been printed, the data light remains on after you press Page to eject the printed page. You can ignore the data light or press Page again to force the printer to eject an empty page and extinguish its data light.

HP LaserJet: The graph resolution looks extremely low.

The HP LaserJet (without the Plus or the Series II) has only 59K of internal memory. This capacity limits printer resolution to 75 dots per inch (dpi).

To print at higher resolutions, you can send the LaserJet a control code, but the graph will be correspondingly smaller. For example, if you double the printed resolution to 150 dpi, the graph will be one quarter as big. If you print at 300 dpi, the graph will be 1/16 as big.

To send the appropriate control code to the printer to increase printing resolution, enter the following as a setup string and print a blank range:

  ESC*t#R. # should be either 100, 150, or 300 (dpi)

HP LaserJet Plus: Splits high-density graphs into two pages.

If you try to print complicated graphs in high-density mode, the memory limit of the LaserJet Plus may cause full-sized graphs to be printed on two pages. To solve this problem, use the low-density driver or feed the same sheet of paper back through to print the remainder of the graph.

HP LaserJet Plus or Series II: Indicates Error 20.

Error 20 indicates that the printer has insufficient memory to print the graph at the size and resolution you specified. Either reduce the size of the graph or use a lower resolution.

HP LaserJet Plus or Series II: Indicates Error Code 21 when printing in landscape orientation.

When printing high-density, full-page graphs sideways on an HP LaserJet Plus or Series II, you may get an error code 21 from the printer, even if you have enough memory and you are using the added memory printer driver.

The problem is caused by the LaserJet's method of printing full page graphics in landscape mode. To solve this problem, change the orientation of the graph to portrait, or in Release 3.0, use /Print Printer Options Advanced Image Rotate. Or, you can print the graph in draft density (150 dpi), which uses less memory.

Problems with Plotters

The two following problems apply especially to printing with plotters.

HP7470A: Occasionally prints reversed graphs.

Turn the plotter off and back on before plotting in 1-2-3 to correct this problem.

HP7475A: The graph begins printing backwards.

A graph will suddenly print backwards if the plotter is reset while PrintGraph is sending graph information to the plotter. This can happen if the plotter is turned off after information begins traveling to the plotter; or the problem occurs if the plotter is not turned on when the PrintGraph begins sending its data.

To solve this problem, turn the plotter off and then back on and try plotting the graph again.

Problems with Color Printers

Several problems occurring with specific color printers are given next with some possible solutions.

Itoh 8510M: Prints wavy lines throughout graph borders and data.

The C. Itoh 8510M is a color printer that is not compatible with the 1-2-3 driver for the C. Itoh 8510. Use the IBM Graphics Printer driver, instead.

Genicom 3404 Color Dot-Matrix Printer: Prints only black and white.

Make sure your Genicom printer uses the process color ribbon, rather than the primary color ribbon. The GE/Genicom 3000 1-2-3 driver does not support the primary color ribbon. The process ribbon has a yellow stripe. When you change the ribbon type, make sure you run the printer's configuration program to set the appropriate ribbon type.

IBM Color Printers: The paper advances 3 inches before printing.

When printing graphs at the default full and half sizes, the printer advances the paper approximately 3 inches before printing. The graph then runs off the bottom of the page. The solution is to set the top margin to zero in PrintGraph (Options Size Manual Top 0), for a paper advance of only 1.25 inches, and the graph will fit on the page.

IBM 3852-1 Model 1 (Color Jetprinter Model 1): Printouts span several pages with "expanded" print style.

The 1-2-3 Color Inkjet driver supports only the Model 2 version of the IBM 3852. This version indicates 3852-Model-2 on the back of the printer. The Model 1 version indicates only 3852 on the back.

Summary

In this chapter, you learned about the types of output devices available for printing and plotting your 1-2-3 graphs. You learned more about what you should expect from current dot-matrix printers and the various laser printers, and when a plotter can be a desirable alternative for graphic output.

Printing with Allways was presented in detail, and the advantages of printing from within 1-2-3 Release 3 were outlined. Common printing problems and possible solutions were presented in a troubleshooting section devoted exclusively to printing.

In the chapter that follows, you learn how to import your 1-2-3 data into other software to increase your range of possibilities for graphic expressiveness.

11

Importing 1-2-3 Data into Graphing Software

In a book entitled *1-2-3 Graphics Techniques,* it sounds at first like heresy to suggest that you might be happier graphing in software other than 1-2-3. But software packages dedicated to graphing can provide capabilities that are complementary to the data analysis strengths of 1-2-3. This chapter demonstrates, by example, all there is to gain by importing 1-2-3 data into dedicated graphics software. Your principal focus will be on two top graphics programs, Freelance Plus and Harvard Graphics. Then you consider the relative merits of other graphics packages that share one common trait: the ability to import data from a 1-2-3 worksheet for the purpose of graphmaking.

Understandably, you may prefer to do initial graphmaking in 1-2-3 to help analyze your data. If so, you many want to consider one of the graphing packages that can import a graph you've made in 1-2-3. These programs can let you embellish a graph from 1-2-3 with such special effects as three-dimensional bars. Or, you can add stylish fonts, images from ready-made clip-art libraries, and informative annotations.

317

Importing completed graphs is covered in Chapter 15, which describes using 1-2-3 PIC files. This chapter covers starting your graphmaking in programs other than 1-2-3, and begins by helping you decide whether you really should take such a dramatic step.

Deciding Whether To Graph Data Outside 1-2-3

Though the graphing software of tomorrow will undoubtedly interpret your data and pick a graph type to suit it, today's graphing software can make many informed and tasteful decisions about how a graph is to be built once you choose its type. The current leading graphics programs help you design presentable graphics with suggested title sizes and positions, axis scaling, and color combinations. For those of us who have little or no art training, these programs automatically select aesthetically appealing colors, fonts, and type sizes for your graph.

Today's programs dedicated to graphing offer other advantages over the graphing built into 1-2-3. Once you settle on an attractive combination of graph elements, you can create a master template, which you can revise again and again. This template can assure that all graphs belonging to a presentation carry uniform characteristics, such as titles, color schemes, and text fonts.

Most presentation graphics software packages give you graph types you do not have in 1-2-3. By some estimates, text presentations, those lists of text items preceded by bullets, make up nearly three quarters of the visual presentations today. Some programs have modules dedicated to nothing more than creating word graphs. Other programs add new business graph styles or provide variants of those found in 1-2-3. Sometimes a graph type provided by one of these programs can simply convey your message more compellingly than a 1-2-3 graph type.

The drawings, annotations, and ready-made images from clip-art libraries found in most graphing software can amplify a graph's meaning considerably. Some graphing packages let you incorporate scanned photographic images or images captured from video. What better way to present a state's demographic data, for example, than to superimpose a bar graph over an image of the state?

To help you structure a presentation, some graphic packages provide an outline-based organizing tool. This framework helps you hang topics and visuals along a carefully thought-out sequence. When it comes down to the actual presentation, some programs prepare your speaker's notes by combining a miniature of your graph with notes to you about the key points to make.

If your presentation is to take place before a few individuals or a group assembled in a room, you can bring along a computer and monitor and run an animated presentation. The better presentation graphics programs include colorful, motion-filled shows that take place right on-screen, with dazzling transitional effects between graphs. Even if your pitch is before a large audience, you can still display an on-screen show with one of the popular computer projectors that display computer screens as if they were slides.

With some graphing programs, you can even produce a self-running demonstration that pauses for user input, has selectable modules, and lets the viewer choose interactive viewing paths.

Most popular graphing programs enable you to import data from a 1-2-3 worksheet, but the better programs go further; they let you establish hot links between the worksheet and the graph. Change numbers in the worksheet and the graph reflects the change the next time it is drawn.

A final benefit of a dedicated graphing program is its output flexibility. Popular graphing programs produce finished graphs on everything from a simple inexpensive black-and-white dot-matrix printer to a complex and high-priced full-color film recorder. Some even support telecommunications links to service bureaus that will make your slides.

Choosing a Graphics Package

Freelance Plus and Harvard Graphics, the two most popular presentation graphics programs, offer most of the advantages you can expect if you leave 1-2-3 to do your graphing elsewhere. Because these programs are prime competitors, each can match the other's features almost one for one.

Both programs work from a fill-in-the-blanks approach. After you supply the content of the chart by importing 1-2-3 data, you check off formatting choices on a series of forms to set how you want the graph to look. Rather than working directly on the graph, you choose from the options that describe graphical elements. For instance, rather than dragging a legend into place with a mouse, you may be asked to place a legend by named location: above, below, left, right, inside, or outside the chart.

Both programs offer a broad range of standard chart types and many variations on these types. Both programs deliver superb on-screen slide shows with special transitional effects between slides. Freelance Plus and Harvard Graphics offer utilities that display on-screen shows independently of the main program. Special runtime modules allow you to take a disk to a presentation with only your charts and a small program that runs the show.

The greatest advantage to using Freelance Plus over other programs is the consistent end-user interface between 1-2-3 and Freelance Plus. The program uses a menu system similar to the horizontal menu bar in 1-2-3. Moreover, at this publishing date, Freelance Plus is the only program that handles the WK3 file format of 1-2-3 Release 3. Finally, with Freelance Plus, you can view a 1-2-3 worksheet on-screen and use commands quite similar to those in 1-2-3, as you point to the data to be graphed. Harvard Graphics forces users to jot down in advance the list of data ranges that will become the chart series, because you cannot view your original 1-2-3 worksheet while you construct a graph.

Perhaps the greatest advantage of Freelance Plus is its superb drawing module. With Freelance Plus, you can zoom into sections of graphs for editing, rotate their elements, and smooth the edges of objects as you see them on the screen. To obtain these capabilities in Harvard Graphics, you need to buy a separate utility, called Draw Partner.

Freelance Plus lets you create a graph on one screen and then lets you page to a second screen. You can pull symbols from the program's extensive clip-art library onto the second page, for example, and transfer them easily to the graph in progress on the first page. You can also organize slides in directories and print a series of graphs by the batch through the Portfolio feature in Freelance Plus.

Harvard Graphics, however, has features not included in Freelance Plus. With Harvard, you have a spelling checker for text charts and automatic speaker's notes for presentations. Extensive calculation capabilities let you calculate new data series based on your existing series. And you can perform a variety of special operations on a series, such as swapping one series with another. Moreover, Harvard Graphics comes with a macro utility that can totally automate graphing. For finished output, Harvard lists extensive choices of drivers for output devices. Transitions from one output device to another are easy.

But even though these two industry-leading graphing programs can fill your day-to-day graphing needs, dozens more business and presentation programs vie for your attention. Some graphing packages attempt to duplicate the suite of features that Freelance Plus and Harvard Graphics give you, but with less success. Still, there are many programs that may uniquely apply to your graphing needs. The last section of this chapter discusses the relative merits of nine graphics programs, all of which import 1-2-3 data.

The upcoming paragraphs detail graphing 1-2-3 data in Freelance Plus and in Harvard Graphics so that you can compare the two programs. Even if you have not yet acquired one of these packages, you may find it helpful to get a sense of how they work.

Graphing 1-2-3 Data with Freelance Plus

You might naturally expect a dedicated graphing program made by the creators of 1-2-3 to reveal its heritage, and, sure enough, you find a common end-user interface between Freelance and 1-2-3, the same menu system and easy transfer of files between the two products. Freelance Plus was written with 1-2-3 users in mind, and it offers them advantages no other graphing product provides. You can view a representation of your 1-2-3 worksheet in Freelance Plus while selecting data series for graphing. You use the same techniques you use in 1-2-3 for selecting ranges of data. But beyond the easy interaction with 1-2-3, Freelance Plus puts at your disposal a truly comprehensive collection of graphing tools and drawing options.

The following section details techniques for importing 1-2-3 data into Freelance Plus for constructing graphs. The section also tells you how to import finished 1-2-3 graphs for enhancement. Unlike many other graphics programs, Freelance Plus can import graphs directly from a 1-2-3 worksheet—if they have been saved using /**G**raph **N**ame **C**reate. When you select a worksheet from which to import a 1-2-3 graph, Freelance Plus searches the worksheet to let you choose from its stored graphs.

Like many graphing programs, Freelance Plus also imports completed 1-2-3 graphs saved as PIC files. But, unlike most other graphing software, Freelance Plus gives you a special choice: you can import PIC files in their "raw" 1-2-3 form or have PIC files converted to all Freelance Plus default characteristics.

Preparing 1-2-3 Data for Graphing in Freelance Plus

Freelance Plus lets you import 1-2-3 worksheet data with minimum advance preparation. As you are filling out the Freelance Plus chart form, you can always refer to the 1-2-3 worksheet by pressing F6 to view the worksheet before you and select a range of numbers or labels.

But, to speed your work, you can name data ranges, label ranges, and the x-axis data range in advance within 1-2-3 using the /Range Name Create command before you save the worksheet. Later, when you supply a worksheet range in Freelance to fill in the chart form, you can press the space bar and choose from a list of worksheet range names. This procedure can be easier and faster than typing long range names.

To try using Freelance, prepare a set of 1-2-3 worksheet data to import by creating the worksheet in figure 11.1. This worksheet compares selected revenues and expenses for Grandma Dorothy's exquisite line of bakery products for the third quarter of a year in question.

```
E18:                                                              READY

          A         B        C        D        E        F        G
 1                         Dorothy's Delights
 2                  Grandma's Own Baking, Shipped Nationwide
 3
 4                  Jul      Aug      Sept     Oct      Nov      Dec
 5
 6   Direct Sales   23000    24350    25000    27000    27000    30000
 7   Mail Order     14250    15000    15500    16750    18100    19500
 8
 9     Total Revenues 37250  39350    40500    44550    45100    49500
10
11   Baking         8200     8450     8600     8925     9300     9100
12   Boxing         5300     6400     6800     7100     7200     7600
13
14     Total Expenses 13500  14850    15400    16025    16500    16700
15
16
17
18
19
20
04-Jan-90  04:45 PM                                           NUM
```

Fig. 11.1. Worksheet for graphing in Freelance Plus.

Using the 1-2-3 /Range Name Create command, set up the following ranges:

Direct: B6..G6
Mail: B7..G7
Revenues: B9..G9
Baking: B11..G11
Boxing: B12..G12
Expenses: B14..G14
Xdata: B4..G4

Notice that you set up a range called Xdata to hold the label entries that would normally be the X data range in a 1-2-3 graph. You'll see that you can specify this range as the Cluster Labels for a Freelance Plus chart.

Now, save the worksheet with the name DOROTHY. You are ready to quit 1-2-3 and proceed into Freelance Plus.

Setting Up a Datalink in Freelance Plus

To create a new graph in Freelance Plus, you must enter the program's Charts and Drawings module by choosing Charts and Drawings from the Freelance Plus Access menu. The first option on the main Freelance Plus horizontal bar menu is Chart. The Edit-data command under Chart summons the first page of the chart form, shown in figure 11.2. Before you proceed, you must choose a chart type so Freelance Plus will know how to set up the remaining pages of the chart form.

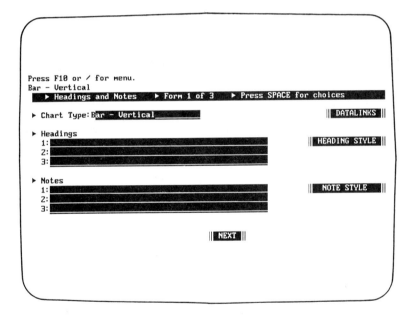

Fig. 11.2. *The Freelance Plus chart form, page 1.*

Vertical bars would be appropriate for this graph so that Grandma Dorothy can compare revenues versus expenses by the month. *Bar - Vertical* is the default chart type, but you may want to press the space bar once to see the pop-up form that shows what other chart types are available. If you do, press Enter to choose Bar - Vertical again and return to the chart form.

Now, you can press the right arrow key or Tab to move the cursor to the box labeled DATALINKS at the right of the screen. To see the Datalinks pop-up form, press the space bar and look for the form you see in figure 11.3.

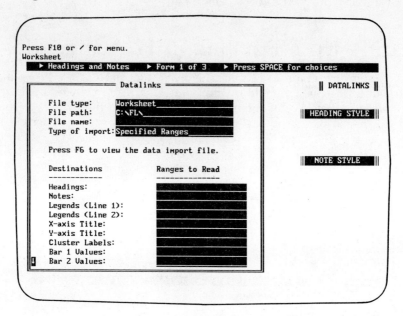

```
Press F10 or / for menu.
Worksheet
  ▶ Headings and Notes    ▶ Form 1 of 3    ▶ Press SPACE for choices
 ═══════════ Datalinks ═══════════              ‖ DATALINKS ‖

    File type:    Worksheet____
    File path:    C:\FL\____                    ‖ HEADING STYLE ‖
    File name:
    Type of import:Specified Ranges____

    Press F6 to view the data import file.      ‖ NOTE STYLE ‖

    Destinations          Ranges to Read
    ────────────          ──────────────
    Headings:
    Notes:
    Legends (Line 1):
    Legends (Line 2):
    X-axis Title:
    Y-axis Title:
    Cluster Labels:
    Bar 1 Values:
    Bar 2 Values:
```

Fig. 11.3. *The Datalinks pop-up form.*

The first three options on the Datalinks form let you specify which worksheet to use:

File type should be set to Worksheet. Press the space bar to see your other file type choices.

File path should be set to the directory that holds your 1-2-3 worksheets. To pick a directory from a list Freelance Plus provides, press the space bar. Freelance will display the directory above the current one in its directory structure and all those below. To choose a directory below the current one, highlight the directory name you want and press Enter. To choose a name above the current directory, select the directory name above the current directory (probably the root: C:\), and then press the space bar again, so that you can pick a directory below the root directory.

You can set the default File path by using the File Options command on the main Freelance Plus menu. To set a default directory for 1-2-3 import worksheets, enter the name of the directory (such as C:\123DATA) at the Other prompt.

File name should be followed by the current worksheet name. To get a list of the worksheets in the current file path, press the space bar. Then, highlight the worksheet you want and press Enter. For this exercise, select the Dorothy worksheet you saved earlier in your 1-2-3 data directory.

The fourth prompt at the top of the Datalinks form, *Type of input*, lets you choose to import specific data ranges or an entire named graph created with /Graph Name Create. Changing the selection here determines how the rest of the page will look. At the moment, the default is Specified Ranges, so the remainder of the Datalinks form shows two side-by-side columns, Destinations and Ranges to Read. If you press the space bar and change Type of Import to Named Graph, the two columns will be replaced by a single prompt requesting the graph name. Leave Type of Import set to Specified Ranges; then you can pull selected data from the worksheet and create the graph in Freelance Plus.

If you choose to import Specified Ranges, your next task is to mate Destinations in the left column with worksheet ranges in the right column on the Datalinks form. To set up a link, you have three choices. First, you can press the space bar to select among any named ranges you set up in 1-2-3. Second, you can manually enter a range address, such as A:B3..H3. Or, third, you can press F6 to view a representation of the worksheet and use the familiar 1-2-3 pointing approach to highlight a range. As you use the third method, Freelance Plus will guide you with instructions at the top of the screen. Follow all the steps below to use a combination of all three methods:

Method One

1. Position the cursor next to the Headings prompt and press F6 to view the worksheet. The worksheet appears as shown in figure. 11.4.

2. Use the right arrow key to move the cursor to cell C1. Notice that you can see only the first nine characters of the cell's entry, but the full entry appears in the control panel at the top of the screen.

3. Press Enter. You will see the range C1..C1 appear as the Range to Read for Headings.

Method Two

4. Position the cursor in the Ranges to Read column next to Notes:

5. Enter B2..B2—the entry for a footnote is one row below and one column to the left of the Heading entry.

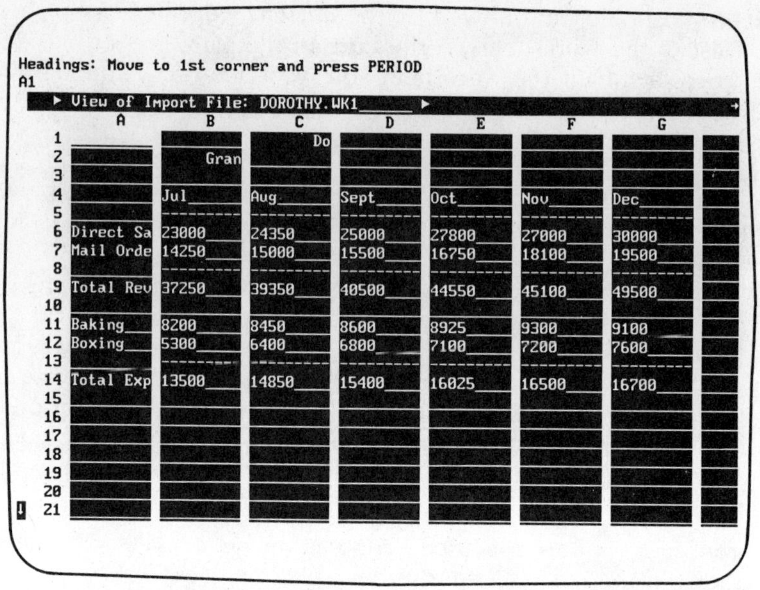

Fig. 11.4. View of a worksheet within Freelance Plus.

Method Three

6. Position the cursor in the Ranges to Read column next to Bar 1 Values and press the space bar.

7. Select Revenues from the list of range names which appears.

8. Position the cursor in the Ranges to Read column next to Bar 2 Values and press the space bar again.

9. Select Expenses from the list of range names which appears.

10. Position the cursor in the Ranges to Read column next to Cluster Labels and press the space bar.

11. Select XDATA from the list of range names which appears.

If the data you need to import is on several worksheets in a 1-2-3 Release 3 multiple worksheet, you can use the same methods for specifying multiple worksheet ranges as you would within 1-2-3. For example, if a range of data to be graphed is in the range A:C1..C:C1 (in cell C1 on worksheets A, B, and C), you can enter A:C1..C:C1 manually, or point to the range by highlighting A:C1; next, press the period key, then use Ctrl-PgUp twice to move up two worksheet levels (to cell C1 in worksheet C), and press Enter.

The Datalinks form should now appear as shown in figure 11.5.

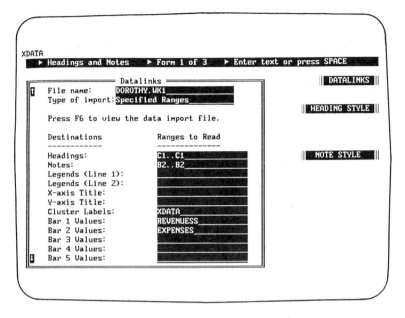

Fig. 11.5 The Datalinks form.

Just as you use a colors or hatches range in 1-2-3 to specify the colors or hatch patterns of graph bars or lines, you can set up a range in a 1-2-3 worksheet that Freelance Plus uses to determine the color and hatch patterns of individual bars. In the 1-2-3 worksheet, you can type Freelance Plus color names into a range with cells that correspond one-to-one to the graphed range. Then, on the Datalinks form in Freelance Plus, you must specify the range as the Bar Colors or Bar Fills range.

You can use the 1-2-3 @IF conditional statement to determine the color of a data point's bar based on the data point's value. This procedure is similar to the Release 3 procedure described in Chapter 6 under the heading "Using Conditional Colors to Highlight Special Results."

To conditionally set the color of a bar portraying a data value in cell D4, for example, you could enter an @IF formula into another cell, in this case, E4. To make the bar green if the data value in D4 is over 100,000, enter @IF(D4>100000,"GREEN","RED"). If the data value is 100,000 or less, the bar appears in red. To make this work, you need to specify this second range of cells as the Bar Colors range on the Datalinks form.

When you finish entering ranges or range names for the applicable Destinations on the Datalinks form, press F10 or position the cursor on the DONE box at the bottom of the list and press Enter. Freelance Plus will ask whether to "Update the chart form with data from the import file?" Select Yes to proceed.

To examine each of the chart's three chart forms, select Edit-Data from the menu at the top of the screen, and then press Ctrl-PgDn repeatedly. Notice on Form 3 of 3, shown in figure 11.6, that Freelance Plus plans to create six clusters (one for each of the months) and two bars per cluster (one bar for revenues and one bar for expenses). Notice also that Freelance Plus displays the correct cluster labels and bar values.

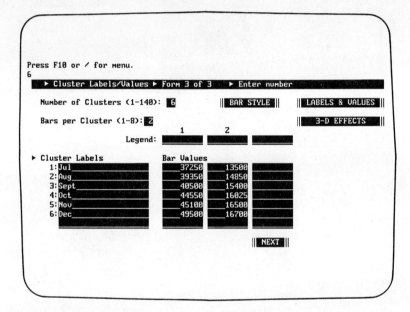

Fig. 11.6. Chart form 3 of 3.

Missing from this page are legends for each of the data series, though. To enter a value directly into any of the entries on a chart form, you can import a label from 1-2-3 directly. This procedure is covered next.

Importing 1-2-3 Data Directly into a Chart Form

To import 1-2-3 cells or ranges into a chart form, position the cursor on the chart-form entry and press F6. When you see the representation of the worksheet, move the cursor to the cell or range you want and highlight it by pointing.

For this graph, position the cursor on the legend entry for series 1, press F6, and then move the cursor to cell A9 (Total Revenues). You should see "A9 Total Revenues" appear in the control panel at the top of the screen, so you can check the entire entry. Press Enter twice to use "Total Revenues" as the legend for the series—once to return to the chart form and once to copy the label "Total Expenses" into the legend entry. Repeat the procedure to make cell A14 (Total Expenses) the legend entry for series 2. The chart form now looks like figure 11.7.

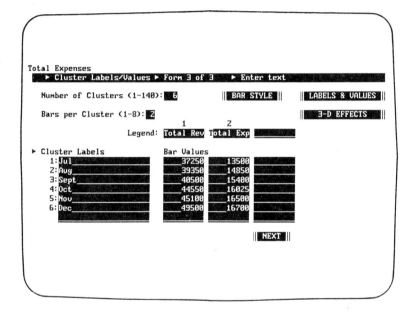

Fig. 11.7. *The completed chart form, page 3.*

When you press Enter to copy a range of cells into a chart form, the range is copied on the chart form in the same orientation. Rows on the worksheet are copied into a series of horizontal entries on the chart form, and columns on the worksheet are copied as chart form columns. If you press Ctrl-Enter rather than Enter, Freelance Plus transposes the data, switching worksheet rows for columns on the chart form.

You can copy data from more than one worksheet into a Freelance Plus chart form. To do so, use the Datalinks pop-up form to change the file name before copying data directly to the chart form. This method allows you to consolidate data from several worksheets into a single graph. The method must depend, though, on your copying data directly to the chart form rather than specifying ranges to import on the Datalinks pop-up form.

When you import 1-2-3 data directly to a chart form, Freelance Plus truncates labels that are too long to fit the space on the chart form; it ignores items that do not match the format expected at the destination; and it rounds the numbers from the worksheet so that they match the Freelance Plus *# of decimal places* setting for that data on the chart form. You can override this action by selecting No for *Round worksheet data when importing* on the Chart Options screen.

If you press F11 to summon the menu while you are working on a chart form, you can use one of the commands under the Range option to move, copy, or erase data. You can also insert blank lines within data and use Date-fill to fill entries on a chart form with a succession of dates.

To view the chart based on the data you have imported, press F11 when the chart form is complete; then select **G**o from the menu. When you see the blank chart drawing screen, press Enter, once to draw the chart and, again, to accept the chart as drawn. Figure 11.8 shows the chart on the main Charts and Drawings screen; Figure 11.9 shows the same chart printed at half-size on a LaserJet Series II laser printer.

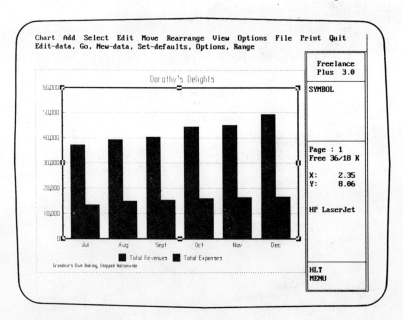

Fig. 11.8.** **The main Charts and Drawings Screen showing the chart.

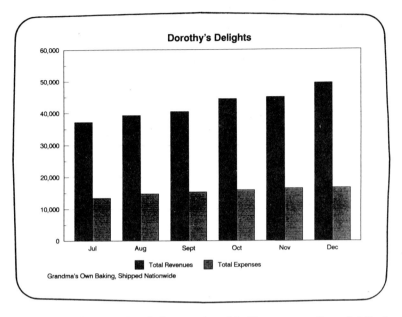

Fig. 11.9. *The completed chart printed half-page on a LaserJet Series II printer.*

Setting Up 1-2-3 Import Options in Freelance Plus

On the Freelance Plus File Options screen (see fig. 11.10), you can determine the default path for the worksheets you import into Freelance Plus. Enter the directory that contains your 1-2-3 worksheets after the Other prompt under Default paths.

When you choose Chart Options from the Freelance Plus menu, you can set a variety of other chart defaults. The Chart Options screen is shown in figure 11.11. The first five entries determine default sizes for chart text in millimeters. The File Importing and Linking options determine a variety of settings for how worksheet data is handled by Freelance Plus.

Import new data when reading chart files lets you determine whether Freelance Plus should update a chart's data from the 1-2-3 worksheet each time you retrieve the chart.

Round worksheet data when importing lets you determine whether Freelance Plus should round data to fit the number of decimal places

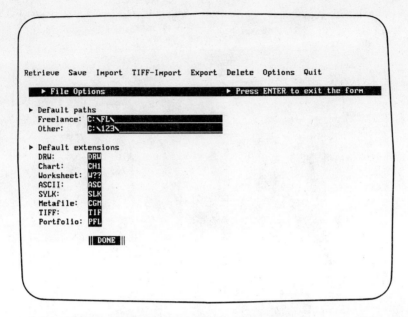

Fig. 11.10. *The Freelance Plus File Options screen.*

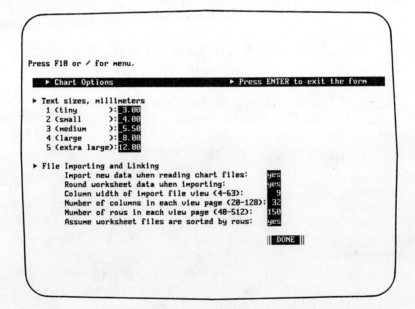

Fig. 11.11. *The Freelance Plus Chart Options screen.*

you chose for the data in Freelance Plus. If you set this option to No, Freelance Plus preserves the full decimal precision of the data.

Column width of import file view lets you determine the width of all columns in the representation of the worksheet you see when you press F6. The default is 9, the same as in 1-2-3.

Number of columns in each view page lets you enter a number between 20 and 128 to set how many data columns Freelance Plus will read from the worksheet when you view a file.

Number of rows in each view page lets you enter a number between 40 and 512 to set how many data rows Freelance Plus will read from the worksheet when you view a file. The larger the number you choose for this and the previous options, the slower your cursor will move on the F6 view worksheet screen.

Assume worksheet files are sorted by rows should be set to Yes if your worksheet file is sorted by rows. Most worksheets are sorted by rows.

Importing a 1-2-3 Graph into Freelance Plus

If you select Named Graph for Type of Import on the Datalinks pop-up form, you can position the cursor next to Name of graph, then press the space bar to see a list of named graphs saved with the worksheet. After you select a named graph and press Enter, Freelance Plus will ask you to confirm that you want to "Update the chart form with data from the import file." Select Yes. Now you can modify any of the entries on the chart forms—or you can press F10 and then **G**o to return to the Freelance Plus drawing screen to see the resulting chart.

Graphing 1-2-3 Data with Harvard Graphics

Harvard Graphics may not have the same close family ties to 1-2-3 as Freelance Plus, but it provides many of the same benefits when importing and graphically presenting 1-2-3 data.

What has endeared Harvard Graphics to so many who create presentation graphics is its combination of power and ease of use. It provides a superb assortment of easily-constructed graph types, an intuitive menuing system and command structure, and built-in blueprints for the most popular business graph types. You need only to provide the ingredients for a graph. Harvard Graphics does most of the work based on its own recipes for attractive, clear graphs. The same ease extends to the task of importing your 1-2-3 graphs and data.

With Harvard Graphics, you have two choices for the source of graphs based on 1-2-3 data. Either you can pull selected data from a 1-2-3 worksheet and create the graph in Harvard Graphics, or you can import a completed basic graph and enhance it with the Harvard options. But, as of this publication date, Harvard Graphics is compatible only with WKS and WK1 worksheet file formats. That means you can use Harvard Graphics with 1-2-3 Release 1A, Release 2.01, or Release 2.2, but Harvard cannot yet interpret Release 3's WK3 worksheet file format. If you are using Release 3, you will not be able to follow along with this example.

The following section covers techniques for importing 1-2-3 data into Harvard Graphics for graphing. It also includes procedures for importing completed 1-2-3 graphs into Harvard Graphics for improvement. Unlike some other graphics programs, Harvard Graphics can pull graphs that have been saved using **/Graph Name Create** directly from a 1-2-3 worksheet. This program does not need a PIC file version of the graph. When you import a 1-2-3 graph and select a worksheet, Harvard Graphics searches the worksheet to let you choose from the graphs saved there.

Preparing 1-2-3 Data for Graphing in Harvard Graphics

If you decide to pull data from a 1-2-3 worksheet and prepare the graph in Harvard Graphics, you should take a few moments to prepare the worksheet while you are still in 1-2-3 to make your later work easier. You can use the 1-2-3 **/Range Name Create** command to assign names to the ranges of data to appear in a graph. Then, when you get into Harvard Graphics, you can specify range names (such as EXPENSES) rather than cumbersome range addresses (such as AC23..AH23) for the data you would like to use for data series in Harvard Graphics.

If your worksheet contains much data, be selective about which data appears in a graph. But you still can leave yourself room for play later, because Harvard Graphics can manage eight data series with as many as 240 data points each. Even if you are not certain you will need a data series, you still may want to import it to Harvard Graphics. If you end up with more data series on the data screen than you need, you can use the Display option on the First Options Page to create a graph or a series of graphs with only certain series selected from the eight.

Whether you decide to use range names or addresses to specify your data, you should jot them down on paper before you leave 1-2-3, because Harvard Graphics offers no way to view a 1-2-3 worksheet to identify range addresses, and it provides no list of the range names available.

To try creating a Harvard Graphics chart based on 1-2-3 data, first set up the worksheet shown in figure 11.12. This is the same worksheet used for the previous section with Freelance Plus. Notice that this worksheet compares selected revenues and expenses for Grandma Dorothy's exquisite line of bakery products for the third quarter of the year in question.

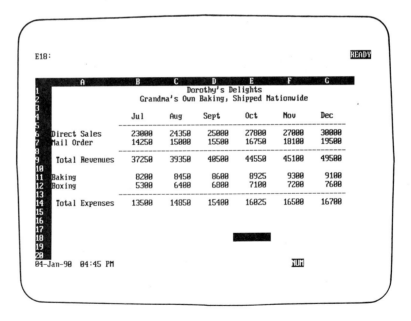

Fig. 11.12. Worksheet for graphing data in Harvard Graphics.

Using the 1-2-3 /**R**ange **N**ame **C**reate command, set up the following ranges:

Direct: B6..G6
Mail: B7..G7
Revenues: B9..G9
Baking: B11..G11
Boxing: B12..G12
Expenses: B14..G14
Xdata: B4..G4

Notice that you set up a range called Xdata that holds the label entries that would normally be the X data range in a 1-2-3 graph. You'll see that you can specify this range as the x-axis labels for a Harvard Graphics chart, as well.

Now, save the worksheet with the name DOROTHY. You are ready to proceed into Harvard Graphics, so quit 1-2-3 and start Harvard Graphics.

Setting Import Defaults in Harvard Graphics

If you keep 1-2-3 worksheets in a single directory on your hard disk, you can tell Harvard Graphics how to locate worksheets by setting a *default import directory.* Although you can choose another directory to search through later, Harvard Graphics will suggest first the default directory. You can even tell Harvard Graphics which worksheet in the 1-2-3 data directory to suggest first, by setting a *default import file.* both of these settings can be seen on the Default Settings screen in figure 11.13.

To get to the Default Settings screen, select *Setup* from the Harvard Graphics main menu and then *Defaults* from the Setup Menu that appears. You will see Import Directory and Import File near the top of the Default Settings screen. Type in appropriate entries, such as C:\123 for a default import directory, and DAILY.WK1 for a default import file of daily results to be graphed. You can press Tab to move to the next entry on the Default Settings screen or Shift-Tab to return to the previous entry. When you are finished, press F10-Continue to return to the Harvard Graphics main menu.

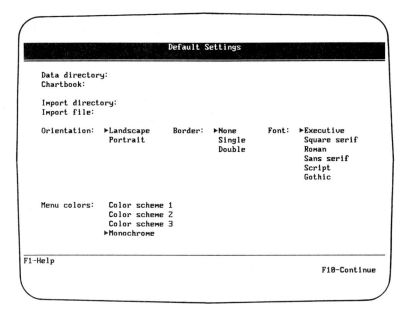

Fig. 11.13. The Harvard Graphics Default Settings screen.

Importing 1-2-3 Data into Harvard Graphics

Before you select *Import/Export* from the Harvard Graphics main menu to import data from a 1-2-3 worksheet, you must set up an appropriate chart type for the data. If you do not, you will see a message that says "Cannot Import Data to Current Chart Type" when you try to import 1-2-3 data.

To set up a chart, select *Create New Chart* from the main Harvard Graphics menu, and then select an appropriate chart type from the resulting Create New Chart menu (see fig. 11.14). To create a chart of the data in the DOROTHY worksheet, select a Bar/Line chart.

The X Data Type menu, which appears next, lets you set up the x-axis of the chart so that it represents appropriate units. For example, if your chart will display data over the passage of time, you can specify days, weeks, months, or a variety of other calendar units for the x-axis. If the x-axis data on the worksheet is in a different time-unit format from those supported by Harvard Graphics, Harvard Graphics will convert the 1-2-3 data to the chart format you specify on the X Data Type menu.

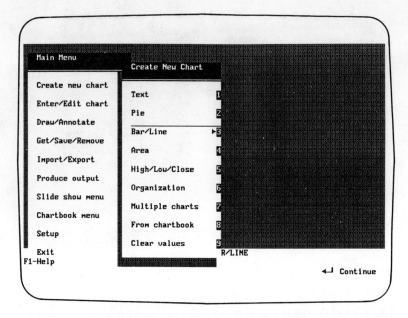

***Fig. 11.14.** The Harvard Graphics Create New Chart menu.*

The DOROTHY chart data is organized by month, so select Month by pressing the space bar repeatedly until Month is highlighted. Normally in Harvard Graphics you enter a first month name at the Starting With prompt and a final month name at the Ending With prompt; then you let Harvard Graphics fill in the months between. For this chart, though, you will import the x-axis labels from 1-2-3, so press Enter three times to pass each of these prompts and the prompt labeled Increment. Figure 11.15 shows the blank Bar/Line Chart Data screen that appears.

If you have a title and subtitle for the chart in mind, you can enter these manually at the top of the Bar/Line Chart Data screen, which appears next. Or, you can wait and pull graph titles from the worksheet later in the process. For this exercise, wait.

With an appropriate chart type set up in Harvard Graphics, you can now return to the main menu by pressing Esc to import chart data from the 1-2-3 worksheet. Select *Import/Export* from the main Harvard Graphics menu; then *Import Lotus data* from the Import/Export menu. If you specified a default import directory, Harvard Graphics now displays a list of the worksheets in that directory; without a default directory, you must use the F3-Select files command to navigate to the proper directory. Highlight DOROTHY.WK1 on the list of worksheets and press Enter. The Import Lotus Data screen appears next (see fig. 11.16).

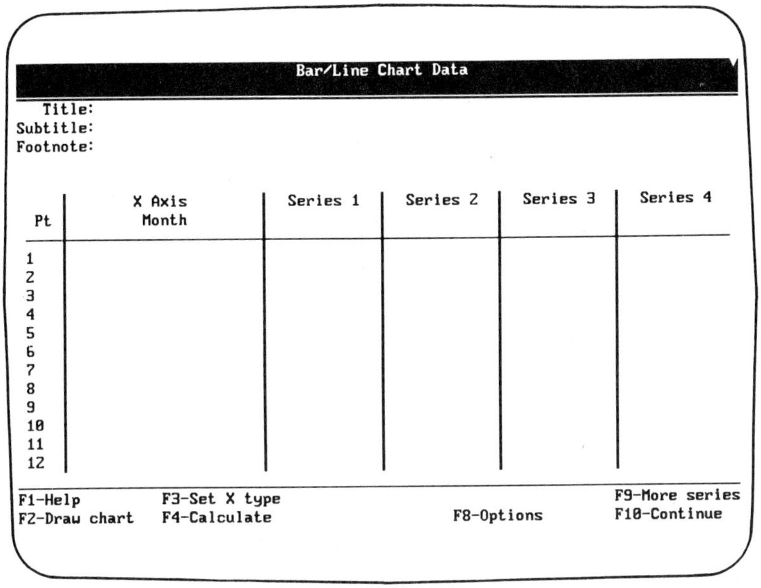

```
                        Bar/Line Chart Data
     Title:
  Subtitle:
  Footnote:

              X Axis       Series 1   Series 2   Series 3   Series 4
   Pt         Month

   1
   2
   3
   4
   5
   6
   7
   8
   9
  10
  11
  12

 F1-Help          F3-Set X type                        F9-More series
 F2-Draw chart    F4-Calculate               F8-Options  F10-Continue
```

Fig. 11.15. *The Bar/Line Chart Data screen.*

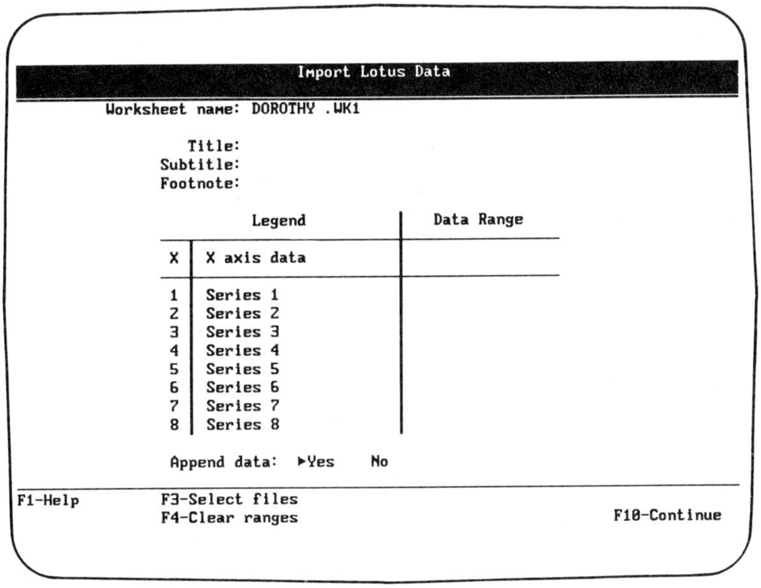

```
                        Import Lotus Data
       Worksheet name: DOROTHY .WK1

                Title:
             Subtitle:
             Footnote:

                    Legend             Data Range

              X │ X axis data

              1 │ Series 1
              2 │ Series 2
              3 │ Series 3
              4 │ Series 4
              5 │ Series 5
              6 │ Series 6
              7 │ Series 7
              8 │ Series 8

              Append data:  ►Yes    No

 F1-Help      F3-Select files
              F4-Clear ranges                        F10-Continue
```

Fig. 11.16. *The Harvard Graphics Import Lotus Data screen.*

At the top of the Import Lotus Data screen you can manually type in a chart title, subtitle, and footnote (which appears at the bottom left of the chart by default). Or, you can enter the cell addresses of these titles on the 1-2-3 worksheet preceded by a backslash (\), just as if you were using worksheet titles for the /Graph Options Titles option within 1-2-3. For this chart, enter \C1 after Title G and \B2 after Footnote; leave the Subtitle entry blank.

Below the titles section of the Import Lotus Data screen is a three-column data entry area. The first column identifies which rows correspond to the x series and the data series 1 through 8. The second column supplies default legends for each of the series. The third column provides space for you to enter data range addresses or range names for each of the series in the graph. Use the Tab key to move from one to the next of these entries. Use the Ctrl-Del key combination to erase an existing entry so that you can enter a new one. Complete the screen to match figure 11.17.

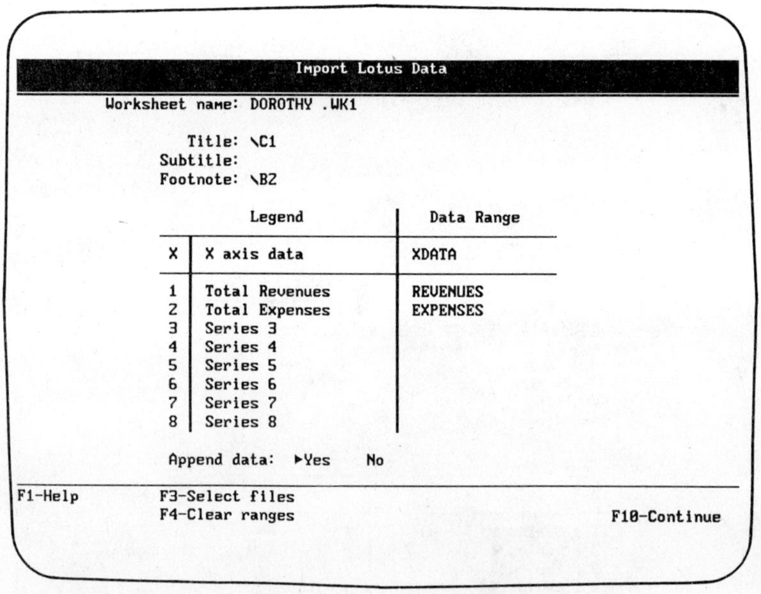

```
                        Import Lotus Data

  Worksheet name: DOROTHY .WK1

          Title: \C1
       Subtitle:
       Footnote: \B2

                  Legend              Data Range

       X | X axis data                XDATA

       1 | Total Revenues             REVENUES
       2 | Total Expenses             EXPENSES
       3 | Series 3
       4 | Series 4
       5 | Series 5
       6 | Series 6
       7 | Series 7
       8 | Series 8

       Append data:  ▶Yes    No

 F1-Help        F3-Select files
                F4-Clear ranges                         F10-Continue
```

Fig. 11.17. The completed Import Lotus Data screen.

Near the bottom of the screen you can choose either Yes or No for Append data. If you choose Yes, the 1-2-3 data you specify will be added to the end of any data already present on the current chart's data screen. If you choose No, the 1-2-3 data will replace any data already on the data screen. For this chart, select No by positioning the highlight on one of the options and pressing the space bar until No is highlighted. Now, press F10-Continue to read in data from the worksheet. You should see the complete data screen as you see it in figure 11.18. This data screen displays only the first four of the six series included. To see the remainder of the series, press F9-More Series. Then, press F9 again to see again the first four series. If you set up the chart titles exactly as you saw them in figure 11.12, the full title text may not fit into the Title and Footnote blanks on the data screen (see fig. 11.11). You will need to manually remove the spaces preceding them and supply any missing characters.

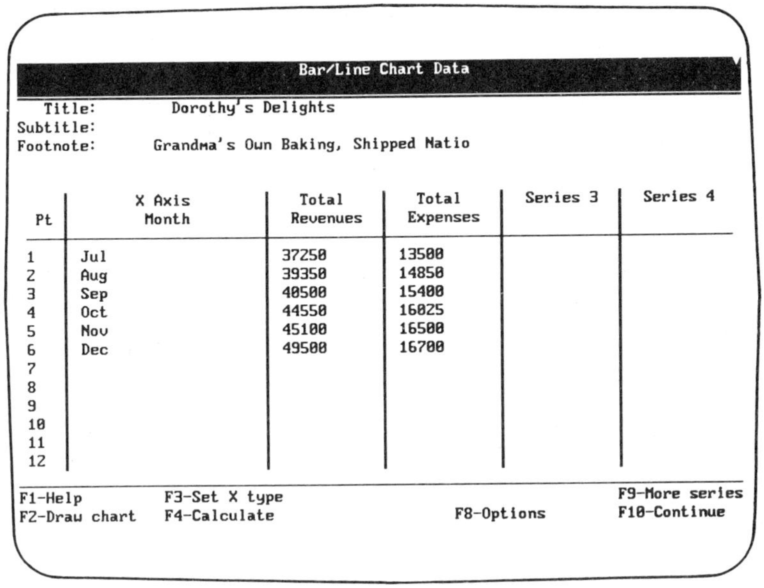

```
                        Bar/Line Chart Data

   Title:        Dorothy's Delights
 Subtitle:
 Footnote:       Grandma's Own Baking, Shipped Natio


         X Axis         Total       Total     Series 3   Series 4
 Pt      Month          Revenues    Expenses

 1       Jul            37250       13500
 2       Aug            39350       14850
 3       Sep            40500       15400
 4       Oct            44550       16025
 5       Nov            45100       16500
 6       Dec            49500       16700
 7
 8
 9
 10
 11
 12

 F1-Help         F3-Set X type                          F9-More series
 F2-Draw chart   F4-Calculate              F8-Options    F10-Continue
```

Fig. 11.18. The 1-2-3 data imported into a Harvard Graphics data screen.

If you press F2-Draw Chart, you get the default bar chart created by Harvard Graphics. This chart should look similar to the one shown in figure 11.19, except that the pictured graph shows the bars filled with patterns rather than colors, so the series can be distinguished in black and white.

Figure 11.20 shows the default bar chart printed at half-size on a LaserJet Series II printer.

After you import data into a Harvard Graphics chart, you can begin a variety of modifications to tailor the chart. Immediate changes you may want to consider are adding axis titles, displaying all or some series as lines rather than bars, selecting 3D as a bar enhancement, and adding a data table to display actual data values in a grid below the worksheet.

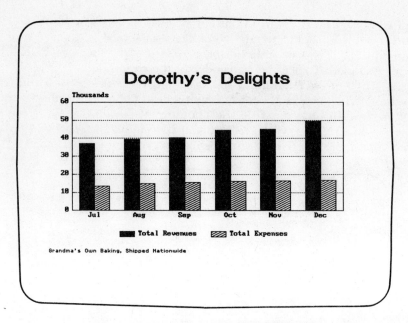

Fig. 11.19. *The default Harvard Graphics bar chart.*

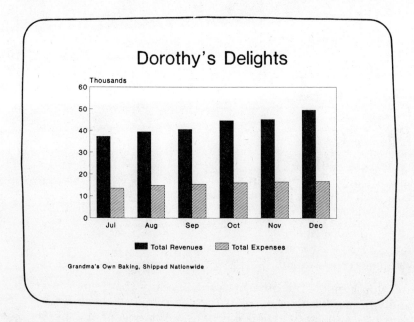

Fig. 11.20. *The bar chart printed half-size on a LaserJet Series II Printer.*

Establishing a Datalink between 1-2-3 and Harvard Graphics

To make a permanent record of the chart on your disk, you can select *Save Chart* after you choose *Get/Save/Remove* from the Harvard Graphics menu. But another selection from the same menu, *Save template,* enables you to establish a permanent marriage between a chart and the worksheet from which its data comes. When you make a change to the data in the worksheet, the chart will reflect the change the next time you load the chart's template using the *Get template* command.

If you merely save the chart using *Save Chart,* it will look the same when you retrieve it, even if you have made changes to the worksheet you imported data from. If you retrieve the template for the chart, instead, the template will reach back out to the worksheet and pull in your new, revised data before it constructs a graph and reproduces your enhancements.

To automate the process one step further, you easily could create a one-keystroke macro that loads the template, saves and then prints the resulting chart. Your macro could even trigger itself at a certain hour and carry out the process before you get to the office in the morning to find your 1-2-3 data has been updated overnight.

Try saving a template of the current chart with a datalink by choosing *Get/Save/Remove* from the Harvard Graphics main menu and then Save template from the resulting menu. The Save Template overlay appears, as shown in figure 11.21.

Type a template name after the Template name prompt. Then, if you like, modify the description derived from the title of the chart. To save the template with the chart's data preserved, change *Clear Values* from Yes to No. To erase the data to make room for new data the next time you load the template, leave Clear Values set to Yes. That way, the revised data pulled from the worksheet by the template will be the only data in the chart.

The last prompt on the Save Template overlay gives you the option to avoid setting up a datalink. The *Import data link* option on your screen is set to Lotus, because you imported data from a 1-2-3 worksheet. Leave it that way by pressing Enter to maintain the link. If you had pulled data from an ASCII file, the option would have been set to ASCII. To break the link between the template and another file that served as the source of data for the chart, you can set Import data link to None. When you press Enter the final time, you will see a warning

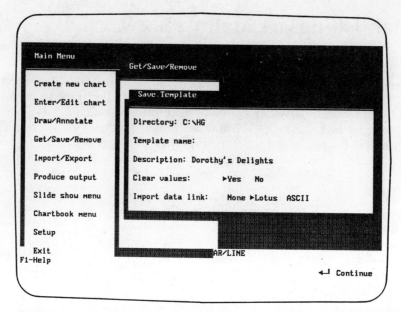

Fig. 11.21. *The Save Template overlay.*

message that says "Chart values are about to be Cleared." Press Enter to let Harvard Graphics clear the data from the template before saving it.

To test the link, exit from Harvard Graphics and return to 1-2-3. Now, modify one of the data entries by adding 100,000 to its value. An extra $100,000 added to one of the expense categories should modify Dorothy's financial picture quite noticeably. Save the worksheet and then return to Harvard Graphics. From the Get/Save/Remove menu, select *Get Template* and then choose the template you saved before.

When Harvard Graphics retrieves a template with a datalink to a 1-2-3 worksheet, it rereads the worksheet data just as it did at first. In fact, Harvard Graphics will tell you it is reading the worksheet before it presents a completed data screen. Once you see the data screen, you can press F2-Draw Chart to preview the chart with all the same options settings you chose for the template. The resulting chart should look something like the chart shown in figure 11.22.

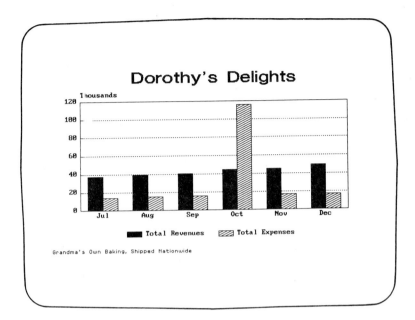

Fig. 11.22. *The bar chart reflecting the 1-2-3 data revision.*

Reordering Data with the Harvard Graphics @REDUC Calculation

Not all data kept in 1-2-3 is ideally organized for import into Harvard Graphics. Data may be formed into rows or columns interspersed with blank spaces or filled with hyphens or equal signs to separate figures into logical groupings. If Harvard Graphics encounters a 1-2-3 label in the middle of an import range, it ignores the label and leaves a blank entry in the resulting Harvard Graphics data screen. The 1-2-3 worksheet data may also be out of order or filled with unwanted duplications. Data that is out of order or that contains blank rows or unwanted duplications on a Harvard Graphics data screen, warrants the quick and easy fix supplied by the @REDUC calculation.

The worksheet shown in figure 11.23 is a sample of data not quite ready for import. Two problems are apparent. First, data is separated into two fiscal quarters by a separator row of hyphens. Second, the last row in the worksheet, row 14, is additional data supplied late for the month of March. You could take the time to delete the row of separator hyphens and add the new March data to the old. The better plan is to import the data as is into Harvard Graphics and use @REDUC to make these changes for you.

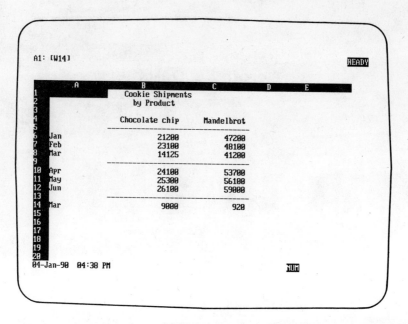

Fig. 11.23. *A worksheet comparing shipments of two cookie varieties.*

To try the @REDUC calculation, recreate the worksheet in figure 11.23. Then you can use the *Import Lotus Data* option on the Import/Export menu within Harvard Graphics to import the two series into a bar/line chart. The completed Import Lotus Data screen should match the one in figure 11.24. The data screen after you perform the import should be compared to figure 11.25.

Notice the blank row 4 and additional March information in row 9. If you preview the chart by pressing F2 now, you will see both of these problems (see fig. 11.26).

To fix this data, position the cursor in the X-Axis, Series 1, or Series 2 column and press F4-Calculate. Press Tab to move the cursor to the *Calculation* prompt on the Calculate overlay which appears. Enter @REDUC for the calculation and press Enter. The completed Calculate overlay appears in figure 11.27.

Now, take a look at the data screen and notice that the blank row has been removed and the two rows of data for March have been added together. The data screen now looks like figure 11.28.

```
                          Import Lotus Data
        Worksheet name: dot.wk1

                Title:  \B1
             Subtitle:  \B2
             Footnote:

                        Legend              Data Range

             X │ X axis data                A6..A14

             1 │ Chocolate chip             B6..B14
             2 │ Mandelbrot                 C6..C14
             3 │ Series 3
             4 │ Series 4
             5 │ Series 5
             6 │ Series 6
             7 │ Series 7
             8 │ Series 8

                Append data:   ▶Yes    No

 F1-Help          F3-Select files
                  F4-Clear ranges                    F10-Continue
```

Fig. 11.24. *The Import Lotus Data screen for the cookie shipment comparison.*

```
                          Bar/Line Chart Data
    Title:       Cookie Shipments
 Subtitle:         by Product
 Footnote:

            X Axis      Chocolate   Mandelbrot   Series 3    Series 4
  Pt        Month         chip

  1    Jan              21200       47200
  2    Feb              23100       48100
  3    Mar              14125       41200
  4
  5    Apr              24100       53700
  6    May              25300       56100
  7    Jun              26100       59000
  8
  9    Mar               9000        9200
 10
 11
 12

 F1-Help        F3-Set X type                         F9-More series
 F2-Draw chart  F4-Calculate           F8-Options     F10-Continue
```

Fig. 11.25. *The Harvard Graphics Data Screen after import.*

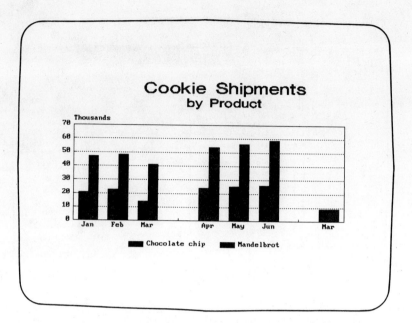

Fig. 11.26. The bar chart based on the data screen in figure 11.25.

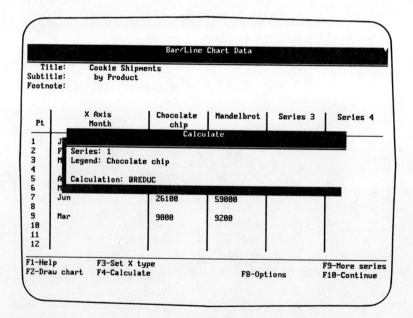

Fig. 11.27. The completed calculate overlay.

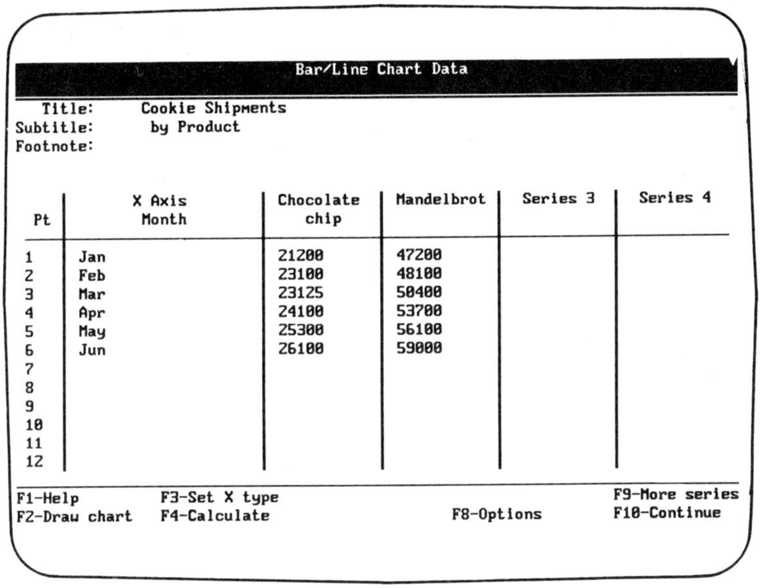

```
                              Bar/Line Chart Data                              ▼
     Title:      Cookie Shipments
   Subtitle:       by Product
   Footnote:

                X Axis       Chocolate    Mandelbrot    Series 3     Series 4
    Pt          Month          chip

    1      Jan                21200        47200
    2      Feb                23100        48100
    3      Mar                23125        50400
    4      Apr                24100        53700
    5      May                25300        56100
    6      Jun                26100        59000
    7
    8
    9
   10
   11
   12

   F1-Help         F3-Set X type                              F9-More series
   F2-Draw chart   F4-Calculate              F8-Options       F10-Continue
```

Fig. 11.28. The data screen after @REDUC.

The @REDUC calculation performs the following tasks:

☐ Sorts data series based on x-axis labels.

☐ Eliminates duplicate x-axis labels.

☐ Eliminates gaps along x-axis caused by blanks.

Importing a 1-2-3 Graph into Harvard Graphics

Rather than creating a graph from scratch in Harvard Graphics, you may prefer to use the basic formatting of a graph you created while still in 1-2-3. Harvard Graphics lets you import graphs you created and named with the /Graph Name Create command.

When Harvard Graphics imports these graphs, it brings the graph's data into a data screen and translates the 1-2-3 graph settings into those compatible with its own options. You may see differences ranging from subtle to pronounced between the the graph in 1-2-3 and the one you see in Harvard Graphics. Harvard Graphics displays a 1-2-3 graph's y-axis indicator above the y-axis rather than to its left, for example. You will also see differences in colors and hatch patterns.

You will see other changes in format. Harvard Graphics does not include the data-labels you added to the 1-2-3 graph with /Graph Options Data-labels. Numbers, as well, may be formatted differently in a Harvard Graphics chart. And, the y-axis in a Harvard Graphics chart may use a different scale.

To import a named graph, select *Import Lotus Graph* from the Import/ Export menu. Harvard Graphics will display a list of available worksheets in the default import directory. When you choose a worksheet, the program will list all named graphs associated with the worksheet. If you haven't saved your graph with a name, you can pick Main from the list. Main is the current chart as set up with the 1-2-3 /Graph menu options.

When you import a graph, you can choose to import only the data from that graph by setting *Import data only* to Yes. If the graph you want is not in the current worksheet, you can choose another worksheet by pressing F3-Select Files.

Harvard Graphics automatically offers the first eight characters of the 1-2-3 graph name as the chart name when you save the chart. If the 1-2-3 graph name includes a space among its first eight characters, Harvard Graphics substitutes an underscore (_) for the space.

After you pull a 1-2-3 graph into Harvard Graphics, you can proceed immediately to the graph's Options pages and begin modifying the graph's details. When you're done, save your work just as you would save any other Harvard Graphics chart.

Graphing 1-2-3 Data with Other Graphing Software

Freelance Plus and Harvard Graphics may be the market-share leaders in the presentation graphics arena, but they are certainly not the only graphics packages worthy of attention. Nearly all major software makers offer one presentation graphics program. And if they don't already, you can be sure they soon will. In only a short time the field of presentation graphics has grown from a new category at the PC level to one of the most dynamic classes of software in the personal computer industry.

You should know about the following nine presentation graphics programs. All share the ability to import and then graph data from 1-2-3 worksheets. These next paragraphs cover each one by one, spotlighting the program's strengths and underscoring its shortcomings.

Lotus Graphwriter II

From the progenitors of 1-2-3 and Freelance Plus comes yet another program with graphics. For people with too much work in too little time, Lotus Graphwriter II focuses on completely automatic graphing. In fact, you can run Autochart, the program's automatic chart generator right from the DOS prompt. Besides completely automatic graph generation, the program features a fully automatic datalink with an ongoing live link to worksheet data. Whenever you modify worksheet data, the graph updates, too.

Graphwriter II may not provide the latitude for artistic expression that programs with more extensive drawing and annotating capabilities do, but it delivers clear and communicative graphs with minimal effort. As you would expect from a Lotus product, Graphwriter II shares 1-2-3's look and feel. It also displays a spreadsheet view right on-screen, just as Freelance Plus does.

Graphwriter II offers an amazing variety of highly professional looking chart types, including two unusual breeds, the bubble chart, which displays data with circular areas whose overlap represents equivalence, and the Gantt chart, used for project management, because it displays a progression of tasks.

Consider Graphwriter II to maintain a consistency of operation with 1-2-3 and to lift the burden of planning professional presentation graphics when you have neither the time nor the inclination to fuss with your visuals.

Graph Plus from Micrografx

Graph Plus, from Micrografx, swings quite the other direction from Graphwriter. The emphasis in Graph Plus is to give you total control over chart design in all its aspects.

First released as Windows Graph in 1987, Graph Plus runs under Microsoft's graphical user interface called Windows. The visually presented concepts of Windows work well in graphmaking. For example, the Graph Plus menus visually present their vast array of chart styles, displaying for you how each chart style will look. If you don't find the chart you need depicted on a menu, you can create a custom chart type and save it in a graph storage area called a *folder*.

Graph Plus imports 1-2-3 data into a huge internal worksheet of 256 rows and 16,384 columns. Based on the data stored there, you can create up to 12 separate graphs simultaneously on twelve 8 1/2-inch x 11-inch pages arranged in a grid. Maintaining so many active graphs makes cutting and pasting among graphs a simple matter.

You can ornament your graphs with clip art from the extensive collection available from Micrografx. And, you can include in your graphs images produced by scanners or paint programs even though these images are in a graphic file format fundamentally different from that created by Graph Plus.

The graphic files produced by devices called scanners, which optically read photographs and other pictures, are always *bit-mapped* files. They are composed of thousands of dots on the screen. Each dot is represented in the computer's memory by one bit (a zero or a one). Simply put, if the bit is a one, the dot on the screen is turned on. If the bit is zero, the dot is dark. Of course, if the image is color, more bits are used for each dot to represent its color.

The graphic files produced by Graph Plus are vector files, instead. Objects on the screen are not stored in the computer's memory dot by dot. Instead, the image is stored mathematically, as a series of simple geometric shapes: lines, boxes, curves, and circles. That's why vector files are often called line art or object-oriented files.

If you regularly use a scanner to convert company logos and other such images into computer files, you'll be pleased with Graph Plus' ability to combine both bit-mapped and vector files.

Another outstanding Graph Plus feature is its superb slide shows, which you organize by arranging thumbnail versions of charts on-screen. Organizing a presentation is facilitated by the program's complete integration of drawing and graphing functions. Other programs provide graphing features in one module and drawing features in another.

Because Graph Plus runs under Windows, it will run on any graphics display supported by Windows. That includes the full 1024 x 768 pixel resolution and 256 simultaneous colors of the IBM 8514/A graphics standard. Other high-speed and high-resolution graphics cards will also display Graph Plus if they include Windows drivers.

But because Graph Plus runs under Windows, you will need more sophisticated hardware to run the program. Windows requires the power of a computer with at least an 80286 processor (an AT-compatible computer). Graph Plus works even more satisfactorily on an 80386 computer.

After you complete a graph in Graph Plus, you can pull the final image into another Micrografx product, Designer, for freehand drawing and annotations. Designer is an illustrator that also runs under Windows. Illustrator programs let you draw easily, using a complete set of tools that perform many of the tasks carried out frequently by professional artists.

Micrografx has been one of the leading developers for the Presentation Manager, the graphical user interface that is part of OS/2, which is IBM and Microsoft's successor to DOS. You can be sure that Micrografx will continue to lead in making versions of its applications available for the OS/2 Presentation Manager.

The major shortcoming of Graph Plus is its lack of automatic word charts, such as lists of text items with bullet points. You can place text on the screen in freeform fashion, but no standard text chart styles are supported.

Choose Graph Plus if you have the disposition to dig in and putter around with your charts. The result can be extraordinary.

Pixie, from Zenographics

Another Windows application called Pixie, from Zenographics, brings fun, impressive ease of use, and low cost to presentation graphics. Pixie may not provide all the features of the market-leading graphics programs—it has no live links with 1-2-3 data, for example—but what it offers, it offers with style.

Pixie is intelligent and responsive to the choices you make. Modify one item and Pixie will modify similar items accordingly. But some might say Pixie makes modifications all too easy. By selecting a bar in a bar chart and increasing its height manually, you can change the underlying chart data. This ability provides easy visual what-ifs, but it also introduces the hazard of inadvertent data modifications.

Pixie can be a stepping stone to the high-end, professional graphics package called Mirage, also from Zenographics. Pixie directly exports a file type that Mirage imports.

Users who have both IBM standard PCs and Macintoshes will be glad to hear that Pixie is available in versions for both machines. That means you can swap Pixie files back and forth between otherwise incompatible machines.

Because Pixie is a Microsoft Windows application, it gives the same benefits as Graph Plus—and the Xerox Windows graphing applications to be described next. Pixie runs comfortably on any graphics device supported by Windows, even IBM's high-resolution 8514/A graphics system.

Pixie's greatest drawbacks are its small built-in clip-art library for adding predrawn images to graphs and its lack of an on-screen slide-show feature. Choose Pixie if your graphing needs are not elaborate, yet you want stylish charts with a minimum of effort.

Xerox Presents

Xerox Presents, a relatively new contender in the category, emphasizes the overall presentation over and above its individual charts. The result is a natural consistency and organization that you must deliberately strive to achieve in most other presentation graphics programs.

In Xerox Presents, you create a file that consists of a series of frames. These frames all possess common characteristics, such as the background color or typeface for text titles. After you complete the components of a presentation, you can organize them into a coherent whole by simply clicking and mouse-dragging your slides in thumbnail sketch versions.

But if Xerox Presents excels at the level of overall presentation, the current version falls short of other graphing programs in creating specific charts. Xerox Presents limits you to six series of data and eight chart styles. The program gives you no method for manually scaling the axes. Those shortcomings and others are more fully addressed in the next product discussed, the even newer Xerox Graph.

Xerox Graph

Xerox Graph, also a Windows application, offers presentation-quality graphs and extensive data analysis in one package. The program offers a vast array of mathematical data manipulations to act on the data maintained in a large built-in spreadsheet. After you import data from 1-2-3 into the spreadsheet, you can perform data smoothing and calculate such statistical results as z-scores and running sums.

Xerox Graph provides no datalink to 1-2-3 worksheets. You can import data from a worksheet to create a graph, but in so doing you sever the relationship between the graph and its 1-2-3 data.

Xerox Graph is also deficient in providing no formal word charts, although its text editing and placement are unusually flexible. And another minus, the program offers no on-screen slide shows.

Choose Xerox Graph if the charts you must create would benefit from the program's unusually complete data calculation, manipulation, and analytical tools.

Microsoft Chart

When Microsoft first introduced its business graphics program, Microsoft Chart, it amazed PC users by what it could do. But since then, it has been overtaken by many newer competitors.

Microsoft Chart offers no drawing capabilities, no clip-art libraries, and no automatic datalink to worksheet data. You can create a link, but you must refresh it manually. Furthermore, the program suffers from minor problems in failure to interpret the format of incoming 1-2-3 data. Microsoft Chart tries to graph labels it finds in the middle of data series, for example, rather than appropriately brushing them off, as other programs will do.

Microsoft Chart still offers an ample variety of chart types and impressive output with an unusually broad range of drivers for output devices, but many other popular programs have surpassed it for graphing 1-2-3 data.

Draw Applause

Ashton Tate's entry in the presentation graphics arena is most noteworthy for its impressive drawing abilities. Yet its palette of chart types is narrower than many other graphing programs. In the Draw Applause drawing module, you can create exciting and interesting special effects, such as a graduated color background or a halo glowing around on-screen objects. But, the program is expensive, and its slide-making resources are limited. It supports only the Matrix PCR film recorder and Ashton Tate's own Ashton Tate Graphics Service, a slide-making service bureau.

GEM Graph Presentation Pack

GEM, the Graphical Environment Manager from Digital Research, has been around for years, and the applications possible with its graphical user interface are some of the most underrated in the industry.

Digital Research has put together a package of three applications dedicated to presentation graphics, GEM Graph, GEM Draw Plus, and GEM WordChart. The three combine well for diverse and complementary graphing abilities.

GEM Graph provides a built-in worksheet with easy editing, and its menu shows you visually all of the available graph types, in the manner of Graph Plus under Microsoft Windows. The program offers a superb variety of graph types, including the unusual symbol graph, which replaces bars with repeated pictographs of cars, airplanes, humans, or other relevant images.

To edit GEM Graph charts, you can pull the completed image into GEM Draw Plus for drawing and annotation. Then, to create the word charts for your presentation, you can use GEM WordChart.

The prime drawback of this presentation package is its lack of support for film recorders. You are obligated to use the MAGIcorp slide-service bureau, instead.

Choose the GEM Presentation Package particularly if you are using Ventura Publisher to desktop-publish documents that incorporate business graphics. Ventura Publisher is a GEM application, also, and GEM Graph files are easily compatible with Ventura.

Aldus Persuasion

At the time of this publication, Aldus Persuasion is available only on the Macintosh. But Aldus has a track record of bringing fine Macintosh products to the PC environment—Aldus PageMaker came from the Mac—and you can look for this precedent to be continued with Persuasion.

Persuasion provides nearly all the benefits of using a dedicated presentation graphics package to create business graphs from your 1-2-3 data. The program offers the same rich tools for organizing a presentation that Xerox Presents does. Persuasion has extensive drawing capabilities, complete text processing tools, a spell-checker, as does Harvard Graphics, and complete slide shows. In addition, the program automatically generates speaker's notes.

Persuasion's major drawback for 1-2-3 users is its lack of a live link between the program's internal spreadsheet and an external worksheet file. You can import 1-2-3 data to Persuasion, but without a mechanism for keeping the data current automatically. But, despite this serious limitation, if Persuasion arrives in the PC market late in 1989, as promised, it may represent state-of-the-art graphing until Software Publishing next updates Harvard Graphics.

Summary

Performing your graphing activities in a dedicated graphing package rather than in 1-2-3 is not so disloyal to 1-2-3 as it may seem. Dedicated graphing packages provide a wealth of benefits that 1-2-3, even 1-2-3 Release 3, just cannot offer. In this chapter you explored first the principal reasons for turning to a dedicated presentation graphics program. You learned the range of options to look for in these special programs.

Next, you considered the relative merits of the two leading graphics packages used with 1-2-3. The portfolios of visual effects offered by Freelance Plus and by Harvard Graphics were examined to give you a fundamental orientation in using dedicated graphics software with 1-2-3. Nine other popular presentation graphics programs were discussed, so that you could sample for yourself the multitude of new programs becoming available, each with particular strengths that might just fit your needs.

In the next chapter, you see how to take your graphics a step further than traditional printed graphs, using the on-screen slide-show feature of some presentation graphics packages. Then the following chapter focuses on animating graphs from your 1-2-3 data, a media enhancement brought within your reach with the new software offerings.

12

Making Slides

The more compelling the medium, the more compelling the message. And few methods can deliver a message with more impact than the eye-catching colors and vivid clarity of 35mm slides. Slides can display your graphs as easily to an auditorium-sized audience as they can to a room-sized meeting. And, well-prepared slides bespeak the professionalism and sophistication that you sometimes need to project. By one estimate, business presentation givers will create more than 180 million computer-generated slides in the year 1990 alone (Hope Reports, Inc.). Slides are easy to carry, simple to control, and they quietly inform an audience of the resources at your disposal. Most importantly, slides can project visual images that make the messages they carry memorably striking.

Slides are not the only means of projecting your graphs onto a screen for audience viewing. Transparencies, when used with an overhead projector, can display a large, easily-seen graphic image, too. Moreover, transparencies are easy to create and edit. You simply photocopy a printed graph onto a transparent page. Or, for color, you put a transparency page into a color plotter. Both methods are simple and inexpensive, and they let you do the work quickly and in-house, leaving open the possibility for last-minute changes and corrections.

But for all their ease, transparencies don't impress many of today's demanding audiences. Transparencies lack the definition and color of slides, and they can be difficult to handle. We've all sat embarrassed, squinting at a bright white screen, while a nervous presenter fumbled trying to find the next page.

Slides, on the other hand, can be sequenced in a tray in advance, to appear quietly and smoothly one after another with a simple press of a button. A uniformly designed series of slides can give quite a different impression from the low-budget look of transparencies. In fact, because slides are so much more professional in appearance than transparencies, many assume they are both difficult and costly to produce. Getting a 35mm slide, the kind that you put into a Kodak Carousel projector, used to be a time-consuming and expensive chore. Only graphic artists could transform your data into impressive visuals. And once the artists had created the visuals, they would photograph their work with a standard 35mm camera and slide film. Then they needed to develop the film and mount the slides to turn out a packaged presentation ready for the most critical of audiences.

Now, as you learn in this chapter, getting a slide of a graph is almost as easy as creating it on-screen. Companies called service bureaus can take a file that contains your 1-2-3 graph, create a slide for you, and return the finished product the following day, no matter where you work, all through overnight delivery services and the telephone.

If you produce many presentations, you can do the same work by acquiring a film recorder. This device connects to your computer and automatically transfers high-resolution images from your computer screen or software program to film. You need only develop the film to obtain professional-looking, colorful graph slides.

As you learn in the next chapter, a challenger for the hearts of business presenters is a new category of hardware and software that makes desktop presentations. Animated on-screen demonstrations generated by these products can be projected before a group with clarity and color. Further, such demonstrations can use television-like transitions, special effects, and interactive pathways. A speaker might stop to explore a particular subject in detail, responding to a question from the audience before returning to the main topic. Slides are static in comparison to the animated presentation, and they best suit a linear presentation that departs little from the script. But slides still hold a commanding lead in both clarity and color.

So, if your choice is to produce slides rather than the less expensive transparencies or the on-screen animated presentation, your next choice is how to process the slides. Should you send your 1-2-3 graph files out to a service bureau for transformation into slides or try doing the work in-house with a film recorder? The factors you must consider are covered next.

Making the Choice: Film Recorder or Service Bureau?

Your decision is not necessarily to use a film recorder exclusively or to routinely turn to a slide service bureau. The decision is first whether to buy a film recorder. You can always take advantage of a service bureau, even if you already own a film recorder. There may be times when sending graphs out to be transformed into slides may be faster than waiting for the recording and film developing process to finish. Service bureaus are equipped for high-volume jobs and quick turnaround times. They may be able to knock out a large presentation with many slides in just a few hours. At other times your film recorder may be overloaded, or you may want to add the artistic touch a graphics professional who is on staff at a service bureau can provide.

Film recorders offer a number of benefits, though. They can save money when you create slides in high volume. Good quality film recorders fall in the $5,000-$7,000 price range, although inexpensive models run as low as $2,000, and top-flight machines cost $25,000 or more. Basic service bureau slides range in price from $8 to $15 each, so you easily can calculate the break-even point for the model you are considering. Beyond the initial outlay for the film recorder purchase and installation, be certain to count in the costs of supplies, maintenance, training, and a staff person to operate the machine. Only after you have included the full costs of operation can you properly compare the relative expenses of the two methods.

After you have factored the relative cost of making slides in-house rather than through a service bureau, your next consideration is the relative turnaround you can expect from the time you have a completed 1-2-3 graph to the time you have a finished slide in hand. Unless you happen to work near a service bureau that offers slides in a matter of hours, your own film recorder usually will deliver faster turnaround. And, in addition, with a film recorder, you can make a last-minute change to a graph and record a new image quickly, usually in 2 to 15 minutes. Remember, of course, that a film recorder simply records images onto a roll of film. You must have the film processed and the slides mounted before your presentation can begin. And, of course, if you are the one doing the work, the extra time spent making the slides yourself is time lost from other work in preparing your presentation.

Service bureaus depend for their livelihood on their ability to deliver completed slides as quickly as possible. But the bureau can return your work to you no faster than you send it. One possibility is to transfer your graphs to a disk, which you send in turn to the service bureau. If you have a modem, you can even transmit your files directly to many service bureaus by telephone. Whether you ship your graphs by mail, messenger, or modem, you can expect to receive completed slides the following day. With some service bureaus, you can take advantage of economy rates if you can wait an extra day or two. And, for a premium, most service bureaus will put a rush on your work, returning it the same day, if geographically possible. Check with your local service bureau to see what discounts and premiums you can expect.

Some people will argue that film recorders let you keep in-house the information that is sensitive to your firm. And it is true that with service bureaus, you are as dependent on their confidentiality as you are with a doctor or therapist. Remember, you may be sending your most highly guarded business strategies off to a remote site, where prying eyes may be a problem. The probable counterargument is that you cannot develop the film you record with your film recorder in-house anyway. Inevitably, you will take the film to a remote site to be developed. Whether you send your graph files out or your exposed film, your information is just as susceptible to loss, whether accidental or not, as soon as it leaves the security of your office.

Can you expect to see a difference in the quality between slides recorded by your film recorder and those produced by a service bureau? Probably so. The $5,000-$7,000 corporate film recorder you may have access to is just a plaything compared to the $250,000 film recorder the larger service bureaus employ. Of course, for many presentations, especially when the projected image is small, the 4,000-line resolution of an in-house film recorder is more than sufficient. When the image is meant for projection in a large auditorium, the difference between a 4,000- line film recorder and an 8,000-line, top-calibre service bureau slide becomes more apparent.

Service bureaus offer options that are unavailable if you are restricted to using an in-house film recorder. If you need something showier than you can achieve on your own, you can employ the scrvices of a professional artist, often on-staff at the service bureau. These graphics experts not only can enhance your graphs, but produce versions of your company logo, special title pages, symbols, and other presentational amenities. For their services you will pay a premium, often $40-$50 per image. If these services are extraordinary, or if you require a complex graphic with much detail or creative artwork, the price you can expect to pay can soar to $100 to $200 per slide.

If you do not need a custom graphic designed expressly for your slides, you may be able to select from a library of graphic images available at the service bureau for incorporation into your slides. These images are like those available in clip-art books in art-supply stores. You can cut and paste any of these onto your own artwork. You can even select special backgrounds to be added to your slides: grids, patterns, or gradient wipes from light to dark or from one color to another. Your service bureau can inform you about the special graphic effects available.

Many service bureaus offer options for output other than 35mm slides. Some offer color ink-jet or thermal transfer printing, laser printing in black and white or color, and even transfer of your images from computer monitor to video tape. Once your images are on videotape, you can edit them into your videotaped presentation.

Of course, as graphics software rapidly improves, fashioning sophisticated visuals becomes easier. With today's newest graphing packages, you can produce gradient background colors, three-dimensional graphs in full perspective, and other design effects that your own in-house film recorder can quickly achieve on film. As the software makes special custom artwork easier, the demand for services by graphics artists at service bureaus will decrease. Even so, you can never replace the trained eye and experience of a graphics professional in finding a unique and eye-catching way to deliver a visual message.

Whether you work with a service bureau or do the job with your own film recorder, you should keep in mind that the slides you get back are never precisely as you expected, despite the best-laid plans of both you and your software. You will see variations in text size and placement, color shifts, and other anomalies. As you gain experience, you will learn to estimate the variations that will occur and adjust your images accordingly.

Evaluating Film Recorders

Slide makers come in several varieties. The most inexpensive simply attach a hood to the front of a camera. The other end of that hood is placed over your computer's screen, so that the camera can get a clear photograph of the screen without reflection. These screen cameras record your actual computer monitor's display, and the slides they produce are limited in quality by the resolution of your screen. Usually, the computer monitor resolution is far lower than the resolution of the more popular slide makers called film recorders, described next.

Most devices that help make slides are more technically sophisticated. Film recorders are so named because their output is not slides but a roll of film to be developed as slides. Like printers and monitors, film recorders respond to the output data coming from a computer and generate their own image. They photograph that image onto film using one of two technologies: analog or digital.

Analog recorders usually connect to a computer's serial port and create an image of your graph on a small black-and-white monitor. A color wheel with the three primary video colors rotates between the internal monitor and the camera, recording the image in three passes; first red, then green, then blue.

Analog recorders have a resolution only slightly greater than that of standard video displays. The Polaroid PalettePlus, for example, the most popular analog film recorder, has a resolution of 640 × 700 screen dots, called *pixels,* compared to the IBM Video Graphics Array (VGA) video standard of 640 × 480 pixels. The result is an image that is sharper than what you see on your computer monitor, but not much. Certainly, you will not get the super-crisp text lettering and graphic lines possible with more expensive film recorders. The advantages to analog film recorders such as the Polaroid are low cost and fast operation.

Digital film recorders operate on a different principle. Whereas these also have a small internal black-and-white monitor and a 35mm camera, they construct an image pixel by pixel, taking as many passes as there are pixels on-screen. Because the resolution typical of the better film recorders is over 4,000 pixels across and over 2,000 pixels vertically, recording the image can take many passes. As a result, digital film recorders are slower than analog models. A film recorder of this resolution is capable of a 4,000-line resolution.

Installing digital film recorders can be more involved than the easily installed analog film recorders. The digital recorders may require the installation of an expansion card within the computer and the setup of special driver software.

Despite the overwhelming popularity of analog recorders, the Polaroid Pallette and its recent sibling, the Polaroid PalettePlus, the more expensive digital film recorders provide the level of resolution that presentation professionals and their audiences want to see. In fact, the 4,000-line resolution these better machines provide is about the maximum resolution available with standard Kodak Ektachrome ASA 100 film, the most-used film in film recorders because of its quality and its easy availability.

The technical proficiency of a film recorder is measured both by resolution and color capacity. The standard is 4,000-line resolution, although 2,000-line film recorders can produce images that are often nearly as impressive. The greatest resolution you will find is about 8,000 lines. The 8,000-line resolution exceeds the capabilities of all but large format film, though, so it is normally employed in those rare circumstances when high resolution overrides all other criteria.

Standard film recorders with a 256-color capacity can produce stunning graphics, but products with a greater color palette can produce smoother transitions from light to dark hues, or from one color to another. For a superbly smooth background gradient, you want a film recorder that can produce at least 1,000 shades of color.

With most film recorders, you can replace the standard film you use with instant print film, so that you can run test prints of your image, checking for size and placement of text and graph components. The capability of your recorder to accept instant print film can be invaluable in your work and can improve your learning curve dramatically as you become aware of the peculiarities of your particular system.

The Path from 1-2-3 Graph to Slide

The path from 1-2-3 graph to slide is littered with confusion, compounded by the literature produced by many film recorder manufacturers. Many companies making film recorders claim compatibility with 1-2-3. But the route, if available at all, is circuitous.

One approach to transmitting 1-2-3 graphs to a film recorder is the route used by the Polaroid PalettePlus. The PalettePlus comes with a software package called OneStep, which captures a graph from the screen and translates it into a format acceptable to the film recorder. That limits the resolution of your slide to the resolution of your computer screen. Lasergraphics offers a utility that translates 1-2-3 graphs to its own graphics language (LL, the Lasergraphics language). The Lasergraphics film recorders then interpret electronically the LL version of the graph and produce an image.

Without any doubt, you are better off using a dedicated software package, such as Harvard Graphics or Freelance Plus as an intermediate link between 1-2-3 and a film recorder. To complete this link, you transfer a 1-2-3 graph saved as a named graph within 1-2-3 to either Harvard Graphics or Freelance Plus. Both of these programs are designed to work with a variety of digital film recorders, although, of the two, Harvard Graphics supports a far greater assortment. Even with little knowledge of either graphing program, you can issue the simple commands needed to send a graph to your film recorder.

After you import a 1-2-3 graph into a dedicated graphing program, further possibilities become available to you for editing and enhancing the image. The previous chapter described in detail the process of transferring a graph from 1-2-3 to either Harvard Graphics or Freelance Plus, and it demonstrated some of the options that programs such as these make available to you.

Figure 12.1 shows the Film Recorder Setup screen in Harvard Graphics, which lists the film recorders for which Harvard provides direct support. Figure 12.2 shows the Installed Devices screen listing the two film recorders for which Freelance Plus provides support.

```
X
┌──────────────────────── Film Recorder Setup ────────────────────────┐

   POLAROID       Palette (CGA)      MATRIX         PCR,QCR
                  PalettePlus (EGA)
                                     AUTOGRAPHIX    Slide Service
   LASERGRAPHICS  RASCOL II/PFR
                  Compatible         VDI            Camera

   BELL & HOWELL  CDI IV,1000        GENERAL        VideoShow
                                     PARAMETRICS    ColorMetric
   PTI            ImageMaker                         GPC file
                  Montage

   Film recorder: RASCOL II/PFR

   Slide file directory:

   Film type:         ▶Ektachrome   Polachrome   669   339
   Use hardware fonts: ▶Yes          No


 F1-Help
                                                        F10-Continue
```

Fig. 12.1. The Harvard Graphics Film Recorder Setup screen.

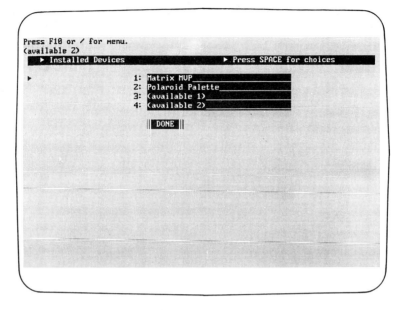

Fig. 12.2. The Freelance Plus Installed Devices screen.

Evaluating Slide Service Bureaus

Service bureaus differ greatly both in their general capabilities and in their ability to process 1-2-3 graphs. Some service bureaus accept 1-2-3 PIC files, but some require that you send an output file from a dedicated graphing program, such as Freelance Plus or Harvard Graphics.

Actually, if you were to look behind the scenes at the service bureaus where 1-2-3 PIC files are accepted, you would find that most use Freelance Plus to convert a 1-2-3 PIC file into a format suitable for use by a film recorder because of the easy communication between the two Lotus products.

Before you commit to a computer service bureau, you should investigate several aspects of its capabilities other than price and delivery time. Check to see if the service bureau has graphics designers who can create custom artwork and special effects for your slides. Check pricing to see if you can save money by using an economy service that may delay your slides for a day or two when time is not a factor. Make certain that the overnight service the firm uses to return slides is acceptable to you.

Contact the service bureau to ask for printed literature with suggestions for best use of the dedicated graphing program you employ. Service bureaus may have documented the most common errors when using a particular package, and this information can save you precious trial-and-error time. Finally, to become thoroughly acquainted with the service, be sure to run a few test slides before you need a rush of slides for an important presentation.

Planning a Presentation

Whether you decide to make slides in-house or to hire an outside service bureau to do the work, the task of designing an engaging presentation still falls squarely on your shoulders. Putting together an interesting presentation may be more art than science, but you can still keep a few suggestions in mind as you prepare slides to inform and entertain your audience.

The easiest way to give a presentation a professional polish is to incorporate uniform design elements throughout. Use a consistent color scheme and text typeface on all your slides. Keep a consistent footnote or subtitle. Add a graphic that repeats on every slide, perhaps your organization's logo. If you fail to maintain consistency in your slides, you may inadvertently give the impression that you've pulled them together by ransacking previous presentations.

The old adage "Keep it short and simple" applies all too well to slides. Slides crammed with text are impediments rather than aids to conveying your point. Don't fill every slide edge to edge with data. Leave some space around your graphs. Position graphs on different sides of the slide for variety, and keep them uncluttered, with text to a minimum. Try to devise short, catchy headlines that capture the one, all-important message in each graph.

If you can mix the graphs you need with text slides summarizing issues or the conclusions you have just presented, you can keep the presentation active and varied. If you can depict different aspects of your data with various graph types—a bar graph first, then a pie graph, then a line graph—all the better. To a viewer, nothing can be more monotonous and sedating than facing one bar graph after the next.

In addition to these few ideas for refining the overall presentation, take note of some of the suggestions in Chapter 2 of this book for improving the appearance of individual graphs. With those recommendations in mind, you'll be set to create presentations that can both impart and inspire.

Summary

Slides are one of today's most prevalent presentation accessories, yet they intimidate many people, who imagine that creating slides is both difficult and expensive. In this chapter, you learned how you can let an outside service bureau do all the work or how you can acquire a film recorder for just a few thousand dollars and make your slides in-house. Using a presentation graphics program such as Harvard Graphics or Freelance Plus is the easiest vehicle for transforming a 1-2-3 graph into an image ready for a slide.

But although you cannot outdo slides for vibrant colors and sharp resolution, another technology is rapidly stealing attention from slides for presentation use. The next chapter covers desktop presentation systems you can use to give your 1-2-3 graphs a different sort of color.

13

Animating 1-2-3 Graphs

U sing slides may give you the most crisp and colorful presentation for your 1-2-3 graphs, but displaying graphs in an animated on-screen presentation can offer benefits no slide show can match. When you create a screen show of graphs that displays right on a computer screen, you can add television-like transition effects between successive graphs. These effects can include such sophisticated techniques as *fades,* which cause the next graph to slowly appear on screen, *wipes,* which reveal the next graph from one side of the screen to the other, and *scrolls,* which slide the graph in from one side of the screen.

Animated screen shows, also called desktop presentations, offer other benefits, too. They let you add motion to the very components that make up each graph. Not only can a graph fade into view, but its bars can grow or its lines can travel across the screen right before the eyes of your audience.

Today's jaded business audiences are going to expect as much. By the time you get to make your pitch, they will have sat through enough slide shows to last a lifetime. The razzle-dazzle effects you create with desktop presentation packages can give your presentation the edge you need to capture their attention. In addition, desktop presentations eliminate the time and expense associated with creating slide presentations, and they easily let you make those inevitable last-minute changes.

Popular desktop presentation programs divide into two groups. The first group is composed of graphing programs that include animated screen shows as just one of their capabilities. The second group is composed of dedicated animation packages that specialize in creating slick desktop presentations.

Graphing programs that are part of the first group, such as Harvard Graphics and Freelance Plus, include basic on-screen presentation capabilities. They let you import and incorporate 1-2-3 PIC files into screen shows, and overlay graphs at successive stages of completion, creating the illusion of building a single graph year by year or product by product.

As an added benefit, graphs are automatically upgraded in appearance when you import them as PIC files into Freelance Plus or Harvard Graphics. The graphs are restyled in more attractive text fonts, colors, and other changes for the better. Then you can use the extensive drawing and annotation features of either program to spruce up your graphs or add consistent design elements throughout a presentation, perhaps placing a company logo in one corner of each graph. But Harvard Graphics, Freelance Plus, and other graphics programs have their downside when it comes to creating animated presentations. Because these multitalented programs include screen shows as just one capability, they fall short of dedicated animation programs, such as IBM's PC Storyboard Plus and Brightbill-Roberts' Show Partner F/X, in offering presentation facilities.

Dedicated on-screen presentation programs give you a more sophisticated technological range than the screen-show modules of charting programs. Consider the options available with IBM's PC Storyboard Plus: you can capture 1-2-3 graphs and wrap them into a show; then add music, sound effects, and voice narration with optional IBM hardware products. Moreover, PC Storyboard Plus and other dedicated animation programs offer far more extensive animation options: you can even animate the individual components within graphs. You can cause certain bars in a bar graph to grow on-screen or to change color. Or, you can make the lines of a line graph snake slowly across the screen, traveling from point to point. You can even converge the slices of a pie graph, drawing them in from all sides to form a completed circle.

The tradeoff to having these capabilities on hand, of course, is the greater effort you must expend to prepare a presentation. Even though dedicated desktop presentation programs make creating sophisticated on-screen effects simple, putting together a complex presentation can be time-consuming, exacting work. Just as professional animators spend days on a sequence that may last a few seconds, you may spend hours putting together a sequence of graphs that remains on the screen for just minutes.

That task may seem more onerous when you learn that most dedicated desktop presentation programs do not import 1-2-3 PIC files. Your choices are to capture graphs as they appear on 1-2-3 screens or to pull PIC files into dedicated graphing programs or translation utilities in order to create an acceptable input file for the desktop presentation program.

Because on-screen presentations run on a computer screen, you may think of them as suitable only for a small group in a meeting room. But such presentations can be just as acceptable before a large group in an auditorium. A wide-screen computer projector can deliver nearly the same dazzling color and moving images at the annual stockholder meeting as a big-screen color monitor can display in a desktop presentation to the board of directors.

This chapter covers the most popular software for creating animated presentations from your graphs, both popular charting programs and dedicated desktop presentation programs. You will learn techniques for creating on-screen slide shows that use animation techniques to switch from one slide to the next and even for creating animated graphs in which the graph bars or lines move on-screen.

Software that enables you to create on-screen presentations is divided into two categories: charting packages that include a screen-show module, and dedicated desktop presentation packages. The category first discussed will be programs with screen-show modules. You will see how two of these programs work, Freelance Plus and Harvard Graphics.

Charting Programs with Screen-Show Modules

Although other charting software provides desktop presentation capabilities, the two most popular software programs in this category are Freelance Plus and Harvard Graphics. Each has its separate strengths. For a description of the relative strengths and weaknesses of the two programs in graphmaking, see Chapter 11, "Importing 1-2-3 Data into Graphing Software."

The following section focuses on the desktop presentation capabilities of each program and recommends specific techniques for using them to their best advantage when presenting 1-2-3 graphs.

Freelance Plus

Freelance was not born with screen-show capabilities. It acquired them as the program evolved. But because the screen-show module in Freelance Plus was developed by animation specialists Brightbill-Roberts, you can expect a variety of dazzling transition effects between drawings and other animation techniques.

Because Freelance Plus imports 1-2-3 PIC files, the transition from 1-2-3 to Freelance Plus is seamless. Neither of the dedicated desktop presentation programs described later in this chapter makes pulling in 1-2-3 graphs so easy.

The fastest way to create a Freelance Plus screen show from 1-2-3 graphs is to follow this orderly series of steps:

1. Save the 1-2-3 graphs that are to become part of the screen show as PIC files in 1-2-3.

2. Import each PIC file into Freelance, enhance it if you wish, and then save it as a Drawing file.

3. Using the Portfolio module of Freelance Plus, convert all Drawing files automatically into the Screen files Freelance Plus needs for screen shows.

4. Add screen-show special effects to the Show List automatically generated by Portfolio.

The process sounds more daunting than it is. To help you examine the screen-show capabilities of Freelance, the text will explain how to create a sequence to be animated. You will create a sequence of screens showing subsequent yearly results. Then you will build a bar chart that incorporates these screens one by one. Before you enter Freelance, though, you must create the sequence of graphs in 1-2-3. Start by setting up the worksheet shown in figure 13.1.

First consider the process you will follow to create the series of individual charts, each with one more year's data than the previous one. You will start by creating the complete graph with the data of all years displayed. You will save the completed graph as a PIC file. Then,

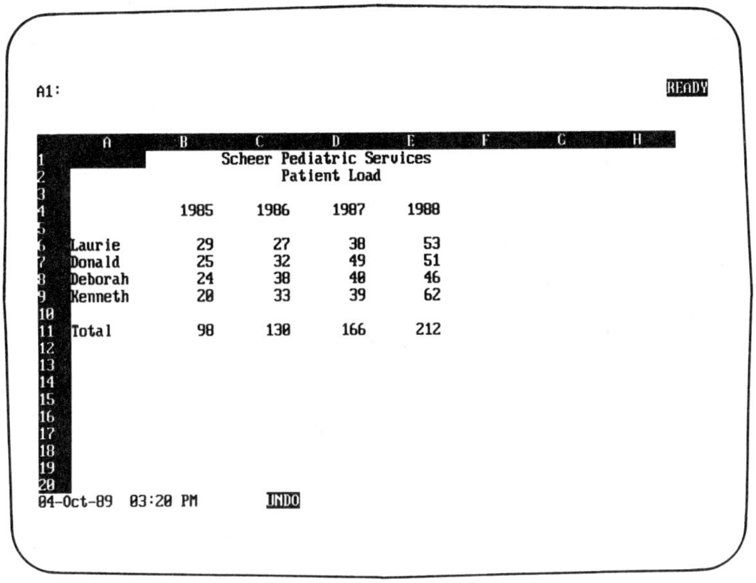

Fig. 13.1. The worksheet for the bar graph.

removing data in reverse chronological order, you will set all the values for the latest year to zero and save the resulting graph as a second PIC file. You will set the year before that also to zero, and save that graph as a PIC file. You will continue setting the values for the previous year in the graph to zero and saving each graph as a PIC file until you have set all data points in the graph to zero. You will save the final graph as a PIC file.

To make this procedure work, you must manually scale the y-axis. Otherwise, 1-2-3 will automatically rescale the y-axis according to the largest remaining value as you begin removing values. If the series of graphs you create have different y-axis scalings, the effect you are about to create will not work.

Here, in detail, is the procedure you should follow in 1-2-3 to create the five PIC files necessary to build this bar graph.

Start by setting up the worksheet shown in figure 13.1 and creating the graph shown in figure 13.2. Notice that the graph has a minimum y-axis value of 0 and a maximum y-axis value of 70. Select /**Graph Options Scale Y-Scale Manual** and set **Lower** to **0** and **Upper** to **70**. Be sure to make the graph black and white by setting **B&W** under /**Graph Options**.

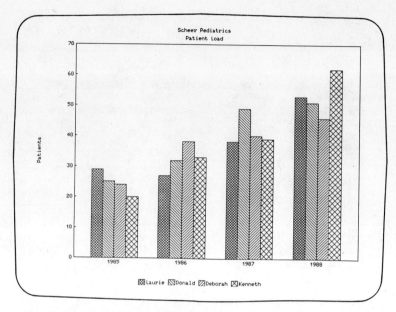

Fig. 13.2. The bar graph created from data in figure 13.1.

1. Save the graph with the manually scaled y-axis as SCHEER5.PIC.

2. Set all values for 1988 to **0** and save the new graph as SCHEER4.PIC.

3. Set all values for 1987 to **0** also and save the new graph as SCHEER3.PIC.

4. Set all values for 1986 to **0** also and save the new graph as SCHEER2.PIC.

5. Finally, set all values in the graph to **0** so that you have a blank graph with no data. Save this final graph as SCHEER1.PIC.

When you create the last graph, your worksheet will look like the worksheet shown in figure 13.3. The resulting graph, shown in figure 13.4, is a blank graph background on top of which you can add sets of bars one by one.

Save the worksheet, if you like, so that you can return to it should you need to; then quit from 1-2-3.

The next phase in the process of producing a screen show is to import the PIC files you have just created into Freelance Plus, where you will save them as Drawing files. After the graphs are saved as Drawing files, you can use the Freelance Plus Portfolio module to automatically create the screen files the program needs for screen shows.

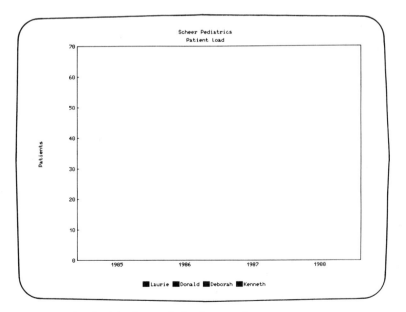

A1:   READY

	A	B	C	D	E	F	G	H
		Scheer Pediatric Services						
		Patient Load						
1								
2								
3								
4		1985	1986	1987	1988			
5								
6	Laurie	0	0	0	0			
7	Donald	0	0	0	0			
8	Deborah	0	0	0	0			
9	Kenneth	0	0	0	0			
10								
11	Total	0	0	0	0			
12								
13								
14								
15								

Fig. 13.3. *The final worksheet with all values set to zero.*

Fig. 13.4. *The blank graph background.*

To import the 1-2-3 PIC files, follow these steps:

1. Select **C**harts and Drawings from the main Freelance Plus menu.

2. Select **F**ile and then **I**mport from the Freelance Plus Charts and Drawings menu.

3. Enter the directory name that contains the 1-2-3 PIC files under the Path prompt and enter the name of the first PIC file, SCHEER1.PIC, under the Name prompt.

4. Press F10 to import the PIC file and return to the main Charts and Drawings menu.

5. Make any enhancements you want on the 1-2-3 graph, but be sure to make changes that you can repeat exactly for the other PIC file graphs. For all the graphs you should remove the fill in the bars and legends.

6. Select **F**ile, **S**ave, and then **D**rawing to save the graph as a Freelance Drawing file with the same name.

7. Repeat the procedure with the remaining 1-2-3 PIC files until you have saved all five as Drawing files.

8. Quit from Charts and Drawings to return to the main Freelance Plus menu.

Now that you have a set of Drawing files saved on disk, you can convert them separately into screen files by using the Print command within the Freelance Plus Charts and Drawings module. A faster approach is to use the Portfolio List Form in the Portfolio module to automatically print screen files from all your drawing files.

Before you use the Portfolio List Form, set the module's Print Options, so that Portfolio will create a new Show List for use by the screen-show module. A *Show List* holds all the screen file names, the transition effects between screens, and other information about the show.

1. Choose **P**rint and then **O**ptions from the Portfolio menu.

2. Set **D**evice to the appropriate device for your screen. If you are using VGA video, for example, set Device to VGA Screen.

3. Press Enter repeatedly to accept all of the default entries on the Print Options form until the cursor gets to Show List file name.

4. Enter a name of up to eight characters for the Show List file. Freelance automatically supplies the filename extension.

5. Type in a comment if you wish describing the Show List file. When you complete the Print Options form, the form should look like the one shown in figure 13.5.

6. Press F10 to return to the Portfolio menu.

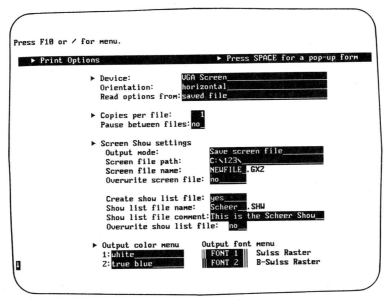

Fig. 13.5. *The completed Print Options form.*

Now, you must add to the Portfolio List the names of all of the Drawing files to be converted. Select **E**dit-list from the Portfolio menu and then enter the Drawing file names in the DRW Filename column. Enter the names in ascending numerical order, starting with SCHEER1 and ending with SCHEER5. When all the names are entered, press F10. To convert automatically all of the Drawing files to Screen files, select **P**rint from the Portfolio menu and then **G**o. The Portfolio module will create the screen files one by one and create a Show List file for the screen-show module. When the process finishes and you see a status report, press Esc to return to the Portfolio menu. **Q**uit from the Portfolio module to enter the screen-show module and prepare the screen show.

The next stage in the process is to create and preview the final screen show. Freelance Plus creates a default screen show without any fancy special effects. If you select **S**creen Show from the main Freelance Plus menu, retrieve the Show List file using **F**ile **R**etrieve, and then select **G**o from the Screen show menu, you will see the five charts replace one another on-screen. You must press Enter after each chart's appearance to continue the show. Because each chart adds an additional year's worth of data, the bar chart will appear to build.

You can create a more impressive version of the same show by using some of the transitional effects possible between successive screen files. When you first see the Show List form, as shown in figure 13.6, you will see the five screen file names in the GX2 filename column and *replace* as the default transition effect in the Effect column. Select **E**dit-list and then move the cursor to the Effect column and press the space bar to examine your choices for effect. Just about any effect that moves up the screen will create an impressive animation, but you may want to try Wipe, which can reveal the image progressively across the screen from top down, bottom up, left to right, or right to left. Leave the effect for the first screen file set to replace so that the legend and frame for the graph will appear quickly on the screen, but set the effect for the remaining four screens to Wipe, so that only the bars appear to grow up the screen.

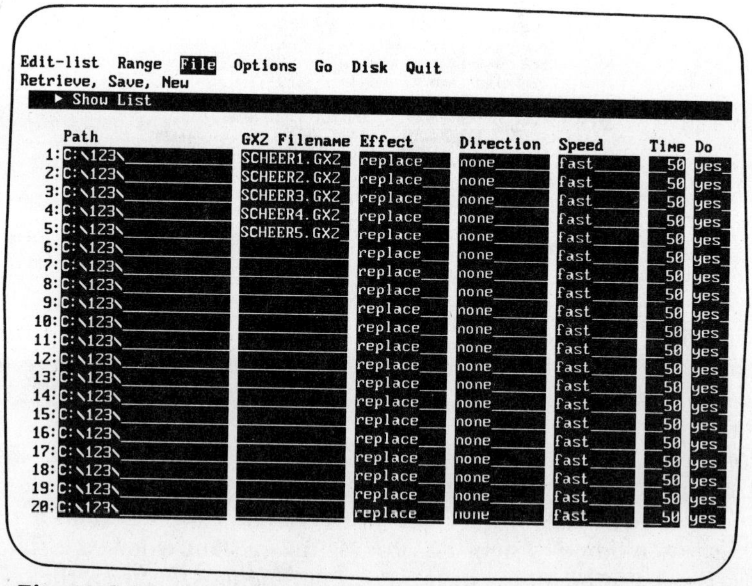
Edit-list Range File Options Go Disk Quit
Retrieve, Save, New
► Show List

	Path	GX2 Filename	Effect	Direction	Speed	Time	Do
1:	C:\123\	SCHEER1.GX2	replace	none	fast	50	yes
2:	C:\123\	SCHEER2.GX2	replace	none	fast	50	yes
3:	C:\123\	SCHEER3.GX2	replace	none	fast	50	yes
4:	C:\123\	SCHEER4.GX2	replace	none	fast	50	yes
5:	C:\123\	SCHEER5.GX2	replace	none	fast	50	yes
6:	C:\123\		replace	none	fast	50	yes
7:	C:\123\		replace	none	fast	50	yes
8:	C:\123\		replace	none	fast	50	yes
9:	C:\123\		replace	none	fast	50	yes
10:	C:\123\		replace	none	fast	50	yes
11:	C:\123\		replace	none	fast	50	yes
12:	C:\123\		replace	none	fast	50	yes
13:	C:\123\		replace	none	fast	50	yes
14:	C:\123\		replace	none	fast	50	yes
15:	C:\123\		replace	none	fast	50	yes
16:	C:\123\		replace	none	fast	50	yes
17:	C:\123\		replace	none	fast	50	yes
18:	C:\123\		replace	none	fast	50	yes
19:	C:\123\		replace	none	fast	50	yes
20:	C:\123\		replace	none	fast	50	yes

Fig. 13.6. *The Show List form.*

If you choose Wipe, the direction for the effect in the next column will automatically be set to Up. Perfect. You may want to vary the speed of the wipe up the screen in the Speed column, though. Select Medium as a starting speed. You can always modify your choice later. For the ultimate in drama, a speed of slow will leave your audience on the edge of their seats waiting for the chart's completion. Finally, set a time for each screen to remain before the next screen appears. Remember, Speed is measured in tenths of a second, so a setting of 100 causes each screen to remain for 10 seconds.

To keep the completed chart on-screen, enter a large value for its Time, perhaps 300 for 30 seconds. Alternately, you can leave the time entry for the last screen blank. The completed chart will stay on the screen until you press any key.

Now, preview the screen show by pressing F10 to return to the menu and then selecting **G**o. You will see each set of bars appear at the bottom of the graph one by one and grow to full height. To save the completed bar chart build, select **S**ave under the **F**ile menu option. Of course, you can add other screens before and after the bar chart build sequence to fashion a complete presentation.

Harvard Graphics

Harvard Graphics, unlike Freelance Plus, does not directly import PIC files. Nor does the program support the 1-2-3 Release 3 WK3 file format. The easiest path to the program starting with a WK1 file is through a named graph. You can, however, pull in 1-2-3 data and generate a graph in Harvard Graphics, if you use 1-2-3 Release 2.2 or an earlier version. Chapter 11 describes the procedures you should follow to create a graph in Harvard Graphics rather than 1-2-3.

The screen shows of Harvard Graphics are very similar to those of Freelance Plus. Following is a rundown of the minor differences.

In Harvard Graphics:

□ You can specify separate effects for drawing a graph and erasing a graph.

□ You can use templates and palette files to modify the formatting of charts in whole sections of a show.

□ You can build a screen show using standard Harvard Graphics chart files.

In Freelance Plus:

□ You must convert your chart files to special screen files.

□ You can vary the duration of a transition effect.

□ You can skip over certain screens with one simple adjustment.

Whether you use Freelance Plus or Harvard Graphics, many of the techniques for creating interesting graph animations are the same. Not only can you display television-like special effects as transitions between the screens, but you can overlay successive graphs to animate the graphs themselves.

The fastest way to present a series of graphs in a Harvard Graphics screen show is to follow these steps:

1. Create the graphs and save them as named graphs within separate worksheet files in 1-2-3.

2. Import the named graphs into Harvard Graphics and save them as chart files.

3. Add the chart files, in order, to a Slide Show list.

4. Add screen-show effects, or transitions between successive graphs.

To try the screen-show capability of Harvard Graphics and compare it to Freelance Plus, you will create the same succession of screens to build a bar graph.

Creating the source 1-2-3 graphs requires a few extra steps in Harvard Graphics. Not only must you save each graph as a named graph, but you must save the worksheet once for each graph you want to include in a screen show.

First, review the process you will follow to create the graph series. To create the same series of graphs you created for the Freelance Plus screen show, you should first create the complete graph with all series displayed. Give the graph a name with /Graph Name Create, and then save the worksheet. Then, removing data in reverse chronological order, set the results of the last year in the graph to zero, give the graph a second name, and save the worksheet with a new name. Repeat the procedure until you have set all data to zero and you have five named graphs stored in five separate worksheets.

You must save the worksheets also, because a named graph saves only the graph settings and not the underlying data. You need to create five separate graphs that display different data, and you can achieve this only by saving five separate worksheets. The named graph is merely the vehicle for transporting the graph settings to Harvard Graphics.

Just as with Freelance Plus, to make this procedure work, you must manually scale the y-axis. Otherwise, 1-2-3 automatically rescales the y-axis according to the largest remaining value as you begin removing values. If the series of graphs you create have different y-axis scalings, you cannot achieve the effect you want.

Here, in detail, is the procedure to follow in 1-2-3 to create the five named graphs and worksheets necessary to build a bar graph.

Start by setting up the worksheet shown in figure 13.1. Then set up the graph shown in figure 13.2. Notice that the graph has a minimum y-axis value of 0 and a maximum y-axis value of 70. Select /Graph **O**ptions Scale **Y**-Scale **M**anual and set **L**ower to **0** and **U**pper to **70**.

Normally, in 1-2-3 you can type \A1 as the legend entry for data range A to automatically enter the label in cell A1. But, when preparing graphs for Harvard Graphics, be sure to type in actual legend names for each of the series, rather than referring to worksheet cells. Harvard Graphics will use the cell references, not the cell contents, when it creates a chart from a 1-2-3 named graph. For your legend entries, you will see \A1, \A2, for example, rather than correct legend entries.

1. Select /Graph **N**ame **C**reate and give the graph the name **SCHEER5**.

2. Save the worksheet as **SHEER5.WK1**.

3. Set all values for 1988 to zero and give the graph the name **SCHEER4**.

4. Save the worksheet as **SCHEER4.WK1**.

5. Continue until you have created a blank graph with no data. Name this graph **SCHEER1** and save the worksheet as **SCHEER1.WK1**.

You now have five named graphs in five worksheets on disk. You can use the Harvard Graphics *Import Lotus Graph* command, described in the following section, to retrieve these worksheets and save each as a Harvard Graphics chart.

Now that you have five named graphs showing a bar graph at successive stages of completion, you need to import each named graph into Harvard Graphics and save it as a Harvard Graphics chart file.

To import a named graph, follow these steps:

1. Select *Import/Export* from the main Harvard Graphics menu.

2. Select *Import Lotus Graph* from the Import/Export menu.

3. Select SCHEER1 as the worksheet from which to import a Lotus graph.

4. Select SCHEER1 as the graph name to import and make sure *Import data only* is set to No.

5. Press Esc when you see the SCHEER1 empty graph and select *Get/Save/Remove* from the Harvard Graphics main menu.

6. Select *Save Chart* from the Get/Save/Remove menu.

7. Accept SCHEER1 as the chart name by pressing Enter twice.

8. Return to the Import/Export menu and select *Import Lotus Graph* again.

9. Press F3-Select Files to select the next 1-2-3 worksheet.

10. Select SCHEER2.WK1 and pull the graph named SCHEER2 from the worksheet.

11. Save the chart as SCHEER2.

12. Continue the procedure until you have five charts saved on disk.

You are now ready to create the actual slide show. When you have the five Harvard Graphics charts saved on disk, you must create a slide show that includes all five charts. Later, you will add screen-show effects to the slide show to create a screen show.

To create a new slide show, follow these steps:

1. Select *Slide Show* menu from the Harvard Graphics main menu.

2. Select *Create slide show* from the Slide Show Menu.

3. Enter SCHEER as the slide show name and type in a description. You will see the Create/Edit Slide Show screen.

4. Use the up and down arrow keys to select SCHEER1.CHT from the list at the top of the screen and press Enter.

5. Select SCHEER2.CHT next and press Enter.

6. Continue until you have added all five charts to the slide show. The completed Create/Edit Slide Show screen should look like the screen shown in figure 13.7.

7. Press F10 to continue.

To see the default screen show, select *Display Screenshow* from the slide-show menu. You will need to press Enter to advance the slide show to the next slide. Press Enter several times until the data for all four years is displayed. When the screen show is complete, you will be returned to the slide-show menu.

The final task is to add the screen-show effects. At this point, you have a default screen show: each time you press Enter, the default screen show replaces the current chart with the next one. You can use more impressive transition effects, though, by selecting *Add Screenshow Effects* from the slide-show menu.

The Screenshow Effects screen, shown in figure 13.8, lets you define a separate draw and erase effect, specify a direction for each effect, and enter a time for each chart to remain on-screen.

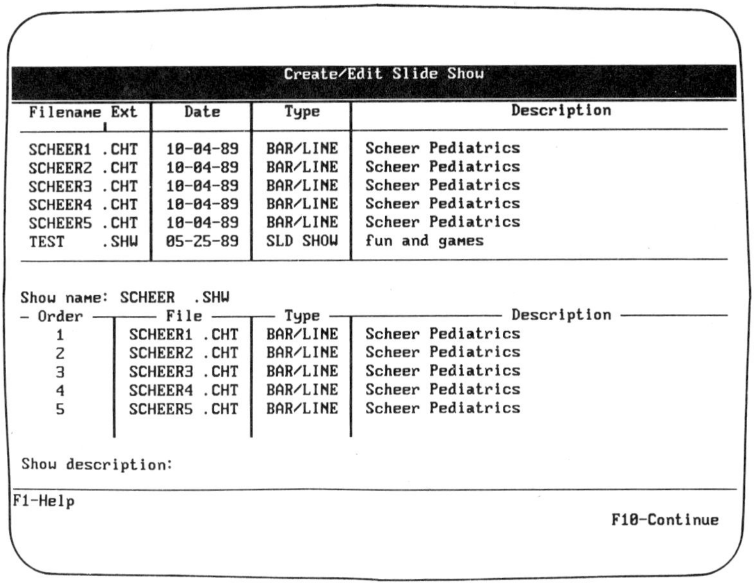

```
                        Create/Edit Slide Show
 ┌───────────────┬──────────┬──────────┬─────────────────────────────┐
 │ Filename Ext  │   Date   │   Type   │      Description            │
 ├───────────────┼──────────┼──────────┼─────────────────────────────┤
 │ SCHEER1 .CHT  │ 10-04-89 │ BAR/LINE │ Scheer Pediatrics           │
 │ SCHEER2 .CHT  │ 10-04-89 │ BAR/LINE │ Scheer Pediatrics           │
 │ SCHEER3 .CHT  │ 10-04-89 │ BAR/LINE │ Scheer Pediatrics           │
 │ SCHEER4 .CHT  │ 10-04-89 │ BAR/LINE │ Scheer Pediatrics           │
 │ SCHEER5 .CHT  │ 10-04-89 │ BAR/LINE │ Scheer Pediatrics           │
 │ TEST    .SHW  │ 05-25-89 │ SLD SHOW │ fun and games               │
 └───────────────┴──────────┴──────────┴─────────────────────────────┘

 Show name: SCHEER  .SHW
 - Order ────── File ──────┬── Type ──┬──────── Description ─────────
      1     SCHEER1 .CHT   │ BAR/LINE │ Scheer Pediatrics
      2     SCHEER2 .CHT   │ BAR/LINE │ Scheer Pediatrics
      3     SCHEER3 .CHT   │ BAR/LINE │ Scheer Pediatrics
      4     SCHEER4 .CHT   │ BAR/LINE │ Scheer Pediatrics
      5     SCHEER5 .CHT   │ BAR/LINE │ Scheer Pediatrics

 Show description:

 F1-Help
                                                        F10-Continue
```

Fig. 13.7. *The completed Create/Edit slide show screen.*

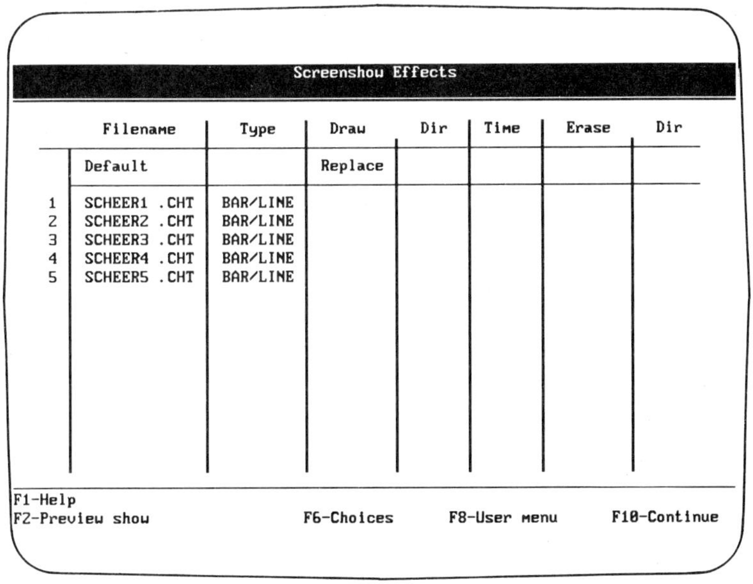

```
                        Screenshow Effects

        Filename    │ Type   │ Draw    │ Dir │ Time │ Erase │ Dir
        Default     │        │ Replace │     │      │       │
     1  SCHEER1 .CHT│ BAR/LINE│
     2  SCHEER2 .CHT│ BAR/LINE│
     3  SCHEER3 .CHT│ BAR/LINE│
     4  SCHEER4 .CHT│ BAR/LINE│
     5  SCHEER5 .CHT│ BAR/LINE│




 F1-Help
 F2-Preview show         F6-Choices      F8-User menu      F10-Continue
```

Fig. 13.8. *The Harvard Graphics Screenshow Effects screen.*

Notice that the default Draw effect is Replace, which causes replacement of the successive charts as you display the screen show. Harvard Graphics uses Replace for any chart for which you do not enter a draw effect.

For this screen show, you want the empty graph frame to appear on the screen suddenly and then be filled by rising bars one year at a time. To create this effect, move the cursor down the Draw column next to SCHEER2 and press F6-Choices. Select *Wipe* from the pop-up box of transition effects and press Enter. Wipe here is the same as it was in Freelance Plus, gradually revealing the chart from one edge of the screen to the other in the direction you choose. Because you want the same effect for all graphs, press Enter to move the cursor down within the column, type **W** and press Enter. Continue until you have set the Draw effect for the remaining charts to Wipe.

Next, move the cursor to the Dir (Direction) column next to SCHEER2 and press F6-Choices again. Select *Up* as the default direction for the remaining graphs.

To display the screen show, move the cursor to the top of the list of charts and press F2-Preview show. Press Enter after each chart to see the next.

For an automatic screen display of successive graphs, enter a time in seconds for the display of each graph. Try entering 0:01 in the Time column next to Default. This sets the default display time for all graphs to one second. Enter 10:00 as the time for the last graph, SCHEER5, so that the final graph chart remains on the screen for ten minutes or until you press a key. The completed Screenshow Effects screen looks like the screen shown in figure 13.9.

A Harvard Graphics template, a completed graph saved only as a template, can format all succeeding graphs in a Harvard Graphics screen show. You can format the titles or add a predrawn figure to the screen, for example, and the same title formatting or figure will appear in all subsequent charts until a new template appears in the slide show list.

To try using a template in a screen show, add the medical symbol to the first chart in the screen show and save the chart as a template. Then, insert the template at the beginning of the show. When you preview the screen show, the medical symbol will appear on every chart.

To add the symbol to the first chart, follow these steps:

1. Use *Get Chart* to retrieve SCHEER1.CHT and then press Esc to return to the main menu.

2. Select *Draw/Annotate* from the main menu and then *Symbol* from the Draw/Annotate Draw menu.

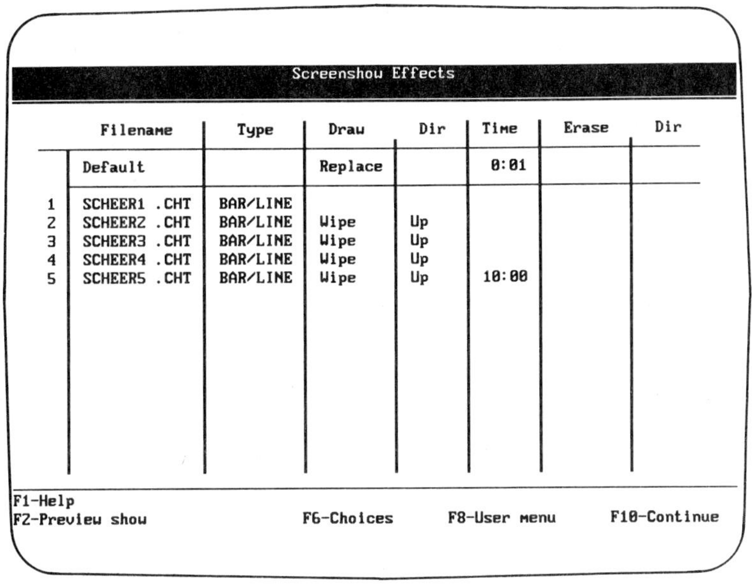

```
┌──────────────────────────────────────────────────────────────┐
│                      Screenshow Effects                        │
│ ════════════════════════════════════════════════════════════ │
│                                                                │
│        Filename    │  Type  │  Draw   │ Dir │ Time │ Erase │ Dir │
│ ──────────────────┼────────┼─────────┼─────┼──────┼───────┼──── │
│      Default       │        │ Replace │     │ 0:01 │       │     │
│ ──────────────────┼────────┼─────────┼─────┼──────┼───────┼──── │
│   1  SCHEER1 .CHT  │BAR/LINE│         │     │      │       │     │
│   2  SCHEER2 .CHT  │BAR/LINE│  Wipe   │ Up  │      │       │     │
│   3  SCHEER3 .CHT  │BAR/LINE│  Wipe   │ Up  │      │       │     │
│   4  SCHEER4 .CHT  │BAR/LINE│  Wipe   │ Up  │      │       │     │
│   5  SCHEER5 .CHT  │BAR/LINE│  Wipe   │ Up  │10:00 │       │     │
│                                                                │
│ F1-Help                                                        │
│ F2-Preview show          F6-Choices    F8-User menu  F10-Continue│
└──────────────────────────────────────────────────────────────┘
```

Fig. 13.9. *The completed Harvard Graphics Screenshow Effects screen.*

3. Select *Get* from the Symbol menu and choose the symbol file INDUSTRY from the list that appears.

4. Point to the medical symbol with the cursor and press Enter.

5. Press the Backspace key so that you can position the symbol freely.

6. Move the cursor to the right of the title and press Enter. Then, move the cursor down and to the right to create a box and press Enter again. The symbol appears on-screen as it does in figure 13.10.

7. Press Esc several times to return to the Harvard Graphics main menu.

To save the revised chart as a template, follow these steps:

1. Select *Get/Save/Remove* and then *Save template* from the Get/ Save/Remove menu.

2. Enter the template name SCHEER1 and make sure *Clear Values* is set to No. Press Enter several times to save the chart as a template.

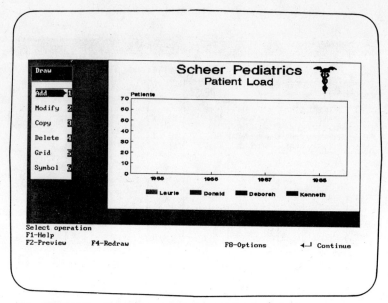

Fig. 13.10. The first chart with the medical symbol.

Your last step is to add the template to the slide show list, which serves as the backbone for the screen show. To add the template, follow these steps:

1. Select *Slide Show menu* from the Harvard Graphics main menu.

2. Select *Edit slide show* from the Slide Show menu.

3. Move the cursor down the list at the top of the screen until you see SCHEER1.TPL, the template you created earlier.

4. Press Enter to add the template to the bottom of the list.

5. Press Tab so that you can rearrange the slide show list order.

6. Make sure the highlight is on SCHEER1.TPL and press Ctrl-up arrow to move SCHEER1.TPL up the list to the top (see fig. 13.11).

7. Press F10-Continue to return to the Slide Show menu.

Now, take a look at the screen show by selecting *Display screenshow* from the Slide Show menu. You will see the medical symbol on every chart.

Templates allow you to enhance an entire series of 1-2-3 graphs by enhancing only the first of the series and including it in the screen show as a template.

```
┌─────────────────────────────────────────────────────────────┐
│                   Create/Edit Slide Show                     │
│  ┌────────────┬──────────┬─────────┬──────────────────────┐  │
│  │ Filename Ext│   Date   │  Type   │    Description       │  │
│  ├────────────┼──────────┼─────────┼──────────────────────┤  │
│  │  HG    .CHT│ 01-24-89 │  CHART  │                      │  │
│  │ SOSEXPEN.CHT│ 01-24-89 │  CHART  │                      │  │
│  │ SOSEXPR .CHT│ 01-24-89 │  CHART  │                      │  │
│  │ TEST   .CHT│ 01-24-89 │  CHART  │                      │  │
│  │ SOSREUS .CHT│ 01-24-89 │  CHART  │                      │  │
│  │ SOSREUO .CHT│ 01-24-89 │  CHART  │                      │  │
│  └────────────┴──────────┴─────────┴──────────────────────┘  │
│                                                              │
│   Show name: SCHEER  .SHW                                    │
│   ─ Order ──┬── File ──┬── Type ──┬───── Description ─────   │
│        1    │ SCHEER1 .TPL │ BAR/LINE │ Scheer Pediatrics    │
│        2    │ SCHEER1 .CHT │ BAR/LINE │ Scheer Pediatrics    │
│        3    │ SCHEER2 .CHT │ BAR/LINE │ Scheer Pediatrics    │
│        4    │ SCHEER3 .CHT │ BAR/LINE │ Scheer Pediatrics    │
│        5    │ SCHEER4 .CHT │ BAR/LINE │ Scheer Pediatrics    │
│        6    │ SCHEER5 .CHT │ BAR/LINE │ Scheer Pediatrics    │
│                                                              │
│   Show description:                                          │
│                                                              │
│  F1-Help                                        F10-Continue │
└─────────────────────────────────────────────────────────────┘
```

Fig. 13.11. The revised slide show list.

Dedicated On-Screen Presentation Packages

Dedicated on-screen presentation packages, often called desktop presentation programs, offer far greater possibilities for animated presentations. Whereas general graphics programs such as Freelance Plus and Harvard Graphics let you overlay images to create the effect of animation, programs like IBM's PC Storyboard and Brightbill-Roberts' Show Partner F/X let you control components of an image to create effects that are much more visually impressive. You won't compete with Disney, but your presentations will surely beat out your competitor's simple slide show.

PC Storyboard Plus

IBM's PC Storyboard was a landmark program when it emerged, introducing excellent animation capabilities to the PC when the PC was just gaining graphics prowess. Now, PC Storyboard Plus, Version 2 carries the tradition forward, offering even more impressive animation techniques and a graphical user interface along with support for high-resolution, full-color video systems.

To use PC Storyboard Plus with 1-2-3 graphics, you must capture 1-2-3 /Graph View screens into special CAP files, because PC Storyboard Plus has no method of importing 1-2-3 PIC files. In fact, the program confuses the issue by using PIC as the filename extension for the bit-mapped graphics files it produces. In other words, though you never create a 1-2-3 PIC file of your graphs, you end up with graphs in PIC files, nonetheless—these are PC Storyboard PIC files.

PC Storyboard comes with five modules that sound confusingly similar: Picture Maker, Picture Taker, Text Maker, Story Teller, and Story Editor. You will need four of the five to animate 1-2-3 graphs:

Picture Taker, a utility that captures images perfectly from all releases of 1-2-3, including Release 3. You can use Picture Taker to capture a graph from a 1-2-3 /Graph View screen into a CAP file.

Picture Maker, an accomplished bit-mapped graphics paint program that lets you edit and save the graphs you capture.

Story Editor, a tool with which you create an animated sequence called a story file.

Story Teller, a small module you can use separately to run a completed story.

If you have additional IBM equipment to complement your PC Storyboard software, you can build a complete system of visuals, music, voice narration, and sound effects. PC Storyboard Plus drives IBM's Music Feature, a synthesizer on an expansion card, and IBM's Voice Communications Option or Personal System/2 Speech Adapter.

PC Storyboard offers complex programming options with which you can create intricate pathways through your presentation tailored to your subjects and audience. You can even create a self-contained demonstration that runs unattended, accepting keyboard input from viewers as they wish to see a particular sequence. You can instruct a story to branch to another and then to another before returning to the original story. You can even branch to a DOS program.

To try the animation capabilities of PC Storyboard Plus, try creating the same bar chart build you created in both Freelance Plus and Harvard Graphics. But this time, rather than overlaying successive charts to create the effect of adding bars year by year, you can make the bars appear and grow on a single chart background.

Before you can begin in PC Storyboard, though, you must capture your 1-2-3 graphs from the 1-2-3 /Graph View screen so that you can transfer them into the graphics program. Capturing graphs from the screen represents no loss in picture quality, as you might think, because you display the graph at the same resolution and with the same colors in PC Storyboard.

For this exercise, you will not need Text Maker, PC Storyboard's program for creating text screens. When you create an actual presentation, though, you may want to use Text Maker to intersperse text screens throughout a presentation to summarize the key points you are making at the podium.

To capture the 1-2-3 graph screens you need, run the utility included with PC Storyboard Plus called Picture Taker. When you run Picture Taker, you will see the Picture Taker Options screen, shown in figure 13.12. On this screen you can change the keystroke combination you use to capture a graph, tell Picture Taker to convert a text screen to a graphics image, and name a file for all your captured screens. You can accept all the defaults by pressing F10 and then responding with a **y** to the Exit (y/n)? prompt that follows.

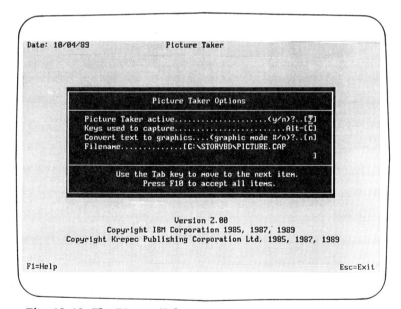

Fig. 13.12. *The Picture Taker screen.*

After you load Picture Taker, it remains resident in your computer's memory, even if you subsequently load 1-2-3. From within 1-2-3, you can press the keystroke combination you selected earlier to invoke Picture Taker and capture any screen in 1-2-3. So load 1-2-3 and create the graph shown in figure 13.14, based on the worksheet shown in figure 13.13. This graph is the Release 3 version of the Release 2.2 graph you completed earlier using Freelance Plus or Harvard Graphics to create a screen show. If you are using Release 2.2, your graph will look like the one in figure 13.2. This time, create a color graph using the /Graph Options Color setting. You can capture color screens just as easily as you can black and white screens.

Notice that the graph has a minimum y-axis value of 0 and a maximum of 70. Select /Graph Options Scale **Y**-Scale **M**anual and set **L**ower to **0** and **U**pper to **70**. In a moment, you will delete the data to leave the background blank, so you want to be sure the y-axis remains the same.

View the resulting worksheet with /Graph View and then press Alt-C. After a moment, you should hear three beeps indicating that Picture Taker successfully captured the screen.

Now, set all data for all four years to zero by entering **0** in one cell and copying it to the remaining cells. View the graph with /Graph View again and note that you see only the frame and blank background of the graph. You'll make bars appear on this blank frame, so press Alt-C again to capture this screen, too. When you hear three beeps, you know the blank graph has been captured.

When you have captured both screens, you should reboot your computer by pressing Ctrl-Alt-Del to clear the Picture Taker utility from memory. You will need as much memory as possible for the PC Storyboard Picture Maker and Story Editor modules.

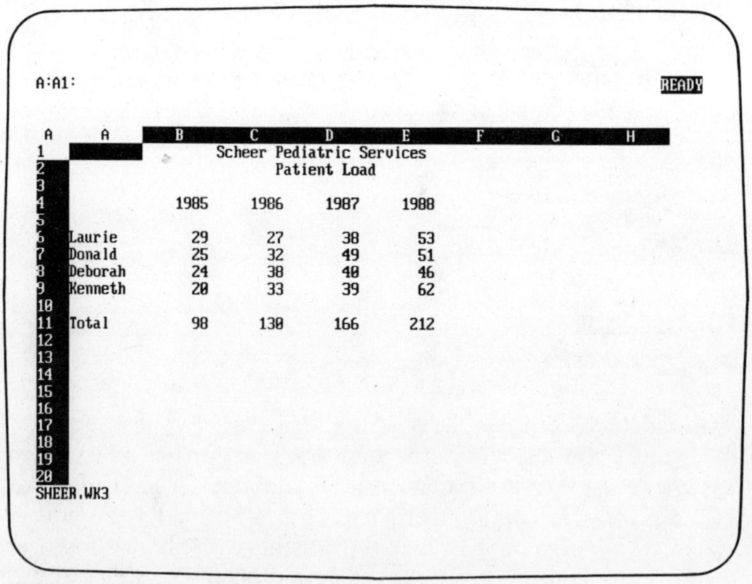

Fig. 13.13. *The worksheet for the bar graph.*

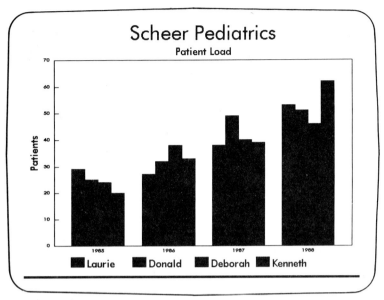

Fig. 13.14.** **The bar graph of the data in figure 13.13.

The next step is to save the graphs as PC Storyboard PIC files. When you capture screens with Picture Taker, they all go into the file you specify in the Picture Taker Options screen. If you don't specify a file name, your captured screens go into PICTURE.CAP.

Although you can pull your images out of PICTURE.CAP in the Story Editor module of PC Storyboard, you may want to extract them from the CAP file in the Picture Maker module, instead. In Picture Maker, you can enhance or modify them before saving them as PC Storyboard PIC files.

When you start Picture Maker, you will see the screen shown in figure 13.15. Picture Maker lets you draw or edit images on the large blank area in the center using the menu options at the top of the screen, the tools on the left, and the colors on the right.

To extract your screens from the CAP file, select Get Picture under the File menu and highlight the .CAP files box. When you do, you will see PICTURE.CAP appear in the filename portion of the dialog box. Highlight PICTURE.CAP, as shown in figure 13.16, and then highlight the Yes button under GET Picture file.

You will see a second dialog box appear listing the contents of the PICTURE.CAP file. 1 - Graphics is your first screen capture, the graph with bars, and 2 - Graphics is the second screen capture, the blank graph. Highlight 1 - Graphics and select Get Picture. You should see the

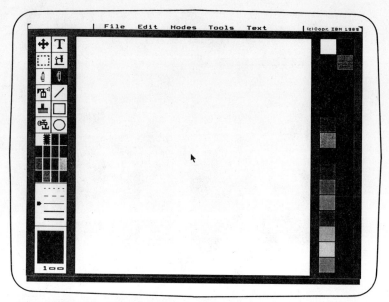

Fig. 13.15. *The Picture Maker screen.*

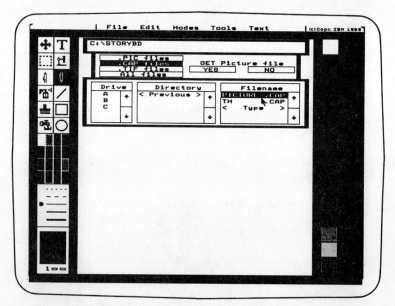

Fig. 13.16. *Getting the PICTURE.CAP file.*

1-2-3 graph with bars appear in the window at the bottom. To see the entire screen, you can select Full Screen under the PC Storyboard Tools menu. When you confirm that you have successfully captured the 1-2-3 screen, select Save Picture under the File menu. If you are looking at the graph full-screen, press the space bar to use the Picture Maker menu.

Under the Filename column highlight <New>, type in **BARS**, and press Enter to save the file. Then, select Get Picture under File again and follow the same procedure to save the second screen capture as a PIC file. To go through these steps in detail:

1. Select Get Picture under the File menu.

2. Make sure .CAP files is highlighted, select PICTURE.CAP as the CAP file to use, and then select Yes under GET Picture file.

3. Highlight 2 - Graphics in the list within the dialog box labeled Get Capture File and select Get Picture. In a moment, you should see the blank graph appear on the screen.

4. Select Save Picture under the File menu.

5. Highlight <New> in the file list at the right, type the filename BLANK, and press Enter.

Now that you have saved both screens as separate PIC files on disk, you can leave Picture Maker and start Story Editor to put together an animated presentation. While still in Picture Maker, though, you can add text annotations, freehand drawings, or library clip-art images, or otherwise edit the 1-2-3 screen before saving it as a PIC file. For now, leave Picture Maker by selecting Main Menu under the File menu.

Next, start Story Editor to begin assembling the animated bar graph. The main Story Editor screen is illustrated in figure 13.17.

Below the horizontal menu at the top of the screen is the story table. Each transition or animated effect in the story has its own line in the story table. At the moment, the table has only two lines, a blank line and a second line labeled "Story Last Line." To build a story, you must put together a list of the screens or parts of screens that will be part of the story and specify any special animation effects for each screen.

The first column of the story table holds an optional label for the story entry. You can use labels to mark certain lines so the story can branch to them later if you create a complicated, interactive presentation. For now, you will create a simple animated graph, so don't worry about entering labels in the label column. You will use the remaining columns to put together the story.

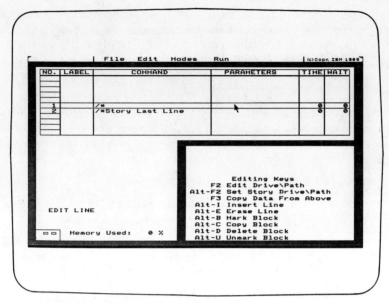

Fig. 13.17. The Story Editor screen.

When you select the current story line in the Command column, Storyboard shows you a list of the possible commands you can enter. Each command has a certain action on the current screen. At the start of the story, you want Storyboard to display the graph background, so select the /DISPLAY command from the list. Next, select the Parameters column and choose Get Existing Name to specify the BLANK.PIC picture file you saved earlier. Verify that .PIC files is highlighted at the top of the dialog box that appears, and then use the up and down arrows that are part of the Filename list to find the PIC file called BLANK.PIC. Because the list is alphabetical, BLANK.PIC is probably showing at the top. Highlight BLANK.PIC and select Yes under GET Picture file.

Your story in progress now displays the graph background and then stops. In fact, it uses the CRUSH display method to display BLANK.PIC. Below the story table at the left, you'll see additional information about story line 1. Notice that Method is Crush and Direction is In-Horizontally, meaning that the graph background will appear from both sides of the screen simultaneously until the image is complete. To see the current state of the story, select Run Story under the Run menu. The empty graph background will appear in the monitor area at the bottom right of the screen. To display the story full-screen rather than in the monitor, select Full Screen under Modes and Run the story again.

But for now, choose Monitor so that you can see both the story table and the story itself simultaneously.

Next, move down the story table to story line number 2. You will overlay a set of bars from the complete graph saved as BARS.PIC on the graph background, so enter /Display in the Command column and select BARS.PIC for the Picture file in the Parameters column. If you Run the story now, you will see the bars all at once using the same Crush dissolve method. Instead, you can instruct Storyboard to add the bars one set at a time, using Push as the dissolve effect and Up as the dissolve direction.

With story line 2 still highlighted, select Push under Method and Up under Direction in the table at the lower left corner of the screen. Take another look at the story. Notice that the entire BARS screen pushes the BLANK screen up and out of the way. Instead, instruct Storyboard to push up only the first set of bars. To do so, make sure the second story line is highlighted and then select Part under Area in the table at the lower left corner of the screen. Select Set on Full Screen under From Picture so that you can select only the first set of bars on the BARS screen.

When the BARS screen appears, you will see a box with a moving marquee at the upper right corner of your screen. Position the pointer just above and to the left of the first set of bars and press the left mouse button. If you do not have a mouse, you can press the plus key on the numeric keypad. The cursor will become a crosshair. Press the left mouse button again and move the crosshair down and to the right until the box encloses the first set of bars and rests just above the horizontal line at the base of the graph. Do not include the horizontal line within the box. This time, press the right mouse button. If you do not have a mouse, you can press the minus key on the numeric keypad, instead. Now, position the pointer within the box and press the left mouse button. In a moment, you will see the BLANK screen. The box on the screen indicates where the bars you selected will appear. Press the left mouse button to accept the current position. Storyboard has automatically entered X-Y coordinates into the From Picture and To Screen entries.

To see the story so far, move the highlight back up to story line 1 by pressing the Home key, and then select Run Story under the Run menu. Notice how fast the bars appeared. For more drama, you may want to increase the duration of the Push effect by entering a number in seconds in the Time column. Make sure story line 2 is highlighted and then select the Time column and choose Input Action Time. When you see a flashing asterisk in the Time column, enter the number 3 and press Enter. Press Home again to return to the top of the story and try running the story again to see the difference. Notice how smoothly the bars appear to grow. You can make the effect even more pronounced by entering a longer time for story line 2, possibly five seconds, but don't make the entire show that slow. Once your audience has been impressed by the effect once, keep the rest of the show from dragging.

To complete the chart, you need to add three more sets of bars from the BARS screen. Each set has its own story line. In effect, you are adding the four sets of bars as four separate effects, even though they all come from the same screen. Because story lines 3, 4, and 5 use the same PIC file as story line 2, you can highlight line 2, press Alt-B to mark it, and then press Alt-C three times to copy it to the next three lines. To finish the story, you need only mark each set of bars as the part of the image to add for that story line. To complete the story, follow these steps:

1. Highlight story line 3.

2. Select Set on Full Screen under From Picture in the table at the lower left.

3. Press the left mouse button to get a crosshair cursor.

4. Position the crosshair above and to the left of the second set of bars and press the left mouse button.

5. Move the crosshair to the bottom right of the bars to enclose them entirely in the box. Do not include the horizontal baseline of the graph within the box.

6. Press the right mouse button and then position the pointer inside the box and press the left mouse button.

7. Press the right mouse button when you see the box positioned correctly on the blank graph screen.

8. Repeat the procedure for story lines 4 and 5, highlighting the next set of bars each time.

Notice that the remaining story lines have the same 3-second time setting as story line 2, because you copied story line 2. Press Home to return to the top of the story, select Full Screen from the Modes menu and then select Run Story from the Run menu to see the story. The story table will reappear as soon as the story finishes. To retain the story on-screen until you press a key, select Key in the Wait column for story line 5. You can also select Key for the other story lines if you want to manually control the progress of the graph build. Or, to add a little more time between the appearance of successive bars, you can enter an Input Wait Delay in seconds in the Wait column. Figure 13.18 shows the completed story table, and figure 13.19 shows a series of screens from the PC Storyboard show as the graph builds.

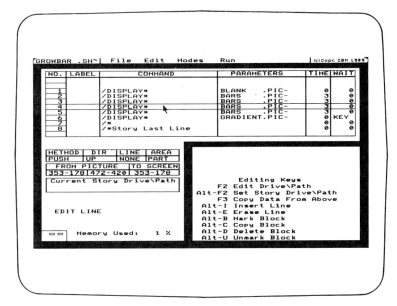

Fig. 13.18. *The completed story table.*

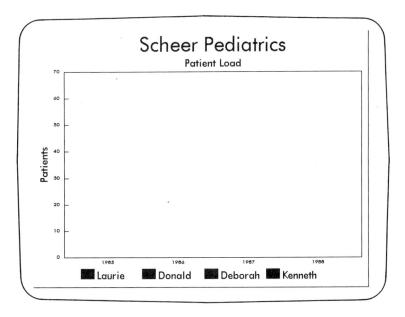

Fig. 13.19a. *The graph as it builds in PC Storyboard.*

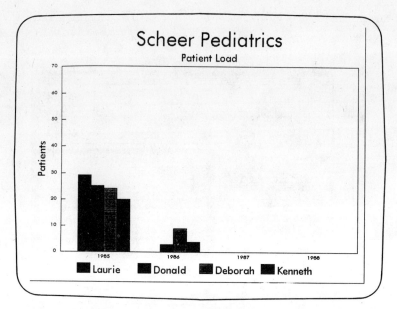

Fig. 13.19b. *The bar graph begins to build.*

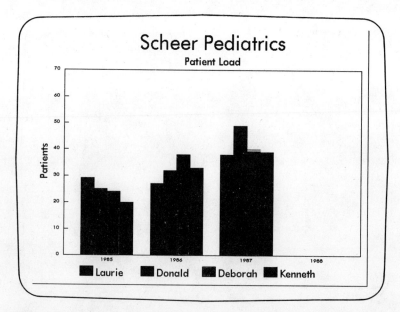

Fig. 13.19c. *Bars are added for the successive years as you watch.*

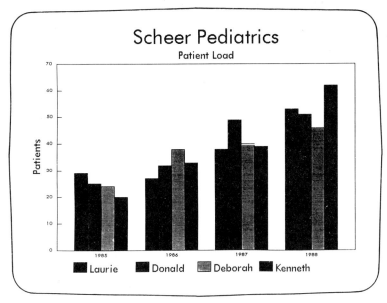

Fig. 13.19d. The bar graph at completion.

Adding a Sprite in PC Storyboard

PC Storyboard comes with a very limited set of canned animations called sprites. Some of the sprites available include a walking man, a walking woman, and a spinning globe. You can add a sprite to a story and have it move across the screen and then disappear.

To try adding a sprite to your existing story, have the walking woman sprite appear to the right of the screen and move across to the left. To add the sprite, highlight story line 2 and press Alt-I to insert a story line for the sprite. In the Command column, select /SPRITE. In the Parameters column, select Get Existing Name and choose the sprite called WOMAN.SPR. In the Sprite Action table at the lower left, set Direction to Right so the sprite will appear from the right.

Now, run the story. Figure 13.20 shows the screen with the sprite of a walking woman. If your data doesn't arrest the audience, the sudden appearance of the sprite will.

Saving the Completed Story

To save the completed story on disk, select Save Story under the File menu, and highlight <New> under the Filename column. Next type in

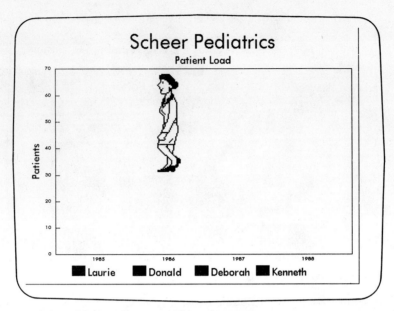

Fig. 13.20. *A sprite enters into the story.*

a name for the story of up to eight characters, such as GROWBARS. Then, select Yes under Save Story file.

To exit from the Story Editor, select Main Menu under the File menu and press Esc at the Story Editor screen that results.

Creating a Gradient Background for the Graph

While your graph images are still in Picture Maker, you can use all the tools in the Picture Maker module to edit or enhance the image. One impressive change is to add a *gradient* background to a graph, a gradual shading from one color to another.

To add a gradient background, you can use the Spread command under the Modes menu. Start by retrieving the BLANK.PIC file with Get Picture under the File menu. Obtain a background color of gray by selecting Background Color under the Modes menu and then selecting gray from the 16 color rectangles at the left of the screen. Press the right mouse button to continue. Then, select the white rectangle and select Spread under the Modes menu. Select the up arrow and press the right mouse button to continue.

Select the Fill icon at the left of the screen (the faucet) and then select Full Screen under the Tools menu to fill the entire graph background with a spread. Position the cursor in the background of the graph and press the left mouse button. You should see a background appear that begins white at the base of the bars and grades into a gray at the top of the graph. The gradient option adds a luminescent effect to your graph.

Save the image as a PIC file called GRADIENT.PIC to include it in the Story you have created. Return to the Story Editor. Retrieve the story you saved earlier and add /DISPLAY GRADIENT.PIC below the previous last story line. Set the Dissolve method for GRADIENT.PIC to Stripe and the Direction to Up. Press Home to return to the top of the show and Run the show to see the change. Figure 13.21 shows the final screen of the revised presentation.

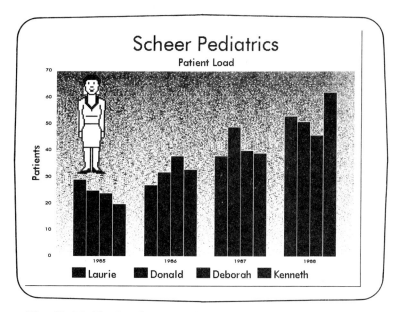

***Fig. 13.21.** The final screen of the revised presentation.*

The specific animation techniques described here are no more than a sampling of what you can accomplish with PC Storyboard Plus. As you work with the program, you'll discover exciting new ways to animate your graphs.

Show Partner F/X

Another program with comparable animation capabilities is Brightbill-Roberts' Show Partner F/X. This program also animates 1-2-3 graphs, but you will have to go through several extra steps getting it to work with 1-2-3.

Show Partner, like PC Storyboard, works best when you capture 1-2-3 graphs from the 1-2-3 /Graph View screen. The program offers no method to import 1-2-3 PIC files. Unfortunately, if you use a VGA display system, Show Partner's capture utility cannot capture Release 2.2 or earlier graphs unless you reinstall the software as though you were using an EGA display system. You can capture 1-2-3 Release 3 graphs only by setting the display to EGA resolution. The screens you capture from a VGA display with either 1-2-3 Release 2.2 or Release 3 are devoid of color. When you pull them into Show Partner's Grafix Editor to restore the color, you may find that the Grafix Editor locks up.

Your only alternative to setting 1-2-3 Release 3 to EGA resolution is to create PIC files of your graphs with any release of 1-2-3, then use a utility such as Hijaak to convert the PIC files to PC Paintbrush PCX files. Using a second utility provided with Show Partner, you can convert PCX files into the GX2 files that Partner uses for its animated presentations. But that is extra work.

After you get the images into GX2 files, it's smooth sailing with some of the flashiest animated special effects possible on a PC screen.

Changing the 1-2-3 Release 3 Video Mode to EGA

Before you can capture 1-2-3 Release 3 graphs with the special screen-capture utility of Show Partner F/X, you must modify 1-2-3 Release 3 so that its display resolution is EGA rather than VGA. If you use an EGA system, you need make no special adjustments.

To change the display to EGA, you must have EGA installed as one of two possible video displays. If you have a VGA system installed, you probably installed only the VGA video drivers, so you need to return to the 1-2-3 installation program and add EGA as a secondary selected display. When you have done so, you can use the /Worksheet Window Display command to select the secondary display driver, EGA resolution.

Capturing the 1-2-3 Release 3 Graphs

Before you start 1-2-3, run the Show Partner F/X Access system by typing FX from within the \FX directory on your hard disk. The Access menu is shown in figure 13.22. DOS Capture is the utility invoked when you press F7, so press F7 and note that DOS Capture is invoked when you press the Ctrl, Alt, and numeric keypad minus keys simultaneously. Press any key to return to the Access menu.

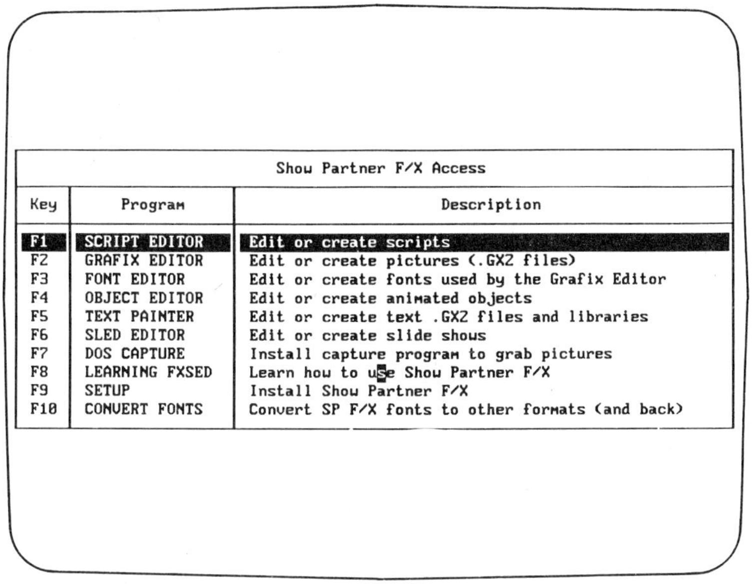

Show Partner F/X Access

Key	Program	Description
F1	SCRIPT EDITOR	Edit or create scripts
F2	GRAFIX EDITOR	Edit or create pictures (.GX2 files)
F3	FONT EDITOR	Edit or create fonts used by the Grafix Editor
F4	OBJECT EDITOR	Edit or create animated objects
F5	TEXT PAINTER	Edit or create text .GX2 files and libraries
F6	SLED EDITOR	Edit or create slide shows
F7	DOS CAPTURE	Install capture program to grab pictures
F8	LEARNING FXSED	Learn how to use Show Partner F/X
F9	SETUP	Install Show Partner F/X
F10	CONVERT FONTS	Convert SP F/X fonts to other formats (and back)

Fig. 13.22. *The Show Partner F/X Access menu.*

To leave the Access menu and start 1-2-3, press Esc and then **Y**. Now, start 1-2-3 and create the graph shown in figure 13.14, based on data from Figure 13.13. This graph is the same graph you created earlier in the section covering PC Storyboard Plus. Remember to manually scale the y-axis to give it a minimum value of 0 and a maximum value of 70.

When you have created the graph, view it using the /**G**raph **V**iew screen and press Alt-Ctrl-Minus to invoke the DOS Capture utility. When you do so, the screen looks like the one in figure 13.23. Notice the current captured and saved modes are 640 x 350 x 16 Graphics. The EGA standard is 640 x 350 pixel resolution with 16 colors.

Enter the filename BARS after the File Name prompt and press Enter several times to bypass the remaining prompts and capture the image. You will overlay the four sets of bars in the Scheer Pediatrics graph one by one on a blank graph background, so you need to create the background separately. In 1-2-3, set all data values to 0 and display the revised graph. The graph still has a legend, but no bars appear. Capture this screen using the DOS Capture utility, and supply the file name BLANK. Now, you can return to Show Partner F/X to begin assembling the Show Partner presentation.

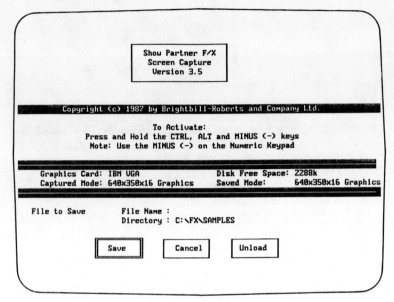

Fig. 13.23. The DOS Capture utility screen.

Assembling a Show Partner Script

A Show Partner presentation is kept in a file called a *script*. You use the Show Partner F/X Script Editor to prepare the script. When you start Show Partner F/X again, select Script Editor from the Access menu by pressing F1. You will see the blank script shown in figure 13.24.

Begin by adding the screen files you need to the script. You can view the available screen files by pressing the left mouse button or the Ins key. Select BLANK from the list first by highlighting the file name and pressing either Enter or the left mouse button. Move the highlight to the second row of the script and view the screen file list again. You must add one BARS screen file for each set of bars you will overlay on the blank graph background. Because you want to overlay all four sets of bars, add four BARS files to the Script.

The remaining columns on the Script Editor screen let you enter more information about the animation effect for the successive images. To see your options for each of these columns, move the cursor to a column and press the Ins key or the left mouse button.

For an added effect, you can use Fade to make the graph background appear gradually. Move the cursor across the first row to the effect column and press F to select Fade. Try pressing Alt-A to see the current

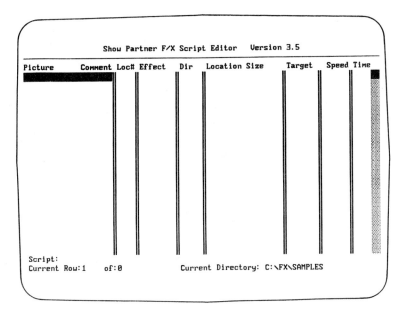

Fig. 13.24. *The blank Show Partner script.*

script in action. Notice that the background fades in slowly, but the four sets of bars appear instantly.

To add suspense to the appearance of the bars, you can use the Wipe Effect and the Up Direction to add each set of bars to the background. The bars will wipe up the screen slowly, appearing to grow. To select Wipe for the Effect, move the cursor to the Effect column in the second row and press the **W** key. To select Up as the Direction, move the cursor to the Direction column and press the **U** key. Repeat the same procedure until you have set the Effect and Direction for all four BARS files.

Next, because each BARS screen listed in the script should contribute only one set of bars, you need to select only a portion of each BARS screen to appear. Move the cursor to the Location and Size column and press the left mouse button or the Ins key. You will see a small crosshair on the screen. Move the crosshair just above and to the left of the first set of bars. If the crosshair seems to jump across the screen when you press an arrow key on the keyboard, you can use the Alt key in combination with a function key to change the speed of cursor movement. Alt-F1 reduces the cursor movement to 1 screen dot per arrow-key press, for example. Alt-F6 increases the cursor movement to 6 screen dots per arrow-key press.

When you have the crosshair at the top left corner of the bars, click the mouse button or press Ins. Move the cursor down and to the right until the box that appears completely encloses the bars. Do not include the horizontal line at the bottom of the bars within the box. Your screen should look like the screen shown in figure 13.25. Note the box enclosing the first set of bars. When the box completely surrounds the bars, click the mouse button or press the Ins key again. Press the mouse button or Ins key again to confirm your choice. In a moment, the graph background will appear so you can position the set of bars. Leave the box exactly where it is and press the mouse button or the Ins key again.

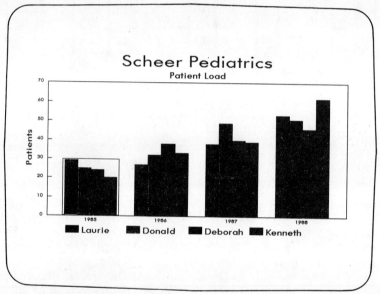

Fig. 13.25. *The first set of bars enclosed in a selection box.*

Repeat the same procedure for the remaining BARS screens, selecting the remaining sets of bars one by one. When you have selected Location and Size for all four BARS screens, your script should look similar to the script shown in figure 13.26. Your X-Y coordinates in the Location and Size columns may show some variation.

Your last step is to modify the speed of the Wipe effect you have chosen for all bars. Set the speed of all four BARS screens to Slow by pressing S with the cursor in the Speed column. To force the last screen to remain visible until you press a key, enter a negative number in the Time column, such as -1. You should see the word Key appear in the fifth row of the Time column.

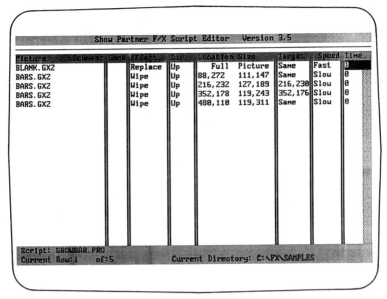

Fig. 13.26. *The Script Editor screen.*

To preview the completed show, press Alt-A. Notice that Show Partner's Wipe effect is different from PC Storyboard's Push effect, even though they create the same overall impression. Show Partner's Wipe reveals more and more of the bars as it moves up the screen. PC Storyboard's Push slides the entire set of bars up the screen, instead.

Saving a Completed Script

When you complete the Show Partner script, you can save the script in a file by pressing Ctrl-F for the File menu. Select Save As . . . and enter a script file name of up to eight characters. Then, press Enter three times to save the file. You can leave Show Partner by pressing Esc and then pressing Enter.

Creating a basic bar graph build is one of the most simple of the wide range of effects you can create within Show Partner F/X. Using the program's special animated-effects commands, you can draw images and have them dance and move across the screen while your bars are growing in the background. When you finish a complicated script, you can create an F/X Master using the F/X Master Maker utility. F/X Master Maker copies all of your screens, your script, and the special F/X Show utility onto a floppy, compresses them, and creates a special batch file to start the presentation. The result is a single disk, which you can duplicate and hand out as independent versions of your 1-2-3 graph animations.

Creating a Slide Show within 1-2-3

1-2-3 offers no formal animation capabilities, but you can put together a slide show of graphs or create the effect of building a single graph by using several /Graph Name Use commands in rapid succession.

/Graph Name Use rapidly displays the graph represented by one complete set of graph settings. So, if you issue a series of /Graph Name Use commands referring to a series of named graphs, you can replace one graph with the next quickly.

1-2-3's macro capabilities can automate display of a slide show. Refer to Chapter 7, "Using Macros for Graphing," for a macro designed especially for creating a slide show.

Summary

In this chapter, you learned about using 1-2-3 graphs to produce animated presentations. You learned about the types of software available to help you create exciting screen shows with sophisticated graphics effects. In the following chapter you will learn more about making suitable hardware choices for your presentations.

14

Choosing Hardware for Graphics Presentations

If your goal is to display finished 1-2-3 graphs to a group, you are ready to consider *presentation hardware,* the devices used to display graphic images to an audience. And at this stage, your choices are at least as abundant as those for making and polishing the graphs: you must decide whether to present with printed materials, slides or overheads, or some of the newer hardware alternatives for displaying your graphic presentation right on the computer screen.

Today's most commonly used technology for presenting graphics to groups is a combination of traditional overhead transparencies and photographic slides. Overhead transparencies are placed on an overhead projector, which projects light through them and onto a screen. Overhead projectors are inexpensive and simple to operate, and their transparencies are easily produced. To make a transparency, you can send standard transparency film through a photocopier and copy onto it a 1-2-3 graph produced with a standard black-and-white printer or with a color printer.

Slides are made either by specialized slide production companies, which record your 1-2-3 graphs onto slide film, or by you in your office with a specialized device called a film recorder. A film recorder captures a 1-2-3 graph and records it on film. You need only to process the film as slides to get the finished visuals for your presentation. Converting 1-2-3 graphs to slides is covered in detail in Chapter 12, "Making Slides."

This chapter starts where transparencies and slides leave off. Both slides and transparencies project static images without motion or sound. Presentations that emanate right from the computer screen can offer what both of these media lack. Your 1-2-3 graphs can become moving images displayed on an oversized computer monitor before a small group or projected before a full auditorium with a computer projection system and a huge screen. But those are only two of today's possibilities. Computer presentation systems, computer-to-VCR hookups, and LCD panels all offer alternatives for displaying series of 1-2-3 graphs with varying degrees of motion, sound, and special effects. This chapter helps you sort through these most recent technologies for presenting 1-2-3 graphs to an audience.

Large-Screen Monitors

Overgrown, large-screen computer monitors make the normal 12- or 14-inch monitor you work with day to day seem puny in comparison. These extra-large monitors, ranging from 19 inches, measured diagonally, to 36 inches and more, can bring a full-color on-screen presentation to a conference room, meeting room, or board room.

Large color monitors deliver the same bright colors as slides with the added potential of animation and video-like special effects, such as fades, pans and scrolls. A group of 12 to 20 people can enjoy the same eye-catching colors and amusing animation that one or two people can enjoy on a standard computer monitor. And, after the presentation, the monitor can be used as an everyday, albeit jumbo, computer display. Someone in your office who works long and hard squinting before a computer screen might enjoy sitting back comfortably and working with a large screen.

Large-scale color monitors that are suitable for presentation graphics are not the same as the large black-and-white screens you see as part of the sophisticated desktop publishing systems. These large desktop publishing screens are extra-high resolution, of such a quality that you can see a full two-page spread yet still read the smallest type. Presentation graphics monitors are comparable to the average computer monitor, but their image is stretched across a much larger display space. Display resolution is measured in the number of pixels on the screen. A *pixel* is a single screen dot. The more dots in an image on the screen, the crisper it appears and so the higher its display resolution.

Many PCs still have Color Graphics Adapter (CGA) add-in cards installed. These early model color cards offer limited color selection and resolution. CGA resolution is only 640 × 200 pixels with four colors on the screen; that's 640 pixels across the screen and 200 pixels down. The most common color graphics display standard used by today's business PCs is IBM's Enhanced Graphics Adapter (EGA) and EGA compatibles made by other manufacturers. These add-in graphics cards can create images with a resolution of 640 × 350 pixels and 16 colors on the screen. A more recent color graphics adapter standard is the Video Graphics Array (VGA). VGA cards can create images with a resolution of 640 × 480 pixels and 16 colors. The additional pixels make text and graphics noticeably more detailed on the screen. You must match the monitor resolution with that of the graphics installed in a PC system.

When you choose a large color monitor, look for the greatest display resolution your computer's graphics card can support. EGA resolution color monitors are popular, but you will see an improvement in picture clarity if you opt for a monitor capable of VGA resolution. A better choice altogether is a monitor capable of detecting and adjusting itself to most of the popular PC graphic display cards. The monitors are enormously popular as normal-sized computer displays, and they are available in extra-large sizes, as well. Multiscanning monitors, or *multisync monitors,* as they are called, accept monochrome, CGA, EGA, or VGA signals, so you can buy a single monitor for any graphics card and not worry about matching your monitor to your graphics card. Some even accept signals produced by Super VGA cards, which have resolutions as great as 800 × 600 pixels. Large scale monitors capable of displaying the resolution of IBM's top-of-the-line PC graphics card, the 8514/A, are another expensive alternative. 8514/A resolution is 1,024 × 768 pixels with a whopping 256-color palette.

A multiscanning monitor means that you can use a variety of computers, from tiny laptops to larger portables to full-scale desktops, to drive your presentation. And, it means that you are less likely to be surprised by incompatibility between your monitor and the graphics card installed in the computer at your presentation site.

As you select a large-scale color monitor, you should also look for controls (brightness, contrast, image positioning) mounted on the front rather than the side or back. You can manage a presentation better without reaching behind an extra-large monitor for adjustments, while craning to see the display in front.

Also look for an anti-glare treatment applied to the monitor screen by the manufacturer. Some computer manufacturers etch the computer screen to dull the glossy surface of a video picture tube. Monitors without anti-glare treatment, especially of this size, will reflect a roomful of light back into your viewers' eyes. Better to have your audience paying attention to your graphs than staring at their own reflections.

For an extra-large color monitor, you can expect to pay between $1,800 and $3,000 retail.

Computer Projection Systems

If the room in which you plan to give a presentation has a computer projection system, you are all set. You need merely to hook up a computer and start the show.

Computer projection systems connect to a computer, sometimes at its serial port and sometimes at its video output connector, and generate an image that is projected onto a large screen. The screen may range from less than 6 feet to more than 25 feet across.

These systems work much like a standard television, which mixes red, green, and blue light beams to form images on a screen. Rather than forming the image on a small screen, though, they project the beams onto a large screen, where an over-sized computer image forms. Because they work with projected light, these systems usually offer less vivid colors than large color monitors, but are suitable for auditorium-style presentations with large audiences. Computer monitors, even the large-screen models discussed in the preceding section, comfortably serve no more than 15 to 20 people.

Computer projection systems suffer several shortcomings. They are not easily portable, and they are far more expensive than most other presentation graphics hardware alternatives. Their lack of portability stems from their weight and size and their sensitivity to movement. With some designs, movement can knock out of alignment the color guns used to project images. In fact, the more fragile systems are often mounted to a ceiling to remain stationary and away from both presenter and audience.

When you choose a computer projector, you can opt for a three-lens system or a single-lens model. The three-lens systems use a separate lens for each color of the computer's primary color set: red, green, and blue. As a result, the images are brighter, but *convergence,* or alignment of the lenses, is critical. If the lenses are slightly out of alignment, the separate color images do not precisely overlap, and a blurry image results. Because moving the projection unit can jar the lenses and cause misconvergence, three-lens systems are more sensitive to being transported than single-lens systems. Most stationary, ceiling-mounted display projectors are three-lens systems. Some three-lens systems require a manual convergence adjustment. Others detect misconvergence automatically and self-adjust.

Single-lens systems mix color signals before projecting them through one lens, so they are not subject to convergence problems. And even though they are heavy and cumbersome, they can more safely be moved.

In a computer projection system, you should look for the same maximum resolution you look for in a large-scale monitor. The resolution of the projection system is limited by the resolution of the video card in the computer that drives the projector, of course. Rather than settling for a projector that supports a specific video standard, you can select a projector with the same multiple-frequency capabilities as *multiscanning monitors.* These projectors automatically detect and adjust to the incoming video signal. This capability, sometimes called *Auto Lock,* enables a projector to work with virtually any video signal available from a standard laptop, portable, or desktop computer, from low resolution CGA to high-resolution VGA and resolutions even greater than standard VGA.

Other features available in computer projectors can affect your presentations. Remote control can free a presenter to move about the room during a presentation. A built-in speaker can bring audio to a presentation. Some desktop presentation software packages include links to music synthesizers and speech modules so that you can incorporate music and narration. Battery backup within the main projection unit can let the unit retain its configuration information even when it is unplugged from a power source. Finally, a variable focus control for three-lens systems can keep the lens in convergence when you change the image size to suit the available screen.

LCD Overhead Panels

Both projection systems and computer monitors have been around for years. They just keep getting better and better. A brand new hardware system for presentation graphics, though, has received attention only recently: the *LCD,* or the Liquid Crystal Display, overhead panel.

The technology used by LCD panels is identical to the technology of LCD display digital watches, portable computers, and other devices that employ LCD screens. Ambient light bounces off the reflective back panel of a digital watch, skipping the darkened dots. This generates a recognizable pattern of characters or graphics. When the LCD panel is placed on an overhead projector, an image of bright areas and darkened dots on the screen forms text and graphics. The shadows on the screen are made by the same simple principle you use to make shadow figures with your hands.

LCD panels are small and light, so they are easily transportable. They are also far less expensive than most other projection technologies. The cost of LCD panels starts under $1,000. Furthermore, the only requirement for an LCD panel is a computer, a darkened room, and the type of overhead projector you find in nearly every room used regularly for presentations. One product even combines the LCD panel and the overhead projector.

Most LCD panels are about 8 inches wide and 5 inches tall, and most are strictly black and white. New panels are appearing, though, with color capabilities. These panels use a technology similar to that used in color LCD miniature televisions. Some LCD panels without color automatically convert colors to shades of gray, as do some LCD displays on portable computers. Other panels either map some colors to black and some to white, or they rely on a presentation prepared in monochrome.

Most panels offer resolution no better than the IBM CGA standard (640 pixels across and 200 pixels down). Because CGA is the standard video output of many inexpensive and lightweight laptop computers, an LCD panel used with a laptop is an easily portable alternative to other presentation devices. When the transportability of a presentation is as important as its professional polish, an LCD panel/laptop combination may be your best choice. CGA is sufficient for text and simple graphs, but more complex graphs and professional presentations demand the resolution of an EGA display. New LCD panels are appearing with full EGA resolution, but of course are more expensive.

You should be aware that the clarity of an image transmitted by an LCD panel is governed by the panel's ability to withstand heat. You may have noticed that the numbers of a digital watch become harder to read if you leave the watch out in the sun. Use a digital watch on the beach and you may never know what time to get out of the sun. As an LCD becomes hotter, its pixels fade. The intense heat from an overhead projector can cause an LCD panel's pixels to fade in a similar fashion, unless the panel dissipates the heat with a fan or a special protective backing. Both techniques are common.

If a panel uses a fan for ventilation, you should look for a model that is easily taken apart for cleaning. Fans can draw in smoke and dust and make regular cleaning a necessity.

Another solution to the heat problem used by some models is an infrared backing on the LCD panel that absorbs heat. Infrared filters may not absorb enough heat, though, to avoid light and dark areas across the panel that are caused by uneven radiation of heat from the projector. One LCD model uses both an infrared backing and a fan for maximum cooling. The more cooling, the brighter the projector light can be, so that the projected image is more easily visible, even if the room is not dark.

The most desirable LCD panels come with software that captures the completed graphs made from your computer screen and displays them in slide-show fashion. These panels also come with remote hand-held controls that communicate with a computer through its serial port. These controls can give you freedom of movement, allowing you to regulate the presentation just as you would with the remote control of a slide projector.

A final characteristic to look for in an LCD panel is a shape that preserves the original length-to-width ratio of a standard computer monitor. Computer monitors have an *aspect ratio,* or length-to-width relationship, of approximately 1.3:1. An LCD panel should have the same aspect ratio; otherwise, the graphs you project will be out of proportion. You may find, for example, that circular pie graphs elongate and present a distorted representation of your data.

Portable Systems

Do not underestimate the effectiveness of displaying graphs on the screen of a laptop that can be hand-carried into a presentation. The displays of today's laptops and portable computers are getting brighter and clearer, and color portable computers have already arrived. Before long, bright and colorful high-resolution displays will be as common on portable computers as currently are LCD screens.

A portable computer lends more to a presentation than simply the presence of an animated screen show. This presentation technique bespeaks both your technical sophistication and the resources available to you. Consider the exciting approach of playing out for a client varying scenarios. With 1-2-3 Release 3, which displays simultaneously a worksheet and a graph on-screen. you can alter the numbers and play what-ifs as part of a presentation.

Many portable computers offer bright, backlit LCD screens with EGA resolution, and a few even offer full VGA resolution. And portable and laptop computers invariably have a video output port on their back panel so that you can connect a client's monitor to your computer for an instant presentation.

The ultimate in portability, though, is to carry your computer presentation on a videocassette. Nearly every office conference room has a videocassette tape player, and most auditoriums can display a video before a large group. Computer to VCR interfaces, covered next, make transferring a complete computer presentation to videotape possible.

Computer to VCR

Back when IBM's Color Graphics Adapter was the only video standard that provided both color and graphics, transferring video images to video tape was easy. Every CGA card came with a standard video output jack, because the CGA signal was so close to standard television video that the conversion was easy. Now that EGA and VGA are today's color graphics video standards, the transfer of computer images to video tape is more complicated. Neither EGA nor VGA is close enough to standard television video to make the conversion easy.

Fortunately, several companies market products that convert high-resolution computer graphics video to a form suitable for input into a standard videocassette recorder. One such product, VGA-TV, from Willow Peripherals, converts VGA video, the video produced by IBM's Personal System/2 computers and VGA cards from a variety of manufacturers into standard video recordable with an everyday VCR.

VGA-TV is a card that fits into a standard PC expansion slot. Two connectors on its back allow you to connect both a standard PC monitor and a standard videocassette recorder. Whatever appears on the computer monitor can be simultaneously recorded on the videocassette recorder.

A more sophisticated VGA-to-VCR hookup is offered by USVideo Inc. in their USVideo Recordable VGA. This product, designed for an IBM AT or compatible, along with a separately available module from the same company, lets you record VGA images mixed with standard video signals on videotape. You might, for example, overlay a 1-2-3 graph showing a factory's output history over a walk-through videotaped tour of the plant.

A third product from Jovian Logic, Inc., called Jovian VIN, attaches to the standard monitor plug of your existing VGA card and sits outside the computer in its own box. The Jovian VIN accepts both VGA and regular video as input and then outputs standard video, the type that a VCR can record. With this unit, also, you can mix computer output and standard video.

With any of these products, you can transfer the animated presentations described in Chapter 13, "Animating 1-2-3 Graphs," to videotape.

Computer Presentation Systems

An intermediate step between real-time computer images displayed on-screen and prerecorded computer presentations on videocassette are such computer presentation systems as VideoShow from General Parametrics and PC Emcee from Computer Support Corporation.

VideoShow

When General Parametrics introduced VideoShow in 1984, this product was one of the only methods for animated presentation graphics on a personal computer. Along with PictureIt, the product's companion software, VideoShow brought the capability of displaying graphs with a variety of slick animated transitions from one image to the next on a standard CGA monitor and with an amazing 1,000-color palette and a resolution of 2000 by 500.

Today, you can use the VideoShow 160, the product's latest incarnation, with an EGA or VGA monitor, but an ordinary CGA monitor is still the best. For an outlay of over $4,000, you get a separate box that connects to a PC, yet has its own disk drive and small, built-in keypad. If VideoShow is connected to a PC, you can store VideoShow graphs on the PC hard disk. But you can use VideoShow by itself, by storing the VideoShow screens on a floppy disk inserted into the drive on the VideoShow.

Harvard Graphics directly supports VideoShow as an output device, enabling you to import graphs from 1-2-3 into Harvard Graphics, enhance them, and then save them as VideoShow screens. Then, you can use VideoShow as a portable presentation system for your graphs.

If you conduct many presentations, you may choose the VideoShow Professional, which uses the AT&T Targa board for 100,000 colors on-screen. With the resolution of the VideoShow system and the Targa's colors, you can display high resolution photographs in your presentation that you have digitized with a color scanner or a video camera.

PC Emcee

PC Emcee, from Computer Support Corporation, is a hardware/software combination that lets you create an animated presentation and play it back on a PC screen. As part of the package, you have the capability to capture graphics screens from other software or to translate graphics files to the PC Emcee format and incorporate them into an animated show (refer to Chapter 13, "Animating 1-2-3 Graphs"). The Show Editor and Show Player programs included with PC Emcee let you create complex scripts with up to 51 transition effects between successive screens.

Along with the software comes an add-in card that fits into a PC, XT, or AT expansion slot or a free-standing box that connects to a computer through its serial port. Both units control a presentation through the computer keyboard or through an infrared remote control you can carry about the presentation area. Both units also control a tape recorder, so that you can create a sound track for a self-running presentation, complete with music, narration, and sound effects. The free-standing box adds connections for hooking up other devices or for connection to a York Controls multichannel switching system that can control 250 devices simultaneously. With the York Controls system in place, you can create an entire multimedia presentation with slide projectors, video projectors, audio tape players, and room lights all controlled by PC Emcee.

A separate product from Computer Support Corporation, On-Que, lets you control conventional software from a remote control unit, just as though you were sitting at the computer's keyboard. By programming a memory-resident module, you can designate particular remote keypresses to be equivalent to specific computer keyboard keypresses or even strings of characters and commands.

Multimedia Presentations

Multimedia, the hot new buzzword in computing, means mixing computer text and graphics with video and audio to create anything from business presentations to interactive educational tools. Multimedia, as a class of PC software and hardware, is still in its infancy, but already rudimentary multimedia is available through the computer presentation systems described earlier in this chapter. With such systems from General Parametrics and Computer Support Corporation, you can mix computer video, audio, and slides.

Down the media pipeline, products will emerge that use a PC as the controlling nucleus for a system that joins high-resolution computer graphics, digital video, and synthesized digital sound. No doubt, graphs originated in 1-2-3 will be integrated into varied multimedia business presentations, merged into a unified presentation by one of the upcoming multimedia control software packages.

Watch for advances in multimedia. Many industry observers are predicting this to be a prime application for computers in the 1990s.

Summary

This and the preceding chapters suggested a host of methods to incorporate 1-2-3 graphs into business presentations. Chapter 13, "Animating 1-2-3 graphs" discussed methods for bringing static 1-2-3 graphs to life by introducing motion into a presentation. This chapter looked at some of the hardware you can use to display your graphs and animated presentations before an audience. The next chapter covers methods and techniques for incorporating 1-2-3 graphs into business documents.

15

Using 1-2-3 PIC Files

This chapter focuses on what you can do with 1-2-3 PIC files, from importing them into a word processor or desktop publisher for adding business graphs to pulling them into an illustration program to add extra flair with freehand drawings, clip-art, and annotations. You will review the procedure for saving a 1-2-3 graph as a PIC file; then you will explore the many uses for the graph saved by this method.

After you have perfected your 1-2-3 graph, you have two choices for a method of storing it. You can name the graph so that you can call it up again any time later, or you can save the graph as a PIC file. A *named graph* resides within the worksheet and is available only when you have the worksheet loaded into 1-2-3. Because it remains an integral part of the worksheet, the graph is constantly updated to correspond to changes made to the data it reflects.

Storing a graph as a named graph using the 1-2-3 /Graph Name Create command saves the current state of all the settings under the /Graph menus. Later, when you retrieve the graph using the /Graph Name Use command, 1-2-3 will reconstruct the graph by recreating all menu settings as they were when you named the graph. When you select

/Graph View, you'll see the graph again just as you left it. A named graph is an inseparable part of a 1-2-3 worksheet. You can't pull a named graph out and import it into a desktop publishing program, for example.

If you save your completed graph as a separate PIC file on disk using the /Graph Save command, you can print the file with PrintGraph—or format the graph with Allways if you are using Release 2.2. As soon as you save the PIC file separately, though, the graph it carries exists only as a snapshot of the worksheet that is frozen at one point in time. The PIC file remains the same despite changes to the data, so the graph may quickly become outdated.

Yet, a PIC file provides some important advantages. You can import a PIC file into any of a multitude of graphics software packages that let you enhance a graph or place it into a document. If the software does not accept PIC files directly, you can translate the file into another graphics file format easily.

Saving a Graph as a PIC File

The procedure described here for making a graph and saving it as a PIC file will help you review how to create PIC files, as well as produce the PIC file used for the examples in this chapter. You will undoubtedly note that the PIC file in this example exceeds the principle of aesthetic simplicity. By adding an array of embellishments to the graph, you can judge how effective these graph elements are in other software.

Start by creating a graph based on the data shown in figure 15.1.

To create the graph, use this series of commands:

/Graph Type Bar

X: B4..D4
B: B6..D6
A: B5..D5
C: B7..D7
D: B8..D8

Options Legend Range
    A: Circulation
    B: Display Advertising
    C: Classified Advertising
    D: Industry Directory Sales

Titles
    First: \A1
    Second: \A2
    X-Axis: **Months**
    Y-Axis: **Dollars**

Grid Horizontal

Data-labels
    A: **B5..D5**
    B: **B6..D6**
    C: **B7..D7**
    D: **B8..D8**

B&W

Quit

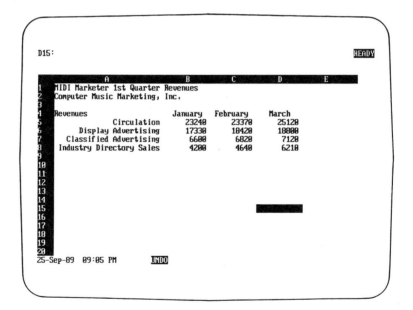

***Fig. 15.1.** Worksheet data for PIC file graph.*

Now, view the graph and note the positioning of its components. In particular, notice the size and placement of its titles, its legend, and its data-labels. See also the colors or hatch patterns used in bars. You may find that some changes are made to the graph when you import it into certain desktop publishing programs or word processors, or when you translate the PIC file to another graphics file format.

If you are using 1-2-3 Release 2.2, the completed graph in black and white (B&W) will look like figure 15.2. If you are using Release 3, your graph in black and white will look like the one in figure 15.3.

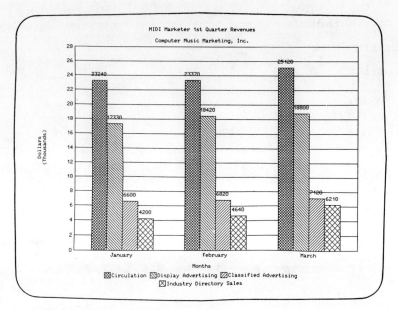

Fig. 15.2. *The sample PIC file 1-2-3 Release 2.2 graph.*

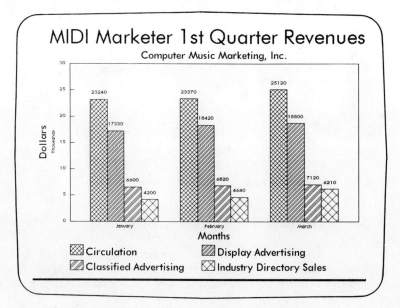

Fig. 15.3. *The sample PIC file 1-2-3 Release 3 graph.*

To create a PIC file, use the /Graph **S**ave command and supply the file name **PICBW**. 1-2-3 will provide the .PIC file extension.

If you are using a color monitor, you may want to return to the graph menu and save another copy of the graph called PICCOLOR.PIC in color by using the color selection on the /Graph Options menu. Then you can try the same exercises in this chapter with both versions of the graph. With the color graph, you can examine how colors translate when the PIC file is imported or translated. And with the black-and-white graph, you can examine how hatch patterns are translated.

Understanding the Benefits of PIC Files

All files that popular graphics programs create fall into two categories, *bit-mapped* graphics files and *vector* graphics files. Bit-mapped files represent an image by storing a map in the computer's memory. This map tells which dots on-screen to turn on and what color each dot should be if the monitor displays color. Vector files, on the other hand, store images as a collection of simple geometric shapes, such as lines, boxes, and filled areas.

1-2-3 PIC files are vector graphics files made up entirely of lines. The advantage of PIC files is that they easily may be resized without gaining or losing any picture resolution. To increase the size of a bit-mapped image on-screen, a graphics program calculates a new map of the image that illuminates more on-screen dots. Of course, enlarging an image composed of dots means calculating larger dots, and larger dots don't provide the same on-screen precision. The effect is to magnify an image's imperfections. Curved lines, text, or diagonal lines may suddenly look jagged.

To enlarge a vector image, on the other hand, a program needs only to extend the length of lines contained in the image. The resulting larger image has all the crispness and clarity of the original.

Bar and line graphs are perfect for vector files. Bar graphs and even pie graphs are composed of collections of lines, and line graphs are obviously well-suited to vector graphics.

Why is it important to understand the distinction between bit-mapped and vector file types? Some graphics programs import and work with only one of the two graphics file types. Paint programs, for example, generally accept and create only bit-mapped files. Drawing and illustrating programs, on the other hand, often import and allow you to edit vector files only. Fortunately, many word processing and desktop publishing programs accept both bit-mapped and vector files, and nearly all accept 1-2-3 PIC files because of the widespread use of Lotus 1-2-3.

Exporting a CGM File in 1-2-3 Release 3

If you use 1-2-3 Release 3, you have another choice for exporting completed 1-2-3 graphs. You can create separate graph files called *Computer Graphics Metafile*, or CGM files.

The CGM standard has become the most widely used graphics file interchange format. Most of the major graphics packages can import and export CGM files, and any desktop publisher or word processor worth consideration for use with 1-2-3 can import CGM files.

The only problem with CGM as a graphics file standard is that there are many implementations of CGM, most being slightly different in minor respects. In other words, as a standard, CGM is not well standardized. You should be able to import a CGM file into any program that accepts the CGM file format, but you may notice subtle differences in the appearance of the graphic, such as variations in the positioning of text or in the color and hatch patterns used in the bars of a graph. The only remedy for these variations is to keep track of them and adjust the graph in 1-2-3 accordingly before you export the CGM file.

To export a CGM file in 1-2-3 Release 3, you must select Metafile as the default file export standard under the /Worksheet Global Default Graph menu. Then, when you use the /Graph Save command, 1-2-3 automatically creates a CGM file rather than a PIC file for the current 1-2-3 session. If you select Update from the /Worksheet Global Default menu to update the 1-2-3 configuration, 1-2-3 will always create CGM files in future sessions.

The remainder of this chapter discusses working with PIC files. If you use 1-2-3 Release 3, you may want to try the same examples with CGM files, as well, to note any differences.

Using PIC Files in Word Processors

Formerly, you expected a word processor to edit text, format your words attractively, and send the finished document to one of a variety of printers. Now, with high-resolution graphics displays and laser printers commonplace, and inexpensive desktop publishing programs encroaching on the word processors' turf, word processors are having to add new capabilities quickly.

One of the most recent improvements to the word-processing repertoire lets you place pictures within text documents. All the best-selling professional word processors now not only can incorporate graphics files into documents but can display the results on-screen before printing them as well.

Most word processors place a graphics file image into an invisible frame within a document. Some let you manually flow text around the frame, and some even provide automatic text wraparound. This section describes the process of importing 1-2-3 PIC files into the most popular word processors.

WordPerfect

WordPerfect 5.1, the latest version of WordPerfect and the most widely used word processing software available, directly imports Lotus PIC files so that you can incorporate 1-2-3 graphs into your documents. After you import a graph in WordPerfect, you can reposition the graph and resize it, flow text around it, and add a caption.

Every graphic file you add to a WordPerfect document goes into a Figure box or a User box, two of the five types of boxes provided by the program. Text and Table boxes are for adding text to a document. Equation boxes are for mathematical and scientific equations. After you set up a box, the PIC file you select fills the box. You won't see the actual contents of the box until you preview the document on-screen with the WordPerfect View Document command.

Setting Up a Box for a PIC File

To set up a box for a PIC file, press Graphics (Alt-F9) and select Figure (1) or User Box (4). WordPerfect will ask whether you want to Create a new box, Edit an existing box, give a box a New Number or modify the current box Options. A new box will use the current options settings, so you may want to select Options (4) first to set box options appropriate to the new box.

When you select Options (4), you see the screen shown in figure 15.4. The first three options on this screen let you set different aspects of each of the box's sides: its left, right, top and bottom. For the first option, Border Style, notice that WordPerfect places a single line on all four sides of the box by default. Your other choices are no lines, double, dashed, dotted, thick, and extra-thick lines.

```
Options: Figure

        1 - Border Style
                Left                            Single
                Right                           Single
                Top                             Single
                Bottom                          Single
        2 - Outside Border Space
                Left                            0.167"
                Right                           0.167"
                Top                             0.167"
                Bottom                          0.167"
        3 - Inside Border Space
                Left                            0"
                Right                           0"
                Top                             0"
                Bottom                          0"
        4 - First Level Numbering Method        Numbers
        5 - Second Level Numbering Method        Off
        6 - Caption Number Style                [BOLD]Figure 1[bold]
        7 - Position of Caption                 Below box, Outside borders
        8 - Minimum Offset from Paragraph        0"
        9 - Gray Shading (% of black)            0%

Selection: 0
```

Fig. 15.4. The WordPerfect Box Options screen.

The next option, Outside Border Space, lets you set the amount of white space padding to appear between the box and the surrounding text on all four sides. Notice that the default space is 0.167 inches.

The third option, Inside Border Space, lets you determine how much space should appear around the edges of the graph within the box. The default is zero. By allowing some inside border space, you can give the graph a little breathing room within the box.

Six other options appear on the Options screen:

The **First and Second Level Numbering Methods** let you turn off numbering or choose from among numbers, letters, or Roman numerals for the figure numbers that WordPerfect automatically provides within figure captions.

Caption Number Style lets you specify how the text in captions will look. Bold is the default.

Position of Caption lets you place a caption either above or below the figure box and either outside or inside the border. The default is "Below box, Outside borders."

Minimum Offset from Paragraph lets you determine the minimum distance between the preceding paragraph and a figure box that WordPerfect will allow when it tries to squeeze a box onto the bottom of a page. The default is zero.

Gray Shading (% of black) lets you fill a box with a gray tint. You can select a percent number from 1 to 100 for the density. For graphs, though, you probably will not want the shading, so leave this option set to 0%.

Creating a Figure Box for a PIC File

After you set the options for the box, press Exit (F7) to return to the editing source. Press Graphics (Alt-F9), select Figure (1), and then select Create (1). You will see the Definition: Figure menu appear, as shown in figure 15.5.

```
Definition: Figure

    1 - Filename

    2 - Contents            Empty

    3 - Caption

    4 - Anchor Type         Paragraph

    5 - Vertical Position   0"

    6 - Horizontal Position Right

    7 - Size                3.25" wide x 3.25" (high)

    8 - Wrap Text Around Box Yes

    9 - Edit



Selection: 0
```

Fig. 15.5. The WordPerfect Definition: Figure menu.

To choose a PIC file for the box, select Filename (1) and then type in the directory name and PIC file name for the graph. You can use List Files (F5) to locate and specify a PIC File.

The Definition: Figure menu has these further options:

2 - Contents lets you indicate to WordPerfect what the box will contain: a graphic image, a block of text, or an equation. But you don't have to use this option. If you designate a graphic file through the Filename (1) option, WordPerfect defaults to Graphics contents. If the box is to contain a graphic image, you have two choices. You can store the graphic image right in the WordPerfect document file, or you can instruct WordPerfect to use a graphic file stored separately on disk.

3 - Caption lets you type in additional caption text for the graph or replace the caption text already there.

4 - Anchor Type lets you choose one of three types for the box: paragraph, page, or character. *Paragraph boxes* stay with the paragraph preceding them. *Page boxes* remain in the same position on the page no matter how the text on the page falls. *Character boxes* are treated as a single character. These flow on the page with the text into which they are embedded.

5 - Vertical Position lets you determine the distance in inches between the preceding paragraph and the top edge of the box.

6 - Horizontal Position lets you choose from among left, right, center, and full. Left, right, and center determine the side-to-side position of the box on the page. Full stretches the box to extend from the left to the right margin.

7 - Size lets you set either the box height or the box width. With this option, you can also rescale the box to the default size or instruct WordPerfect to calculate the appropriate height-to-width ratio for the box.

8 - Wrap Text Around Box lets you determine whether text should flow around the edges of the box or continue below it. If you center the box, text will flow down only the left side of the box and continue underneath. To make text flow on both sides of a centered box, you must use columns. You can wrap text around up to 20 boxes in a single file. After that, text no longer wraps around but begins to flow through boxes.

9 - Edit lets you rotate, scale, and display a portion of a graphic image. If you are working with a Text box, you use this option to type text that should appear within the box. As you proceed, you can use WordPerfect's formatting commands to format the text. You can even use the Graphics command (Alt-F9) to rotate the text 90, 180, or 270 degrees (to print rotated text, your printer must be capable of rotating fonts). You won't see the text in the box until you use the View Document command to preview the final document.

Editing a Box That Holds a PIC File

To edit a box, press Graphics (Alt-F9), select the type of box, and select Edit (2). Enter the figure number of the box you want to edit and make any changes you need in the Definition: Figure menu. Select Exit (F7) to return to the document.

Editing a PIC File within a Box

WordPerfect provides a limited set of commands for making changes to the PIC file within the box. Although you cannot actually modify the contents of the PIC file, you can move the PIC file within the box, display only a portion of the PIC file, rotate or mirror the PIC file, and reverse the colors so that black areas become white.

Viewing a Document with an Embedded PIC File

To get a sense of the final appearance of the printed page with an embedded PIC file, display the page on the screen, select Print (Shift-F7) and then select **6-View Document**. You will see the layout of the text elements and the actual 1-2-3 graph on the page. To end View Document, press Exit (F7). Figure 15.6. shows the WordPerfect View Document screen.

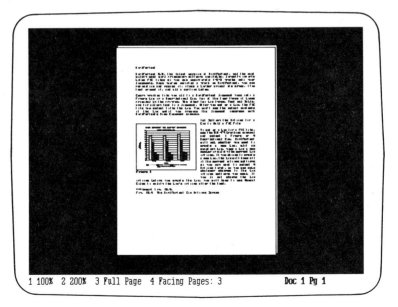

Fig. 15.6. *The WordPerfect View Document screen.*

Figure 15.7 shows the black-and-white 1-2-3 Release 2.2 PIC file printed from within WordPerfect.

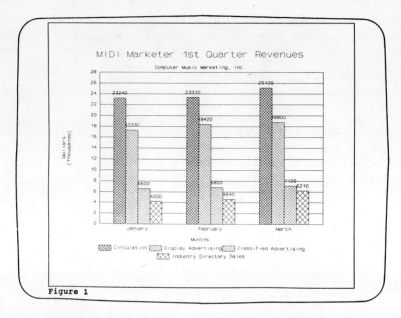

Fig. 15.7. *The black-and-white 1-2-3 Release 2.2 PIC file printed from within WordPerfect.*

Microsoft Word

Microsoft Word 5.0 imports more than a dozen different graphics file formats, including Lotus PIC files. Each graphics file is imported into a frame that you can reposition and resize. Word even lets you specify a certain white space around a picture, which is measured as a distance between the edge of the frame and the surrounding text.

Normally, you see only a line of text inserted into the document that tells the size and positioning of the graphic frame and its contents. With Word's Show Layout command, you can see the precise positioning of the graphic frame and edit the document as necessary. And, with Word's Page Preview mode, you can see a full graphic representation of the printed page that shows the actual 1-2-3 graph on the screen.

Importing a PIC File

To import a 1-2-3 graph into a Word document, position the cursor in the document where you want the graph to be; then use the **Library**

Link Graphics command to import a PIC file. When you specify PIC as the file extension, Word automatically recognizes that you are importing a Lotus PIC file. Word places a line in the document at the position of the cursor that starts with .G. (the Word code for Graphic) and continues with the PIC file's name, size, and the graphic file type, which in this case is Lotus PIC.

The .G. line is its own paragraph, and the .G. is formatted as hidden text. You will not see the .G. unless Show Hidden Text is set to Yes. If you were to import the PIC file named PICBW.PIC into a Word document, the Word screen would look like the screen in figure 15.8 with Show Hidden Text set to Yes.

```
    ═ L0·[······1·········2·········3·········4·········5·······]·········7···
    ·······································································
T1     (d) Microsoft Word¶

T1     ¶

T1     Microsoft Word imports more than a dozen different
       graphics file formats, including Lotus PIC files. Each
       graphic file is imported into a frame that you can
       reposition and resize. Word even lets you specify a
       certain white space around a picture measured as a
       distance between the edge of the frame and the surrounding
       text.¶

          .G.C:\1232\PICBW.PIC;5.8";4.188";Lotus PIC¶

T1     Normally, you see only a line of text inserted into the
       document which tells the size and positioning of the
       graphic frame and its contents. With Word's Show Layout
       command, though, you can see the precise positioning of
       the graphic frame and edit the document as necessary. And,
       with Word's Page Preview mode, you can see a full graphic
       representation of the printed page which shows the actual
       1-2-3 graph on the screen.¶

T1     ▌
                                                    ─123GT15S.DOC─
    Pg6 Li19 Co3      {¶}              ?            Microsoft Word
```

Fig. 15.8. *A Microsoft Word file with PICBW.PIC embedded.*

The Library Link Graphics menu provides a number of options for formatting the PIC file. By default, Word suggests a width for the graphic frame equal to the width of the current column. The graphics height for the frame Word suggests is the appropriate height to maintain the image's original shape. This shape is called its aspect ratio or width-to-height ratio. You can left-align, right-align, or center the PIC file within its frame using the option called "alignment in frame," and you can supply a space before and after the graphic frame just as you can supply a space before and after any paragraph.

Previewing the Document

After you import a PIC file into a Word document, you can check the appearance of the file by using one of two methods.

Show Layout shows the true appearance of the document on-screen but still lets you edit the document's text and graphic positioning. The placement of each PIC file is indicated by a dotted box that contains within its bottom edge the PIC file's name, size, and file type (Lotus PIC).

Print Preview displays exactly how the document will look when printed. When you select Print Preview, you can see all characteristics of the document including its headers, footers, margins, fonts, and the actual embedded 1-2-3 graphs. But you cannot edit a document while Print Previewing it.

To view an accurate representation of a document with an embedded PIC file, set Show Layout to Yes on the Options menu or press Alt-F4. You will see a dotted box appear, which represents the PIC file. If you have added a border to the frame holding the PIC file, the border will show up on the screen.

While you are looking at the Show Layout representation of the PIC file embedded within the document, you can edit the document's text or edit the contents of the line within the bottom of the PIC file frame.

To see the actual appearance of the printed document, you can use the Preview option under the Print command or press Ctrl-F9. Print Preview displays the entire page or a set of facing pages, and shows not only the positioning of the PIC file, but the actual 1-2-3 graph on-screen. Figure 15.9 displays the Print Preview screen.

Adjusting Size and Placement of Graphs

To position a PIC file precisely on a page, you can use Microsoft Word's **F**ormat **PO**sition command. The choices on the Format Position menu provide a wide variety of PIC file frame positions relative to a column on the page, the margins of the document, or the edges of the entire page. You can add more white space around the PIC file than the default 1/6 inch by setting a larger measurement for distance from text field. To leave white space around a PIC file within its frame, add space above and below the graphic and make the graphic width narrower than the width of the frame.

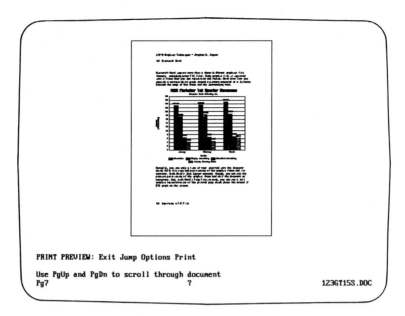

Fig. 15.9. *Microsoft Word Print Preview displaying a PIC file embedded within a document.*

Adding a Border to the Graph

To add a border around a PIC file, position the cursor on the .G. line that describes the PIC file, and select Format **B**order. With the Format Border command, you can pick a variety of border types, line styles, and shading intensities.

Adding a Caption to the Graph

You can add a caption under a graph by adding the caption as separate text immediately after the graphic frame. Or you can position the cursor at the end of the .G. line, press Shift-Enter to start a new line, and then type the caption text. You can then format the caption just as you would format any paragraph.

Printing a Document with Graphs

To print a document with a PIC file, your printer must be capable of printing graphics. Under the Print Options menu, you can choose the graphics resolutions available to your printer. The higher the resolution, the cleaner and less jagged the lines of the printed graph. Use lower resolutions for faster draft printing and the higher resolutions for the final draft. Figure 15.10 shows the sample black-and-white PIC file printed from within Microsoft Word.

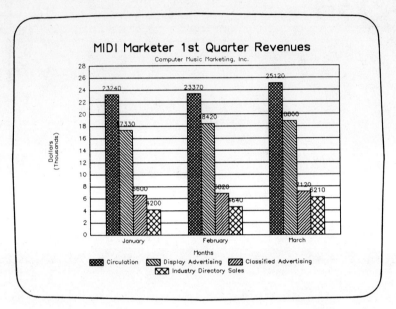

Fig. 15.10. The sample black-and-white PIC file printed from within Microsoft Word.

WordStar

WordStar users can integrate 1-2-3 PIC files into their documents using the special program Inset from Inset Systems. Inset, covered in the following section, allows you to merge graphics files into word processing documents. WordStar provides special shortcuts for entering the appropriate codes to use Inset.

Inset

Inset, from Inset Systems Inc., is not a word processor, but it gives word processors without the ability to integrate text and graphics a handy method of including 1-2-3 PIC files in documents.

Inset runs as a memory-resident program behind 1-2-3 or your word processor. While you are viewing a graph with the 1-2-3 /Graph View command, you can pop up Inset and capture the graph into a special

Inset file that has the extension .PIX. If you have Hijaak, a file translator made by the same company, you can translate a graph saved as a PIC file directly into an Inset PIX file, instead. The advantage of translating directly from PIC to PIX is a higher resolution. The image you capture with Inset is limited in resolution to that of the video card and monitor you use.

Once you have a graph in a PIX file, you can use the tools of Inset to edit the graph. PIX files are bit-mapped, so you can perform pixel-by-pixel editing. Among the edits possible are drawing geometric shapes, adding text, copying, moving, and erasing portions of the screen. PIX files translated from PIC files by Hijaak are better left unedited. You can crop them to display only a portion of the image, but if you edit them, Inset will reduce their resolution to the resolution of the screen.

To place an Inset PIX file that displays a 1-2-3 graph into a word-processing document, you must first create the space for it within the document by using the space bar or Tab key. Then, you can type the name of the PIX file you want enclosed by square brackets, such as [PICBW.PIX], to give the file a *PIX tag*.

If you invoke Inset while you are within the word processor when the PIX tag nears the top of the screen, Inset displays a box on-screen showing the size and positioning of the PIX file. Resize and reposition the box using Inset's commands and then press Enter to lock in the graphic.

To see both the document text and the graphic, you can use Preview under Inset's Modify menu option to see on the screen both your 1-2-3 graph and text as they will appear when printed.

To print a document with both text and PIX files added with Inset, simply print your document as you normally would while Inset is memory resident in the background. Inset will take care of all the work, merging 1-2-3 graphs into a document just as you instructed.

Using PIC Files in Desktop Publishing Programs

Being able to import PIC files into word processors lets you intermingle text and 1-2-3 graphs in memos, letters, and proposals. As you've seen, the better word processors even give you the tools to design documents with more complicated layouts suitable for newsletters and fliers. Word processors of this caliber depend on more advanced formatting commands and a visual page preview for on-screen inspection before printing.

Desktop publishing programs go several steps further. Rather than limiting your view of the final document to a quick peek before printing, most popular desktop publishing programs let you actually work on a graphical view of your document. You see the document's text on-screen with its final fonts, and you see 1-2-3 graphs and other images on-screen.

Aldus PageMaker and Xerox Ventura Publisher, the two most popular desktop publishing programs today, both easily import 1-2-3 PIC files. But you'll achieve better results with either package if you keep a few considerations in mind.

☐ Text that you create in the desktop publishing program always looks better than the text you supply within 1-2-3 for titles and other labels within the graph. The desktop publisher gives you absolute control over the positioning, size, and typeface of the added text. You are better off, therefore, to create a 1-2-3 graph without main graph titles and axis titles. Add these elements after you import the PIC file into a desktop publisher.

☐ A desktop publisher gives you no greater control than a word processor over the actual design of the graph. A 1-2-3 graph comes into word processing and desktop publishing programs as a complete and finished file. You can make no modifications to the colors of a graph's bars, for example, or to the positioning of its axis labels. What a desktop publishing program does provide is far greater control over the formatting of the document into which you have imported the graph.

☐ With most desktop publishing packages, the final look of the 1-2-3 graph on paper depends on the type of output equipment you use. Because PIC files are line-oriented in nature, printers and typesetting equipment that use the line-oriented PostScript page description language will print a cleaner, crisper copy of the graph. Dot-matrix and laser printers that are compatible with the Hewlett-Packard LaserJet series create a bit-mapped image based on the PIC file, and the translation introduces the same distortion and somewhat jagged lines and text often found in bit-mapped graphics images. You'll see this effect most visibly when you print a 1-2-3 pie graph. Depending on how large you make the pie, the circular boundary of the graph may become jagged.

Aldus PageMaker

Aldus PageMaker makes adding a 1-2-3 graph to a document easy. You need only select the PIC file and draw a rectangular frame to hold it on the page. PageMaker interprets the PIC file and automatically recreates the graph on-screen. It sets up the axes, makes the bars or lines, and positions and chooses fonts for the graph's text. But PageMaker's interpretation of a PIC file differs from the original graph as viewed with the 1-2-3 /**Graph V**iew command in a variety of ways.

☐ The bars of a bar graph may be empty if you try importing a PIC file that was made with the color option in 1-2-3.

☐ The graph's main titles and x- and y-axis titles may be out of position, and the font PageMaker supplies for them may not be what you expected. This is true especially if the titles are composed of many characters.

☐ Text that is rotated, such as the y-axis indicator, will be interpreted by PageMaker as a graphic element rather than as text. PageMaker will have difficulty positioning the text, and you will find it improperly aligned along the y-axis.

☐ If you use a PCL printer (an HP LaserJet or compatible), the text in the graph's legend may be missing, the graph's title may be out of position, and the axis titles may be in a larger font size than you chose in 1-2-3.

Figure 15.11 shows the sample 1-2-3 Release 2.2 color graph as interpreted by PageMaker and printed on an HP LaserJet Series II. Notice that the bars are blank, the title is left-aligned, and the subtitle is out of position and far too small. Notice also that the legend is pushed to the left and the y-axis label and indicator are legible but positioned improperly. If you are using a PostScript output device, the result on-screen and on the printed page should be substantially better. Figure 15.12 shows the black-and-white version of the same graph.

The Release 3 version of the same graph, but in black and white, fared better in PageMaker, but it has similar problems. Figure 15.13 shows the 1-2-3 Release 3 graph. Notice that a graph with the B&W option turned on displays hatch patterns in its bars. The color version of the 1-2-3 Release 3 graph had the same problem with blank bars as did the 1-2-3 Release 2.2 version.

1-2-3 Release 3 offers CGM as an alternate graphics output file format. Because CGM is a graphics file format accepted by PageMaker, you may want to use it as the link between the two programs. 1-2-3's CGM files, when displayed in PageMaker, suffer similar problems to those of PIC

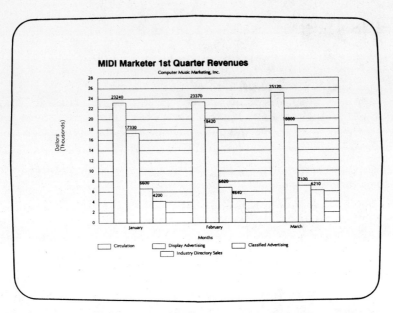

Fig. 15.11. *The sample 1-2-3 Release 2.2 color graph as interpreted and printed by PageMaker.*

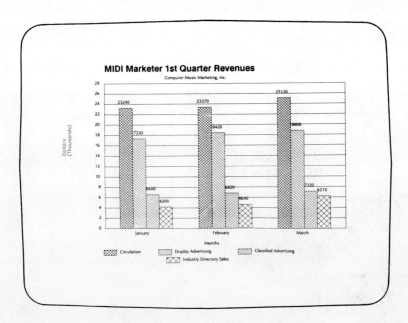

Fig. 15.12. *The 1-2-3 Release 3 B&W Graph as interpreted and printed by PageMaker on an HP LaserJet Series II.*

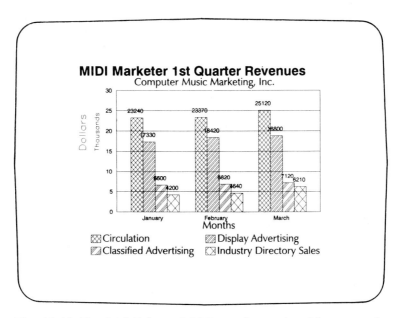

Fig. 15.13. *The 1-2-3 Release 3 B&W graph as printed by PageMaker on an HP LaserJet Series II.*

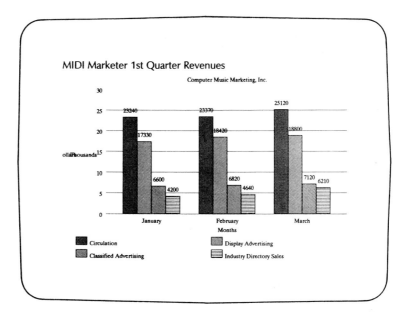

Fig. 15.14. *A 1-2-3 Release 3 CGM output file as interpreted and printed by PageMaker.*

files. Figure 15.14 displays the CGM version of the sample graph printed by PageMaker. You'll notice that the y-axis titles are not rotated and that the title and indicator overwrite each other. PageMaker also interpreted the title font in the CGM file as Optima, a soft font for the LaserJet installed in one copy of Windows/286, Version 2.1.

Unfortunately, there is no simple one-shot solution to the maladies of all of these graphs. But there are steps you can take to work around some of them. First, when you create the 1-2-3 PIC file, be sure to use B&W rather than Color on the /Graph Options menu. The data series of black-and-white graphs are differentiated by hatch patterns rather than colors, so you should be able to use the hatch patterns in PageMaker to distinguish among the series, too.

Second, before you save the PIC file, delete any titles you have set. The resulting PIC file will have only the graph's axes, legend, and bars or lines. If the PIC file represents a pie graph, only the slices of the pie will be part of the file. After you import the graph into PageMaker, you can add graph titles, axis titles, and even a footnote and caption below the graph, using the PageMaker text tool. You can then format the text added in PageMaker, just as you would format any document text. That means you can choose any available font for the text. Then you can position the text with PageMaker's precise text-alignment options. If you add free-floating text for a graph's title, be sure to add the text somewhere within the top edge of the frame containing the 1-2-3 graph. If you don't, the text may flow around the edge of the graph.

If you must use the titles from Release 3, rather than creating titles in PageMaker, reducing the number of characters or choosing a smaller size for the text may automatically center the titles in the PIC or CGM file you create rather than left-aligning them.

Ventura Publisher

One of Xerox Ventura Publisher's strongest features is its linking of graphics files to desktop-published documents. Rather than incorporate a PIC file permanently into one of Ventura's chapters, the program pulls a fresh copy of the PIC file from the PIC file's original directory each time you load a Ventura publication. The result is that you can swap a new PIC file right into Ventura. As long as you give the new PIC file the same name and put it into the same directory as the original, Ventura will blindly use it rather than the PIC file you loaded before. That means you can update the 1-2-3 graph's PIC file periodically and see the update reflected the next time you call up the Ventura document.

Xerox Ventura Publisher is far more successful than PageMaker at recreating a 1-2-3 graph based on a PIC file, but it suffers some of the same problems. Rather than trying to interpret the rotated text of the y-axis title and y-axis indicator, Ventura may ignore it altogether. Ventura also misaligns the main graph titles, pushing them too far to the left. Figure 15.15 displays the sample black-and-white PIC file as printed by Ventura Publisher 2.0 on a Hewlett-Packard LaserJet Series II.

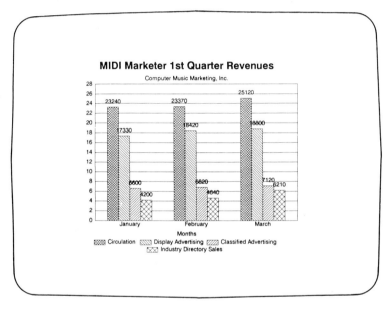

Fig. 15.15. *The sample black-and-white 1-2-3 Release 2.2 PIC file as interpreted and printed by Ventura 2.0 on an HP LaserJet Series II.*

In other respects, Ventura is faithful to the 1-2-3 PIC file and sometimes even improves on the original. Rather than ignore the colors in a color PIC file, as PageMaker does, Ventura displays them in all their glory and even translates them to shades of gray when it prints the graph on a black and white printer (see fig. 15.16). Ventura also translates the hatch patterns in 1-2-3 Release 3 PIC files to hatch patterns that are more easily distinguished when they are side by side.

Ventura has significant problems interpreting other aspects of 1-2-3 Release 3 PIC files, though. You may find missing altogether the graph's frame, the box that encloses the graph's bars or lines. The graph's first title may be way out of alignment, pushed far to the left, as seen in figure 15.17. This figure displays the sample PIC file generated by 1-2-3 Release 3 printed by Ventura Publisher 2.0 on a Hewlett-Packard

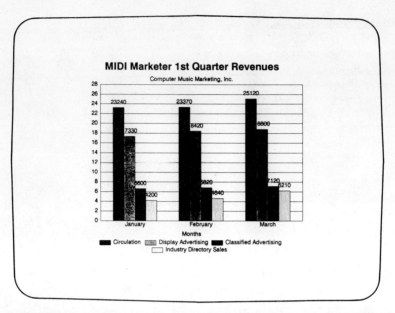

Fig. 15.16. *The sample color PIC file as interpreted and printed by Ventura Publisher 2.0 on an HP LaserJet Series II.*

LaserJet Series II. Figure 15.18 shows the CGM version of the same graph printed by Ventura.

Some users find that all the text on their PIC file graphs looks impossibly tiny when displayed in Ventura. If this happens to you, Ventura has selected 2 point Swiss as the font for your graph's text.

As with PageMaker, your best bet to solve the title alignment errors and incorrect text-font style and size problems is to omit as much text as possible when you create the PIC file in 1-2-3. Add the text to the graph within Ventura, instead. You can attach text to a graph file using Ventura's Box Text option in the program's built-in graphics module.

Adding Text with Ventura's Box Text Feature

After you load a PIC file into a Ventura frame, you can add text to the image using Ventura's Box Text feature. To use Box Text, first select the frame containing the PIC file in Ventura's Frame Setting mode. This will attach the box text to the graph frame. Then, select Ventura's Graphic Editing mode and select the icon labeled Box Text, which appears at the left side of the screen. Draw a box on the screen and you will see the words "Box Text" in the box. Use Ventura's Text

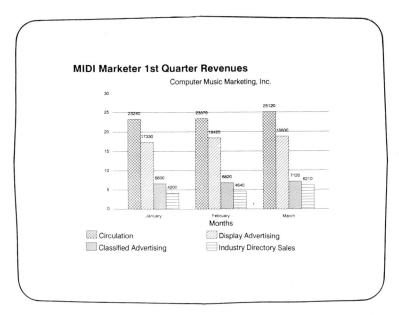

Fig. 15.17. *The sample 1-2-3 Release 3 black-and-White PIC file as printed by Ventura 2.0 on a LaserJet Series II.*

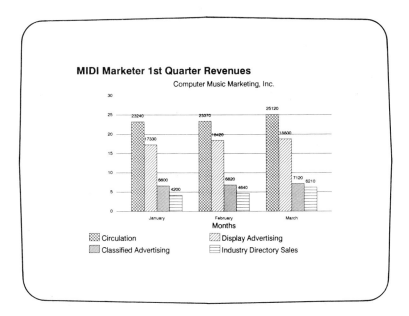

Fig. 15.18. *The sample 1-2-3 Release 3 CGM file as printed by Ventura Publisher 2.0 on an HP LaserJet Series II.*

Editor to replace "Box Text" with a line of text for the graphic, perhaps one of the titles. You can position the box on top of the graph frame by placing the cursor in the middle of the box, holding the mouse button down, and dragging the box to a new location.

Now, with the box still selected (you should see frame handles surrounding the box) select Line Attributes from the Graphic menu and set Line Thickness to None. This eliminates the box around the box text frame and leaves free-floating text on the screen.

Box text is text you can tag like any other paragraph text. By default, Ventura creates a tag called Z_Box Text for all box text in the chapter. You can modify the attributes of the Z_Box Text tag. Or you can create a new tag for any particular box text to change any of the text attributes, such as font, alignment, or spacing. You can attach as many box text frames to the PIC file frame as you need. If you move the frame, the box text will move, too.

Eliminating Color from B&W Graphs

Even when you have created a black-and-white PIC file with the 1-2-3 /Graph Options B&W setting, Ventura Publisher 2.0 may still display the bars, lines, or pie slices of your graph with both hatch patterns and colors. To suppress the display of colors, you can use the Define Colors option under the Ventura Paragraph menu.

When you select Define Colors on the Ventura 2.0 Paragraph menu, Ventura shows a dialog box display of the color composition of each of the defined screen colors. You can see all the colors by advancing and decreasing the color number, using the right and left arrows next to Color Number. For each color, set the percentage of black to 100%. This makes every color black, and, as a result, black-and-white graphs appear in black and white on the screen.

Inexpensive Desktop Publishing Systems

The battle is fierce between the foremost word-processing packages and the inexpensive desktop publishing programs described here. As word processors have gotten more capable at formatting pages—mixing text and graphics, and even dressing up the page with lines and boxes—the distinction between desktop publishing and word processing has begun to blur. These inexpensive desktop publishing packages muddy the waters further by lacking some of the fancy features that so clearly distinguish such top-notch desktop publishing programs as PageMaker and Ventura Publisher.

Nevertheless, the two programs described in the following paragraphs which both work with 1-2-3 PIC files let you see your document on-screen as you are preparing it rather than waiting for a final preview mode.

Byline

Ashton-Tate's Byline is a pared-down and inexpensive version of desktop publishing. Byline does not even require a mouse as an input device. The program works through simple keyboard commands. Byline accepts 1-2-3 PIC files directly as one of its graphics file import formats.

In Byline, you can expect to get many of the capabilities of more elaborate desktop publishing systems, foregoing such niceties as automatic footnoting or automatic hyphenation. When it comes to PIC files, Byline lets you resize a PIC file on-screen and even choose only a portion of the PIC file to view.

Byline, like Ventura Publisher, creates a link between a PIC file and a document. That means you can update a PIC file and the update will be reflected automatically within the Byline document.

GEM Desktop Publisher

Using GEM Desktop Publisher, from Digital Research, is like using a paperback version of Xerox Ventura Publisher. GEM Desktop Publisher provides the essential subset of Ventura commands in a fashion that is reminiscent of Ventura because it runs under the same graphical user interface, GEM. But GEM Desktop Publisher is far easier to use.

GEM Desktop Publisher, unlike Byline, lets you directly edit a graphical image of your document. But, also unlike Byline, it does not directly support importing 1-2-3 PIC files. To prepare a PIC file for GEM Desktop Publisher, you must use an optional graphics file translator called The Graphics Link, discussed later in the section "Translating PIC Files."

Illustrating PIC Files

A brief detour for your 1-2-3 PIC files through a PC drawing package can produce a makeover so dramatic that you may not recognize your graphs when they emerge. Drawing programs have been around nearly as long as the PC has had graphics capabilities. Yet the Draw category has evolved recently into one of the hottest new areas in PC graphics, illustration software for graphics professionals.

With many illustration programs, you can import a PIC file, break the graph into its components, and then begin dressing up each graph element through the powerful capabilities of the illustrator. You can modify the color or shape of any component of the graph. You can change the size, font, or placement of text, for example, or move the graph's legend to another, more suitable location. But these are only some of the changes possible with illustration software.

Some illustrators let you add gradually shaded backgrounds to add style or include text annotations that give your graph greater meaning. Other options allow you to define a path along which words should flow so that you can bend words around an object on-screen or make text appear to recede into the distance. If your artistic ability permits, you can draw freehand on the graph with an illustrator. If your imagination is better than your drawing hand, you can make subtle changes to the graph's design and then pick predrawn images from the illustrator's library of clip-art.

Because illustrators are vector-based graphics programs and PIC files are vector-based graphics files, the mating of the two is usually smooth and easy. Some illustrators import PIC files directly. Many import CGM files, one of the output formats available in 1-2-3 Release 3. If the illustrator imports neither of these formats, you can use one of the translator utilities described later in this chapter to translate your PIC file to an acceptable vector file format.

Most illustrators are particularly strong in generating presentation-quality output. Many can create four-color separations for color printing. Some provide drivers and can send completed images to film recorders for slide-making. Nearly all work best with PostScript laser printers or PostScript typesetting devices.

If your goal is to use an illustrator to spruce up a 1-2-3 graph on its way to a desktop publisher, most illustrators can offer you a variety of output graphics file formats, any of which can be imported into most desktop publishing programs. The following section describes some of the most popular illustration programs.

Arts & Letters

The Arts & Letters Composer, from the Computer Support Corporation, lets you directly import a 1-2-3 PIC file and immediately access any of its components, just by pointing to the element and clicking with the mouse. Each line on the screen is a separate element, but you can select groups of objects and change their attributes simultaneously. Using the Arts & Letters menu options, for example, you can change the interior colors of the slices of a pie and add patterns to the pie slices, as well.

Arts & Letters, despite its strong drawing capabilities, is not usually grouped with other illustrators. The program is most noted for its unusually extensive library of symbols. Arts & Letters Composer comes with thousands of professional-looking clip-art images. You can draw your own or modify the existing images with the optional Arts & Letters Graphics Editor, also available from Computer Support Corporation.

In the Arts & Letters clip-art library you find a truly huge assortment of images, some of complete objects representing animals and buildings, and others of graphic shapes and borders such as boxes, arrows, and stars. You can combine any of these images with your graph or use an image as a border or background to the graph.

Arts & Letters also provides a starter selection of 15 outline typefaces to replace the titles of your graph or annotate an aspect of the graph's information.

Arts & Letters is easy to use, and it even includes sections in its manual detailing the procedures for transferring Arts & Letters images into the desktop publishing programs PageMaker and Ventura Publisher.

GEM Artline

GEM Artline, an application that runs under the Graphical Environment Manager (GEM) user interface by Digital Research, is a particularly appropriate intermediate step for your PIC files between 1-2-3 and Ventura Publisher. Ventura Publisher runs under GEM, also, and uses the same graphics file format as Artline.

Artline's most noted attribute is its superb handling of type, but its drawing capabilities are also top-notch. Artline comes with three typeface families from Bitstream, the same company supplying typefaces for PageMaker and Ventura Publisher, but you easily can add more. You can place text on top of a PIC file imported onto the screen, break down the text into its individual characters, and modify each character separately as though it were an individual drawing.

You can also modify each aspect of a PIC file graph or group together elements of the graph and modify them together. Artline offers moving, copying, rotating, scaling, mirroring, patterning, and coloring of any object on its screen.

Artline provides a capability called picture tracing. You can import a bit-mapped image from a paint program or a bit-mapped picture read in with a scanner and instruct the program to trace its outlines and create a vector graphic. Once the graphic is vector, you can easily stretch or shrink it and perform any of the modifications possible with vector graphics images. Artline comes with its own libraries of predrawn symbols, and it provides easy export to both Ventura Publisher and PageMaker.

Micrografx Designer

PIC file import is a new feature of Designer 2.0. For Lotus users this is a more compelling argument than ever for using Micrografx's superb illustration program to embellish a 1-2-3 graph. You no longer need to translate a 1-2-3 PIC file into another file format before importing it into Designer.

Designer is acknowledged as one of the foremost illustration programs available on the PC and a challenger of some of the truly outstanding illustration programs available for the Apple Macintosh computer. Its tools for professional illustration are top-notch. It provides unparalleled control over color and curve drawing, a variety of output device drivers, and the same automatic image tracing as Gem Artline. Its optional clip-art libraries include over 12,000 images for embellishing a 1-2-3 graph.

If Designer has a shortcoming, it is in the program's text handling. Unlike some illustrators that treat each character in a line of text as a separately drawn object, Designer treats each line of text as an editable object. Moreover, the text you see on-screen is a representation of the final text that will be printed. Although the text will represent the size and position of the final type, you may not see the precise font you have chosen.

Adobe Illustrator

Adobe Illustrator 1.0 for the PC is a direct descendent of Adobe Illustrator 88 for the Apple Macintosh computer. Unfortunately, it lacks some of the most popular features of the Macintosh version. Moreover, Illustrator on the PC is sluggish and demands more in computer hardware than other illustration programs. For example, the program virtually demands the speed of an 80386 computer, and it requires at least 256K of expanded memory.

Illustrator provides no support for color in illustrations, and its control over text is more limited than other illustrators. Although Illustrator directly imports 1-2-3 PIC files, you may prefer other illustration programs to enhance your 1-2-3 graphs until Adobe comes out with an improved PC version of its software.

Corel Draw!

Corel Draw! has had an immediate and strong impact on the illustration market since its recent arrival. Its capabilities are so superb that the program is constantly rated among the very best illustration software, along with Micrografx Designer.

Corel Draw! has an innovative user interface that delivers a wealth of command options with a minimum of screen clutter. The program's capabilities for working with text are unmatched. Corel Draw! comes with 50 typefaces, and it lets you break lines of text into characters for individual editing, just as GEM Artline does. You can modify characters individually or describe a path for a line of text to follow in order to bend text around objects on-screen.

Corel Draw! is also one of the least expensive of the illustration programs. You will be able to set up a 1-2-3 graph embellishment system at a relatively low cost.

Translating PIC Files

If you can get your data into any kind of computer file, some utility can translate it into the format you need. This is as true with graphics files as it is with text. When you format your data and save it as a PIC file graph, you are not restricted to using the graph in only those programs directly importing PIC files. Several useful utilities can act as the missing link between the PIC file format of 1-2-3 and the dozens of other graphics file formats used by today's graphics software.

Some graphics file format converters can accept 1-2-3 PIC files as input and can produce an output file in one of a dozen or more file types. Some require that you capture the 1-2-3 /Graph View screen, instead, translating the resulting bit-mapped file into another bit-mapped file format.

Hijaak

Hijaak, from Inset Systems, accepts PIC files as direct input. From your PIC files, Hijaak can create more than 22 types of output files. Hijaak supports GEM Paint IMG files, CompuServe GIF files, HP LaserJet HPC files, Microsoft Paint MSP files, PC Paintbrush PCX files, PostScript PSC files, NewsMaster SHP files, Scanner TIFF files, and text files. With Hijaak, you can convert a 1-2-3 PIC file into an Amiga IFF file or a Macintosh MacPaint file for use on those two computers. You can also use Hijaak to convert your PIC file into one of six different fax file formats, in order to fax a PIC file directly from an internal PC fax card.

You can use the Hijaak menu system to select translation formats and input and output files, or you can instruct Hijaak to perform the translation by detailing the type of translation you need right at the DOS command line.

Graphics Transformer

The Graphics Transformer is another version of Inset System's Hijaak software, described earlier. Formerly called Reflection, Graphics Transformer is available from International Microcomputer Software, Inc. (IMSI).

The Graphics Link Plus

The Graphics Link Plus, from Harvard Systems, provides file conversion among 17 different bit-mapped file formats. Although you cannot directly translate Lotus PIC files, you can use the built-in screen capture utilities to capture 1-2-3 graphs from the /Graph View screen. The Graphics Link Plus will capture a 1-2-3 graph in any screen mode 1-2-3 supports.

The resolution of graphics files translated from these captured screens will not be as good as the resolution of graphics files translated from PIC files. Yet the Graphics Link Plus offers a host of features for processing bit-mapped files that may more than compensate for the difference in resolution.

If you are using a black-and-white printer, for example, you can capture a color graph and perform an automatic color-to-gray scale conversion. The colors in your color graph will be translated to shades of gray. You can also rotate the image, size, scale, stretch, and compress it, and reverse the colors of a black-and-white image.

PICture-PICTure

PICture-PICTure works with the Apple File Exchange utility and translates a Lotus PIC file into a standard Macintosh PICT file. Whereas Hijaak and Graphics Link Plus enable you to translate a PIC file to a Macintosh-compatible paint file, PICture-PICTure lets you convert a PIC file to a Macintosh PICT vector graphics file. You can edit the resulting vector files in drawing programs on the Macintosh such as MacDraw. In MacDraw and other Macintosh draw programs, you can edit each object in the chart, including the chart text and colors.

Summary

This final chapter has explored a variety of directions to consider for use and enhancement of 1-2-3 graphs. PIC files are the method of transmitting a 1-2-3 graph from one software package to another. Think of PrintGraph, in 1-2-3 Release 2.2 and prior releases, as just another piece of software that imports PIC files and does something valuable with them. After you have a graph in PIC file format, you can integrate it into a variety of other graphics and documents.

Index

N–O

P

More Computer Knowledge from Que

Lotus Software Titles

1-2-3 Database Techniques	24.95
1-2-3 Release 2.2 Business Applications	39.95
1-2-3 Release 2.2 Quick Reference	7.95
1-2-3 Release 2.2 QuickStart	19.95
1-2-3 Release 2.2 Workbook and Disk	29.95
1-2-3 Release 3 Business Applications	39.95
1-2-3 Release 3 Quick Reference	7.95
1-2-3 Release 3 QuickStart	19.95
1-2-3 Release 3 Workbook and Disk	29.95
1-2-3 Tips, Tricks, and Traps, 3rd Edition	22.95
Upgrading to 1-2-3 Release 3	14.95
Using 1-2-3, Special Edition	24.95
Using 1-2-3 Release 2.2, Special Edition	24.95
Using 1-2-3 Release 3	24.95
Using Lotus Magellan	21.95
Using Symphony, 2nd Edition	26.95

Database Titles

dBASE III Plus Applications Library	24.95
dBASE III Plus Handbook, 2nd Edition	24.95
dBASE III Plus Tips, Tricks, and Traps	21.95
dBASE III Plus Workbook and Disk	29.95
dBASE IV Applications Library, 2nd Edition	39.95
dBASE IV Handbook, 3rd Edition	23.95
dBASE IV Programming Techniques	24.95
dBASE IV QueCards	21.95
dBASE IV Quick Reference	7.95
dBASE IV QuickStart	19.95
dBASE IV Tips, Tricks, and Traps, 2nd Edition	21.95
dBASE IV Workbook and Disk	29.95
dBXL and Quicksilver Programming: Beyond dBASE	24.95
R:BASE User's Guide, 3rd Edition	22.95
Using Clipper	24.95
Using DataEase	22.95
Using Reflex	19.95
Using Paradox 3	24.95

Applications Software Titles

AutoCAD Advanced Techniques	34.95
AutoCAD Quick Reference	7.95
AutoCAD Sourcebook	24.95
Excel Business Applications: IBM Version	39.95
Introduction to Business Software	14.95
PC Tools Quick Reference	7.95
Smart Tips, Tricks, and Traps	24.95
Using AutoCAD, 2nd Edition	29.95
Using Computers in Business	24.95
Using DacEasy	21.95

Using Dollars and Sense: IBM Version, 2nd Edition	19.95
Using Enable/OA	23.95
Using Excel: IBM Version	24.95
Using Generic CADD	24.95
Using Harvard Project Manager	24.95
Using Managing Your Money, 2nd Edition	19.95
Using Microsoft Works: IBM Version	21.95
Using PROCOMM PLUS	19.95
Using Q&A, 2nd Edition	21.95
Using Quattro	21.95
Using Quicken	19.95
Using Smart	22.95
Using SmartWare II	24.95
Using SuperCalc5, 2nd Edition	22.95

Word Processing and Desktop Publishing Titles

DisplayWrite QuickStart	19.95
Harvard Graphics Quick Reference	7.95
Microsoft Word 5 Quick Reference	7.95
Microsoft Word 5 Tips, Tricks, and Traps: IBM Version	19.95
Using DisplayWrite 4, 2nd Edition	19.95
Using Freelance Plus	24.95
Using Harvard Graphics	24.95
Using Microsoft Word 5: IBM Version	21.95
Using MultiMate Advantage, 2nd Edition	19.95
Using PageMaker: IBM Version, 2nd Edition	24.95
Using PFS: First Choice	22.95
Using PFS: First Publisher	22.95
Using Professional Write	19.95
Using Sprint	21.95
Using Ventura Publisher, 2nd Edition	24.95
Using WordPerfect, 3rd Edition	21.95
Using WordPerfect 5	24.95
Using WordStar, 2nd Edition	21.95
Ventura Publisher Techniques and Applications	22.95
Ventura Publisher Tips, Tricks, and Traps	24.95
WordPerfect Macro Library	21.95
WordPerfect Power Techniques	21.95
WordPerfect QueCards	21.95
WordPerfect Quick Reference	7.95
WordPerfect QuickStart	21.95
WordPerfect Tips, Tricks, and Traps, 2nd Edition	21.95
WordPerfect 5 Workbook and Disk	29.95

Macintosh/Apple II Titles

The Big Mac Book	27.95
Excel QuickStart	19.95
Excel Tips, Tricks, and Traps	22.95
Using AppleWorks, 3rd Edition	21.95
Using AppleWorks GS	21.95
Using dBASE Mac	19.95
Using Dollars and Sense: Macintosh Version	19.95
Using Excel: Macintosh Verson	22.95
Using FullWrite Professional	21.95

Using HyperCard:	24.95
Using Microsoft Word 4: Macintosh Version	21.95
Using Microsoft Works: Macintosh Version, 2nd Edition	21.95
Using PageMaker: Macintosh Version	24.95
Using WordPerfect: Macintosh Version	19.95

Hardware and Systems Titles

DOS Tips, Tricks, and Traps	22.95
DOS Workbook and Disk	29.95
Hard Disk Quick Reference	7.95
IBM PS/2 Handbook	21.95
Managing Your Hard Disk, 2nd Edition	22.95
MS-DOS Quick Reference	7.95
MS-DOS QuickStart	21.95
MS-DOS User's Guide, Special Edition	29.95
Networking Personal Computers, 3rd Edition	22.95
Norton Utilities Quick Reference	7.95
The Printer Bible	24.95
Understanding UNIX: A Conceptual Guide, 2nd Edition	21.95
Upgrading and Repairing PCs	27.95
Using DOS	22.95
Using Microsoft Windows	19.95
Using Novell NetWare	24.95
Using OS/2	23.95
Using PC DOS, 3rd Edition	22.95

Programming and Technical Titles

Assembly Language Quick Reference	7.95
C Programmer's Toolkit	39.95
C Programming Guide, 3rd Edition	24.95
C Quick Reference	7.95
DOS and BIOS Functions Quick Reference	7.95
DOS Programmer's Reference, 2nd Edition	27.95
Power Graphics Programming	24.95
QuickBASIC Advanced Techniques	21.95
QuickBASIC Programmer's Toolkit	39.95
QuickBASIC Quick Reference	7.95
SQL Programmer's Guide	29.95
Turbo C Programming	22.95
Turbo Pascal Advanced Techniques	22.95
Turbo Pascal Programmer's Toolkit	39.95
Turbo Pascal Quick Reference	7.95
Using Assembly Language	24.95
Using QuickBASIC 4	19.95
Using Turbo Pascal	21.95

For more information, call

1-800-428-5331

All prices subject to change without notice. Prices and charges are for domestic orders only. Non-U.S. prices might be higher.

Using 1-2-3 Release 3
Developed by Que Corporation

Only the spreadsheet experts at Que can bring you this comprehensive guide to the commands, functions, and operations of new 1-2-3 Release 3. Includes a comprehensive Command Reference, a useful Troubleshooting section, and easy-to-follow instructions for Release 3 worksheets, graphics, databases, and macros.

Order #971
$24.95 USA
0-88022-440-1, 862 pp.

Using 1-2-3 Release 2.2, Special Edition
Developed by Que Corporation

Learn professional spreadsheet techniques from the world's leading publisher of 1-2-3 books! This comprehensive text leads you from worksheet basics to advanced 1-2-3 operations. Includes Allways coverage, a Troubleshooting section, a Command Reference, and a tear-out 1-2-3 Menu Map. The most complete resource available for Release 2.01 and Release 2.2!

Order #1040
$24.95 USA
0-88022-501-7, 850 pp.

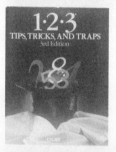

1-2-3 Tips, Tricks, and Traps, 3rd Edition
by Dick Andersen

Covering all releases of Lotus 1-2-3—including 2.2 and 3—this updated version of a Que classic presents hundreds of tips and techniques. Covers 3-D spreadsheet capability, new graphics features, and enhancements to the database and command language.

Order #963
$22.95 USA
0-88022-416-9, 550 pp.

1-2-3 Macro Library, 3rd Edition
Developed by Que Corporation

Includes companion disk! From simple keystroke macros to complex macro programs, *1-2-3 Macro Library*, 3rd Edition, helps users automate spreadsheet applications. Also teaches how to develop sophisticated macro programs for database and financial applications.

Order #962
$39.95 USA
0-88022-418-5, 600 pp.

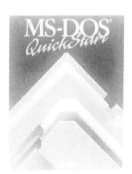
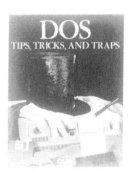

1-2-3 Release 2.2 Business Applications

by Thomas Miezejeski

Book and disk set! Combining ready-to-run business applications with an easy-to-follow, illustrated text, *1-2-3 Release 2.2 Business Applications* teaches successful techniques for building spreadsheet and database applications. Covers Releases 2.01 and 2.2.

Order #1065
$39.95 USA
0-88022-516-5, 550 pp.

1-2-3 Release 3 Business Applications

by Edward M. Donie

This new book/disk combination contains a series of business models in ready-to-run form. Release 3 features are incorporated, including 3-D spreadsheets and enhanced graphics

Order #972
$39.95 USA
0-88022-439-8, 550 pp.

1-2-3 Database Techniques

by Dick Andersen

Concepts and techniques to help users create complex 1-2-3 database applications! With an emphasis on Release 3 features, this book introduces database fundamentals, compares 1-2-3 with traditional database programs, offers numerous application tips, and discusses add-in programs.

Order #835
$22.95 USA
0-88022-346-4, 450 pp.

Upgrading to 1-2-3 Release 3

Developed by Que Corporation

This versatile text helps you elevate your upgrading needs, then gets you up and running with the new features of 1-2-3 Release 3. Covers hardware and operating system requirements, plus helpful techniques and troubleshooting tips.

Order #1018
$14.95 USA
0-88022-491-6, 388 pp.

Upgrading and Repairing PCs

by Scott Mueller

The ultimate resource for personal computer upgrade, repair, maintenance, and troubleshooting! This comprehensive text covers all types of IBM computers and compatibles—from the original PC to the new PS/2 models. Defines your system components and provides solutions to common PC problems.

Order #882
$27.95 USA
0-88022-395-2, 750 pp.

Networking Personal Computers, 3rd Edition

by Michael Durr and Mark Gibbs

The most in-depth coverage of local area networks! Learn LAN standards, LAN hardware, LAN installation, and practical solutions to common LAN problems. The text also covers networking IBM-compatible PCs with Macintosh machines.

Order #955
$22.95 USA
0-88022-417-7, 400 pp.

Using Novell NetWare

by Bill Lawrence

An inside look at the leading local network sofware. NetWare users will appreciate this thorough guide to installation, network management, and advanced NetWare topics.

Order #1013
$24.95 USA
0-88022-466-5, 400 pp.

Managing Your Hard Disk, 2nd Edition

by Don Berliner

Learn the most efficient techniques for organizing the programs and data on your hard disk! This hard-working text includes management tips, essential DOS commands, an explanation of new application and utility software, and an introduction to PS/2 hardware.

Order #837
$22.95 USA
0-88022-348-0, 600 pp.

Using Computers in Business
by Joel Shore

This text covers all aspects of business computerization, including a thorough analysis of benefits, costs, alternatives, and common problems. Also discusses how to budget for computerization, how to shop for the right hardware and software, and how to allow for expansions and upgrades.

Order #1020
$22.95 USA
0-88022-470-3, 450 pp.

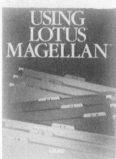

Using Lotus Magellan
by David Gobel

The ultimate book on Lotus' new file management software! Covers Magellan's file viewing capability and shows how to edit and print files, organize data, index files, use "fuzzy searching," work with macros, and set up Magellan for network use.

Order #980
$21.95 USA
0-88022-448-7, 400 pp.

Introduction to Business Software
Developed by Que Corporation

A useful introduction to the best-selling IBM-compatible software programs. Discusses the basics and benefits of each application.

Order #1034
$14.95 USA
0-88022-496-7, 400 pp.

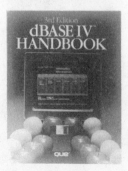

dBASE IV Handbook, 3rd Edition
by George T. Chou, Ph.D.

A complete introduction to dBASE IV functions! Beginning users will progress systematically from basic database concepts to advanced dBASE features, and experienced dBASE users will appreciate the information on the new features of dBASE IV. Includes Quick Start tutorials.

Order #852
$23.95 USA
0-88022-380-4, 785 pp.

Using WordPerfect 5

by Charles O. Stewart III, et al.

The #1 best-selling word processing book! Introduces Word-Perfect basics and helps readers learn to use macros, styles, and other advanced features. Also includes **Quick Start** tutorials, a tear-out command reference card, and an introduction to Word-Perfect 5 for 4.2 users.

Order #843
$24.95 USA
0-88022-351-0, 867 pp.

WordPerfect QuickStart

Developed by Que Corporation

WordPerfect QuickStart **shows** how to produce common documents and leads users step-by-step through the most essential features of WordPerfect 5.

Order #871
$21.95 USA
0-88022-387-1, 350 pp.

Using Professional Write

by Katherine Murray

Quick Start tutorials introduce word processing basics and help readers progress to advanced skills. Discusses macros, printing techniques, and how to use Professional Write with other programs. Packed with easy-to-follow examples!

Order #1027
$19.95 USA
0-88022-490-8, 400 pp.

Using DisplayWrite 4, 2nd Edition

by David Busch

Features **Quick Start** lessons and timesaving shortcuts. Also discusses how to use DisplayWrite 4 in the OS/2 environment.

Order #975
$19.95 USA
0-88022-445-2, 438 pp.

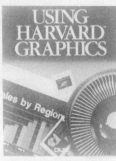

Using Harvard Graphics

by Steve Sagman and Jane Graver Sandlar

An excellent introduction to presentation graphics! This well-written text presents both program basics and presentation fundamentals to create bar, pie, line, and other types of informative graphs. Includes hundreds of samples!

Order #941
$24.95 USA
0-88022-407-X, 550 pp.

Using PFS: First Publisher

by Katherine Murray

From word processing basics to advanced layout features, this text is power-packed with program and design tips! Includes a Quick Start lesson, step-by-step explanations of the program's capabilities, and coverage of DeskMate.

Order #937
$22.95 USA
0-88022-401-0, 388 pp.

Using PageMaker: IBM Version, 2nd Edition

by S. Venit and Diane Burns

Updated for the IBM-compatible version of PageMaker 3.0, this popular text now covers the cover separations capabilities of the program. An ideal introductory text, *Using PageMaker* presents both program basics and basic design concepts. Soon you'll be producing professional publications—just like the dozens of detailed examples presented in this book!

Order #953
$24.95 USA
0-88022-415-0, 511 pp.

Using Freelance Plus

by Jim Meade

A systematic approach to sophisticated presentation graphics! *Using Freelance Plus* includes **Quick Start** tutorials, advanced techniques, and numerous examples to help users produce effective, eye-catching presentations.

Order #1050
$24.95 USA
0-88022-528-9, 450 pp.

Free Catalog!

Mail us this registration form today, and we'll send you a free catalog featuring Que's complete line of best-selling books.

Name of Book _____

Name _____

Title _____

Phone (___) _____

Company _____

Address _____

City _____

State _____ ZIP _____

Please check the appropriate answers:

1. Where did you buy your Que book?
   - ☐ Bookstore (name: _____)
   - ☐ Computer store (name: _____)
   - ☐ Catalog (name: _____)
   - ☐ Direct from Que
   - ☐ Other: _____

2. How many computer books do you buy a year?
   - ☐ 1 or less
   - ☐ 2-5
   - ☐ 6-10
   - ☐ More than 10

3. How many Que books do you own?
   - ☐ 1
   - ☐ 2-5
   - ☐ 6-10
   - ☐ More than 10

4. How long have you been using this software?
   - ☐ Less than 6 months
   - ☐ 6 months to 1 year
   - ☐ 1-3 years
   - ☐ More than 3 years

5. What influenced your purchase of this Que book?
   - ☐ Personal recommendation
   - ☐ Advertisement
   - ☐ In-store display
   - ☐ Price
   - ☐ Que catalog
   - ☐ Que mailing
   - ☐ Que's reputation
   - ☐ Other: _____

6. How would you rate the overall content of the book?
   - ☐ Very good
   - ☐ Good
   - ☐ Satisfactory
   - ☐ Poor

7. What do you like *best* about this Que book?

   _____

   _____

8. What do you like *least* about this Que book?

   _____

   _____

9. Did you buy this book with your personal funds?
   - ☐ Yes   ☐ No

10. Please feel free to list any other comments you may have about this Que book.

    _____

    _____

    _____

QUE

Order Your Que Books Today!

Name _____

Title _____

Company _____

City _____

State _____ ZIP _____

Phone No. (___) _____

Method of Payment:

Check ☐ (Please enclose in envelope.)

Charge My: VISA ☐   MasterCard ☐

American Express ☐

Charge # _____

Expiration Date _____

Order No.	Title	Qty.	Price	Total

You can **FAX** your order to **1-317-573-2583**. Or call **1-800-428-5331, ext. ORDR** to order direct.

Please add $2.50 per title for shipping and handling.

Subtotal _____

Shipping & Handling _____

Total _____

QUE

BUSINESS REPLY MAIL
First Class Permit No. 9918   Indianapolis, IN

Postage will be paid by addressee

11711 N. College
Carmel, IN 46032

BUSINESS REPLY MAIL
First Class Permit No. 9918   Indianapolis, IN

Postage will be paid by addressee

11711 N. College
Carmel, IN 46032